Trading in Genes

Trading in Genes

Development Perspectives on Biotechnology, Trade and Sustainability

Edited by
Ricardo Meléndez-Ortiz and Vicente Sánchez

London • Sterling, VA

First published by Earthscan in the UK and USA in 2005

ISBN-10: 1-84407-028-X paperback
          1-84407-027-1 hardback
ISBN-13: 978-1-84407-028-2 paperback
          978-1-84407-027-5 hardback

Typesetting by JS Typesetting Ltd, Porthcawl, Mid Glamorgan
Printed and bound in the UK by Bath Press
Cover design by Yvonne Booth

For a full list of publications please contact:

Earthscan
8–12 Camden High Street
London, NW1 0JH, UK
Tel: +44 (0)20 7387 8558
Fax: +44 (0)20 7387 8998
Email: earthinfo@earthscan.co.uk
Web: **www.earthscan.co.uk**

22883 Quicksilver Drive, Sterling, VA 20166-2012, USA

Earthscan is an imprint of James and James (Science Publishers) Ltd and publishes in association with the International Institute for Environment and Development

A catalogue record for this book is available from the British Library

Library of Congress Cataloging-in-Publication Data has been applied for

Printed on elemental chlorine-free paper

Contents

PART TWO – TRADE IN BIOTECHNOLOGY: NEW CHALLENGES IN AN OLD PLAYGROUND

APPENDICES

List of Boxes, Figures and Tables

BOXES

FIGURES

TABLES

List of Acronyms and Abbreviations

AAR   Applied Agricultural Research (Malaysia)
ABE   Agricultural Biotechnology in Europe
ABSP   Agricultural Biotechnology Support Project (US)
AFIC   Asian Food Information Centre
AGERI   Agricultural Genetic Engineering Research Institute
AIA   advance informed agreement
ANVISA   Agência Nacional de Vigilância Sanitária (Brazil's national agency for health)
ANZFA   Australia–New Zealand Food Authority (now FSANZ)
ANZFSC   Australia–New Zealand Food Standards Council
APHIS   Animal and Plant Health Inspection Service (operated by USDA)
AQIS   Australian Quarantine and Inspection Service
ARC   Agricultural Research Council (South Africa)
ASEAN   Association of Southeast Asian Nations
ATCC   American Type Culture Collection
BAC   Biotechnology Advisory Center
BINAS   Biosafety Information Network and Advisory Service (operated by UNIDO)
BIO-EARN   East African Regional Programme and Research Network for Biotechnology, Biosafety and Biotechnology Policy Development
BPI   Bureau of Plant Industry (the Philippines)
BSE   Bovine Spongiform Encephalopathy
BSWG   Working Group on Biosafety
Bt   *Bacillus thuringiensis*
CBD   Convention on Biological Diversity
CENIT   Centro de Investigaciones para la Transformación (Argentina's centre of research for transformation)
CFIA   Canadian Food Inspection Agency
CG   Compromise Group
CGIAR   Consultative Group on International Agricultural Research
CGRFA   Draft Code of Conduct on Biotechnology as it relates to Genetic Resources for Food and Agriculture
CIAT   Centro Internacional de Agricultura Tropical (International Center for Tropical Agriculture)

CIBio	Comissões Internas de Biossegurança (Brazil's internal biosafety commission)
CIBIOGEM	Comisión Intersecretarial de Bioseguridad y Organismos Genéticamente Modificados (Mexico's intersectoral commission for biosafety and GMOs)
CIDA	Canadian International Development Agency
CIGB	Centro de Ingeniería Genética y Biotecnología (Cuba's centre of genetic engineering and biotechnology)
CIMMYT	Centro Internacional de Mejoramiento de Maíz y Trigo (International Maize and Wheat Improvement Center)
CIP	International Potato Center
CIPR	Commission on Intellectual Property Rights
CNBS	Conselho Nacional de Biossegurança (Brazil's national biosafety council)
COMESA	Common Market for Eastern and Southern Africa
CONABIA	Comisión Nacional Asesora de Biotecnología Agropecuaria (Argentina's national advisory commission on agricultural biotechnology)
CONAMA	Conselho Nacional do Meio Ambiente (Brazil's national environmental council)
COP	Conference of the Parties
CORPOICA	Corporación Colombiana de Investigación Agropecuaria (Colombia's corporation of agricultural research)
CPB	Cartagena Protocol on Biosafety
CRIFC	Central Research Institute for Field Crops
CRSP	Collaborative Research Support Program
CTD	Committee on Trade and Development
CTE	Committee on Trade and Environment
CTNBio	Comissão Técnica Nacional de Biossegurança (Brazil's national technical biosafety commission)
DANCED	Danish Cooperation for Environment and Development
DANCEE	Danish Cooperation for Environment in Eastern Europe
DBT	Department of Biotechnology (India)
DFID	Department for International Development (UK)
DGIS	Directorate-General for International Cooperation (The Netherlands)
DGSV	Dirección General de Sanidad Vegetal (Mexico's general directorate of plant health)
DNA	deoxyribonucleic acid
DPVCTRF	Direction de la Protection des Végétaux, des Contrôles Techniques et de la Répression des Fraudes (Moroccan Ministry of Agriculture's division for plant protection)
DSB	Dispute Settlement Body

DSM	Dispute Settlement Mechanism
DSU	Dispute Settlement Understanding
ECACC	European Collection of Cell Cultures
Embrapa	Empresa Brasileira de Pesquisa Agropecuária (Brazil's agricultural research corporation)
EPA	Environment Protection Agency (US)
EPC	European Patent Convention
EPO	erythropoietin
ERS	Economic Research Service, US Department of Agriculture
ETC	action group on Erosion, Technology and Concentration
ExCOP	Extraordinary Conference of the Parties
FAO	Food and Agriculture Organization
FAS	Foreign Agriculture Service, US Department of Agriculture
FDA	Food and Drug Administration (US)
FFP	for direct use as food or feed, or for processing
FSANZ	Food Standards Australia New Zealand (formerly ANZFA)
GATT	General Agreement on Tariffs and Trade
GDP	gross domestic product
GEAC	Genetic Engineering Approval Committee (India)
GEF	Global Environment Facility
GM	genetically modified
GMO	genetically modified organism
GT	glyphosate tolerant
GURT	genetic use restriction technology
HIV	human immunodeficiency virus
IAEA	International Atomic Energy Agency
IBAMA	Instituto Brasileiro do Meio Ambiente e dos Recursos Naturais Renováveis (Brazil's institute of the environment and renewable natural resources)
IBS	ISNAR Biotechnology Service
ICA	Instituto Colombiano Agropecuario (Colombia's institute for agriculture and livestock)
ICCP	Intergovernmental Committee for the Cartagena Protocol
ICGEB	International Centre for Genetic Engineering and Biotechnology
IDEC	Instituto Brasileiro de Defesa do Consumidor (Brazil's consumer protection institute)
IDRC	International Development Research Centre
IFIC	International Food Information Council
IFPRI	International Food Policy Research Institute
IGF	Institut für Genbiologische Forschung
IICA	Inter-American Institute for Cooperation on Agriculture
IITA	International Institute for Tropical Agriculture
INASE	Instituto Nacional de Semillas (Argentina's national seed institute)

IPGRI	International Plant Genetic Resources Institute
IPM	integrated pest management
IPPC	International Plant Protection Convention
IPR	intellectual property rights
IRRI	International Rice Research Institute
ISAAA	International Service for the Acquisition of Agri-biotech Applications
ISNAR	International Service for National Agricultural Research
ISO	International Organization for Standardization
ISPM	International Standards for Phytosanitary Measures
ITSC	Institute of Tropical and Subtropical Crops
JUSSCANNZ	Japan, the United States, Switzerland, Canada, Australia, Norway and New Zealand
KARI	Kenyan Agricultural Research Institute
LAC	Latin America and the Caribbean
LMG	like-minded Group
LMO	living modified organism
MADR	Ministerio de Agricultura y Desarrollo Rural de Colombia (Colombia's Ministry of Agriculture and Rural Development)
MAFF	Ministry for Agriculture, Forestry and Fisheries (Japan)
MEA	multilateral environmental agreement
MHLW	Ministry of Health, Labour and Welfare (Japan)
MNC	multinational corporation
MOFA	Ministry of Foreign Affairs, The Netherlands
MOP	Meeting of the Parties
MSU	Michigan State University
MSV	maize streak virus
MTA	material transfer agreement
NEDA	Netherlands Development Assistance (formerly Directorate-General for International Cooperation, DGIS)
NEDO	New Energy and Industrial Technology Development Organization
NEPAD	New Partnership for Africa's Development
NGO	non-governmental organization
OAPI	Organisation Africaine de la Propriété Intellectuelle (African Intellectual Property Organization)
ODA	official development assistance
OECD	Organisation for Economic Co-operation and Development
OIE	Office International des Épizooties (World Organisation for Animal Health)
OSTP	Office of Science and Technology Policy (US)
PBA	Programa Colombiano de Biotecnología Agrícola (Colombia's agricultural biotechnology programme for small farmers)

PBR	plant breeders' right
PGRFA	International Treaty on Plant Genetic Resources for Food and Agriculture 2001
PIC	prior informed consent
PP	precautionary principle
PPM	process and production methods
R&D	research and development
RCGM	Review Committee on Genetic Manipulation (India)
REDBIO/FAO	Red de Cooperación Técnica en Biotecnología Vegetal para América Latina y el Caribe (technical cooperation network on plant biotechnology in Latin America and the Caribbean, under the sponsorship of FAO)
RIIA	Royal Institute of International Affairs (London, UK)
RR	Roundup Ready
RRIM	Rubber Research Institute of Malaysia
S&T	science and technology
SADC	Southern African Development Community
SAGARPA	Secretaría de Agricultura, Ganadería, Desarrollo Rural, Pesca y Alimentación (Mexico's agricultural ministry)
SAGPyA	Secretaría de Agricultura, Ganadería, Pesca y Alimentos (Argentina's agricultural ministry)
SARB	South Africa Regional Biosafety Program
SAREC	Department for Research Cooperation (of Sida)
SDA	Secretaria de Defesa Agropecuária (Brazil's ministry for plant protection)
SDC	Swiss Agency for Development and Cooperation
SENASA	Servicio Nacional de Sanidad y Calidad Agroalimentaria (Argentina's national phytosanitary service)
Sida	Swedish International Development Cooperation Agency
SIDS	small island developing states
SME	small and medium-sized enterprises
SPM	sanitary and phytosanitary measures
SRISTI	Society for Research and Initiatives for Sustainable Technologies and Institutions
TBT	technical barriers to trade
TK	traditional knowledge
TRIPS	trade-related aspects of intellectual property rights
UNCED	United Nations Conference on Environment and Development
UNDP	United Nations Development Programme
UNEP	United Nations Environment Programme
UNESCO	United Nations Educational, Scientific and Cultural Organization

UNIDO	United Nations Industrial Development Organization
UNITAR	UN Institute for Training and Research
UPOV	International Union for the Protection of New Varieties of Plants
USAID	United States Agency for International Development
USDA	United States Department of Agriculture
WFP	World Food Programme
WHO	World Health Organization
WIPO	World Intellectual Property Organization
WSSD	World Summit on Sustainable Development
WTO	World Trade Organization

List of Contributors

Heike Baumüller is Programme Manager, Environment and Natural Resources at the International Centre for Trade and Sustainable Development (ICTSD). Among other areas, she has coordinated the biotechnology-related activities of ICTSD since 2000. She is the Managing Editor of the ICTSD publication BRIDGES Trade BioRes and has published on a range of issues related to trade, biotechnology and sustainable development. She holds a Master's degree in Environmental Studies from Macquarie University, Sydney.

Eugenio Cap is Director of the Institute of Economics and Sociology (IES) at Argentina's National Institute of Agricultural Technology (INTA). Previously he has served as Director of Strategic Planning at INTA. His research work has included the development of quantitative tools for the analysis of the agricultural sector with emphasis on technological variables and the impact assessment of agricultural research. He has worked as a consultant for the Food and Agriculture Organization, The World Bank, the Inter-American Development Bank and the Inter-American Institute for Cooperation in Agriculture. He holds a PhD in Agricultural and Applied Economics from the University of Minnesota.

Paul Chavarriaga is Research Associate with the International Center for Tropical Agriculture (CIAT), Cali, Colombia, where he focuses on the use of genetic transformation as a tool to introduce new traits into cassava cultivars selected by farmers and adapted to different environments in Colombia. From 1993 to 1997 he taught Biology and Botany at the University of Georgia (Athens, Georgia), for which he received the 1997 Outstanding Graduate Teaching Award. His current research receives the support of the Ministry of Agriculture of Colombia, the Department for International Development (UK) and the Directorate-General for International Cooperation (The Netherlands).

Daniel Chudnovsky holds a DPhil from Oxford University and is Director of the Centro de Investigaciones para la Transformación (CENIT) in Buenos Aires and Full Professor at the University of San Andrés. His previous work experience includes several years as an Economic Affairs Officer in the Technology Division of United Nations Conference on Trade and Development (UNCTAD) and as Director of the Center for International Economics in Buenos Aires. He has written extensively on trade, foreign investment, environment and technology issues.

Carlos C Correa is Director of the postgraduate courses on Intellectual Property and of the Masters Programme on Science and Technology Policy and Management at the University of Buenos Aires. From 1984 to 1989 he was Under-secretary of State for Informatics and Development in the Argentine national government. He was Director of the United Nations Development Programme (UNDP)/United Nations Industrial Development Organization (UNIDO) Regional Programme on Informatics and Microelectronics for Latin America and the Caribbean from 1990 to 1995, and has also served as director of research projects sponsored by the International Development Research Centre of Canada.

Padmashree Gehl Sampath joined United Nations University Institute for New Technologies (UNU-INTECH) in the autumn of 2002, before which she was a research associate at the Institute for International and European Environmental Policy in Berlin. At UNU-INTECH Padmashree is working on research initiatives in the area of biotechnology with a particular emphasis on pharmaceuticals/health, in addition to coordinating UNU/INTECH's series of public lectures and seminars. She is a Doctoral Scholar from the Graduate College for Law and Economics, University of Hamburg.

Kakoli Ghosh is Genetic Resource Officer with the Seed and Plant Genetic Resources Service of the Food and Agriculture Organization (FAO). Ghosh trained as a biotechnologist and is now working in capacity building for policy development in biotechnology and plant genetic resources for food and agriculture. Born in India, she joined FAO in 1999 after completing a DPhil in Plant Molecular Biology at the University of Oxford.

Joseph Muchabaiwa Gopo is Biotechnology and Biosafety Adviser at the Namibian Ministry of Higher Education, Training and Employment Creation, and Former Director of the Biotechnology Research Institute of the Zimbabwe Scientific Research Development Center. He held fellowships of the Jaques Monod Institute of Molecular Genetics and the University of Maryland, where he was also appointed Adjunct Professor between 1990 and 1995. Between 1986 and 1991 he served as Chair of the Department of Biological Sciences of the University of Zimbabwe while between 1991 and 1995 he served as Deputy Dean for the University's Faculty of Science. He has consulted with the International Center of Insect Physiology and Ecology and the International Development Research Centre of Canada.

Maria José Amstalden Moraes Sampaio joined the Brazilian Agricultural Research Corporation (Embrapa) in 1976. In 1983, she began work at Embrapa's Genetic Resources and Biotechnology Center in Brasilia and helped to build the Biotechnology Unit. She was the Head of Research and Development from 1989 to 1995 when she moved to Embrapa's headquarters to work on policy making in different areas related to genetic resources, intellectual property rights, biotechnology and biosafety. She spent two years (1998–2000) at the University of Cornell, US, working in the fields of technology transfer and intellectual property rights. She holds a PhD from the University of Dundee, Scotland, where she worked in the fields of biochemistry and enzymology of nitrogen fixation.

Calestous Juma is Director of the Science, Technology and Innovation Program at the Center for International Development at Harvard University. He is former Executive Secretary of the United Nations Convention on Biological Diversity and Founding Executive Director of the African Center for Technology Studies in Nairobi (Kenya). He has won several international awards including the 1991 Pew Scholars Award in Conservation and the Environment and the 1993 United Nations Global 500 Award. He holds a PhD in Science and Technology Policy Studies from the Science Policy Research Unit of Sussex University (England).

Patricia Kameri-Mbote is a senior lecturer and Acting Dean at the Faculty of Law, University of Nairobi. She teaches Intellectual Property Law, Law, Science and Technology, and Gender and the Law. She is also the Programme Director for Africa at the International Environmental Law Research Centre. She has published widely in the areas of environmental law, intellectual property and women's rights and is the author of a book entitled *Property Rights and Biodiversity Management in Kenya*.

Atul Kaushik is a civil servant with the government of India, appointed as Deputy Secretariat of the Cabinet Secretariat since 2001. He has worked in the Trade Policy Division of the Ministry of Commerce and Industry as Under-secretary and Deputy Secretary since 1995, focusing on World Trade Organization (WTO)-related issues. His responsibilities included formulating India's position in the Committee on Trade and Environment and the TRIPS Council. He represented India as a negotiator on the drafting of the first report of the CTE in 1996 as well as in the delegation to the 1999 WTO Ministerial at Seattle.

Veit Koester holds a Master's degree in Law and Administration (Copenhagen University). After admission to the Bar in 1962 he turned to government administration in 1967. In the Ministry of the Environment of Denmark, he was the Head of the Ecological Division of the National Forest and Nature Agency for 20 years. He is now heading the section for Multilateral Cooperation of the Agency. He serves as examiner at the University of Copenhagen (since 1980) and Roskilde University Centre (since 1985), and as External Professor at Roskilde University Centre (since 1997).

Victor Konde is a lecturer at the Chemistry Department of the University of Zambia. He held a postdoctoral fellowship in the Science, Technology and

Innovation Program at Harvard University. His research interests include the application of agricultural biotechnology to developing countries and finding new biotechnological solutions to the nutritional and environmental problems specific to African agriculture. He received his PhD in Biochemistry from Brunel University in the UK.

Dr Jakkrit Kuanpoth is a senior lecturer at the Faculty of Law, University of Wollongong, Australia. Before coming to Wollongong, he taught at the School of Law, Sukhothai Thammathirat Open University, Thailand. He has published widely in the areas of intellectual property law, international economic law, and law and technology. He holds a LLB (Hons) from Ramkhamhaeng University, Thailand, 1983; a Barrister-at-Law from the Institute of Legal Education Thai Bar Association, Thailand, 1984; a LLM from the International Economic Law department, University of Warwick, UK, 1992; a PhD from the University of Aberdeen, UK, 1995; and a post-doctoral fellowship from the Max Planck Institute for Foreign and International Patent, Copyright and Competition Law, Munich, Germany, 1996.

Maurício Antônio Lopes is Manager of the Genetic Resources Theme Group in the Genetic Resources and Biotechnology Center of the Brazilian Agricultural Research Corporation (Embrapa), which he joined in 1986. At Embrapa, he was Leader of the Maize Breeding Program (1993–1995) and Head of Research and Development (1995–1999) in the Maize and Sorghum Center. From January 2000 to April 2003 he was the Head of Embrapa's Research and Development Department. He holds an MSc in Genetics (1989) from Purdue University and a PhD in Molecular Genetics (1993) from the University of Arizona.

Andrés López is Principal Researcher at the Centro de Investigaciones para la Transformación (CENIT) and Professor of Development Economics at the University of Buenos Aires. He has several publications in specialized journals and books on technological change, foreign investment and sustainable development issues. He holds a PhD in Economic Sciences from the University of Buenos Aires.

Arturo Martinez is Service Chief at the Plant Genetic Resources Service of the Food and Agriculture Organization. Previously he worked as a senior adviser to the Government of Argentina on issues and international negotiations related to biological diversity. Between 1990 and 1993 he served as Director of the Institute of Biological Resources within the Argentina National Institute of Agricultural Technology. He has been a convener and delegate to numerous meetings of the Convention for Biodiversity. He holds a PhD from the Department of Agriculture and Botany at Reading University in the UK.

Juan Mayr currently serves as a member of the UN High Level Panel on Civil Society. Formerly Minister for the Environment in Colombia (1998–2002), he served as Vice-President of IUCN and as Regional Representative from Latin America on the IUCN Governing Council (1993–2000). In 2000, Juan Mayr was President of the Extraordinary Session of the Convention on Biological Diversity, which led to the adoption of the Biosafety Protocol, and Chairman of Session VIII of the Commission on Sustainable Development.

Ricardo Meléndez-Ortiz is Executive Director of the International Centre for Trade and Sustainable Development (ICTSD). He was the Co-founder and General Director of Fundacion Futuro Latinoamericano (FFLA) in Quito, Ecuador (1994–1996). Formerly, he was the First Secretary at the Permanent Mission of Colombia to the United Nations Office, Geneva, Switzerland (1990–1994), Principal Adviser on international negotiations to the Minister of Economic Development (1988–1990) and Chief of Administration at the Office of the President of Colombia, Bogotá (1987–1988).

Douglas Pachico has been Director of Research at the International Center for Tropical Agriculture (CIAT) in Cali, Colombia, since 1981. His responsibilities in the centre evolved from Marketing Economist, Cassava Program to Program Leader for the Bean Program, and subsequently Director of Natural Resource Management and of Strategic Planning. He holds a PhD from Cornell University where his research focused on modelling small farmer decision-making.

Vicente Sánchez is Senior Adviser on Environment to the National Chamber of Commerce of Chile. Formerly he was Senior Fellow of the International Centre for Trade and Sustainable Development (ICTSD) and Consultant on Capacity-building on Biotechnology and Biosafety funded by the Rockefeller Foundation. He was Executive Director of the South Centre in Geneva (2000–2001), before which he was Elected Chairman of the Negotiations for the Convention on Biological Diversity (CBD) from its beginning in 1991 until the Convention entered into force. From 1975 to 1978 he was First Director of the United Nations Environment Programme (UNEP) for Latin America and the Caribbean. He is also author of more than 40 publications on environmental issues in journals and has published several books dealing with environment and development, among them one with Calestous Juma entitled *Biodiplomacy: Genetic Resources and International Relations.*

Adriana Soto works as an international consultant for environmental issues, having formerly been Head of the Global Change Office at the National Institute of Hydrology, Meteorology and Environmental Studies in Colombia. She was the Biosafety Adviser to the Colombian Deputy Minister and the Minister of the Environment from 1995 to 2000, and was the Colombian Chief Negotiator throughout the biosafety negotiations until 1998. She served as the Spokesperson for the Latin American and Caribbean Group during the Madrid meeting and the Second Conference of the Parties to the Convention on Biological Diversity.

Joe Tohme is Head of the Biotechnology Research Unit at the International Center for Tropical Agriculture (CIAT) in Cali, Colombia, where he coordinates Agrobiodiversity and Biotechnology projects. His work on cassava and rice genome mapping has attracted international funding from the Rockefeller Foundation since 1992. Between 1993 and 1997 he also received a grant from the government of Belgium for the molecular characterization of *Phaseolus vulgaris*. He has received numerous international awards including the Outstanding Paper on Genetic Resources by the Crop Science Society of America and the 1984 Dr R. P. Mericle Memorial Scholarship in Michigan State University.

Eduardo J Trigo is Director of Grupo CEO SA, a consulting group in agricultural and natural resources development policy issues. He has served on the Board of Trustees of the Agency for the Promotion of Science, Technology and Innovation and the National Advisory Committee for Agricultural Biotechnology Policy of Argentina. Prior to these roles he was Director of the Technology Programme at the Inter-American Institute for Cooperation on Agriculture (IICA) in San José, Costa Rica, and Director of Research at the International Service for National Agricultural Research in The Hague, The Netherlands. His research work is focused on science and technology policy with emphasis on the agricultural sector. He holds a PhD in Agricultural Economics from the University of Wisconsin.

Jayashree Watal works in the Intellectual Property Division of the World Trade Organization (WTO). She has been a Fellow of the Indian Council for Research in International Economic Research, New Delhi and Visiting Fellow of the Institute for International Economics, Washington DC. She was Director of the Trade Policy Division of the Ministry of Commerce, New Delhi. Watal was responsible for TRIPS negotiations in the Uruguay Round from 1989 to 1991. She has recently completed a comprehensive study, *Intellectual Property Rights in the WTO and Developing Countries*, published in 2001 by Kluwer Law International.

Christiane Wolff is Project Manager in the Agriculture & Natural Resources Division of the KfW Bankengruppe (a German banking group). She is currently on leave from her position as an Economics Affairs Officer with the Agriculture and Commodities Division of the WTO, where her work focused on providing support to the Committee on Sanitary and Phytosanitary Measures, assisting dispute settlement panels and offering technical support to developing countries. Prior to the WTO she consulted with the International Food Policy Research Institute as well as the United Nations Economic Commission for Latin America and the Caribbean. She holds an MS in Agricultural, Resource and Managerial Economics from Cornell University (Ithaca, New York state) where her research focused on smallholder oil palm production in Mexico.

Preface

This book's origin sprang from a captivating and intense dialogue we jointly convened in late 2000 at the South Centre in Geneva. Vicente Sánchez was then serving as the first Executive Director of Julius Nyerere's South Centre and had invited his kith and kin to seek responses to the challenges posed to developing countries by rapidly advancing bio-based technologies and emerging global policy frameworks and controversies. To the bright Southern minds that have accompanied this debate for over a decade, such as Joseph Gopo, Mohamed Hassan, Calestous Juma, Arturo Martinez, Banpot Napompeth, Sandra Wint and A. H. Zakri, we added Katheryn Stokes and Mongi Hamdi, who, from the platform of the United Nations Conference on Trade and Development (UNCTAD)-served Commission on Science and Technology for Development, have been assisting developing countries to flesh out their views on these issues. Michael Lesnick and Todd Baker of the Meridian Institute participated as observers. The two-day discussions resulted in an array of ideas, underscored by the shared concern about the scarce capabilities of developing countries in several fields, ranging from the technological, institutional and scientific capacity for the safe use of biotechnology to the ability to set up domestic regulatory frameworks and effectively participate in multilateral negotiations.

The eventful World Trade Organization (WTO) Ministerial Conference in Seattle at the end of 1999 had seen a serious row between countries, including some European ones, on the treatment of biotechnology-related trade issues. Some strongly favoured gambling on the premature insertion of yet another complex issue area into the multilateral trade governance system. Many, if not most, governments as well as observers intuitively felt frightened by such a prospect. A sense of uncertainty and a feeling of vertigo seemed to reign among trade negotiators, and many civil society observers vividly expressed strong opposing views. Following the difficult disputes there, ministers of environment and trade negotiators worked intensely in Montreal in early 2000 to bridge over years of differences and finalize the crafting of an internationally binding treaty on the transboundary movement of living modified organisms in the form of the Cartagena Protocol on Biosafety. This all took place against a backdrop of tension in transatlantic relations, which had escalated over the strife generated by loss of consumer confidence and environmental suspicion about imports of transgenic crops from the US into Europe. In the midst of this, developing countries were seen to make faltering attempts to find a place in the international debate and to responsibly articulate their national interests.

Insufficient information and analysis, reflected in controversies at the domestic level, in both developed and developing countries, were (and continue to be) of concern and frustration to policy makers. Indeed, the debate on public policy objectives of biotechnology and the treatment of its trade aspects remain unsatisfactory. It is not only the lack of technical, scientific and financial capabilities – characteristic of the departing policy environment in many developing countries – that holds back the emergence of sound policy in this specific field, it is also a persistent failure in the policy formulation processes, not uncommon in international trade, to consider the concerns and deepen the knowledge of stakeholders.

As a result of this situation, a pragmatic approach is gaining weight. Evidence of this can be found in the various schemes and models of research, production or import regimes for biotechnology that we have seen tossed around and aside in developing countries over the past few years. Surveys of trade negotiators in Geneva confirmed to us that most of them appreciate the urgency of effectively involving themselves in this debate in an informed manner. Many also point to the frustration with the lack of response to this need from their colleagues in their capitals. The trade agendas are more than full and little time is left for reflection in missions in Geneva. In an effort to make this reality more bearable and modestly contribute to its improvement, the International Centre for Trade and Sustainable Development (ICTSD), under the leadership of Vicente Sánchez, convened in June of 2001 a second dialogue in Bellevue, Switzerland. This time we used the form of a seminar, with developing country experts as resource presenters, and focused on developing country trade negotiators (see Appendix III).

This book borrows mainly from presentations at that seminar. It has been enriched by other contributions on aspects that participants felt required more attention. The collection as a whole remains a non-partisan endeavour to assist in and incite the development of the essential knowledge to make policy specifically related to the intersection of trade, biotechnology and sustainable development in the South. It does not advocate any single approach on precaution, risk assessment and management or handling of bio-based technologies or products. Contributors have been selected in an attempt to cover some of the most relevant aspects of the debate and represent various perspectives. Their views are theirs and not those of any institution or the editors. We clearly understand that the chapters here are modest in their coverage and may not do justice to the complexity and variety of public policy and individual concerns; we also acknowledge the dynamic nature of policy environments, particularly when they refer to science. We hope to be in a position in the future to contribute further to the development of vital policy in this area.

Part One features a series of chapters highlighting the links between biotechnology, trade and sustainable development. Calestous Juma and Victor Konde place the issues into the broader context of the *global bioeconomy*. Using industrial biotechnology as an example, they highlight elements of a global biotechnology governance regime that can help developing countries to participate more actively in the new bioeconomy. Carlos Correa assesses the many economic factors that drive developing countries' competitiveness in biotech production. He notes the continuing inability of these countries to exploit the opportunities provided by biotechnology in the pharmaceutical and agricultural sectors, suggesting avenues for developing countries to get more actively engaged in these fields.

Joseph Gopo and Patricia Kameri-Mbote highlight barriers preventing the South from benefiting from biotechnology, pointing to constraints within developing countries as well as external forces. They stress the need to deal with safety concerns that continue to surround this technology and point to loopholes in the Biosafety Protocol that need to be addressed. Heike Baumüller considers the response of several countries, including some within the EU and the US as well as selected developing countries, to increase trade in agriculture biotechnology products from a 'collective preferences' analytical stance, with the aim of contributing to a better understanding of the basis for differing positions on biotech trade. Padmashree Gehl Sampath assesses the potential of agricultural biotechnology for the South. She highlights intellectual property rights and limited scientific and technological capacities as important constraints faced by developing countries, identifying strategies and options to address these concerns.

Chapter 6 sets out the different approaches to biotechnology taken by Brazil and Argentina. Maurício Antônio Lopes and Maria José Amstalden Sampaio outline the long and arduous process of developing Brazil's biosafety framework and assess the potential economic impact of adopting transgenic crops in the country. Eugenio Cap, Daniel Chudnovsky, Andrés López and Eduardo Trigo give an account of Argentina's experience with genetically modified soy, maize and cotton and look ahead towards the future of biotechnology in the country. Paul Chavarriaga-Aguirre, Douglas Pachico and Joe Tohme describe the example of transgenic cassava in Colombia. They outline the plant's potential to address challenges of tropical agriculture in the region while taking into account issues related to the trade in cassava products.

Part Two includes a series of chapters that address the challenges for current regulatory frameworks to address trade in biotechnology and highlight options to address these constraints. Jayashree Watal takes a closer look at the intellectual property regime and in particular the Agreement for Trade-related Aspects of Intellectual Property Rights (TRIPS). She notes opportunities for developing countries to use the provisions of the TRIPS Agreement to access the new technologies, which might be more effective than reopening negotiations. Jakkrit Kuanpoth addresses issues of access to genetic resources and traditional knowledge, and the sharing of benefits derived from them. He notes that the current intellectual property system does not suit the needs of developing countries and outlines alternative ways of protecting biological resources and associated knowledge.

Juan Mayr and Adriana Soto provide an account of the hard, but heartening, negotiating process of the Cartagena Protocol on Biosafety. They highlight difficulties in balancing trade and biosafety interests, stressing the importance of a negotiating format that matches the realities of the different positions. Veit Koester analyses the potential for conflict between the Cartagena Protocol on Biosafety and multilateral trade rules, and the extent to which the Protocol's provisions would be respected in a WTO dispute. He concludes that trade-regulating measures under the Protocol are unlikely to cause conflict with WTO rules or be disregarded in a dispute. Arturo Martinez and Kakoli Ghosh outline the capacities needed for developing countries to reap the benefits and manage the potential risk of biotechnology. They assess a range of capacity building activities already under way, stressing the need for such activities to be complemented by the transfer of appropriate technologies.

Christiane Wolff focuses on relevant WTO agreements and how they relate to the trade in biotechnology products. She outlines current debates at the WTO on labelling and import restrictions, and assesses the role of science in a possible WTO dispute. Atul Kaushik looks at the main trade concerns that have been voiced by developing countries with regard to biotechnology and how these would be covered by the current rules. He outlines the various WTO fora where these concerns might be raised and assesses which forum might best serve developing countries' interests.

Appendix I sets out relevant international legal frameworks for biotechnology, biosafety and trade. Appendix II describes the status of biotech approvals in a number of key countries and their national biotechnology frameworks, including regulations for the environmental release of genetically modified crops, the import and sale of biotech foods, risk assessment, and labelling requirements. A list of selected readings rounds off this collection, providing pointers to useful resources on issues related to trade and biotechnology.

Many people have been involved in this project in addition to the contributors, whom we thank sincerely for making their writing available to the public. We are grateful above anybody else to our very able and dedicated Assistant Editor, Heike Baumüller at ICTSD. From her entry position at the time of the South Centre's dialogue, Heike has been a supportive pillar of this effort. Her tolerance, patience and sound understanding of the issues and her sensitivity towards the various political and scientific views involved have been instrumental in taking this project to fruition. We would also like to extend our special thanks to Sofia Spirou, who provided invaluable editorial support in putting this publication together, as well as Sarah Mohan for helping us put on the finishing touches. Constanza Martinez ably arranged, on a shoestring and with little notice, the December 2000 dialogue. Christophe Bellmann, Heike Baumüller, Jeanette Tantillo, Jennifer Ngai and other colleagues at ICTSD made the dialogue in Bellevue possible. Our thanks also go to Jonathan Sinclair-Wilson and his able team at Earthscan who provided their tireless support to make this book a reality.

Finally, we are particularly grateful to the Rockefeller Foundation, which kindly sponsored the Bellevue meeting, and the Dutch Minister of Housing, Spatial Planning and the Environment, who provided the necessary financial support for this publication.

Vicente Sánchez
Universidad Bolivariana

Ricardo Meléndez-Ortiz
Executive Director, ICTSD

PART ONE

WEIGHING BIOTECHNOLOGY ON THE SCALES OF SUSTAINABLE DEVELOPMENT

Developing Countries in the Global Bioeconomy: Emerging Issues[1]

Calestous Juma and Victor Konde

Emerging technologies offer new prospects for bringing a large number of developing countries into the global economy. This chapter examines the ability of developing countries to play a significant role in international trade in industrial biotechnology, a sub-sector of what is referred to here as the *global bioeconomy*. Sustaining the new bioeconomy requires adoption of a global biotechnology governance regime that helps to bring a large number of developing countries into the global trading system. Limited participation of the developing countries in the emerging global bioeconomy can be expected to intensify public opposition to biotechnology. Such opposition is likely to be fuelled by presumptions about possible market dislocation and apparent features of technological disparities between nations. The elements of such a governance system include improvements in market access, development of technological capabilities, access to technology and the management of risks and benefits associated with its use.

THE GLOBAL BIOECONOMY

The promise of biotechnology, a set of revolutionary techniques, has been the subject of public policy aspirations for the last two decades. In a call tempered by realism and caution, Agenda 21, the work programme adopted by the 1992 United Nations Conference on Environment and Development, asserted that biotechnology:

> *promises to make a significant contribution in enabling the development of, for example, better health care, enhanced food security through*

> *sustainable agricultural practices, improved supplies of potable water,*
> *more efficient industrial development processes for transforming raw*
> *materials, support for sustainable methods of afforestation and reforesta-*
> *tion and detoxification of hazardous wastes.* (UN, 1992, p136)

The decade following the adoption of these commitments has shown little progress in the application of biotechnology in the developing world despite visions of a promising future.[2] Instead, the international community has devoted considerable resources to managing perceptions of biotechnology risks rather than exploring new opportunities for its use (Pardo et al, 2002). Despite this, a careful examination reveals biotechnology inroads into nearly all major fields of human endeavour (Pew Initiative on Food and Biotechnology, 2001). It is now a decade since world leaders signed Agenda 21. Since then, three major developments have occurred. First, the institutions of globalization that were being crafted at the time of the adoption of Agenda 21 are now in place and their influence on the international trading system has become a subject of considerable debate. Second, biotechnology products have made their debut on the international market and it is now possible to assess the performance of biotechnology in the global economy. Third, advances in biology (especially molecular biology) signal the prospect of a new generation of products and services that were not conceivable a decade ago.

This chapter explores the ability of developing countries to play a significant role in what is clearly an emerging field, involving the wider application of modern biotechnologies in fields such as agriculture, medicine and industry. We refer to the confluence of modern biotechnologies and the market niches that they occupy in the global bioeconomy. The new bioeconomy will benefit from advances in other fields, especially informatics, and it will take root in countries and regions that take deliberate steps to create an enabling environment for its adoption.

Advances in biotechnology-related fields such as genomics, genetic engineering, chemical engineering and cell technology are transforming the industrial process and management landscape. Advances in biotechnology are having particularly far-reaching impacts on the chemical industry.[3] Micro-organisms, enzymes or their products are replacing processes that depended heavily on chemicals, many of which are implicated in environmental damage. However, much discussion on biotechnology currently focuses on agricultural applications (and to some extent biomedical uses). The generic nature of biotechnology techniques makes it possible to create a new bioeconomy with greater prospects for the commercialization of new biotechnology products and wider participation of the developing countries.[4] This global market inclusion model will differ from the current one in which technology is concentrated in a small number of countries and resistance to new products is widespread.[5]

Since its emergence, modern biotechnology has been associated with debates concerning benefits and risks. The ability to transform life itself to generate new products and services has been classified as a revolutionary technology with the same societal impacts as the information and communications revolution. With these high expectations have come fears and concerns, which have captured public and policy attention worldwide. Concealed in the narrower debates about the impacts of biotechnology on human health and the environment are wider concerns about socio-economic considerations, which arise from concerns over market translocations.

Indeed, early concerns about agricultural biotechnology focused on the possible impacts of genetic engineering on shifting the locus of production of raw materials and its potential to reduce the participation of developing countries in the global economy. Little attention was paid to the ability of the developing countries to use the same technologies to diversify their produce and become players in the new global bioeconomy (Serageldin, 1999).[6] The debate over the distribution of biotechnological capabilities is evident in the field of agriculture, where only a handful of countries are producing genetically modified (GM) crops. This narrow distribution of capabilities is also a major source of international concern and a key factor in opposition to GM foods worldwide. Responses to the challenge will entail greater international cooperation in the field of biotechnology in general and in industrial biotechnology in particular (Juma, 2002). Such increased technology cooperation will also require greater participation by the developing countries in the global economy.

Although scientific advances in biotechnology appear to be concentrated in a small number of industrialized countries, there are various factors that would allow for the wider participation of developing countries in the new bioeconomy:

- the growing recognition that the current patterns of globalization are untenable if they do not increasingly include developing country products. These countries depend on industries that are based on natural resources and therefore can benefit from the use of modern biotechnology;
- the fact that many of the techniques used in biotechnology research are becoming readily available because of scientific familiarity and are therefore relatively easy to acquire through sustained capacity development and enterprise development efforts; and
- the fact that much of the initial research and development (R&D) expenditure has already been borne by the industrialized countries and what are needed are effective international technology partnerships.

Taking advantage of these opportunities, however, will depend on the level of domestic technological capacity in the developing countries and the kind of global biotechnology governance system that emerges from the current policy debates. A global governance system that provides opportunities for market access will help to foster the commercialization of new technologies, especially those that threaten to alter the patterns and loci of production. In other words, resistance to new technologies is likely to be reduced by perceptions of access to the new technologies, as well as to their markets. This, indeed, has not been the case with agricultural bio-technology, which involves worldwide exports with the potential for product displacement, while leaving wide margins of uncertainty for technological followers.

Wider participation in the bioeconomy will also foster greater interest in the harmonization of regulatory practices among countries. This view is based on the claim that regulatory practices evolve from the practical management of technology. In other words, those who have the capacity to use modern biotechnology are also the ones who would have the means and interest to develop regulatory systems for that technology. An alternative scenario involves a small number of biotechnology exporters and a large number of countries that are likely to consider restrictive regulatory practices. This seems to be a possible scenario in the field of GM foods.

The fears of technological exclusion are growing. The skills and detailed knowledge, from biology to engineering, needed for countries to become players in modern biotechnology are diverse and comprehensive. In addition, equipment sophistication and finance must be globally competitive (Visalakshi, 2001). Responses by developing countries to these requirements will vary considerably, depending on prior capabilities in relevant fields, existing strategies for enhancing national competitiveness in biotechnology and the degree of integration into global technological networks through joint ventures, strategic alliances and export opportunities (Dieter and Mytelka, 1998).

The new bioeconomy is characterized by the emergence of institutional structures, as well as rules, that demand alternative technology cooperation approaches. First, the new bioeconomy has emerged concurrently with international trading rules that reinforce the market dominance of leaders in particular technological fields. These rules are reinforced by greater emphasis on instruments such as the Agreement on Trade-related Aspects of Intellectual Property Rights (TRIPS) under the World Trade Organization (WTO), which have the potential to reduce the prospects for technological spill-overs to developing countries. Second, globalization has intensified interactions among firms in the developed world and contributed to technological convergence among firms in this region at the expense of linkages with firms in developing countries. Third, the new bioeconomy is driven largely by complex interactions between government, industry and academia with specific emphasis on the role of private enterprises. The growing role of the private sector in the industrialized countries demands a similar shift in the developing countries. This suggestion does not entail a reduction in the role of the public sector. However, it necessitates a review of the role of the public sector in a globalizing world (Juma and Calo, 2002). On the whole, a new technology governance regime is needed to foster technological cooperation, expand market opportunities for all major players and expand the prospects for wider acceptance of biotechnology products.

TRENDS IN INDUSTRIAL BIOTECHNOLOGY

This century promises to open new avenues for increasing the use of renewable resources in the global economy. These trends will give rise to new opportunities for the participation of developing countries in the global bioeconomy. But promise and reality are different. In the case of agricultural biotechnology, for example, only a handful of developing countries have so far managed to become players in the global economy. The rest have little hope of playing significant roles in the near future. As in other technological fields, participation in the global bioeconomy will be uneven and limited to those countries that make the necessary investments in technological development.

So far, much of the research on policy aspects of biotechnology has focused on agricultural and pharmaceutical biotechnology. The field of industrial biotechnology remains under-studied. Industrial biotechnology covers two distinct areas. The first area is the use of renewable raw materials (biomass) to replace raw materials derived from fossil fuels. The second is the use of biological systems such as cells or enzymes (used as reagents or catalysts) to replace conventional, non-biological methods.

One of the main prospects of industrial biotechnology is controlled production of biological catalysts. These biocatalysts are more specific and selective than their non-biological counterparts and their applications are being extended to non-conventional media.[7] As a result, they offer greater potential for cleaner industrial production. In other words, biocatalysts generate fewer by-products and can start with relatively unprocessed natural raw material. One of their applications is in waste treatment (OECD, 1998; OECD, 2001). But despite these advantages, biocatalysts are generally fragile and they have to be present in large quantities to produce the reaction wanted. Over the years, however, incremental technological innovations and new bioreactor designs have helped to improve the industrial performance of biocatalysts (Bolon et al, 2002). With incremental improvements in biocatalysts and the emergence of new design concepts, biotechnology's capacity to diffuse in the industrial sector will be strengthened. This prospect is enhanced by the growth in the biological sciences, as well as complementary fields such as chemistry and informatics.

The use of biomass for energy and industrial uses has been on the agenda of many governments for nearly two decades. Much of the interest was triggered by the oil crises of the 1970s. Although interest in the field waned with the decline in energy prices, advances in the biological sciences have continued to enhance the prospects for technological improvement and wider application. In addition to energy, living plants can be used to produce chemicals such as citric acid, lysine and lactic acid. Genetic modification offers new possibilities for utilizing plants as bioreactors or sources of raw materials for chemicals or even finished products. Monsanto, for example, has experimented with a genetically modified cress plant to produce a biodegradable plastic using a gene extracted from a bacterium,

Ralstonia eutropha. Chemical firms around the world are undertaking similar research activities. One of the most advanced efforts is a pilot plant constructed by Cargill Dow Polymers to produce 140,000 tons a year of polylactide (a biodegradable plastic) using lactic acid fermented from maize.

Improvement in enzyme technology is raising prospects for broadening the base of industrial biotechnology through increased use of micro-organisms.[8] Much of this world remains underutilized largely because micro-organisms have so far been poorly studied and documented. With the advent of DNA sequencing, micro-organisms will become an important addition to industrial activities through scientists' discovery of new biocatalysts (Lorenz and Schleper, 2002). The field of genomics is therefore likely to extend its influence from medicine and agriculture to industrial production and environmental management. Methods such as directed evolution and rational design would continue to be used to discover new enzymes for industrial use (Zhao et al, 2002). In addition, methods such as gene shuffling are helping firms to optimize their bioprocessing activities.

The genomes of a wide variety of micro-organisms of relevance to industrial production will be sequenced in the coming years and this will add significantly to the library of industrial biotechnology resources. Prospecting for biological organisms of industrial value will increase as bioprocessing gains acceptance. The network of agreements between bioprospecting firms such as Diversa and biotechnology-related firms such as Dow, Aventis, Glaxo and Syngenta are an example of the growth taking place in this field. These technological developments will result in new generations of chemicals and polymers that will compete directly with bulk petrochemical products.

MARKET OPPORTUNITIES FOR DEVELOPING COUNTRIES IN INDUSTRIAL BIOTECHNOLOGY

Although bioprocessing, using enzymes and biological methods, can cut costs while making production cleaner, its adoption by various developing country industries remains controversial at least in the near future. The heaviest polluters such as mining, paper and pulp and textile as well as leather manufacturing are prime opportunities for curbing pollution and lowering costs of production through the application of biotechnology. Still, a cluster of factors conspire to keep the biotechnology industry closed to the developing countries, including its complex structure, riddled with inter-corporate linkages and mergers that keep the sector in the hands of a few large corporations.

However, as the market expands at a rapid pace, so will the opportunities for new players to enter into industrial biotechnology. For example, enzymes are estimated to hold a world market value of US$1.6 billion, of which North America and Europe account for 35 per cent and 31 per cent, respectively. The share of the enzymes market in the textile and detergents sectors shrank, while that in animal feeds, specialty chemicals and food applications, increased at least five-fold, between 1992 and 1998.

In the sub-sector of bioengineered food additives, Asia has the fastest growing market currently estimated to be over US$6 billion globally, followed by Latin America. Amino acids and vitamins account for about US$3 billion, digestive enhancers, about US$1.3 billion and disease-preventing agents, US$480 million. It is estimated that the amino acid and digestive enhancers market will continue to grow. The market for probiotics should continue to grow, following the introduction of legislation in Europe and other countries to prohibit the use of antibiotics in animal feed.

However, it is also important to note that a number of the current biotechnological products are more expensive than their traditional equivalents. Biopesticides are still lagging behind chemical pesticides due to target specificity (which is bad for business, but good for the environment), instability and batch (potency) variation. This makes the marketing and production of biopesticides difficult and their use by farmers, households and industry unattractive.

Bioplastics and bio-fuels have been more expensive than traditional plastics and petroleum-derived equivalents in developed countries. Although the gains to the environment made by the use of these products are hard to determine, bioplastics and bio-fuels remain worthwhile areas for development, especially since costs of production are dropping. Bioplastics are now commonly used in hospitals and in home products and disposable utensils. Further, the costs of petroleum products in developing and developed countries are different, which makes them attractive in the former. It is along these lines that genetic modification may increase the value, but reduce the cost of production of these products.

DEVELOPING COUNTRY EXPERIENCES IN THE NEW BIOECONOMY

The potential role of developing countries in the bioeconomy is illustrated by the case of Biocon India. The firm was established in 1978 in Bangalore as a joint venture between Biocon Biochemicals of Ireland and local entrepreneurs. It began with the sale of simple fermentation products and later embarked on its own R&D programme that has made it a major international actor in the biotechnology field. One of its first R&D efforts was to develop a local alternative to Konji – a fermented mass of cooked soybean meal and roasted wheat – imported from Japan. Konji is a good source of amylases and proteases, which are essential in the hydrolysis of carbohydrates and enzymes.

Right from the beginning, Biocon India defined itself as a research enterprise and mastered a number of complicated fermentation techniques leading to innovations that improved the production process. The big breakthrough for Biocon India came as it developed Plafractor, a solid phase fermentation platform

(Suryanarayan, 2003). The patented bioreactor won the 2001 Biotechnology Product and Process Development Award from the Indian Department of Biotechnology in the Ministry of Science and Technology.

The story of Biocon India illustrates the importance of international partnerships. While Biocon India focused on innovation and production, Biocon Ireland established the market for its products, providing the newly formed firm with a regular flow of income while eliminating marketing costs. In 1989, Biocon Ireland and its 30 per cent share in Biocon India were acquired by Unilever whose financial strength and global standing gave Biocon new linkages and access to funds.

Biocon India has expanded its operations and moved into fields such as pharmaceutical research, developing rapidly through strategic partnerships with corporate clients of its products. Biocon has used its association with global companies to expand its markets and product range. All these lessons have helped the company consolidate its position, identify funding opportunities and take advantage of market availability. The creation of autonomous, individual companies has spurred its expansion, depth of research and product development. Overall, Biocon India is a model of biotechnology commercialization and international partnership that should encourage the development of industrial and environmental biotechnology.

Market inclusion through international alliances is also illustrated by Cuban experiences in biotechnology commercialization. It was not until the early 1980s that the Cuban government started to focus policy attention on biotechnology as a source of pharmaceutical products by supporting the creation of research centres. Cuba's centre of genetic engineering and biotechnology, the Centro de Ingeniería Genética y Biotecnología (CIGB), employs about 1200 scientists and technicians and has 192 laboratories, equipped with the best instruments from countries such as Japan, Germany and Sweden. These facilities produce vaccines for meningitis B and hepatitis B and are developing vaccines for HIV, haemophilia and cholera. In diagnostics, CIGB has produced analytic systems capable of detecting HIV, hepatitis B, herpes simplex, chagás, leprosy and other diseases. It has also produced probes for plant diseases, about 50 enzymes (some of which are produced only in Cuba) and 160 medical and pharmaceutical products (Elderhorst, 1994; de la Fuente, 2001).

Cuba moved into the commercialization of biotechnology products through the creation of a semi-private enterprise, Herber Biotech. By 1998, Herber Biotech was recording annually about US$290 million in sales of hepatitis B vaccines and pharmaceuticals in 34 countries. Nationally, biotechnology was placed just behind tourism, nickel and tobacco in terms of export earnings. The company now is extending its partnerships with other developing countries. In 2001, it established a joint marketing venture with Kee Pharmaceuticals of India that aims to access the Indian market through special pricing and technology transfers. Kee Pharmaceuticals launched Cardiostrep, owned by Herber Biotech, a streptokinase used for the hydrolysis of coronary clots or prevention of heart attacks. The market for streptokinase is valued at about US$11 million per year and is expected to grow by 30 per cent annually.

Cuba recognizes that participating in the global market involves forging alliances with a wide range of enterprises, especially those that have extensive marketing networks. Cuba's biotechnology industry demonstrates the importance of political leadership on technological matters, domestic funding for research activities, creation of appropriate research institutions and international alliances for product commercialization. Its future will depend on the degree to which these elements are maintained, especially in the face of worsening economic conditions that might divert resource allocation and political commitment to other sectors.

International policy options

The wider application of industrial biotechnology on a global level will depend on the strengthening of an international governance system for the new bioeconomy that is based on the principles of market inclusion. For developing countries to participate effectively in the new bioeconomy, at least four key areas of the governance system will need to be adjusted: market access; international biotechnology alliances; intellectual property protection; and risk management. This section outlines some of the key recommendations that pertain to these areas of global governance.

Market access

Market access represents the greatest hurdle to international trade and consequently to accessing and accepting technology. It serves as a critical signal to the potential for benefiting from investment in technological innovation in developing countries. Although liberalization of markets has increased over the last 50 years following the numerous trade negotiations and integration of economies, many barriers to trade still exist, especially in labour-intensive sectors that are of interest to developing countries. The two major barriers are high tariffs and standards (sanitary and phytosanitary requirements). Agricultural products and industrial product exports to developed countries suffer most from tariff peaks.[9] The EU and Japan have the highest number of tariff peak products for agricultural imports, while the US and Japan have the highest number for industrial and electronic product imports. These products represent about 15 per cent of the exports of the least-developed to the developed countries.

Other than tariff peaks, these products also suffer from tariff escalation. For example, exports of finished textile and clothing products to Canada attract about 16 times the tariff on raw materials for the same industry. Other products that suffer from incrementally applied tariffs by stage of production include leather, rubber, metal, wood and paper. These are all products where developing countries have particular interest. In manufacturing, developing countries products face tariffs of about 70 per cent higher than those faced by developed countries.

Taken together, tariff peaks and escalations reduce the desire in developing countries to export finished products, thereby reducing diversification and skill accumulation. Because of high levels of subsidies to agriculture and export products in developed countries, most developing countries continue to be marginalized in international trade.[10] In the absence of open markets, it is not surprising that developing countries do not invest heavily in export industries linked to the processing of raw materials. Their inability to invest in product improvement further weakens their capacity to compete in the global economy.[11]

Non-tariff restrictions, such as quota allocation, voluntary export restraints and non-automatic licensing, continue to impact on exports from developing countries. Products affected by these measures include textiles, sugar, rubber, minerals, machinery and precious stones in both developing and developed country markets. There are also fears that once these measures are phased out, they are likely to be substituted by other measures such as anti-dumping or other technical barriers.

The requirement for exporters to meet product standards similar to those found in the importing countries is a critical element in international trade. However, if the exporter's home market standards are different from that of the export market, then extra cost has to be incurred to meet the demands. Many developing countries do not have sufficient facilities and personnel to conform to industrialized countries' market demands. Developing countries often import products that are banned in industrialized countries, while developed countries are more restrictive when it comes to imports from developing countries. The implications of these restrictive measures and other trade inhibitory mechanisms such as countervailing duties, safeguards, customs and administrative red tape on industrial biotechnology are potentially large. These measures will affect products such as polymers, fuels, paints, lubricants, fertilizers, plastics and many others derived from biomass using industrial biotechnology.

Market access is an essential element of market liberalization and special efforts are needed to create better trading opportunities for developing countries. In the absence of such improvements, trust in global markets will remain low and the mistrust is likely to hinder the wider application of emerging technologies such as industrial biotechnology and cleaner production methods. Efforts to promote the wider use of industrial biotechnologies should involve measures aimed at reducing barriers to market entry for products originating from developing countries. This should be done in the context of measures aimed at fostering the emergence of the new bioeconomy.

Biotechnology alliances

One of the most significant developments in the structure of the global biotechnology industry is a network involving partnering activities (Mytelka, 1999). These networks are products of complex links between a wide range of enterprises, links that are designed to reduce the risks associated with the development of new products, as well as to facilitate information exchange. More specifically, these partnering arrangements help to provide sources of financing through licensing and up-front fees for R&D expenses, reimbursement of expenses for partnered products and services, royalties, profits and other success fees associated with the achievement of certain milestones. Such arrangements are particularly important in areas with limited access to other forms of financing, such as venture capital. Even where venture capital is available, these arrangements still serve an important risk-reducing function.

Partnering activities are naturally more concentrated in the industrialized countries, but these arrangements are being extended to developing countries, especially in agricultural biotechnology. Similar arrangements could be considered in industrial biotechnology. In addition to the risk-reducing benefits outlined above, partnering arrangements could also play a key role in the development of technological capabilities in the firms and institutions in developing countries. Such capacity would be specialized and related to specific products and services. Furthermore, such partnering would also be useful in promoting the adoption of good management and industrial production standards in developing countries. It is therefore recommended that partnering models that are relevant to developing countries be identified and promoted as part of the expansion of the new bio-economy.

Creating flexible intellectual property systems

Emerging technologies are associated with strong regimes of intellectual property protection. Biotechnology is a particularly interesting area for two reasons. First, the patenting of living forms is a recent development that is specifically linked to policy measures to foster the establishment of the biotechnology industry (Sechley and Schroeder, 2000). There are differences of opinion on the exact impact of patent protection on the evolution of the biotechnology industry. What is evident, though, is that complementary institutions such as venture capital would not have evolved to the extent that they did without the existence of an intellectual property regime that provides comfort to investors and inventors alike.

In this regard, intellectual property protection has co-evolved with the biotechnology industry and is one if its key institutional attributes. There are, of course, many areas of industrial biotechnology in developing countries that have developed through the use of public domain technology and have therefore not been affected by increased intellectual protection barriers. This, however, is going to change as more countries are brought under the auspices of the TRIPS Agreement, its successor arrangements and extra-juridical measures.

Practice suggests that the impact of intellectual property rights on the ability of developing countries to participate in the new bioeconomy varies considerably, depending on the nature of the research, level of technological development and enterprise size.[12] Public sector research programmes remain particularly vulnerable to changes in the intellectual property regime because of their traditional dependence on public domain technologies and lack of knowledge of intellectual property practices. Although this situation is starting to change, many developing countries are still far from mastering the detailed legal aspects of invention activity. Ironically, however, these same rules might affect their ability to be players in the new bioeconomy.

Furthermore, most developing countries are still in the early stages of technological learning where access to patented technologies is essential for industrial development. The more advanced of them need to maintain their interest in having access to protected technologies as soon as possible, while preserving the possibility that any of their future inventions will be protected. There are no general models that would enable countries to reflect these various balances in one strategy. However, there are specific areas that require policy attention. First, developing countries will need to ensure that they meet the minimum requirements for intellectual property protection and create suitable environments for inventive activity. In turn, industrialized countries should help increase the level of trust in the intellectual property system by seeking to balance strong intellectual property protection with the need to broaden the base for technological partnerships with developing countries. Agricultural biotechnology firms are exploring ways of sharing their patented technologies with developing countries under special institutional arrangements, including flexible licensing arrangements. Similar measures may be needed in the field of industrial biotechnology.

Economic risks and benefits

One of the main sources of resistance to the adoption of a new technology is failure to manage its risks. Institutions that deal with some aspects of risk and benefit management, such as anti-trust legislation, do not deal with seemingly benign product displacement. However, the pace of diffusion could undermine the benefits that the technology promises to bring. The use of pest resistant crops, for example, could be seen as offering a wide range of economic and health benefits. But those who rely on the chemical industry for their livelihoods are likely to be direct and indirect sources of resistance to the new technology.[13]

Managing technological transition is not easy, partly because of the competitive nature of market behaviour and the dominant view of losses as part of the institution of free markets. However, in the absence of measures that reduce radical market impacts, resistance to new technologies is likely to emerge and undermine the potential benefits to society. Intra-industry and inter-industry consultations are an essential element of such a technological transition strategy. Such consultation should lead to measures that promote market inclusion, particularly of the most vulnerable income groups that may be exposed to increased job insecurity during the course of economic restructuring. Early efforts to identify potential winners and losers are an important part of the technology development strategy. With this identification, it should be possible to manage both the risks and the benefits in a way that allows for relatively smooth technological transitions.

CONCLUSIONS

The wider adoption of industrial biotechnology as a growing segment of the new bioeconomy will depend largely on the extent to which global economic govern-ance provides adequate space for the emerging technologies. Of particular relevance is the ability of developing countries to participate in the new bioeconomy. The chapter has stressed the importance of a more open market access system, flexible enforcement of intellectual property rights in industrialized countries and adher-ence to minimum protection standards in developing countries, wider technology partnerships through corporate alliances and more effective systems for managing the economic risks and benefits associated with the introduction of new technologies.

NOTES

1   This paper first appeared in *Environment*, 'Industrial Applications for biotechnology –
    opportunities for developing countries', Juma, C and Konde, V, vol 44, no 6, p24–33,
    July–August 2002. Adapted with permission of the Helen Dwight Reid Educational
    Foundation. Published by Heldref Publications, 1319 18th Street, NW, Washington,
    DC 20036-1802. Copyright © (2002). It builds on an earlier version prepared for the
    United Nations Conference on Trade and Development, Geneva. We are indebted to
    Derya Honca and Karen Fang (Center for International Development at Harvard
    University) and Alexey Vikhlyaev (United Nations Conference on Trade and Develop-
    ment, Geneva) for their support, additional information and comments on an earlier
    version of this paper.
2   'Information technology now crosses all disciplines and impacts on all walks of life. The
    integration of biotechnology with materials sciences has the potential to have a similar
    impact; this will lead to the creation of new disciplines in which the biology and
    materials science community will be at ease with one another in technical discourse.
    We believe successful business impact will require an integrated approach of combining
    the traditional chemical and polymer sciences with biotechnology. Such interaction is
    most likely to provide valuable products to society, as indicated by other game-changing
    innovations that have occurred at the interface of several apparently separate disciplines,
    such as magnetic resonance imaging, heart pacemakers and so on.' (Miller and
    Nagarajan, 2000)
3   'The emergence of biotechnology in the chemicals and materials arena has begun. The
    biological world produces a vast array of polymers. Biologists routinely engineer
    proteins, polysaccharides, nucleic acids, polyhydroxy alkanoates and so on. Synthetic
    polymer chemistry has produced a plethora of polymers with wide ranging function-
    alities.' (Miller and Nagarajan, 2000)

4   Models of biotechnology commercialization in small economies may be of relevance to most developing countries. See, for example, Marsh, 2000.

5   This view also takes into account key dimensions of international politics. See for, example, Pownall, 2000.

6   For a discussion on the role of technological innovation in the global economy, see Archibugi et al, 1999.

7   'The conventional notion that enzymes are only active in aqueous media has long been discarded, thanks to the numerous studies documenting enzyme activities in non-aqueous media, including pure organic solvents and supercritical fluids. Enzymatic reactions in non-aqueous solvents offer new possibilities for producing useful chemicals (emulsifiers, surfactants, wax esters, chiral drug molecules, biopolymers, peptides and proteins, modified fats and oils, structured lipids and flavour esters).' (Krishna, 2002)

8   'Enzymes catalyze chemical reactions with great specificity and rate enhancements. These reactions are the basis of the metabolism of all living organisms . . . and provide tremendous opportunities for industry to carry out elegant, efficient and economical biocatalytic conversions.' (van Beilen and Li, 2002; see also Ogawa and Shimuzi, 1999)

9   Tariff peaks are tariffs of 15 per cent or higher, or three times the tariff in developed countries. Tariff escalation refers to tariffs that increase with level of downstream processing.

10   The Organisation for Economic Co-operation and Development (OECD) support to agriculture is estimated at US$1 billion per day.

11   For a study of the failure of the African countries to complete in the global economy, see Lall and Pietrobelli, 2002.

12   For a more extensive treatment of this subject, see Watal, 2000.

13   For further analysis on the sources of technological resistance, see Mokyr, 2002 and Randall, 1986.

REFERENCES

Archibugi, D, Howells, J and Michie, J (1999) 'Innovation systems and policy in a global economy', in Archibugi, D, Howells, J and Michie, J (eds) *Innovation Policy in a Global Economy*, Cambridge University Press, pp1–15

Bolon, D N, Voigt, C A, Stephen, L and Mayo, S L (2002) '*De novo* design of biocatalysts', *Current Opinion in Chemical Biology*, vol 6, no 2, pp125–129

de la Fuente, J (2001) 'Wine into vinegar: The fall of Cuba's biotechnology,' *Nature Biotechnology*, vol 19, no 10, pp905–907

Dieter, E and Mytelka, L (1998) 'Technological capabilities in the context of export-led growth', in Ernst, D, Ganiatsos, T and Mytelka, L (eds) *Technological Capabilities and Export Success in Asia*, Routledge Press, New York, pp5–45

Elderhorst, M (1994) 'Will Cuba's biotechnology capacity survive the socio-economic crisis?', *Biotechnology and Development Monitor*, no 20, pp11–13

Juma, C (2002) 'Biotechnology and international relations: Forging new strategic partnerships', *International Journal of Biotechnology*, vol 4, no 2/3, pp115–128

Juma, C and Calo, M (2002) 'Government and technological innovation: The case of agricultural biotechnology in the United States', in Norberg-Bohm, V (ed) *The Role of Government in Technology Innovation: Insights for Government Policy in the Energy Sector*,

Belfer Center for Science and International Affairs, Kennedy School of Government, Harvard University, Cambridge, Massachusetts, pp83–107

Krishna, S H (2002) 'Developments and trends in enzyme catalysis in non-conventional media,' *Biotechnology Advances*, vol 20, nos 3–4, p239

Lall, S and Pietrobelli, C (2002) *Failing to Compete: Technology Development and Technology Systems in Africa*, Edward Elgar, Cheltenham, UK

Lorenz, L and Schleper, C (2002) 'Metagenome – a challenging source of enzyme discovery', *Journal of Molecular Catalysis B: Enzymatic*, vols 19–20, pp13–19

Marsh, D (2000) *Fostering Innovation in a Small Open Economy: The Case of the New Zealand Biotechnology Sector*, Eighth International Joseph A Schumpeter Society conference, 28 June, Manchester, UK

Miller, J Jr and Nagarajan, V (2000) 'The impact of biotechnology on the chemical industry in the 21st century,' *Trends in Biotechnology*, vol 18, no 5, p191

Mokyr, J (2002) *The Gifts of Athena: Historical Origins of the Knowledge Economy*, Princeton University Press, Princeton, NJ

Mytelka, L (1999) 'New trends in biotechnology networking', *International Journal of Biotechnology*, vol 1, no 1, pp30–41

OECD (1998) *Biotechnology for Clean Industrial Products and Processes: Towards Industrial Sustainability*, Organisation for Economic Co-operation and Development, Paris

OECD (2001) *The Application of Biotechnology to Industrial Sustainability*, Organisation for Economic Co-operation and Development, Paris

Ogawa, J and Shimuzi, S (1999) 'Microbial enzymes: New industrial applications from traditional screening methods,' *Trends in Biotechnology*, vol 17, no 1, pp13–20

Pardo, R, Midden, C and Miller, J D (2002) 'Attitudes towards biotechnology in the European Union', *Journal of Biotechnology*, vol 98, no 1, pp 9–24

Pew Initiative on Food and Biotechnology (2001) *Harvest on the Horizon: Future Uses of Agricultural Biotechnology*, Pew Initiative on Food and Biotechnology, Washington, DC

Pownall, I E (2000) 'An international political economy view of the biotechnology industry', *Electronic Journal of Biotechnology*, vol 3, no 2, pp1–20

Randall, A J (1986) 'The philosophy of Luddism: The case of the West of England woolen workers, ca 1790–1809', *Technology and Culture*, vol 27, no 1, pp181–197

Sechley, K A and Schroeder, H (2000) 'Intellectual property protection of plant biotechnology inventions', *Trends in Biotechnology*, vol 20, no 11, pp456–461

Serageldin, I (1999) 'Biotechnology and food security in the 21st century', *Science*, vol 285, pp387–389

Suryanarayan, S (2003) 'Current industrial practice in solid state fermentations for secondary metabolite production: The Biocon India experience', *Biochemical Engineering Journal*, vol 13, pp189–195

UN (1992) *Earth Summit Agenda 21*, United Nations, New York

Visalakshi, S (2001) 'Manpower requirement in biotechnology and strategies to achieve them – international and Indian experiences', *International Journal of Biotechnology*, vol 3, no 1/2, pp199–216

van Beilen, J B and Li, Z (2002) 'Enzyme technology: An overview', *Current Opinion in Biotechnology*, vol 13, no 4, p338–344

Watal, J (2000) 'Intellectual property and biotechnology: Trade interests of developing countries', *International Journal of Biotechnology*, vol 2, nos 1–3, pp44–55

Zhao, H, Chockalingam, K and Chen, Z (2002) 'Directed evolution of enzymes and pathways for industrial biocatalysis', *Current Opinion in Biotechnology*, vol 13, no 2, pp 104–110

2

From Biotech Innovation to the Market: Economic Factors Driving the South's Competitiveness in Biotechnology

Carlos M Correa

Biotechnology offers a wide range of techniques that can be applied in the areas of agriculture, industry, energy, the environment and human and animal healthcare.[1] The diffusion of such techniques has not given rise to a *biotechnology industry*, but they have significantly influenced research and innovation in various sectors, notably the seeds and pharmaceutical industry. Rising numbers of new transgenic crops and drugs under clinical trials testify to the economic transformation triggered by the new technologies (Dhar and Chaturvedi, 2000, p10).

Biotechnology has been regarded as opening a window of opportunity for developing countries to enter new fields, such as biopharmaceuticals, or to add value to existing production, such as agriculture. However, so far the capacity to develop and industrially exploit biotechnology has been strongly concentrated in developed countries and even in a few countries and firms among them. In the case of genetically modified (GM) seeds, for instance, half a dozen large firms have research and development (R&D) capacity, patent portfolios and seeds distribution networks that allow them to dominate the industry (Falcon and Fowler, 2002, p204). In the area of biopharmaceuticals, large US and European companies have also been the main beneficiaries of modern biotechnology (Gambardella, 1995).

In fact, with some notable exceptions, developing countries have not been able to become significant players in the development of new biotechnology-based products and processes. However, some countries are important users of modern biotechnology developed elsewhere, as shown by the diffusion of GM crops in Argentina, South Africa and other developing countries. Both the capacity to industrially develop and to apply biotechnology and utilize biotechnological products and processes may have important implications on the competitive position of countries in world markets.

THE MANY ECONOMIC CONDITIONS NEEDED FOR A BIOTECH SECTOR TO TAKE OFF

There are a number of supply side factors that crucially influence the creation of an innovation capacity in biotechnology. These include the availability of qualified personnel (Waithaka, 1992; Sasson, 1993, p26), good industry–university linkages (Kenney, 1986; Correa et al, 1996; Cassier, 1999), funding, particularly subsidies and venture capital,[2] legal framework for R&D, including intellectual property, national policies to support start-ups, small and medium enterprises (SMEs), the commercialization of R&D results (Senker and Van Zwanenberg, 2001), and general industrial and services infrastructure (Sasson, 1992).

In addition, there are various demand side factors that may greatly influence the development of biotechnology, such as market size, procurement policies of, for example, pharmaceuticals by national healthcare systems, public perception and consumer attitudes and biosafety regulations (Senker and Van Zwanenberg, 2001, p10).

The interplay of the above-mentioned factors determines the incentives given to biotechnological development. For instance, a good science basis and industrial infrastructure, a supportive government policy, combined with muted public opposition to genetically modified organisms (GMOs), can provide a suitable environment for such development. A strong public opposition may constitute in some areas (notably agriculture) a barrier to development as strong as the absence of good science and entrepreneurship. National policies may also be a key element for the development of a biotechnology-based industry. Some developing countries have established, with very diverse scope and funding, national policies on the matter (see Box 2.1) .[3]

Sercovich and Leopold (1991) discussed various strategies for the entry of developing countries into biotechnology. These include supply-led strategies, which may be science-led, as in Cuba, industry-led, as in Argentina, or market-driven approaches, as in Brazil. Dominant strategies may promote research but scarcely succeed in turning scientific output into industrial production. Sercovich and Leopold conclude that 'the key to effectively exploiting leapfrogging potential does not lie in mastery of the scientific underpinning of a technology, but rather in the mastery of the engineering, industrial and commercial skills and capabilities that make it possible to reach the market competitively' (quoted in Sasson, 1992, p115).

In addition, there are sector-specific factors that need to be considered. The cases of pharmaceuticals and agro-biotechnology are briefly considered below.

BOX 2.1 NATIONAL POLICIES ON BIOTECHNOLOGY IN DEVELOPING COUNTRIES

The Ministry of Science and Technology of the *Republic of Korea* has established a set of plans to help entrepreneurs, scientists and technicians set up 600 biotechnology-related venture firms by the end of next year. The ministry decided to allot 323.8 billion Won (US$259 million) into research and development of biotechnology related to DNA, protein and bio-information. It also announced a plan to set up a National Genetic Research Centre and to introduce a life science ethics law in order to lay the groundwork for genome studies (CropBiotech Update, 2002, 16 August).

South Africa has designed a national biotechnology strategy to enable it to catch up with the progress of other developing countries. Key recommendations include the establishment of a government agency to champion biotechnology, proactive investment in human resources development and the strengthening of scientific and technological capabilities (Ngubane, 2002; CropBiotech Update, 2002, 6 September).

Singapore announced in June 2000 its National Biomedical Science Strategy, which would provide for an estimated US$2 billion over the next five years into new institutes, academic research and training in the life sciences, as well as tax incentives for both multinational pharmaceutical companies and homegrown biotech start-ups (Normile, 2002).

Malaysia aspires to become one of the key biotechnology hubs in the world while reaping the greatest potential benefits from its greatly diversified bio-resources. The government has indicated in its Eighth Malaysia Plan, that biotechnology will become a major component, supporting Malaysia's overall strategy for sustainable growth in the knowledge-based economy. The main instrument for the country's biotechnology development programme is *BioValley Malaysia*. It is intended to be a catalyst and test-bed for the development of Malaysia's biotechnology industry. *BioValley* will be designed to enable the location of a critical mass of researchers, industry workers and entrepreneurs in an environment created to facilitate networking, sharing of information and ideas and the development of commercial activities pertaining to biotechnology (CropBiotech Update, 2002, 13 September).

The Federal Government of *Nigeria* will spend around US$19 million a year for three years on biotechnology, through its National Biotechnology Development Agency. Nigeria's biotechnology development programme objectives include ensuring self-reliance in the development and production of biotech products and services critical to national economy. It also aims to ensure access to safe, ethical and profitable uses of biotech products and services (CropBiotech Update, 2002, 13 September).

Sources: CropBiotech Update, 2002; Ngubane, 2002; Normile, 2002

BIOPHARMACEUTICALS: WHY LARGE FIRMS DOMINATE THE MARKET AND KEEP DEVELOPING COUNTRY START-UPS IN THE MARGINS

Modern biotechnology may be applied in the pharmaceutical sector both to advance research[4] and as a means of producing medicines that replicate substances pre-existing in nature (such as growth hormones, interferon and erythropoietin) or to develop other medicines and vaccines. In fact, biotechnology is reported to have already yielded a large number of new drug candidates.[5] Few firms in developing countries have the technical capacity and can fund the substantial investments in R&D[6] needed to compete at the frontier of the biotechnological development. However, biotechnology has also been regarded as opening a window of opportunity for developing countries to enter the pharmaceutical sector. Several reasons have underpinned this belief:

- First, the application of biotechnology is heavily dependent on scientific knowledge and some developing countries have a good basis in biosciences. In addition, the techniques of genetic engineering have become routine and can be applied in production following the experiences of pioneer companies.[7]
- Second, capital requirements for production are relatively low in comparison to other activities in the pharmaceutical sector. In some cases, such as interferon, an important protein helping the human body fight off viral infections, the domestic and even world demand may be satisfied with a low volume of production given that required doses are minimal.
- Third, biological materials – cloned genes, cloning vectors which are DNA-vehicles for the transfer of traits from one cell to another, recombinant viruses which are similarly used to insert DNA into a host-cell – are generally available in the market at reasonable cost. Modern equipment and software makes it possible to perform economically and rapidly tasks that in the past were lengthy and costly, such as the synthesis of nucleotides, one of the basic building blocks of DNA. Some specialized firms offer kits with specified properties to clone a desired gene or undertake gene-cloning on request, for a small fee. In other words, the diffusion of knowledge and the market availability of biological inputs and specialized services and equipment have considerably facilitated gene-cloning and thereby reduced the entry barriers for new firms.

There are, however, many important constraints for developing countries as well. Though laboratory techniques can be mastered, industrial scaling up generally poses important technical challenges and requires considerable investment. Industrial microbiologists and other specialists in the downstream activities are scarce or non-existent in most developing countries. Hence, while the scientific aspects of certain processes may be mastered, developing an acceptable product may be out of reach, particularly due to the stringent requirements imposed for the manufacture and commercialization of medicines. The level of purity (close to 100 per cent) required, for instance, for commercially selling recombinant erythro-poietin requires sophisticated technical capacity and productive experience that is generally not available in domestic firms, universities and other R&D public institutions.[8]

Further, the quality of the general infrastructure available in a country is important for modern biotech production. For example, since most enzyme and other materials are unstable at ordinary temperatures, facilities for cold transporta-tion and storage are essential, not to mention more basic requirements regarding water and electricity supply. As in other undertakings, the overall industrial infrastructure for equipment repair, recruitment of technical staff for laboratories and so on are equally important to ensure efficient production.

In addition, a set of new techniques has been developed in the last ten years, the application of which may require significant learning and investment. They include, inter alia, genomics, or technologies deciphering the precise functions of genes, proteomics, meaning the discovery of the function of proteins, combina-torial chemistry, meaning new techniques to select promising drugs and high throughput techniques, that is, new methods of automating and hugely accelerat-ing drug discovery by testing thousands of chemical reactions in a miniaturized, automated chemistry laboratory (Wolff, 2001, p13).

The commercialization of pharmaceutical products requires the approval by the national health authority in each country in which the product is to be sold. Obtaining such approval is a complex task under many jurisdictions particularly in those, such as Australia, the US and the European Union, where legislation grants the first firm to get commercialization approval exclusive rights over the test data for a given period that varies from five years in the US to six to ten years in the EU (Correa, 2002). Biotech firms in developing countries, like start-ups in the developed world, lack the capacity to undertake the long pre-clinical and clinical trials necessary to put a new drug on the market.[9]

The commercial exploitation of biotechnology-based pharmaceutical products is also problematic. While small firms may master the process of production, they would need significant resources to establish and maintain the sales network necessary to reach doctors. In fact, the experience of biotech start-ups in the US shows that very few companies were able to become pharmaceutical companies on their own, due to lack of sufficient capital and experience in the pharmaceutical market.

Another important barrier is now emerging as a result of the expansion and strengthening of intellectual property rights. In response to pressures from industrialized countries and in order to conform to the standards adopted under the Agreement on Trade-related Aspects of Intellectual Property Rights (the TRIPS Agreement) negotiated during the Uruguay Round, developing countries have introduced patents on pharmaceutical products. They must also protect micro-organisms, which are often understood under national patent laws in developed countries as comprising cells and sub-cellular components, such as genes.[10]

Though some domestic institutes and firms in developing countries have entered the complex field of patenting in biotechnology, firms in industrialized countries control most biotech patents. US-based Celera has filed around 10,000 gene patent applications. Another US-based firm, Incyte Pharmaceuticals, has about 500 gene patents granted and more than 7000 applications. US-based Human Genome Sciences has received 200 patents and applied for 8000 more. And US-based Millennium Pharmaceuticals with strong presence in the UK too, has applied for 1500 patents. The US Patent Office was reported to have 30,000 biotech patent applications pending, 20,000 of them gene related. As noted by Wolff, many gene patent applications are based on a mere hypothetical computer-made – and potentially worthless – analysis of gene functions. Using specialized software, genomics companies turn the problem of postulating a gene's function over to computers. The computer makes a guess about the gene's probable function and a patent application is filed (Wolff, 2001, pp14, 67).

Finally, strategic alliances have become crucial in biotechnology (Barbanti et al, 1999). The possibility of exploiting complementary assets with other firms is key to the competitive strength in this area. Biotechnology has in fact been one of the areas where strategic alliances became more frequent. One of the most common forms of strategic alliances in biotechnology has been agreements between a small biotechnology firm and a major drug company where the former contributes a new product or therapy and the latter funding for further R&D[11] as well as experience in carrying out trials and procedures for marketing approval. The ability to resort to an established sales force and to large manufacturing capabilities, are other distinct contributions that large companies can make to an alliance with smaller biotech firms. Entering into such alliances is not easy, if possible at all, for firms in developing countries since they cannot offer complementary assets sufficiently attractive to potential partners from developed countries.

As a result of these limitations and barriers, not surprisingly, few firms from developing countries have so far seriously succeeded in entering the biopharma-ceutical field. One such case is Biosidus in Argentina, which produces, inter alia, erythropoietin (EPO), a hormone that stimulates the production of red blood cells, for the domestic and foreign markets. Another one is the Genetic Engineering and Biotechnology Centre (CIGB) of Cuba, which has reached a significant develop-ment and commercial success in foreign markets (Correa, 1998, p295). Instead, the R&D investment in DNA products is reported to be below 2 per cent of the total investment of the biotechnology industry in India, despite the fact that the country's pharmaceutical industry has become a major world supplier of generic drugs (Dhar and Chaturvedi, 2000, p16).

HIGH RESEARCH COSTS AND MARKET RISK RAISE SCEPTICISM ON THE FUTURE OF GM CROPS

Conventional breeding can only mix plants that are by nature capable of inter-breeding and producing offspring. Genetic engineering permits going beyond these limits, by artificially merging DNA from one or more organisms into the inherited genetic code of the plant's genome. Genetic engineering thus permits incorporation of new traits into plants either by using genes from other organisms and changing plant phenotypes, such as herbicide tolerance and insect resistance,[12] or by modifying the gene expression of plants, as with the use of anti-sense technology, which blocks the expression of unwanted traits.[13] It also permits altering the capacity of seeds to germinate, as in the case of the so-called *terminator* technology (Swanson and Goeschl, 2002, p177).

Most of the transgenic crops developed and marketed so far have incorporated only a very limited number of genes in order to obtain herbicide resistance or insect resistance. Some transgenic crops of greater potential interest for developing countries have also been developed, such as transgenic rice of high iron content developed by transferring the ferritin gene from soybean to rice, or transgenic rice producing provitamin A. However, very few applications with direct benefits to poor consumers or to resource-poor farmers in developing countries have been introduced (Byerlee and Fischer, 2002, p931).

Genetic engineering in plants is largely dominated, as mentioned, by a few large companies. Due to increasing R&D expenses as well as costs and complexity of patent protection, which has led to extensive and costly litigation and the search for control of the whole cycle of seed production, a process of unprecedented concentration has taken place in the agro-biotechnology field. A few major multinational agricultural biotech companies control the basic technologies and research tools and hold the largest portfolio of the growing number of patents in this field.[14] Such companies also control a large proportion of the supply of commercial seed. For instance, in Brazil, Monsanto increased its share of the maize seed market from 0 to 60 per cent between 1997 and 1999. It acquired three locally based firms, including Cargill, as the result of an international deal, while Dow and AgrEvo (now Aventis) also increased their market share by acquisition. Only one Brazilian-owned firm remained with a 5 per cent market share. This trend seems widespread in developing countries (CIPR, 2002, p65).

Transgenic plant varieties have been disseminated in some developing coun-tries, because of field testing or use in cultivation of some crops. Around a quarter of land grown with GM crops in 2002 was in developing countries, notably in Argentina, China, South Africa and Mexico.[15] *Bacillus thuringiensis* (Bt) cotton or Bt maize is now grown in at least five developing countries (CIPR, 2002, p64). However, in all of Africa, the only nation to have given commercial planting approval for any GM crops so far has been South Africa (for GM maize and GM cotton). In all of developing Asia, the only significant commercial GM crop planting approvals so far have been for cotton (in China, Indonesia and, as of 2002, in India as well) and to a lesser extent maize (in the Philippines).[16]

The economic and agronomic implications of the use of GM seeds remain extremely controversial. Some evidence, mainly on their economic impact, is emerging in industrialized[17] and some developing countries.[18]

The degree of diffusion of transgenic varieties in developing countries is far more significant than their participation in R&D in this field. The largest part of agricultural R&D in such countries is funded and executed by the public sector.[19] Some developing countries, Argentina, Brazil, India, China, Mexico and South Africa, have strong capacity in molecular biology, often located in universities, and have undertaken R&D in genetic engineering of plants, occasionally with external support,[20] but R&D on genetically engineered seeds is in its early days. The latter generally takes place in the framework of public institutions, with limited funding.[21] Moreover, the R&D agenda in plant genetic engineering is often being largely determined by the transnational corporations, which mainly focus on export crops[22] and on herbicide, insect and virus resistance.

Domestic firms in developing countries, which in some cases excel in conventional breeding, have made little contribution in the area of genetic engineering, where their capacity is very limited.[23] The private sector is a major player in developing countries for R&D on hybrid crops, such as maize, even in markets with relatively small farms. For non-hybrid crops, private companies are mostly conducting biotechnology research in a few developing countries with large seed markets and where intellectual property rights can be enforced (Byerlee and Fischer, 2002, p932). Some local companies have started work in GM crops, often in association with foreign partners. Thus, Biosidus has worked on transgenic potato in Argentina. Rallis India is working on various vegetable crops to introduce insect resistance based on foreign technology. The joint venture between Proagro and Plant Genetic Systems of Belgium (Proagro PGS) is working on crops like mustard, cauliflower, cabbage, tomato and aubergine to introduce genes of insect resistance and male sterility (Dhar and Chaturvedi 2000, p30).

Can developing countries become competitive in the field of plant biotechnology? So far, as mentioned, their capacity in this field is quite limited. In those countries that accept the planting of GM crops, one possible approach may be to exploit the complementarities between genetic engineering and conventional breeding. In fact, in some developing countries the capacity of public institutions and domestic firms in conventional breeding has opened routes of cooperation with biotechnology companies (mostly large multinationals). A commercially successful GM variety combines the best of an existing plant modified to incorporate a desired new characteristic. Such elite basic plant material can often be provided by local institutions and seed companies. For instance, in Argentina, one of the world's largest producers of transgenic soybean, the most successful commercial transgenic varieties resulted from the cooperation between Monsanto, providing the Roundup

Ready (RR) gene which gives plants pesticide resistance, and domestic seed companies, providing high yielding germplasm well adapted to local agricultural needs.[24]

Another approach would obviously be to intensify efforts to develop transgenic added value products. This would require considerable investment and scientific capacity. Questions arise, however, as to whether developing countries should expand their capacity in this field, or rather concentrate their efforts in conventional breeding, in view of the still uncertain impact of GMOs on the environment and the reluctance of major markets (notably Europe) to accept GMOs.

The competitive advantages that the use of GM plant varieties may bring about, if they exist at all, may be neutralized by consumers' attitudes vis-à-vis GM food in potential export markets. Such attitudes vary considerably from country to country. While US consumers generally accept GMOs,[25] and this apparently is also the case in some developing countries,[26] rejection is strong in major markets such as European countries. As noted by Paarlberg (2002), most developing countries' authorities have recently adopted a go-slow approach toward this controversial new technology. They are deciding, for the moment at least, to hold back on the planting of any GM food or feed crops for fear of losing their access to key export markets in the industrialized world – particularly Europe and Japan. The most important barrier to getting GM seeds into the hands of farmers in poor countries is now the consumer and policy resistance toward GM food that has become pervasive in wealthy countries that import food and animal feed. In developing countries, labelling capacity is weak and it will cost too much in any case to try to segregate farm products into separate GM versus non-GM marketing channels. The cheapest way to compete for the business of anti-GM food and feed customers in Europe or Japan is to remain entirely GM-free. The commercial benefits of this strategy are already being seen. Because Brazil has not yet introduced GM maize, it was recently able to capture a premium of US$6–7 per ton against US maize in the markets of Spain and Japan.[27]

In addition to problems posed by limited resources and environmental and commercial risk, R&D in new transgenic varieties may face important obstacles emerging from patent legislation, particularly the patenting of research tools. For example, development of a GM insect resistant crop may involve using a protected plant variety as well as patents related to the selected marker gene and the insecticidal gene, the transformation technology, the promoter and other regulatory elements needed for adequate gene expression in the plant cells. To develop a single transgenic plant may involve nearly 100 protected elements or processes (Ruane and Zimmermann, 2001, p75). The multiplicity of patents embedded in a biotechnology product can block research projects, make the product expensive and jeopardize commercialization in those markets where the patents are in force.

Even a single patent holder can block the development and commercial exploitation of a transgenic variety. It has been observed that in many cases research tool patents have not been applied for and obtained in developing countries. This would give local institutions and companies the freedom to operate and use those patents for products for the domestic market and other markets where the patent has not been issued. In some cases, however, such institutions and companies may be inclined to respect the intellectual property on a particular gene – even if the patent were not granted in the country – in order to prevent retaliations from the intellectual property rights owner or to avoid jeopardizing other collaborations. Moreover, if the product finally developed contained a component patented in one country, but not patented in the country where the development took place, the patent owner could block exports, because of the patents granted in the importing country.[28] Unless a licence to use such a component were obtained, this would certainly reduce the interest in undertaking research in export crops with uncertain commercial benefits.

DIVERSITY PREVAILS OVER DEVELOPING COUNTRY POSITIONS ON RISKS AND OPPORTUNITIES OF GM CROPS

The development and diffusion of biotechnology, particularly in agriculture, has raised serious concerns about the implications on health and the environment of the release (intended or not) of GMOs. Governments, scholars and non-governmental organizations (NGOs) have taken different and in some cases quite opposite views on the possible impact of such a release. As a result, what is deemed a *safe use* varies considerably depending on the point of view adopted. Some countries have issued strict regulations covering research, production and use of GMOs, while others follow more liberal approaches, as examined elsewhere in this book (see Appendix II).

Given the still largely unknown implications of biotechnology for health and the environment, its application needs to be subject to monitoring and scientific evaluation. However, applying biosafety regulations may be more difficult in developing countries than in industrialized ones. Developing countries possess limited funds, scientific infrastructure and expertise and do not have the capacity to monitor experiments or the products of such experiments. Furthermore, they are generally ill-equipped to deal with any environmental disasters emanating from these products. This could be the case even in a country with a strong biosafety system in force, such as India (Ruane and Zimmermann, 2001, p18).

The methodologies and techniques necessary to comply with biosafety rules are not so complex in themselves,[29] but they are still evolving[30] and adequate infrastructure and institutional arrangements are needed.[31] Thus genetically modified plant varieties may easily contaminate non-modified varieties,[32] for instance, through normal processes of pollination. A country wishing to supply non-modified products (which may receive a premium price in GMO-averse countries) may find it difficult or impossible to keep a GMO-free production.[33] An example is provided by the case of Brazil, a major agricultural producer. Though the government authorized the release of genetically modified varieties,[34] GMO opponents have succeeded so far to obtain judicial measures that prevented such release.[35] However, for several years farmers in the south of Brazil have imported and reproduced soybean transgenic (herbicide resistant) seed from Argentina. Today a significant production of soybean in different regions of Brazil is based on such transgenic seed, leading the government to issue Provisional Measures in 2002, 2003 and 2004 allowing the sale of GM crops for a limited amount of time (see Chapter 7).

In other developing countries an ambivalent approach towards GMOs prevails. Though the risks of GMOs are clearly perceived, governments do not want to miss the opportunities offered by GMOs in terms of increased yield or productivity. This ambivalence is well reflected by a recent statement by the Malaysian Prime Minister: 'foods derived from GMOs hold great promise but we continue to verify their effects as quickly as science will allow us . . . It would be unfortunate indeed, if millions must die because the rich have decided to reject GM food in favour of the more costly normal products' (CropBiotech Update, 2002, 4 October).

Finally, there are implications of GM crops and food products for trade that are often overlooked:

> the main developing countries exports are tea, coffee, cocoa, cotton and sugar, while Africa and China are big cereals importers. If GM crops (or substitutes), grown in industrialized countries, raised the supply of a beverage crop by 20 per cent, a price fall of about 60 per cent would be needed to clear the market. Such a development would threaten to devastate low-income exporters of beverage crops such as Ghana and Sri Lanka. Conversely, failure to achieve rapid cereal output increases in Africa or Asia would, in view of the pending growth of demand and population, mean explosive rises in food import needs and some rise in the price at which such imports would be available. We consider that such trade effects, while seldom quantified, are potentially very damaging. (Nuffield Council on Bioethics, 1999, p66)

Conclusions

While biotechnology may be applied in a wide range of activities in developing countries and generate new industrial and trade opportunities, the most visible and profitable industrial applications, such as in pharmaceuticals, have largely been beyond the reach of developing countries. A few cases show that with the appropriate infrastructure and policies, some developing countries have been able to participate modestly in the emerging market of biopharmaceuticals. Significant efforts from the private and public sector would be required, however, to exploit such opportunities, especially in order to catch up with new developments in genomics and other technologies.

Opportunities to reap benefits of agricultural biotechnology remain equally out of reach for developing countries. Though it will be up to each country to define its own policy on this matter, it seems clear that current R&D trends in biotechnology may not benefit developing countries in the long term. This will be particularly true if:

- only slow progress continues to be made in those GM crops that enable poor countries to be self-sufficient in food;
- advances are directed at crop quality or management rather than at drought tolerance or yield enhancement;
- innovations that save labour costs (for example, herbicide tolerance), rather than those which create productive employment, are emphasized; and
- industrialized countries are able to produce, or substitute for, GM crops now imported in conventional (non-GM) form from developing countries (Nuffield Council on Bioethics, 1999, pp66–67).

Developing countries face serious challenges in the field of agricultural biotechnology, including the possible risks posed to health and the environment by the release of GMOs, the potential negative impact of GMOs' diffusion for exports to GMO-averse markets, and the risk of substitution of local produce by GM crops grown in developed countries. The use of biotechnology in agriculture raises some fundamental dilemmas for developing countries, in view of the risks but also the potential for increased production and poverty alleviation.

NOTES

1   Though biotechnology encompasses a broad set of mature and intermediate technologies, the term is used in this chapter in relation to more modern techniques based on genetic engineering.
2   Biotechnology has emerged as an industry largely because of one economic institution: venture capital (Kenney, 1986, p133).
3   For agricultural biotechnology policies and priority setting see Cohen, 1999.
4   Biotechnology has substantially changed the R&D paradigm in pharmaceuticals where the *rational drug design* has substituted to a large extent *mass screening* methods. See Gambardella, 1995, pp23, 79.
5   Most of these new drugs are aimed at so-called *big target diseases* that would generate high revenue returns. For heart disease and stroke, 96 drugs are in development; for the many forms of cancer, 316 new treatments are progressing; 122 drugs are being developed to fight AIDS; 29 new approaches to treat arthritis are being tested and Alzheimer's disease has 17 new treatments in the pipeline. In 2000, the US Food and Drug Administration approved 32 new biotech drugs, vaccines, and other therapeutic innovations; the total number of successful biotech products on the market was approaching 110 (Wolff, 2001, p22).

6   The Biotechnology Industry Organization reported that in 1999 American biotech companies spent more than half of the sector's revenues (US$11 billion) on R&D (Wolff, 2001, p16).

7   One Argentine firm, for instance, was able to produce recombinant interferon based on published scientific information and a well-qualified staff in contact with foreign research institutions. Given that the genetic sequence of interferon was already known and published, the firm developed a method of isolation, without entering into the costly and lengthy screening process that the first firm to produce recombinant interferon had to undertake.

8   A study on biotechnology production in Latin America, for instance, showed that only one domestic firm had been able to master the science and technology necessary to produce and commercialize recombinant pharmaceutical products. It also showed that while public institutions mastered the use of cloning techniques for obtaining the protein, they were not well equipped to undertake purification and other processes required for testing and production (Correa et al, 1996).

9   The costs and complexities of such trials explain to a great extent the process of takeovers in the biotech industry globally, especially the acquisition of small and medium biotech firms by large established pharmaceutical companies.

10 However, developing countries need not adopt this expansive interpretation since, strictly interpreted, micro-organisms only include *organisms* not visible to the naked eye such as bacteria, fungi or viruses.

11 Alliances in biotech take many different forms. One of the most common is an agreement between a smaller biotechnology firm and a major drug company:

> to share the future profits from a promising new therapy in development by the junior partner in return for periodic cash infusions called milestone payments. Typically, the Big Pharma partner pays the biotech ally a set amount when the smaller company achieves certain predefined goals in the discovery and drug-testing process. The biotech company benefits by receiving enough cash to carry on and the Big Pharma partner also stands to profit by gaining access to promising new developments without the enormous effort, investment and risk involved in starting a discovery program from scratch (Wolff, 2001, p63).

12 Herbicide tolerance has so far been the main plant biotechnology application, such as in commercial soybean varieties resistant to glyphosate. Another group of important applications is related to the resistance to biotic stress conditions caused by insect, fungi, and virus attacks. Insect tolerance is the most important application, in particular, wide use of genes derived from Bacillus thuringiensis (Banchero et al, 2001).

13 In the case of transgenic tomato, for instance, due to the inhibition of the polygalacturonase enzyme expression, tomatoes do not soften at ripening.

14 For instance, it has been reported that of the roughly 270 patents related to genes of the soil bacterium *Bacillus thuringiensis* granted from 1986 to 1997 in industrialized countries, about 60 per cent were owned by only six corporations (Ruane and Zimmermann, 2001, pp64–65).

15   Of the 81.0 million hectares of GM global area in 2004, some 58.6 million (72 per cent) were planted with crops modified for tolerance to a specific herbicide; 15.6 million hectares (19 per cent) were modified to include a toxin-producing gene from a soil bacterium, *Bacillus thuringiensis*, while 6.8 million hectares (9 per cent) were planted with crops having both herbicide tolerance and insect resistance (James, 2004).

16   In March 2002, the Indian Genetic Engineering Approval Committee (GEAC), cleared Bt cotton for commercial planting, in spite of the legal challenges to its planting pending in the Supreme Court alleging irregular testing. Some Indian States, however, have banned the sale of Bt cotton seeds. The potential risk of genetically modified cotton for India is that, unlike other countries, oil is extracted from cotton seed and used for cooking and the residue is fed to cattle, raising the possibility of the toxic genes entering the human food chain. GEAC has also moved to grant approval for the large-scale farming of genetically modified mustard seed developed by Aventis/Proagro and promoted by Proagro PGS (India), a subsidiary of the Belgium-based Hoechst Schering AgrEvo (SUNS, 27 September 2002). See also Gahukar, 2002. In December 2002, the Bureau of Plant Industry in the Philippines approved the first biotechnology crop (insect-protected GM maize) for commercial release (Monsanto, 2002).

17   Another study was conducted by the George Morris Center to determine the impact of glyphosate tolerant (GT) soybeans in Ontario. Farmers using GT technology had made, on average, 1.7 fewer passes over their fields for herbicide application. Further, they used less of the implements usually associated with soil erosion. Producers perceived that GT technology saved labour and fuel and lowered herbicide costs. In terms of environmental impact, Ontario producers were split on whether GT technology had positive or negative impact on biodiversity (Brethour et al, 2002)

18   In South Africa, GM crops such as Bt cotton have been planted by large and small farmers. Among the large farmers the most important benefit of Bt cotton cited was the savings on pesticides and application costs followed by peace of mind about bollworms. For small farmers who adopted the technology, the most important reason was pesticide saving. Increased yield benefit was seen as more important by small farmers. Large farmers saw it more as a bonus (Kirsten and Gouse, 2002). See also Ismael et al, 2002.

19   While worldwide private agricultural R&D expenditures totalled US$11.5 billion in 1995, only US$0.7 billion was attributable to developing countries (CIPR, 2002, p60).

20   The UK Department for International Development (DFID) was reported to have funded a GB£13.4 million programme to create a new generation of GM animals, crops and drugs in developing countries. Funding would include about 80 GM projects involving 24 countries in four continents, ranging from long-life bananas to fast-growing pigs and fish, from disease resistant rice to stopping tsetse flies carrying sleeping sickness (CropBiotech Update, 2002, 27 September).

21   R&D investment by the centres of the Consultative Group on International Agricultural Research (CGIAR) should also be considered in this context. The centres invest around US$25 million annually in biotechnology, representing 7.7 per cent of the total CGIAR budget (Byerlee and Fischer, 2002, p934).

22   Research on alfalfa and tomato are an exception to this rule in the case of Argentina.

23   In India, for example, investment in the development of transgenic crops was below 14 per cent of the total investment in the agro-biotechnology sector (Dhar and Chaturvedi, 2000, p16).

24 Monsanto intended to produce RR soybean in Brazil through its subsidiary Monsoy in the states of Sao Pablo, Minas Gerais, Mato Grosso and Mato Grosso do Sul, where field trials were carried out. The five varieties were developed in Brazil from the crossing of local varieties by FT-Semillas de Paraná, a company owned by Monsanto.

25 The International Food Information Council (IFIC), 2002, finds that opinions on food biotechnology are holding steady. Nearly three-quarters (71 per cent as against 65 per cent in 2001) of those surveyed said they would be likely to buy produce that had been enhanced through biotechnology for protection from insect damage and required fewer pesticide applications. In addition, more than half (54 per cent) of American consumers would be likely to purchase the same produce if it had been enhanced to taste better or fresher, a number that has remained stable since October 1999.

26 A survey by the Asian Food Information Centre (AFIC) in China, Thailand and the Philippines about GM foods indicated that of the consumers surveyed, 66 per cent believed that they would personally benefit from food biotechnology during the next five years. Sixty-one per cent of the respondents believed they had eaten GM foods recently and of those who believed they had eaten GM foods, 90 per cent were satisfied with the situation and took no action to avoid it (CropBiotech Update, 2002, 27 September).

27 See Paarlberg, 2002, p249. These concerns were illustrated by the cases of Zambia, Zimbabwe and Mozambique, which refused to accept GM grain as aid from the US, notwithstanding an impending famine which threatened millions of people. Fears related to effects on the region's biodiversity and to the introduction of GMOs jeopardizing southern African countries' future ability to export to each other and Europe (Lamont, 2002).

28 For instance, a recent review of the patent pedigree of enhanced vitamin-A rice identified 44 potential patents related to this rice in the United States, while the number of relevant patents in developing countries varied by country from 0 to 11. But even countries with no relevant patents (such as Thailand, Uruguay and Pakistan) would face difficulties in using the relevant tools, since they are major rice exporters to countries where patents are held (Byerlee and Fischer, 2002, p936).

29 See, for example, Ahmed, 2002. In the case of Bt, industry and scientists have argued for a high-dose/refuge strategy to combat resistance to Bt crops. The foundations of this strategy are to have Bt crops express enough toxins to kill all but the most resistant pests and for farmers to plant a portion of their acreage to refuge where the Bt is not used for pest control. Refuges allow susceptible pests to thrive and mate with resistant pests, thereby reducing selection pressure and slowing the proliferation of resistance (Hurley et al, 2001, p117).

30 The US Office of Science and Technology Policy (2002) announced federal actions to update field test requirements for biotechnology-derived plants and to establish early food safety assessments for new proteins produced by such plants. The measures are aimed at preventing low levels of biotechnology-derived genes and gene products from being found in commercial seed, commodities, and processed food and feed until appropriate safety standards can be met. Under this new system, the Food and Drug Administration will review data packages while crops are still in small acreage plots and determine whether there is a basis for allergenicity or toxicity concerns.

31   In some cases (such as Kenya) slow approval of GMOs has resulted in part from weak
     scientific and administrative capacity to conduct the elaborate and expensive case-by-
     case biosafety screenings that wealthy donor countries now insist upon as one condition
     for financial or technical assistance (Paarlberg, 2002).

32   In Mexico, for instance, it has been reported that native varieties of maize in remote
     regions of the country have been contaminated by transgenic DNA (Quist and
     Chapela, 2001).

33   With regard to the costs of segregation and identity preservation of non-GMOs, see
     Bullock and Desquilbet, 2002.

34   The Brazilian research agency Embrapa has also opened new facilities to assess the
     food safety of GMOs, with an investment of 1.2 million Real (US$320,000). See
     CropBiotech Update, 2002, 27 September.

35   The *Roundup Ready* (RR) soybean was the first GMO release approved by the National
     Technical Biosafety Committee (CTNBio). Monsanto filed the application on June
     10, 1998. Imported seeds were planted for trials, which were subject to oversight, by
     the Ministry of Agriculture in different states. CTNBio released the RR soybean
     through Regulation no 54, on September 29, 1998. However, the Brazilian NGOs and
     Greenpeace filed complaints with the Federal Courts and RR soy was commercially
     banned. The CTNBio was able to partially revoke the judgement. However, in another
     decision (June 2000) the court ordered the Federal Government to undertake an
     environmental impact assessment before allowing the release of any GMO.

REFERENCES

Ahmed, F (2002) 'Detection of genetically modified organisms in foods', *Trends in
    Biotechnology*, vol 20, no 5

Banchero, C, Correa, C and Bergel, S (2001) *Diffusion of Biotechnology in Argentina and
    Brazil: The Case of the Transgenic Plants*, University of Buenos Aires, Buenos Aires

Barbanti, P, Gambardella, A and Orsenigo, L (1999) 'The evolution of collaborative
    relationships among firms in biotechnology', *International Journal of Biotechnology*,
    vol 1, no 1

Brethour, C, Mussel, A, Mayer, H and Martin, L (2002) *Agronomic, Economic and
    Environmental Impact of the Commercial Cultivation of Glyphosate Tolerant Soybeans in
    Ontario*, George Morris Centre, Calgary, Canada

Bullock, D S and Desquilbet, M (2002) 'The economics of non-GMO segregation and
    identity preservation', *Food Policy*, vol 27, no 1, pp81–99

Byerlee, D and Fischer, K (2002) 'Accessing modern science. Policy and institutional options
    for agricultural biotechnology in developing countries', *World Development*, vol 30,
    no 6

Cassier, M (1999) 'Research contracts between university and industry: Co-operation and
    hybridisation between academic research and industrial research', *International Journal
    of Biotechnology*, vol 1, no 1

CIPR (2002) *Integrating Intellectual Property Rights and Development*, Commission on
    Intellectual Property Rights, London

Cohen, J (1999) *Managing Agricultural Biotechnology. Addressing Research Program Needs
    and Policy Implications*, Biotechnology in Agriculture Series, CAB International, The
    Hague

Correa, C M (1998) 'The South–South dimension in partnering: Strategic alliances in the biotechnology sector', *New Approaches to Science and Technology Cooperation and Capacity Building*, ATAS XI, New York and Geneva

Correa, C M (2002) *Protection of Data Submitted for the Registration of Pharmaceuticals. Implementing the Standards of the TRIPS Agreement*, South Centre/WHO, Geneva

Correa, C M, Díaz, A, Burachik, M, Jeppesen, C, Gil, L, Moreno, F, Sorj B and Sutz, J (1996) *Biotecnología: Innovación y Producción en América Latina*, Centre for Advanced Studies (CEA), Buenos Aires University

CropBiotech Update (2002) Newsletter, produced by Global Knowledge Center on Crop Biotechnology, International Service for the Acquisition of Agri-biotech Applications (ISAAA)'s SEAsiaCenter

Dhar, B and Chaturvedi, S (2000) *Recent Trends in the Biotechnology Sector in India: The Role in Intellectual Property Rights*, UNCTAD, Geneva

Falcon, W and Fowler, C (2002) 'Carving up the commons – emergence of a new international regime for germplasm development and transfer', *Food Policy*, vol 27, no 3, pp197–222

Gahukar, R T (2002) 'Status of genetically modified food crops in India', *Outlook on Agriculture*, vol 31, no 1, pp43–49

Gambardella, A (1995) *Science and Innovation. The US Pharmaceutical Industry During the 1980s*, Cambridge University Press

Hurley, T, Babcock, B and Hellmich, R (2001) 'Bt corn and insect resistance: An economic assessment of refuges', *Journal of Agricultural and Resource Economics*, vol 26, no 1, pp176–194

IFIC (2002) *US Consumer Attitudes Toward Food Biotechnology*, study conducted by Wirthlin Worldwide for International Food Information Council (IFIC), Washington, DC

Ismael, Y, Bennet, R and Morse, S (2002) 'Farm-level economic impact of biotechnology: Smallholder Bt cotton farmers in South Africa', *Outlook on Agriculture*, vol 31, no 2

James, C (2004) 'Preview: Global status of commercialized transgenic crops: 2004', *ISAAA Briefs No 32*, ISAAA, Ithaca, NY

Kenney, M (1986) *Biotechnology: The University–Industrial Complex*, Yale University Press, New York

Kirsten, J and Gouse, M (2002) *Bt Cotton in South Africa: Adoption and Impact on Farm Incomes Amongst Small and Large-Scale Farmers*, Information Systems for Biotechnology, Virginia, US

Lamont, J (2002) 'Zambia biotech food warning', *Financial Times*, 17 September 2002

Monsanto (2002) *Monsanto's Insect-Protected Corn Approved for Planting in the Philippines*, Monsanto Press Release, 5 December 2002

Ngubane, B S (2002) *Welcoming Address by the Minister of Arts, Culture Science and Technology of the Republic of South Africa*, Dr B S Ngubane, at the AfricaBio seminar on 'The role of biotechnology in sustainable development', 31 August 2002, Johannesburg

Normile, D (2002) 'Can money turn Singapore into a biotech juggernaut?', *Science*, vol 197, pp1470–1473

Nuffield Council on Bioethics (1999) *Genetically Modified Crops: The Ethical and Social Issues*, London

Paarlberg, R (2002) 'The real threat to GM crops in poor countries: Consumer and policy resistance to GM foods in rich countries', *Food Policy*, vol 27, no 3, pp247–250

Quist, D and Chapela, I (2001) 'Transgenic DNA introgressed into traditional maize landraces in Oaxaca, Mexico', *Nature*, vol 414, pp541–543

Ruane, J and Zimmermann, M (2001) 'Agricultural biotechnology for developing countries – results of an electric forum', *FAO Research and Technology Paper No 8*, FAO, Rome

Sasson, A (1992) 'Prospects for biotechnology in selected Asian countries', in *Biotechnology and Development: Expanding the Capacity to Produce Food*, United Nations Department of Economic and Social Development, United Nations, New York

Sasson, A (1993) 'Biotechnologies in developing countries: Present and future. Volume 1: Regional and national survey', *Future-oriented Studies*, UNESCO Publishing, Paris

Senker, J and Van Zwanenberg, P (2001) *European Biotechnology Innovation Systems: EC Policy Overview*, Science and Technology Policy Research Unit (SPRU), University of Sussex, UK

Sercovich, F C and Leopold, M (1991) *Developing Countries and the New Biotechnology: Market Entry and Industrial Policy*, International Development Research Center, Ottawa

SUNS (2002) *South North Development Monitor*, Third World Network, 27 September 2002

Swanson, T and Goeschl, T (2002) 'The impact of GURTs on developing countries: A preliminary assessment', in Swanson, T (ed) *Biotechnology, Agriculture and the Developing World: The Distributional Implications of Technological Change*, Edward Elgar, Cheltenham, UK

US Office of Science and Technology Policy (2002) *Proposed Federal Actions to Update Field Test Requirements for Biotechnology Derived Plants and to Establish Early Food Safety Assessments for New Proteins Produced by such Plants*, notice, from the Federal Register Online via GPO Access, vol 67, no 149

Waithaka, K (1992) 'Requirements for biotechnology development', *Biotechnology and Development Expanding the Capacity to Produce Food*, ATAS series, United Nations Publications, Issue 9, New York

Wolff, G (2001) *The Biotech Investor's Bible*, John Wiley & Sons, New York

3

Biotechnology: A Turning Point in Development or an Opportunity that Will Be Missed?

Joseph Gopo and Patricia Kameri-Mbote

While rapid changes are taking place in the life sciences sector that could have far-reaching positive influences on development, the South still has to bridge the gap preventing it from reaping the benefits of biotechnology. Despite exceptions such as India, Brazil and China, many developing economies do not have an extensive tradition of investing in science. More importantly lack of political commitment of Southern leaders to science and technology (S&T), combined with limited financial and human resources, lack of consumer and producer support, low capacity, and high entry costs to S&T activity threaten to keep the developing world an outsider to the international biotech development. However, it is only at their own peril that developing countries give up biotechnology entirely, as it may hold promise for sustainable growth in agriculture, pharmaceutical and healthcare sectors in the South. At the same time developing countries are vulnerable to the controversial facets of the new technology that have to be addressed effectively if the South is to reap the benefits of the safe application of biotechnology. While the Cartagena Protocol on Biosafety has made progress in ensuring that the science that produces biotech-goods is a safe one, it leaves important loopholes that can compromise developing countries' interests. Analysing the concerns of the South that lie at the centre of the debate on biotechnology and development is therefore undertaken to draw insights on where lies the road for the South in the globalized bioeconomy.

Will the South take the biotech leap?

Lack of adequate capacity building is partly due to the inability of the governments to allocate adequate financial resources to research and development (R&D) as well as an overall lack of a commitment to S&T. Many African governments do not commit even 0.01 per cent of their GDP to S&T funding. In fact, very few African governments even have an S&T policy. The usual reasons given range from declining economics to servicing of the debt burden. Closer examination, however, reveals that those developing countries that do not contribute meaningfully to S&T are simultaneously, in fact, big spenders in the procurement of antiquated military hardware. At the end of the day, the real problems are *misallocation* of resources due to poor prioritization for national developments. One might even say that politicians are often more concerned with staying in power through the barrel of the gun than offering science-based development through well-funded biotechnology coupled with effective biosafety regulations.

Developing a biotechnology sector would mean taking steps to upgrade technological infrastructures, enhance human expertise and set up regulatory frameworks. It would take vast R&D investments with distant and uncertain payoffs. Developing countries would have to enter into complex public–private partnerships and develop the legal, institutional and executive acumen that is necessary to foster biotechnological innovation and its application. In addition, they would have to contend with a public that is apprehensive of genetic engineering in principle, and all the more so in practice. Rapid advances in knowledge pose a formidable challenge for developing countries' capacity to update their technological stock. High concentration of market power in the hands of a few life science giants also poses a serious problem for the development of biotechnology in the South. Biotech start-ups in the South lack industrial capacity to bring a product through all stages of certification and large-scale marketing. All these factors combine to produce very high barriers to the entry of Southern biotech players into the global market for biotechnological products.

Even as constraints facing developing countries in building biotechnology sectors are severe, choosing to remain outsiders may not be a viable option either. In Asia, for instance, estimates are that the introduction of genetically modified (GM) rice could increase production by up to 25 per cent. For the biodiversity-rich South the challenge is to transform this natural resource into biotechnological products for agriculture and healthcare that meet local needs and incorporate existing knowledge and skills, including traditional knowledge. Biotechology may be a powerful strategy for sustainable development in prospect for the 21st century, but this potential is dependent upon effective government action to provide incentives, research and regulation. If the opportunity is missed, developing country citizens risk being bypassed by the benefits of biotechnology.

THE PROMISES OF SAFE BIOTECHNOLOGY

Transgenic crops for food security

Developing countries can and should adopt and use transgenic crops that can put more food on the market and bring more cash to the farmer. Biotechnology may not be the silver bullet to end malnutrition and hunger, but it holds the promise of increased, sustainable, environmentally friendly and economically profitable agricultural growth. Developing countries have high hopes for the potential of high yield transgenic crops to reduce threats to food security. In sub-Saharan Africa, for instance, where maize is the staple to millions, food security depends on the ability of farmers to increase maize yield per unit area of land tilled. When harvests are affected by drought stress, infested by insect pest and viral and fungal diseases, the result is severe crop loss. The potential of agricultural biotechnology for sub-Saharan countries lies in producing hardier crops that can withstand these natural risks. This biotechnology can only deliver, though, given simultaneous action on other problems that prevent agricultural growth, including trade rules, rural infrastructure and government investment. The area's abundant biodiversity resources offer a wide range of possibilities for sources of new desired genetic traits that could be embedded in transgenic crops through well-funded and innovative research and regulatory processes that facilitate the creation of environmentally friendly, diversity-preserving new varieties that are hardier than conventional varieties.

Cases of scientific breakthrough in agro-biotechnology in developing countries have shown that biotechnology can transform the local economy and alleviate food security concerns. The most famous example of technology's beneficial impacts on agricultural yields is the green revolution. More recently, Kenyan scientists for instance have made significant progress in developing agro-biotechnology that matches local farming needs. Modified sweet potato with added resistance to parasites achieved a high trial yield increase of 15 per cent. Sweet potato is staple to millions of Africans and takes up an area of 12 million hectares annually. Translating the increased productivity into profits would create a financial benefit of US$495 million annually for Kenya. The transgenic sweet potato of the Kenyan Agricultural Research Institute can be used in the rest of Africa to improve productivity (Cook, 2002). Moreover, what is true for sweet potato can be true for a large variety of other crops. New generations of crops, such as maize, cotton, potatoes, lettuce, tobacco, banana and tomato, could be used to reverse the negative trends in food security throughout the world.

Agricultural biotechnology has, in some situations, helped economies grow. Experiences from the US show that transgenic crops can boost farmers' incomes as disease-fighting costs decrease while yields and chances that all goes well increase. Annual savings on foregoing insecticide together with increased profits from higher yields in transgenic cotton in the US amounted to US$61 million in 1996 and

US$81 million in 1997. In the case of transgenic maize, increased yields in the range of 9 per cent translated into a benefit of US$19 million in 1997 (James, 1999). Figures do not only speak of the success of biotechnology but also of the perils of ignoring it. As a result of being infected with stock borer disease, conventional maize harvest in the US in 1996 led to over US$1 billion losses.

Protecting biodiversity and the environment

Mugabe and Clark suggest that technology, and specifically biotechnology, is critical to the achievement of the objectives of the Convention on Biological Diversity (CBD), in particular Articles 8(g), 16 and 19, namely conservation and sustainable utilization of biological resources and the fair and equitable sharing of benefits arising from their use (Mugabe and Clark, 1996). While Agenda 21, adopted at the Earth Summit in Rio in 1992, acknowledges that biotechnology by itself 'cannot resolve all the fundamental problems of environment and development', it points to the significant contribution the technology can make 'in enabling development of, for example, better healthcare, enhanced food security through sustainable development processes for transforming raw materials, support for sustainable methods of afforestation and reforestation, and detoxification of hazardous waste' (Robinson, 1993). In this context, Agenda 21 lists opportunities for a global partnership between biodiversity-rich countries, which lack experience and investments necessary to exploit resources for economic development, and industrialized countries, which possess the necessary technological know-how. Emphasis is placed on conditions to guarantee successful and environmentally safe application of biotechnology in agriculture, environment and human health through international cooperative mechanisms.

Many other potential environmental benefits have been attributed to the use of biotechnology (see for example GM Science Review Panel, 2003). Some examples include the creation of bacteria that biodegrade environmental pollutants, developing GM plants with the capacity to absorb metals, the production of biodegradable plastics using oilseed rape, plants that require less fertilizers and are resistant to pests, and the production of coloured cotton to reduce the use of synthetic dyes.

Healthcare in the age of biotechnology

Unlocking life's code in 2000 by decoding the human genome opened up virtually unlimited possibilities in medical diagnosis and early cure. As the functioning of genes is understood better, it also becomes possible to identify disturbances to healthy genes earlier on. So healthcare promises to become more preventive in the future. New diagnostic tools made out of bits of DNA embedded on silicon chips will soon be able to test for hundreds of thousands of genetic conditions that reveal what an individual is predisposed to. In turn this will help determine what individuals might do to prevent disease in the course of their lives.

Another promise of pharmaceutical biotechnology is the development of more powerful drugs with fewer side effects. A key feature of tailor-made drugs is high precision in identifying the problem and setting the target (Carr, 2000). Recent reports show that the gene responsible for development and control of speech has now been identified by a UK-based research team (Whitfield, 2001). Genes for longevity, disease resistance genes and other special protein genes are among a repertoire of rare genes that are now identifiable using biotechnology. As a result, future drugs will concentrate their action on a much smaller number of targets within the organism, hence reducing the side effects.

Molecular pharming

Just as plants can be engineered to have higher nutritional value, they can also be designed to have higher medicinal value, or high content of key enzymes. The growing of crops to extract medicinal substances is a highly promising sector. The mechanism is simple. By reprogramming the plant's genes, a number of therapeutic substances including antibodies and vaccines can be produced within the crop (Erickson, 1996, p47; Wayt Gibbs, 1997, p23).

Among the diseases targeted by this technology is hepatitis B. One of the plants currently on trial as an edible vaccine that will switch on the body's defence to hepatitis is tomato (*China Daily*, 2002). Similar experiments with plant vaccines are being carried out with genetically modified potato and soybean, which target rabies and colon bacillus, a germ that induces severe diarrhoea. To be vaccinated in the future, one may hope developing country citizens might not need to see a doctor; rather, they may only need to consume a tomato.

Just as plant genes can be modified to produce medicines, animal genes can also be used to produce medicinal substances. One of the ways this technology would reach consumers would be by transferring medicinal substances through animal produce consumed daily, such as milk and other dairy products. Antibodies that can serve as natural medicines might for instance be included in a glass of milk. Researchers are even trying to use mosquitoes to inject immunity-boosting substances to humans they bite.

Blurring the distinction between high value pharmaceuticals and low value animal husbandry will transform business. This is especially so when animals are used to fight diseases such as cancer or HIV/AIDS that take massive tolls on societies. For instance, multi-million dollar factories used to produce drugs could soon be replaced by a single herd of goats.

Animal husbandry

Modern biotechnology offers great potential for improving the efficiency of animal breeding. Biotechnological methods have an advantage over traditional breeding methods in that they allow identification of the most successful breeding combinations at younger stages of an animal's life. Recent advances in molecular genetics, specifically genetic markers, are being used to tag parts of the chromosome where the genes of interest reside. Besides, biotechnology has also led to improved animal husbandry through the use of embryo transfers and artificial insemination as well as animal cloning.

RISKS OF BIOTECHNOLOGY

The scientific community and the corporate biotechnology sector have over the years selectively over-emphasized the technology's potential benefits at the neglect of the technology's potential hazards. In the past few years, consumer advocacy has resulted in public rejection of GM foods in Europe and some parts of the US. The public rejection is based on a range of concerns about the potential adverse impacts of GM foods on human and animal health and on the environment. Other concerns are on the potential adverse impact on biological diversity, as well as ethical issues and the technology's impact on indigenous people and their knowledge. In the EU, farmers, retailers and supermarket suppliers are now trying to meet consumer demands by using organic non-GM foods. Below are specific examples of scientific uncertainties raising deep concerns about biosafety.

Environmental risks

Although engineered crops and agriceuticals have potential globally, the fundamental *living* nature of the new inventions puts them in a risk category of their own. Unlike physical inventions of the past, a mistake in biotechnology would be able to replicate itself. This creates genuine worries about genetically modified organisms (GMOs) escaping control and entering the food chain and humans, plants and animals with unknowable consequences. The contamination of native Mexican maize varieties by transgenic DNA, which occurred despite a ban on the import of GM maize into Mexico since 1998, has highlighted the risks to biodiversity of the introduction of GM crops (Quist and Chapela, 2001). Technological fixes created ostensibly to deal with this threat, notably genetic use restriction technology (GURT), have proven to be highly controversial, raising concerns over the corporate control of the world's food supply (see Box 3.1)

BOX 3.1 GENETIC USE RESTRICTION TECHNOLOGY (GURT): BIOSAFETY OR BIOBUSINESS?

While developments in modern biotechnology have great potential, they can also be potentially harmful. A good and highly controversial example is the genetic use restriction technology (GURT), which has led to the applications of so-called *Terminator and Traitor* technologies in the global seed business. On 3 March 1998, the US Department of Agriculture and a seed corporation, Delta and Pine Land, were jointly awarded patent code named the *Terminator Technology*. Patent applications have been filed in at least 78 countries. This technology enables the seed companies to genetically alter seed so that it does not germinate if replanted. A more recent and serious development in the use and application of GURT is the so-called *Traitor Technology*. This technology uses an inducible promoter system where the coding sequence for a protein is under the control of a chemically inducible promoter. This system can be used to turn on and off any plant genetic trait with the application of an external chemical catalyst. Plant molecular biologists have used this technology to develop the ability to control a wide range of traits such as insect resistance, tolerance to herbicides, flowering period, fruit ripening, flavour, nutritional qualities and male or female sterility.

On the face of it, this sounds like an asset of modern biotechnology. Some believe that GURT could have applications for world consumers, growers and the environment. They argue that GURT could be used to prevent transgenics from spreading to closely related wild plant species by preventing germination of any crossed seeds. The technology could prevent and eliminate the problems of volunteer plants in agriculture that appear from the seed left in the field after harvest. The engineering of sterility in crops offers a built-in safety feature because the escape of such sterile seed will not produce any new crops. It would appear that these technologies could particularly benefit developing countries, that lack the financial and scientific capacity to monitor and enforce biosafety regulations. Some of the proponents of the terminator seed technology include the US National Research Council, the UK Advisory Committee on Release to the Environment and several National Academies of Science. However, like any other scientific advancement, it depends on the intended use and application.

The introduction of *Terminator Technology* and other GURT in 1998, which brought forth to the general public the concept of *suicide seeds*, aroused widespread condemnation. It suggested to the public that commercial biotechnology was not principally aimed at feeding the hungry and providing food security in the developing world, but at maximizing profits to satisfy corporate greed because the *Terminator* enables corporations to force farmers to buy seed from them year after year, rather than being able to re-use and share seed year after year as is customary practice in many countries. A few multinational companies will control the food supply of the world; this will adversely affect biodiversity, leading to loss in biodiversity and genetic resources. The *Terminator Technology* is owned by Syngenta (Novartis), Syngenta (Zeneca), Delta and Pine Land/ US Department of Agriculture (USDA), BASF, LLC/Iowa State University, Du Pont (Pioneer Hi-Bred), Pharmacia (Monsanto), Cornell Research Foundation and Purdue Research Foundation/USDA. The new *Traitor Technology* is owned by Syngenta (Novartis) and Du Pont (Pioneer). It is very clear that the ultimate goal of genetic seed sterility is not biosafety as is claimed by some governments and the corporate seed giants, but seed biotrade leading to control of global agriculture. An additional possible hazard associated with *Traitor Technology* is the link between the chemical industry and the seed industry. Farmers will be completely dependent on both the seed giants and the agrochemical giants who in most cases will be the same. The immediate winners are major corporations and the losers are the small-scale farmers in developing countries because the technology will destroy farmers' seed sovereignty, potentially threaten biodiversity and jeopardize food security in developing countries where the world's poor depend on the right to re-use their seed. Farmers in developing countries of the world would be totally dependent on the profit motives of global corporations for their food security.

Source: ETC Group (formerly RAFI), 1998, 2001

Extensive studies recently conducted in the United Kingdom identify various potential environmental risks that may result from the release of GM crops and how likely they are to occur (GM Science Review Panel, 2003; Firbank et al, 2003). One of the major concerns identified is that they may be more invasive of natural habitats than their conventional counterparts, in particular, those with traits to increase their fitness. The GM Science Review highlights the difficulty inherent in predicting the potential for invasiveness on the basis of traits alone, given the complex relationship between the biological traits of a plant species and the likelihood of a species becoming invasive when introduced into a new habitat.

Another concern associated in particular with herbicide tolerant weeds is that the inserted genes may 'escape' from the crop by being transferred to another crop or wild relative which in turn may become 'super-weeds' that are difficult to control and could impact on the functions and biodiversity of the ecosystem that they invade. While gene flow can occur from GM crops to sexually compatible wild relatives and to agricultural weeds, the GM Science Review points to important gaps in our understanding of the potential consequences of gene flow and the effect of particular traits on the fitness of the weed or wild relatives. This is of particular concern to developing countries given that they include some of the most biodiversity-rich areas on the planet, such as rainforests, in which environmental testing of gene flow and its impact upon food chains and biodiversity has been minimal.

Another concern associated with plants engineered to produce a toxin relates to the unintended harm to non-target species – making the plant 'toxic' to wildlife that feeds on the crop – or indirect effects on ecosystem dynamics resulting, for instance, from changes in the availability or quality of the target pest as prey for other species. The GM Science Review found little evidence for significant adverse ecological impacts on non-target wildlife resulting from toxicity of GM plants. The Review, however, cautions that research has so far focused on small-scale field studies and that detailed studies on the population dynamics of target and non-target organisms are still lacking.

It has been argued that the evidence of actual or potential harm to the environment is not enough to justify a moratorium on research, field trials and controlled release of genetically modified products into the environment (Nuffield

Council on Bioethics, 2003). The possibility of this happening, it has been proposed, is minimal and overall the benefits of genetically modified products far outweigh the potential minimal risks. At the same time, significant uncertainties persist regarding the possible environmental impacts of introducing GM crops and the evidence that currently exists for one country might not necessarily be relevant for another (GM Science Review Panel, 2003, pp24–25). GM crops will have to be judged on a case-by-case basis and in relation to non-modified crops grown in conventional, organic or other lower intensity farming systems.

Reinforced antibiotic resistance – a health concern

Another cause of serious concern over GM crops is the possible spread of antibiotic resistant genes from living modified organisms (LMOs) to humans and animals. The current method for checking that transfer of a desired trait in an LMO has succeeded is through the so-called *marker gene*, which is usually a gene that confers resistance to antibiotics. This is done by inserting the antibiotic resistance trait as well as the desired trait into the LMO. Once the crop sprouts, it is treated with antibiotic. If the crop shows antibiotic resistance, it means that transfer of the antibiotic resistance gene has succeeded and by implication transfer of the desired trait has also succeeded.

The health risk linked to the use of antibiotic marker genes is that through eating GM crops the marker gene might be transferred from the crop to bacteria in the stomach, thereby making potentially harmful bacteria resistant to antibiotics. Scientists agree that this risk factor is very low because enzymes of the digestive tract would largely break up the antibiotic resistance strains. Moreover, the chances that the few remaining antibiotic resistance strains become integrated into the human and animal genetic code are also very low. In this respect, current practices, such as using antibiotics as feed additives, raise much higher concern than the possible transfer of antibiotic resistance through consumption of GM crops. Nonetheless, the risk of gene transfer cannot be ruled out, so if the application of biotechnology is to be safe, new technologies that do not use antibiotic marker genes have to be developed.

Ethical concerns

In the area of medicine, biotechnology is not only raising questions of safety, but also ethical and moral concerns. Such concerns have been voiced, for instance, with regard to the use of human tissue in biotechnology research, including the way tissue is obtained (see Box 3.2). Research in embryonic stem cells is a particularly controversial example. Stem cells have a high potential to cure degenerative diseases such as cancer or heart disease. This is possible due to the high renewal ability stem cells possess. The embryonic stem cell harvest, however, results in the sacrificing of the embryo. Is it moral and ethical to sacrifice any embryo for whatever benefit?

When does life really begin? Can humanity justify the termination of one life to save another? These are all pertinent questions that must be asked when questioning the larger impacts of biotechnological innovations.

BOX 3.2 HUMAN TISSUE BANKING AND TRAFFICKING

The practice of human tissue banking is now common in developed countries and examples of this practice include the US American Type Culture Collection (ATCC) and the European Collection of Cell Cultures (ECACC). Developing countries need to develop the capacity to conduct modern biotechnology research into human tissue because of the dire ramifications of the trade in these tissues, the research into the human genome and the international tissue culture industry. Human tissue, cells and genes and their components are crucial areas for investigation in the search for treatments of diseases and genetic disorders. A critical study of the genetic diversity between individuals and among human populations is required to resolve current and future health problems. In the US, cell cultures are becoming increasingly important to manufacturing in the biotechnology industry. Many transnational pharmaceutical companies, with the support of universities, human genome sequencing activities, computer software and hardware companies and blood and tissue banks, including the Red Cross, are active in the human tissue trade. The sources of human tissue, cells and genes are in the developing countries of Africa, Asia and Latin America. The multi-million dollar industry that trades in human tissue has developed international human tissue exchange routes that are open to corporate businesses in the public and private sector as well as the military. These are being developed without patient confidentiality or prior informed consent with regard to commercialization and patenting. In some cases, the material that has been collected is subjected to mass reproduction for commercial purposes. There is an urgent need to assess and, where necessary, strengthen the policy and legal frameworks to protect the countries where these tissues originate and to ensure that ethical considerations are respected in human tissue research.

Sources: ETC Group (formerly RAFI), 1997; Nuffield Council on Bioethics, 1995

THE CARTAGENA PROTOCOL ON BIOSAFETY

We have shown that biotechnology holds potential promise for both developed and developing countries. It is a technology for the new millennium, but the technology also has the potential to harm human society. The world community will only be able to derive maximum benefits from biotechnology when adequate, transparent and internationally enforceable safety instruments governing broad control procedures in the movements of LMOs are put in place. Such safety procedures should include, among others, primary considerations of the organisms and the LMOs and should build upon the principles of familiarity and substantial equivalence applied in a flexible framework that take into account national and regional requirements, starting with a step-by-step and case-by-case approach. The objective should be to ensure safe development, application and transfer of biotechnology and its products in industrialized and developing countries, through the use of international agreements based on principles for risk assessment and risk management as they apply particularly to issues on human health and to environmental safety. The application of such a biosafety instrument must also take into account the issues of ethical considerations and indigenous and traditional knowledge.

The Cartagena Protocol on Biosafety, which was adopted in January 2000 and entered into force in September 2003, represents a milestone in managing the risks of biotechnology. Does this Protocol provide an adequate instrument for safe development and use of biotechnology? A closer examination shows that the Protocol does not sufficiently address important concerns of developing countries.

THE PROTOCOL'S LOOPHOLES

The scope of the Cartagena Protocol – Article 4

The Article states that the Protocol 'shall apply to the transboundary movement, transit, handling and use of all living modified organisms that may have adverse effects on the conservation and sustainable use of biological diversity, taking also into account risks to human health'. The concern that some developing countries have is that the scope of the Protocol is too narrow as it concerns itself mainly with the transboundary movements of LMOs. The scope must be expanded to include the safe production of LMOs. The science which produces the LMOs must be a safe science and be governed by internationally agreed safeguards, which must include safe laboratory practices, safe disposal and storage rules for chemicals, constructs and antibiotic resistance genes as well as the transgenes. The science of genetic modifications is still full of uncertainties, which require some agreed methods of containment. It is important that such an international biosafety protocol must include the areas of safety in biotechnology and not concern itself with transboundary movements only.

The scope of the Cartagena Protocol is also considered narrow because it concerns itself only with the LMOs and not with their products. The issue of the products of LMOs is very critical to developing countries where LMOs and their products have entered the food chain. In southern Africa, maize meal is a staple to millions who consume it for breakfast, lunch and supper. What will be the cumulative effects of eating *Bacillus thuringiensis* (Bt) maize? Any adequate biosafety instrument must include the safe use of the products of LMOs. Besides Bt maize meal, there are many other products of LMOs that are already in the food chain. Is the consumption of such products considered safe? The question of the safety of GM foods has not been resolved. The science is still uncertain. It is necessary therefore that the scope of the Cartagena Protocol be expanded to include the safe movement, transit, handling and use, as well as safe production at a scientific level, of the LMOs and their products.

Lack of liability provisions is another defect of the Protocol's scope. Since the biotechnology industry is almost a Western monopoly, the lack of liability provisions within the Protocol squares with industrialized countries' interests at the expense of consumers in poorer countries. Developing countries' concerns over the possible risks of the new technology are underpinned by a lack of capacity to deal with potential damage. The failure to tie responsibility to suppliers of the LMOs in industrialized countries for damage that might occur leaves developing countries exposed to unknown harmful impacts of the new technology.

Pharmaceuticals – Article 5

The Cartagena Protocol in Article 5 exempts from risk assessments all LMOs that are pharmaceuticals intended for human consumption because they are or may be addressed by other relevant international agreements. This is not acceptable because it makes this Protocol subservient to other protocols, and thus, at a minimum, Cartagena should specify its relationship to the other protocols. The current state of scientific knowledge may be such that it is not possible to conclude with any certainty the absolute safety of any pharmaceutical. Risk assessment must be conducted by the exporter and in some cases by the importer to be sure that such pharmaceuticals are safe. For the protection of people in developing countries, all pharmaceuticals must be subjected to a risk assessment, using procedures which are agreed upon by the international community. The Cartagena Protocol's Article 5 must be amended to include mandatory risk assessment on pharmaceuticals.

Advance Informed Agreement – Articles 6 and 7

In Article 6, the Protocol must be expanded to require Advance Informed Agreement procedures to apply to any transboundary movement of LMOs and their products, not just to LMOs for intentional introduction into the environment. This is even more important in Article 7(2), which exempts the movement and export of commodities for direct use as food or for food aid. People in the developing world, whether starving or not, have the right not only to know, but to chose whether to eat GM foods. This Article gives the right to exporting countries to move LMOs and their products as commodities for trade or for food aid. This Article must be amended to require not only Advance Informed Agreement, but also the labelling of the LMOs and their products.

Labelling and identification provisions

The Protocol's current labelling regime does not give consumers sufficient information to make a choice regarding produce containing LMOs. The extent to which food on the shelves might contain LMOs remains unknown as identification rules require products derived from LMOs, which may be food aid items, to be identified as 'may contain LMO'. This regulation governing food intended for human consumption as well as animal feed poses a real problem for countries considering whether they should accept food aid in times of crisis. The decision whether the food that reaches consumers is safe should not be left in the hands of the biotechnology industry even in times of severe food stress.

Protecting biotrade rather than biosafety?

The focus of the Cartagena Protocol seems to be on what some have come to call *biotrade*. The Protocol is concerned primarily with transboundary movement of genetically modified commodities and food aid from exporting countries, mainly being industrialized countries, to the consumers in the developing countries. The Protocol in its present format does not provide adequate protection to people in the developing world who are now faced with the trade-related issues of bio-technology. Rather, it demonstrates that the industrialized world – represented by the so-called Miami Group (Argentina, Australia, Canada, Chile, Uruguay and US) during the negotiations of the Protocol – wanted a *Biotrade Protocol* rather than a Biosafety Protocol. The Miami group was influenced by the fact that they already have a number of transgenic crops, such as Bt maize, Bt cotton, herbicide resistant soybeans and others on the international commodity markets. In the end it is LMO exporters, including corporations, that are protected by the Protocol, rather than the consumers and the environment in the developing world.

PATENTS AND BIOPIRACY OBSTRUCT THE SOUTH'S POTENTIAL BIOTECH BENEFITS

The biotechnology industry advertises its technology as a solution to hunger, but some of the crucial questions remain open. Will the poor be able to afford and access the benefits of GM crops? For the time being, the answer is no. The technology faces the risk of being a Western monopoly blind to developing country needs and centred on profit.

Biotechnology is the brainchild of US corporate culture. Mapping the human genome, initially a large state project, was hijacked eight years into its life by the fast and young private biotech sector in 1998. By 2000, the private sector had beaten the US government to the task five years ahead of the initial schedule and at a lower cost. Agricultural biotechnology is also essentially a US invention. The first transgenic crop introduced in the US in 1992 was a tomato genetically engineered to delay ripening. By contrast, the participation of the developing world in transgenic crops remains low, although a growing number of countries, including Argentina, Brazil, China, Paraguay, Uruguay, India, Mexico, the Philippines and South Africa, have taken up the technology (James, 2004).

The major problem for developing countries is the patenting of biotechnology by corporations in the West. Nearly every core technology used in crop biotechnology is the intellectual property of companies such as Dow, DuPont, Monsanto and Novartis. These patents on life forms are a core controversy between countries. The Agreement on Trade-related Aspects of Intellectual Property Rights (TRIPS) of the WTO in fact states that countries 'are allowed to exclude animals and plants from patents where the prevention within (national) territory . . . is necessary to protect *ordre public* and morality' (Article 27.3(b)). In the US, however, where the hand of the corporate biotechnology sector is stronger than in any other country, the industry has managed to get patents on life forms approved.

So if India or Uganda wanted to distribute a product such as the hypothetical hepatitis-vaccinating tomato described above, they would first have to negotiate with various companies for the gene transfer, gene promoter and selectable marker technologies that were used in its development. Historically, on the other hand, information on new technologies was routinely exchanged between companies and public and not-for-profit research institutes, allowing developing countries access to them. Today this access is denied, as most poor countries simply do not have the financial resources or the scientific or legal acumen to wade through this complex patent maze.

Moreover, the US corporate sector is at work for profit and that means designing crops for richer parts of the world where prices are high and agriculture is capital intensive. This means that developing countries will be faced with very high prices of biotech seed and that engineered crops may not meet local needs. The principal transgenic crops grown today are soybean, maize, cotton and canola (James, 2004). To meet developing countries needs, however, attention to crops such as rice, cassava and millet are needed. Moreover, GM crops for developing countries have to take into account the high labour and low capital intensity character of farming. This is extremely important for the developing world where as much as 65 per cent of livelihoods are closely bound to agriculture (ITDG, 2003). A technology that makes farming labour redundant may not be sustainable in the developing world.

Sharp opposition to patents is raised on the grounds that these intellectual property tools end up denying local communities the rights to their natural resources. While developing countries hold most of the primary genetic material, the exclusive property rights end up being held by corporations in the North. It is estimated that around 83 per cent of the total biodiversity lies within the developing world. However, patents are almost exclusively held in industrialized countries, so that the South gets locked out of its own wealth.

Developing countries seem to be in an impossible position. On the one hand they cannot close their borders to the biotechnology firms that bring employment and money. The Plant Genome Research Initiative for instance has received recently more than US$40 million to investigate the genomes of economically important plants in the South (Macilwain, 1997). On the other hand they cannot use litigation against cases where their genetic resources are subjected to illegal intellectual property claims pressed by richer countries because, unlike them, developing countries lack the means to carry through expensive litigation. The Convention on Biological Diversity attempts to prevent such 'biopiracy' by asserting the sovereign right of states to their biological resources, to their determination of how such resources are to be used and to their share in the profits gained thereby.

These concerns raise important questions for the future of biotechnology in the developing world, which have yet to be resolved. What is the role of the private sector, particularly the dominance of multinationals in the biotechnology sector? What are the role and potential ramifications of transgenic crop technology on global food security and more especially food security in developing countries (James, 1999)?

THE DUMPING CHARITY – GM FOOD AID

Developing countries' mistrust of the biotechnology industry was recently reinforced by controversy over the food aid issue, when a number of southern African countries rejected imports of food aid containing GM maize. Developing countries argue they should not be used as dumping grounds for potentially unsafe food, nor be pushed to take long-term decisions on food security they are not prepared for. GM food aid raises concerns about the effects on human health and the environment of developing countries. Moreover, there are trade arguments justifying developing countries' hesitation to accept GM food aid.

In the case of food aid involving shipments of seeds, a contamination of the natural environment may occur. This might be accidental, but it may also be as a result of farmers sowing food aid grains instead of consuming them. The release of LMO strains into the natural environment could prove a disaster if it limited the developing country's ability to trade with countries such as those within the EU that have a stringent LMO import policy. Developing countries dependent on agricultural trade with the EU may prefer to weather the current famine without accepting GM food aid if their future trade is at stake. Moreover, developing countries are bound to keep to a cautious policy route, since they are well aware of their poor position in dealing with potential damages.

With respect to food aid, the Cartagena Protocol on Biosafety is a weak protector of developing countries. On the contrary, it defends the interests of the six multinationals that control GM crops that are used for food aid. Novartis,

Monsanto, AgrEvo, Delta and Pine Land, Dow-Agroscience and Du Pont dominate the research and market of genetically modified crops whose expected value by 2010 is US$25 billion. The Protocol's current labelling regime does not give countries prior information through the Advance Informed Agreement procedure regarding GM crops that may have been used in food or feed, let alone in food aid. Moreover, when the LMOs in question are processed food or feed, the procedures for informed consent prior to import are less strict than for seeds.

Genetically modified food aid reflects an unjust policy towards developing countries. The rationale of donors, for instance, that unknown risks of GM food are better than the certainty of starvation, is flawed because donors are not qualified to decide that on behalf of developing country citizens. It is important to realize that, even in cases of severe food shortage, consumers or the government which represents them should still be the ones to decide whether to eat GM food or not. Toward this, donors must provide adequate information on the GM content of food aid. Under the current Protocol on Biosafety, donors are only required to state whether the export *may* contain LMOs, which gives rise to uncertainty and fears that public health, the economy and the environment may be subjected to unknown quantities of risks.

What is more, African countries suffering from the current famine do not agree with the US official position that the only crops available as food aid were US GM crops. This is untrue, as excess stockpiles of maize around the world, in Europe, Brazil and India, run into many tens of millions of tonnes, which is more than enough to stop the famine. The real reason behind US insistence lies in subsidies behind US farm production used as food aid. One of the targets of the US Agency for International Development (USAID) is to integrate GM into the local food systems. The famines will only help GMO exporters to further their business interests.

THE ROAD AHEAD

Biotechnology has been dubbed the new nuclear industry. If its potential is harnessed, great threats to humankind's well-being, such as malnutrition and hunger, may be greatly reduced through bioengineered crops. In order to achieve maximum benefits, however, the science that produces biotechnology must be a safe one. And while the Biosafety Protocol has gone some way to protect humans and the environment from unintended risks of LMOs, the safety question remains unsettled.

There is need to put in place an international biosafety protocol which does not focus mainly on the trade interests of Western corporate business, but is a biosafety protocol which is designed to promote biotechnology for safe applications and safe sustainable uses of the products of the technology. Developing countries must insist upon a review of the Cartagena Protocol on Biosafety with the aim of changing the focus of the Protocol from *biotrade* to *biosafety*. The precautionary principle that governs the *transboundary movement* of LMOs should be expanded to govern the *safe use and production* of LMOs. The scope of the Protocol itself must be expanded to protect humans and the environment from risks of production and use of LMOs.

Moreover, transparent identification, including labelling, has to be adopted to show the LMO content of goods intended for food, feed or processing. The pressure of the international community must be brought to bear on this clause and its serious and significant consequences on developing countries' sovereignty over the crucial issue of food security and food aid. Genetically modified maize is undoubtedly useful in combating severe food crises. However, even severe food shortages do not justify the damage to consumer choice allowed currently by the Protocol's labelling regime. The prevailing rules dismiss consumers' right to know the real LMO content of food on the shelf.

Responsibility for unintended harm caused by the use of LMOs must be fixed on the biotechnology industry that supplies the technology. The current Protocol fails to address the issue of liability, which is crucial to developing countries that are in a poor position to redress potential damage.

Developing countries face serious ramifications and constraints in accessing and developing modern biotechnology R&D because of declining economies and increasing debt burden, their relatively small industrial base and the lack of capacity in human resources and physical infrastructure. Nevertheless, the South needs modern biotechnology because it has the potential to increase agricultural productivity by using transgenic crops such as Bt maize, Bt cotton, Bt soybeans and others. Biotechnology can increase the economic productivity of developing country genetic resources.

If the developing world is to benefit from biotechnology, the industry must make available, on a royalty-free basis, the technology on food crops selected by developing countries such as rice, cassava and millet. This reflects a general scheme of dividing global markets into areas where intellectual property rights are enforced to a lesser extent and those where such rights are fully enforced. Within this the poorest countries would not be subject to international intellectual property restrictions while the rest of the world would have stronger patent protection. Patents would still have their function of encouraging innovation, as inventors would still receive royalties from consumers in the industrialized world. At the same time, poor nations would have affordable access to a wider variety of high-technology goods. The result would be a better intellectual property protection scheme for all involved (Graff and Zilberman, 2001).

On the other hand, developing countries cannot afford to remain bystanders in the transformation taking place under the *gene revolution*. Like the green revolution, it has an immense potential to improve food security. Unlike the green revolution, access to the gene revolution is barred by corporate interests. As life scientist C. S. Prakash of Tuskegee University said, 'nobody should expect

Monsanto to end world hunger; that is like counting on Microsoft to wipe out illiteracy' (Prakash, 2000).

Governments in the South must create the conditions for consensual policy-making among scientists and decision makers. As biotechnology is a knowledge industry, the role of scientists will be crucial in developing a biosafety approach at the national and local levels. That includes compiling information databases, procedures for risk evaluation and conditions of release of LMOs into the environment. Scientists can further help with designing and implementing monitoring of regulations. There should also be a direct commitment in capacity building to provide skilled human resources in biosafety in the developing world. At the same time, there is a need to develop the necessary infrastructural capacity to provide state-of-the-art laboratories and state-of-the-art equipment to enable scientists in developing countries to conduct meaningful research in biotechnology and biosafety. In all these issues, the safety concerns should be fully addressed. Developing countries need to implement such strategies if they are to benefit from the technology.

REFERENCES

Carr, G (2000) 'The human genome', *Economist*, 1 July 2000

China Daily (2002) 'Tomato vaccine on trial', *China Daily*, 28 November 2002

Cook, L J (2002) 'Millions served', interview with Dr Florence Wambugu, *Forbes Magazine*, 23 December 2002

Erickson, L (1996) 'Edible vaccines – transforming alfalfa for TGEV immunity', *Agrifood Research in Ontario Magazine*, vol 19, no 2, p47

ETC Group (former RAFI) (1997) 'The human tissue trade', Action Group on Erosion, Technology and Concentration, communiqué, January–February, pp1–12

ETC Group (former RAFI) (1998) 'Terminator Technology', Action Group on Erosion, Technology and Concentration, communiqué, April, pp1–6

ETC Group (former RAFI) (2001) '2001: A seed odyssey – Annual update on terminator and traitor technology', Action Group on Erosion, Technology and Concentration, communiqué, Issue no 68

Firbank, L G, Perry, J N, Squire, G R, Bohan, D A, Brooks, D R, Champion, G T, Clark, S J, Daniels, R E, Dewar, A M, Haughton, A J, Hawes, C, Heard, M S, Hill, M O, May, M J, Osborne, J L, Rothery, P, Scott, R J and Woiwod, I P (2003) *The Implications of Spring-Sown Genetically Modified Herbicide Tolerant Crops for Farmland Biodiversity: A Commentary on the Farm Scale Evaluations of Spring Sown Crops*, Department for Environment, Food and Rural Affairs (DEFRA),UK

GM Science Review Panel (2003) *GM Science Review – First Report: An Open Review of the Science Relevant to GM Crops and Food Based on Interests and Concerns of the Public*, GM Science Review Panel, UK

Graff, G and Zilberman, D (2001) 'Intellectual property clearing house for agricultural biotechnology', *Intellectual Property Strategy Today*, no 3

ITDG (2003) 'Technology for sustainable livelihoods', T4SL homepage, http://livelihood technology.org, as viewed on 10 February 2003

James, C (1999) 'Achievements of plant breeding and its contribution to global food security', Proceedings of the World Seed Conference, Cambridge, UK, September 1999

James, C (2004) 'Preview: Global status of commercialized transgenic crops: 2004', *ISAAA Briefs No 32*, ISAAA, Ithaca, NY

Macilwain, C (1997) '$40m plant genome sequencing effort targets the best science', *Nature*, vol 390, pp539–540

Mugabe, J and Clark, N (1996) *Technology Transfer and the Convention on Biological Diversity: Emerging Policy and Institutional Issues*, African Centre for Technology Studies, Kenya

Nuffield Council on Bioethics (1995) *Human Tissue Trade: Legal and Ethical Issues*, Nuffield Council on Bioethics, London

Nuffield Council on Bioethics (2003) *The Use of Genetically Modified Crops in Developing Countries*, Nuffield Council, London

Prakash, C S (2000) 'Hungry for biotech', *Technology Review*, July/August, p32

Quist, D and Chapela, I H (2001) 'Transgenic DNA introgressed into traditional maize landraces in Oaxaca, Mexico', *Nature*, vol 414, pp541–543

Robinson, N A (1993) 'Agenda 21: Earth's action plan – annotated', *IUCN Environmental Policy & Law Paper*, no 27, Oceana Publications, London, Rome.

Wayt Gibbs, W (1997) 'Plantbodies: Human antibodies produced by field crops enter clinical trials', *Scientific American*, vol 277, no 5, p23

Whitfield, J (2001) 'Language gene found', *Nature*, Science Update, Nature News Service, 4 October 2001

4

Trade in Biotechnology: Development and the Clash of Collective Preferences

Heike Baumüller

As tariffs rates are progressively being reduced in the context of ongoing trade liberalization talks, the relevance of non-tariff policy tools is likely to increase, including standards and technical regulations setting out specific characteristics of a product or the way a product is labelled, packaged or produced. To some extent, this trend is a logical consequence of the growing trade volumes and diversification of traded goods that will need to be regulated to comply with the importing countries' standards. Protectionist intent can be expected to lie behind some measures as countries try to shield domestic industries increasingly exposed to foreign competitors. However, as competition becomes fierce and international rules on fair competition become smarter and more stringent, countries, to discourage measures taken to protect specific commercial interests, would increasingly be left with non-tariff measures of the type motivated by public policy objectives, such as protecting human health, the environment or societal values, which trade liberalization is increasingly bringing into play.

This trend is clearly apparent in the growing biotech trade, which is increasingly subject to labelling and testing requirements of varying strictness and scope. These variations can often be traced back to countries' differing attitudes to or 'collective preferences' regarding genetic modification and risk. Collective preferences – introduced as a concept into the trade debate by the former European Trade Commissioner, Pascal Lamy – can be loosely defined as social values or choices that form the basis of a community's practical decisions and actions (Lamy, 2004). Lamy acknowledges that articulating collective preferences could be ambiguous and open to dispute given that they are not always rational and evolve over time from cultural and religious values, political considerations, historical factors and the level of development. Regarding biotechnology, Lamy identifies consumers' wish to decide what they are eating and a precautionary approach to the technology as some of the collective preferences prevailing in Europe (Lamy, 2004; Lamy and Laïdi, 2002).

The basic concept underlying collective preferences, namely that policy making is not only guided by objective, measurable facts but also needs to account for legitimate societal and ethical values, is not necessarily new. The need for broader considerations to be taken into account has frequently been raised during discussions on the ethical issues in food and agriculture – and specifically biotechnology – which include issues related to risk, precaution, environment, health and equity (FAO, 2000). The concept is also reflected in debates on risk analysis where commentators have been arguing over the apparent dichotomy between 'objective', quantitative risk assessment and the 'subjective' (and often thought of as irrational) perceptions of the public (the 'qualitative' dimension) that need to be taken into account when managing the risk (Marris, 2001).[1]

The belief in the quantifiable nature of risk is reflected in the rules of the multilateral trading system. While some provisos have been built in to provide countries with a certain amount of leeway to accommodate societal choices (which will be discussed later), they are unlikely to be sufficient to easily accommodate trade-related measures that are based on collective preferences. Disagreements over countries' import regulations for biotech products are an interesting case in point. The dispute at the World Trade Organization (WTO) between the US, Argentina and Canada on the one side and the European Union on the other has brought to the surface fundamental differences in attitudes to assessing and managing risks as well as to the nature and application of biotechnology. At the same time, many developing countries are pursuing widely differing approaches to biotechnology, ranging from Zambia's extreme caution towards genetically modified (GM) food aid to Brazil's mixed response vis-à-vis the technology to Argentina's rapid, commercially driven adoption of GM soy.

This chapter will try to consider the response of several countries, including EU countries and the US as well as selected developing countries, to increased trade in agriculture biotechnology products from a 'collective preferences' analytical stance with the aim of contributing to a better understanding of the basis for differing positions on biotech trade. Such an attempt will necessarily have to be a preliminary one (given the limited scope of this chapter), which will hopefully provide a general framework for further discussions and analysis. The chapter will then look at the extent to which existing WTO rules account for these collective preferences and where they might be insufficient. Finally, possibilities will be suggested for better accommodating collective preferences in multilateral trade discussions and relations.

Assessing collective preference on biotechnology

Three sources of information underlie this preliminary discussion of collective preferences on biotechnology: the results of public opinion surveys; the role and behaviour of non-state actors (including farmers, public interest groups and the private sector); and specific country's domestic policy decisions. While the third criterion might appear to be a circular argument, its use is based on the assumption that the policies of democratically elected governments are thought to (more or less) reflect the will of the people – an assumption that is of course open to debate (Dye, 1990). The suitability of the criteria will be discussed later in the chapter.

European Union

Extensive public surveys have been carried out in the EU member states on biotech-related issues (ABE, 2002; ABE 2003). Overall, the awareness of biotechnology was found to be reasonably high (48 per cent). A survey carried out in 2002 found that 58 per cent of consumers would not buy a product if it were labelled to contain GM ingredients while 27 per cent would continue to buy it. Among their main concerns, consumers fear that the introduction of genetically modified organisms (GMOs) could harm the environment (49 per cent), put too much control in the hands of GMO-producing companies and destroy the quality and flavours of foods (14 per cent respectively). Also contributing to this reluctance is the general attitude to food in Europe. Food is seen by Europeans 'through a humanistic and aesthetic lens', functioning almost like a measure of national and cultural identity (Runge et al, 2001, p222).

However, to conclude that Europeans are opposed to biotechnology would be too simplistic; rather, opinions appear to be fairly differentiated. Opinion polls found opposition to be lower for products that were perceived to be useful, such as GM crops that support environmental practices. Also, the source of information on the safety of a biotech product was found to be relevant. Consumer organizations and the medical profession (26 and 24 per cent) were regarded as the most trusted sources, while the lowest ratings went to international organizations and national public authorities (3 and 4 per cent). A number of food scares that have haunted Europe over the past few decades, most recently the spread of mad cow disease (bovine spongiform encephalopathy or BSE), have certainly contributed to the declining trust in the capacity of national governments and regulatory bodies to deal with such crises (Runge et al, 2001).

The anti-GMO lobby has been particularly active in Europe. Environmental groups such as Greenpeace and Friends of the Earth, have been at the forefront of these protests. They reacted angrily to Monsanto's unrelenting efforts in the mid-1990s to introduce GMOs in Europe despite signs of growing consumer rejection (Charles, 2001). Opposition was particularly strong in Germany, where views on biotechnology continue to be among the most negative (ABE, 2003). Civil society groups have also become increasingly more active in the UK and France, culminating in the destruction of GMO field trials that have brought field research in Europe virtually to a halt. Today even after the EU had introduced stringent labelling and traceability regulations, every decision in Brussels on the approval of a new GM variety for use as food, feed or environmental release is accompanied by protests.

The anti-GM movement also found support from the private sector, notably the supermarkets and food retailers (Runge et al, 2001).[2] In the UK, a number of major companies, including Sainsbury, Tesco, Marks & Spencer, Burger King and McDonalds, responded to these consumer concerns in 1999 by banning GMOs from their shelves and menus. In Spain, Pryca, the largest importer of soy-based GMOs and producer of GM maize, announced it would no longer use GMOs in its brands. Similarly Swiss-based Nestlé temporarily abandoned the use of GMOs in it products. In contrast, the pro-GM camps, including the farmers, remained relatively quiet. Moreover, in response to the widespread opposition, a number of major biotech companies, including Monsanto, DuPont, Bayer Cropscience and Syngenta, have decided to close their crop research in the UK. While farmers in some European countries have adopted GM crops, notably in Spain and (somewhat surprisingly) in Germany, they clearly recognize that there is little use in fighting to grow a crop that does not have a market.

It has also been suggested that competitiveness considerations might play a central role in determining Europe's stance on biotechnology (Anderson et al, 2004). The argument here is that the comparative advantage of using biotechnology for US farmers over their European competitors, who due to the comparatively small size of their farms are unlikely to reap the same benefits as their large-scale counterparts, provides an incentive for European farm groups to lobby for stringent regulations, thereby keeping the more efficient producers out of the market. In other words, 'when firms lobby policy makers to influence standards and consumers and environmentalists care about the choice of standard, it is also possible that increased competition can lead to strategic incentives to raise standards' (Anderson et al, 2004, pp4–5).

In the face of these developments, it is not surprising that the EU has opted for a stringent and comprehensive risk assessment and approval process, including the world's most rigorous labelling and traceability system which even covers products produced from but no longer containing GMOs (such as soy oil made from GM soy). The regulations are based on the precautionary approach – an integral part of EU policy making since 1994 – which allows precautionary decisions to be taken in the absence of sufficient scientific evidence. Approvals had been put on hold since 1998 while the system was developed. While a number of GMOs have been authorized since early 2004, the decision was usually left to the Commission after member states failed to reach an agreement, highlighting the continued tensions within the EU on how to move forward on biotechnology.

United States

Although the use and sale of GM crops and product is now widespread in the US, awareness among consumers of biotechnology is generally low (36 per cent) and 58 per cent of respondents were convinced that they had not eaten GM food (Pew Initiative, 2003). While a sizable proportion of respondents expressed their opposition to biotech foods (48 per cent), the intense opposition witnessed in Europe has not formed. This has been attributed to the generally 'utilitarian' view of food that focuses on food in nutritional terms (Runge et al, 2001). What clearly distinguishes the American from the European consumer is the widespread trust in food safety authorities, notably the Food and Drug Administration which many consumers would like to see play a central role in regulating biotech foods (89 per cent). This support continued even after the Starlink crisis in which GM maize approved only for feed use was found in food products, allegedly evoking allergic reactions among some consumers.

Already in 1994, GM foods had been quietly introduced in the US market in the form of the Flavr Savr tomato, genetically engineered for delayed ripening. Their arrival evoked few reactions and open opposition to GM foods remains comparatively limited. Nevertheless, a number of public interest groups are leading a continued campaign, focusing in particular on labelling, and several states have seen (so far unsuccessful) efforts to institute legislation to regulate the introduction of GMOs or require GM food products to be labelled. Moreover, Mendocino County became the first county in the US to ban the growing of GMOs and several other counties are likely to follow suit. These efforts, however, remain scattered and it is the farm lobby and industry groups that have to date been most vocal in their support for GMOs. Farmers in the US have been quick to adopt the new technology: in 2003, GMOs covered 47.6 million hectares, making up 59 per cent of the global area of transgenic crops (James, 2004)

The regulatory system in the US clearly reflects the widespread perception among policy makers and supporters of GMOs that modern biotechnology is just another form of genetic modification that has been practised by farmers ever since they started to cross-breed plants. Genetically modified organisms are seen as 'substantially equivalent' to their conventional counterparts unless shown otherwise. Biotech products thus fall within the scope of existing regulations that are monitored by the various government bodies depending on the intended use of the GMO. Risk assessments are usually carried out by the companies seeking approval. Labelling for GM products is not required although producers are free to label their products as GM-free if they comply with the government-approved standard.

Selected developing countries

Assessing the attitudes to biotechnology in other countries or regions around the world is much less straightforward. In most countries, few opinion polls have been carried out and, particularly in poorer regions, many consumers, farmers and often even policy makers remain ill-informed about the risks and benefits of biotechnology. Despite these caveats, it is possible to provide at least some tentative observations of certain developing countries' collective preferences on biotechnology.

In general, it has become clear that the biotechnology-related priorities in most developing countries differ from those in the EU and the US. This is not to say that the concerns are necessarily fundamentally different; rather the prioritization of concerns in relation to each other and to other policy priorities are often not the same. Thus, emphasis is usually placed on the need to ensure access to seed for poor farmers, to take into account local environments and constraints when assessing and managing risk, to meet the needs of the domestic as well as the demands of the export markets, and to strengthen their own capabilities on research and development to adapt GMOs to local needs. These concerns can be illustrated with specific examples from India, Mexico, Brazil and Zambia.

India

In India, biotechnology was received rather cautiously due to concerns that GM crops could in fact threaten food security by encouraging cash crops or could negatively affect agricultural exports to key markets (Dhar, 2001). As the decision drew nearer on whether to allow the growing of GMOs (in particular GM cotton), it was concerns over corporate control of the seed market rather than biosafety that became the focus of the debate (Paarlberg, 2002). The possibility that the 'terminator technology' – used to produce sterile seeds that can not be replanted – might be introduced into the country evoked strong reactions from civil society and farmers groups who saw this as an attempt to increase farmers' dependence on the seed companies by threatening farmers' right to replant seeds. In a largely agriculture-dependent society such as India with its significant number of small-scale subsistence farmers, this right is seen as a fundamental prerequisite for food security. Despite these protests, the government allowed the commercial planting of GM cotton in 2002. Food crops, however, including soy, sunflower and rapeseed used for India's oilseed meal exports, have not yet been approved for commercial release (Paarlberg, 2002).

Mexico

In Mexico, concerns over the contamination of native maize varieties have been at the heart of the biotech debate. Despite a ban on the planting of GM maize imposed in 1998, native varieties were found to contain transgenic DNA. This discovery is of particular importance to Mexico, which is the centre of origin for maize. Thus any contamination not only affects local farmers, but might also affect the world's seed supplies given that crop improvements depend on the diversity of genes in existing varieties. In response to the discovery, the Mexican Congress, environmental groups and farmer organizations called for a ban on the GM maize imports that have been identified as the most likely source of the contamination. However, an extensive consultative study carried out by the North American Commission for Environmental Cooperation concludes that introgression of a few individual transgenes is unlikely to have any major biological effect on genetic diversity in maize landraces, in particular, compared to other factors such as modern agricultural practices (CEC, 2004). Nevertheless, the report points to the 'significant cultural, symbolic and spiritual values' (p15) of maize for most Mexicans, stressing that 'risk assessment of transgenic maize in Mexico is inextricably linked to the central role of maize in Mexico's history and culture, including the beliefs and value systems of indigenous peoples' (p16).

Brazil

The debate in Brazil has been particularly divisive, requiring policy makers to accommodate widely opposing attitudes and preferences. Thus, while in particular the previous government and industry have been pushing for the introduction of GMOs, environmental groups have fought an extensive campaign to keep Brazil free from GMOs. The approach to GMOs today, however, is not so much a result of informed national debate, but rather a legal battle between civil society groups and the government (Toni and von Braun, 2001). Environmental groups in 1999 lodged a complaint against the government's approval of GM soy for commercial release, thus effectively charging the court to be de facto arbiter between the opposing camps. The court ruled in favour of the complainants, leading to a 'judicial moratorium' on the commercial release of GMOs. Farmers in the south, however, voted with their ploughs by growing GM soy smuggled from Argentina in defiance of the court's decision. The government acknowledged the widespread use of GMOs in 2003 by granting an amnesty to soy farmers and allowing the sale of the crop. Subsequently, the permission to use authorized GM soy was explicitly included in Brazil's Biosafety Law of 2005. The uncertainty over the future of biotechnology and the increasingly complex regulatory processes have raised concerns among Brazilian scientists over negative impacts on research and development in the country (see also Chapter 6).

Zambia

Zambia provides a stark contrast to the countries discussed so far. In a country afflicted by widespread poverty, public awareness of biotechnology remains very low as a result of the high level of illiteracy, the absence of dialogue on science policy, and a media dominated by politics and fragmented information about the implications of GM crops for local agriculture (Chinsembu and Kambikambi, 2001). At the same time, Zambia has found itself at the heart of the biotech debate, being forced to take decisions without the necessary information and regulatory frameworks. Along with several other southern African countries, Zambia in 2002 refused the importation of food aid containing GM maize because of biosafety concerns and fears that the inadvertent growing of the maize could harm Zambia's exports. While the other countries in the end accepted the food aid provided it was milled before or upon arrival, Zambia continues to reject it. Efforts by the government to develop a regulatory framework have been marred by a lack of political will to invest in science and technology, the continued economic crisis, lack of specialized human resource capacity and a highly differentiated agricultural sector (Lewanika, 2001).

The situation in Zambia is not uncommon for other countries in sub-Saharan Africa, which continue to be torn between the supporters and opponents of biotechnology. While Africa probably has most to gain from the appropriate and safe use of biotechnology, countries in the region plead for the right to make their own choice based on an assessment of their needs and priorities. At the same time, they are acutely aware that they are lacking the necessary information and capacity to take these decisions. Risk analyses have largely focused on temperate zones and little information is available on the risks of GMOs in tropical, humid countries, where the high levels of biodiversity pose an additional complexity (Egziabher, 2003). They call for greater capacity building efforts, including the transfer of necessary technologies, to allow them to make comprehensive risk assessments and to enable them to improve crops of importance to them with traits that respond to their needs. Like other developing countries, many African countries have raised concerns over corporate control of the seed supply facilitated by patents. Any regulatory framework will need to take into account their specific realities, including a highly informal seed market which relies on farmers' ability to exchange seeds freely and makes monitoring of environmental impacts of GM crops virtually impossible (Morris and Koch, 2002).

COLLECTIVE PREFERENCES AND WTO RULES

As Lamy notes, WTO rules do provide some (albeit limited) leeway for countries to address their constituents' values or collective preferences by allowing for exceptions to be made on the grounds of public health, public order, public morality, the environment or national security (Lamy, 2004). Moreover, the WTO's Dispute Settlement Mechanism continues to be faced with the need to strike a balance between legitimate preferences and protectionist measures, not least in the biotech dispute.

With regard to health or environmental risks, application of WTO rules is comparatively straightforward. Most recently, the preamble of the WTO Doha Ministerial Declaration adopted in 2001 clearly recognizes 'that under WTO rules no country should be prevented from taking measures for the protection of human, animal or plant life or health, or of the environment at the levels it considers appropriate'. Specific exceptions were also enshrined in Article XX of the General

Agreement on Tariffs and Trade (GATT) of 1994, which allows countries to take measures 'necessary to protect human, animal or plant life or health' (paragraph b) and 'relating to the conservation of exhaustible natural resources' (paragraph g). It is important to note, however, that both the preamble of the Doha Declaration and Article XX include caveats stipulating that measures should not be discriminatory or constitute disguised restrictions on international trade, thereby limiting the range of measures that can be implemented (but without clearly defining the limit). Moreover, Article XX (b) introduces a 'necessity' test, which has been interpreted as requiring countries to show that the measure employed was the least trade-restrictive alternative reasonably available to achieve the objective (Marceau and Trachtman, 2002).

The Agreement for the Application of Sanitary and Phytosanitary Measures (SPS) encourages Members to base their SPS measures 'necessary for the protection of human, animal or plant life or health' on international standards, thus favouring countries agreeing on what could be described as 'universal preferences'. However, the Agreement also provides countries with the flexibility to institute measures that achieve a higher level of protection than those based on relevant international standards. These measures, however, are subject to certain criteria, including a risk assessment, non-discrimination, proportionality and consistency, which again limit the range of measures that can be applied. The Agreement also allows countries to take provisional measures in light of insufficient scientific evidence, provided that the measure is reviewed within a reasonable period of time and efforts are made to obtain further evidence.

Standards and technical regulations not covered by the SPS Agreement fall under the Agreement on Technical Barriers to Trade (TBT). The scope of TBT measures is defined rather broadly as necessary to pursue 'legitimate objectives', including human safety or health, the protection of animal and plant life or health, and the protection of the environment. The TBT Agreement also encourages the use of international standards unless they would be ineffective or inappropriate (for instance by running counter to collective preferences) to fulfil the measure's objective. Contrary to the SPS Agreement, measures that deviate from international standards do not need to be justified scientifically (although they are still subject to the other conditions mentioned above).

Both the SPS and the TBT Agreements recognize that countries may wish to employ different approaches to achieving a certain level of protection (which could, among other reasons, respond to different collective preferences).[3] The SPS Agreement encourages Members to accept each others' measures as long as they ensure the same level of protection, while the TBT Agreement simply calls on Members to give 'positive consideration' to accepting other Members' measures as equivalent.

The provisions described above are based on the assumption that the objectives pursued by certain measures, be they health or environment-related, are somewhat measurable and verifiable. Problems arise, however, when this assumption does not hold, which tends to be the case for most policy decisions. As outlined in the previous section, consumer attitudes to biotech products are only partly based on fears for their own safety or on environmental concerns; many other factors that are far more difficult to grasp play an important role in people's choices and governments' policy stands. Current WTO rules provide little guidance on how to deal with these situations, although some relevant provisions can be identified.

The TBT Agreement, for instance, leaves the permissible 'legitimate objectives' underlying a certain measure undefined, providing room for governments to argue for broader policy objectives or consumer choice. As noted above, the Agreement also does not require scientific justification if measures are not based on inter- national standards, thereby providing a certain degree of flexibility for how to achieve a certain objective. However, the SPS Agreement does not provide the same amount of leeway, nor does the definition of risk assessment in the Agreement leave much space to take into account considerations outside the realm of science. This is of particular relevance to biotech-related measures, which will often respond to a variety of concerns, some of which are likely to fall under the scope of the SPS Agreement.

Also relevant is the requirement in the GATT 1994 and the TBT Agreement that measures must not discriminate between 'like' products. While the agreements leave the concept of 'like' undefined, four criteria are commonly used to determine likeness, namely the products' physical properties, end-uses, tariff classification and consumers' tastes and habits (Musselli and Zarrilli, 2002).[4] It is the last of these criteria – consumers' tastes and habits – that could be argued to provide an opening for countries to bring in consumers' collective preferences. If they did, one test that might be applied is the extent to which a government might have influenced the 'creation' of these preferences (as was argued in the sardines case).[5]

The Agreement on Agriculture and the Doha Declaration stress the need to take into account non-trade concerns when making new commitments in the context of further agriculture trade liberalization. While mentioning food security and environmental protection as possible examples, the Agreement does not elaborate further on the nature of possible concerns. It could be argued that such concerns also include certain collective preferences, such as the preference for precautionary measures to ensure that conventional, GM and organic crops do not cross-breed in the field. While these provisions are not of immediate use as they relate primarily to the ongoing negotiations, they still provide an opening for Members to ensure that the outcomes of these negotiations leave sufficient leeway for them to pursue their collective preferences.

Finally, in addition to the environment- and health-related exceptions men- tioned above, GATT 1994 Article XX(a) also allows for measures 'necessary to protect public morals'. The scope of this provision is left undefined and has not yet been tested in the dispute settlement system. This option would likely be subject to the same test of proportionality (or level of trade-restrictiveness) as Article XX(b) mentioned above.

ADDRESSING COLLECTIVE PREFERENCES IN TRADE POLICY

It is clear that multilateral trade rules were not negotiated with 'collective preferences' at the forefront of countries' minds. Rather, the trading system aims to fit possible exceptions that might require special treatment into a rules-based framework that leaves little leeway for the more intangible attitudes and priorities. This section will assess a number of options that might be used to better accommodate such preferences in trade policy.

The need for a broad definition

For Lamy, collective preferences seem to be primarily a 'Northern' concept. He argues that 'sensitivity to collective preferences is one of the features of development' and that 'the very formation of collective preferences is dependent on income levels', namely the trade-off between environmental protection and the reduction of inequalities that becomes necessary when societies become more affluent (Lamy, 2004, p6). This is based on the assumption that collective preferences are fundamentally 'non-market', and related to, for instance, the environment, the social clause[6] or agriculture (Lamy and Laïdi, 2002). Thus, it is 'the North's defence of its collective preferences . . . which stands in the way of the South's development' (p3).

There is no reason to assume, however, that only rich countries have collective preferences that guide their policy making. Many developing countries might be poor, but it does not follow that their societies do not make collective choices towards a common objective or do not have different values and priorities that need to be balanced. If the wish to choose what to eat is a collective preference, so is the wish to eat. Or the wish to keep out GMOs until the country has built up its capacities to deal with them. The same applies to different agriculture systems and in particular to different systems for handing seeds, as in India, for instance, where the right to save seed can be regarded as a cultural preference just like Europe's support for multifunctionality (Shiva, 2004). Thus, there is a need to broaden the debate on collective preferences from Lamy's Eurocentric concept into a much more holistic approach to identifying values and priorities. Indeed, the dichotomy between 'rich' and 'poor' countries in this context might be too simplistic, given that effects of collective choices on others can occur irrespective of development levels (although the actual impacts are bound to be different).

ASSESSING COLLECTIVE PREFERENCES

Identifying collective preferences will likely be the greatest challenge, which is precisely the reason why the WTO has so far tried to skirt round the issue. The indicators listed above for assessing preferences on biotechnology all have their weaknesses. While opinion polls and public consultations certainly provide some insights, they are often subject to some fundamental flaws. Althaus (2003) found opinions expressed in surveys frequently to be 'shallow, coarse, vacillating, and illogical' (p7). He notes that political awareness tends generally to be low (although people are still willing to give an opinion) and spread unevenly across social groups, diminishing the quality and representativeness of surveys.

On a practical level, the order and language of the questions can already have an impact on the results. The term 'genetically modified food', for instance, tends to evoke a negative reaction, while consumers are usually less sceptical of using biotechnology for 'food production' (ABE, 2003). The sample, such as gender balance or levels of education, can also impact on the result.[7] In the UK consultations, participants in the public consultations were found to be far more critical of biotechnology's potential for developing countries than those participating in the randomly selected focus groups.[8] This difference could be explained by the fact that the open consultations attracted certain segments of the public and in particular the opponents of biotechnology.

Opinions also do not always correspond to actions, as is apparent from the success of sales in paste, clearly labelled as made from GM tomatoes, in the UK despite the public's negative attitude to biotechnology (ABE, 2002). The source and type of information is also crucial for the formation of public opinion. The UK consultations, for example, had shown that people who became more engaged in the GM issues also became more negative. This result is not surprising given that participants in the survey were left to find the information themselves, primarily on the internet which is clearly dominated by negative publicity. Had participants instead been given a series of balanced and informative lectures on the risks and benefits of biotechnology, the attitude change would likely have been different.

Some of these pitfalls also apply to using election results as a measure of public support for government policies. While biotechnology might be a decisive factor in some countries, such as possibly the UK or Germany, in most countries it is not, particularly in developing countries. Additionally, only a limited proportion of citizens usually participate in elections and not all interests are equally represented. Also, the activities of interest groups cannot always be seen as a definitive indicator of public concerns since it is uncertain whether all relevant voices are indeed included in the group system or that groups truly represent the people in whose interest they claim to act (Althouse, 2004). The destruction of authorized and monitored field trials in France, for instance, did not find broad support among the general public (ABE, 2002).

Despite these drawbacks, it should not be concluded that opinion polls could not be useful; rather they have to be put into perspective and be carefully designed to ensure a representative result. It is also important to bear in mind that a low level of knowledge among ordinary citizens remains an inherent shortcoming of many opinion polls (Althouse, 2004), requiring balanced and comprehensive information provision, including through the media. The aim is not to achieve a certain result (such as a greater support for biotechnology) but rather to ensure that the survey results better reflect the public's collective preferences. Well-designed sustainability impact assessments, as suggested by Lamy, could provide one possible tool in this effort, as long as they combine factual research and analysis with a thorough public consultation process.

Adapting WTO rules to better integrate collective preferences

Lamy has suggested the use of a special safeguard mechanism to integrate collective preferences into WTO rules, which he believes would only rarely need to be used (Lamy, 2004). This would enable other instruments to function more effectively and stop the issue from 'paralysing the entire debate on trade policy' (p10). He identifies two major provisos that would have to accompany such a clause. First, it would be necessary to show that the measure was consistent with a real social demand, based on an internal review of the underlying collective preferences. Second, the measure would still be subject to the usual conditions, such as transparency, non-discrimination, national treatment and proportionality, and could not be used to sanction customs duties. Lastly, protection granted by the safeguard clause would only be temporary (although Lamy does not specify a maximum time or when/how it would be revoked).

Another more radical approach to dealing with the specific facets of biotechnology, including prevailing uncertainty and ethical concerns, has been put forward by Perdikis (2000). He believes that WTO rules are fundamentally not suited for dealing with GMOs, in particular the SPS and TBT Agreements, which were established to address comparatively straightforward issues. New institutions and agreements are needed, he argues, to monitor and decide on the legitimacy of consumer concerns. Such a framework would need to be open and transparent, with discussions based on a comprehensive assessment by an independent body of experts. Penalties should be set high so as to discourage dubious requests.

It might also be worth exploring additional avenues involving existing rules. One possibility could include some form of guidelines to be used in the interpretation of WTO rules by the dispute settlement mechanism, specifying the leeway countries have to pursue their collective preferences. Such guidelines are one of the options raised during the ongoing negotiations on clarifying the relationship between WTO rules and multilateral environmental agreements (MEAs). They could be used to define the flexibility of countries to put in place trade measures to achieve their 'universal preferences' defined in MEAs within the context of WTO rules (although it remains open to debate to what extent it should be the WTO's role to define this flexibility).

Broadening the concept of risk assessment in the WTO

Another way of better accommodating collective preferences might be to broaden the concept of risk assessment in the WTO. As previously noted, the SPS Agreement provides far less flexibility to take 'non-scientific' factors into account than the TBT Agreement. This is in part due to the narrow definition of risk assessment applied in the Agreement, which focuses on the 'likelihood of entry, establishment or spread of a pest or disease' and the 'associated potential biological and economic consequences', or the 'potential adverse effects on human or animal health' arising from additives, contaminants, toxins or disease-causing organisms in food, beverages or feedstuffs (Annex A). Some additional factors can be taken into account, primarily related to science, ecology, regulatory processes and economics.

Some rulings of the WTO Dispute Settlement Body have already gone some way towards broadening this narrow definition of risk assessment, although only on a case-by-case basis. The Appellate Body in the *hormones* case, for instance, noted that factors for risk assessment outlined in the SPS Agreement did not 'exclude *a priori*, from the scope of a risk assessment, factors which are not susceptible of quantitative analysis by the empirical or experimental laboratory methods commonly associated with the physical sciences' (WTO, 1998b, p99). The report also notes that 'there is nothing to indicate that the listing of factors that may be taken into account in a risk assessment of Article 5.2 was intended to be a closed list' (p72). The risk that is to be evaluated in a risk assessment, the report adds, 'is not only risk ascertainable in a science laboratory operating under strictly controlled conditions, but also risk in human societies as they actually exist, in other words, the actual potential for adverse effects on human health in the real world where people live and work and die' (p72).

The need for formalizing a more holistic approach to risk assessment under current trade rules is well argued in the *amicus curiae* brief submitted by a group of academics to the panel examining the biotech dispute (Busch et al, 2004). The group notes that risk assessments tend to be subject to certain constraints, including the maturity of scientific knowledge, the scientific and cultural contingencies that shape the assessment by determining the analytical foci, and the wider background assumptions and value commitments that are embedded within scientific knowledge. They note that these complexities are particularly apparent in the context of biotechnology, which scores low on both of the fundamental variables that define risk situations, namely certainty and consensus.

The group calls on the panel to recognize that risk assessments conducted in a specific national or institutional context are necessarily limited and partial, constrained by the decision-making culture in which they are produced. Thus, public consultation and review processes should be an integral part of risk assessments, especially in cases of low certainty and consensus. Such a broad approach to risk assessment, as advocated in the brief, would provide additional room for integrating the more intangible facets of people's collective preferences when evaluating the risks and benefits of biotechnologies and the most suitable measures to address them. It could also help to assess the level of *acceptable* risk, which often differs with historical, cultural and socio-economic circumstances or as a result of possible 'trade-offs' between perceived risks and benefits.

A balanced system for addressing potential negative impacts on exporters

Even after a society's collective preferences have been identified and factored into the risk assessment, the question remains how countries should deal with the impacts of the preferences on their trading partners, in particular on developing countries. Lamy (2004) proposes to establish a compensation mechanism which would help to test countries' determination to pursue their preference and at least partially compensate the affected exporters. Compensation should take into account the nature of the interests affected (including the differing abilities to adapt to the measures in say the US and Africa) and should take the form of payments or, in the case of developing countries, complementary policies, such as technical assistance or building capacities to meet the importer's standards.

This proposal presumes the previously mentioned distinction between Northern preferences and Southern development needs. It seems appropriate for countries such as the US and the EU where attitudes and expectations are linked to a high level of development, turning the preferences into luxuries rather than necessities. It would only be fair and equitable for rich countries to compensate the poor under these circumstances. For poor countries, this approach however would not be feasible. It would be hardly fair to require a country like Senegal to pay compensation should it decide to halt biotech imports from the US. Any system to deal with the impact of preferences will need to provide a balanced approach to ensure that poor countries are not disproportionately penalized for pursuing their societal preferences while minimizing negative impacts of rich countries' collective choices.

TOWARDS 'UNIVERSAL PREFERENCES'?

As much as possible, countries should aim to find common ground among their collective preferences at the international and regional levels. This approach is also encouraged by WTO rules and practices. As noted above, the SPS and TBT Agreements encourage the use of internationally agreed standards. WTO jurisprudence also favours a consultative approach to resolving conflicts, apparent for example in the *shrimp–turtle* case where the Appellate Body encouraged countries to seek an internationally agreed solution to the 'preservation of globally shared environmental resources', for instance, in the form of a multilateral environmental agreement (WTO, 1998a, p25).

Arriving at such 'universal preferences' – or 'universal public goods' (Lamy and Laïdi, 2002) – is not always possible, however, nor does it necessarily lead to universally satisfactory results. Often, negotiated outcomes reflect the lowest common denominator rather than the preferences with which countries entered the negotiations. In the Codex Alimentarius Commission, for instance, countries, after long debates over the meaning of 'product tracing' for biotech foods, in the end left the definition so vague that it is of little use for resolving their differences. Moreover, the political clout of the negotiating partners and their capacity to participate effectively vary widely, with developing countries left on the margin. Even where countries succeed in reaching an agreement, the result is often open to interpretation, as in the case of the Cartagena Protocol on Biosafety where the US and the EU continue to be deeply divided over the extent to which the Protocol incorporates the precautionary principle.

A multilateral approach to reconciling collective preferences assumes that countries are indeed representing their constituents' values and choices, which might not always be the case. Thus, it will be crucial to ensure effective participation of all interested parties during the formulation of countries' negotiating positions. At the same time, there is a need to build the capacity of developing countries to engage in the negotiations so as to ensure that their constraints are taken into account in the decision-making process and that capacity gaps to implement their obligations are identified and addressed. Moreover, any 'universal preferences' will still need to leave sufficient space for countries to preserve their own specific collective preferences.

CONCLUSION

More so than for most other technologies, differing (and often intangible) preferences, attitudes and values lie at the root of the different approaches to biotechnology. Food safety, environmental and ethical concerns prevalent in the EU stand in contrast to the utilitarian, ostensibly science-based approach of the US. These priorities again differ from the concerns of many developing countries, where issues related to food security and poverty alleviation form the focus of the debate. The various preferences and priorities are equally valid and countries should be given the flexibility to pursue them (and adapt their policies to possible changes in these preferences). Where this pursuit affects others, care must be taken to minimize detrimental impacts on their economic and development interests. In a globalizing, interdependent world, many choices also affect outsiders and the costs and benefits of these decisions should be distributed fairly. The challenge, however, begins with the clear identification of the collective preferences so as to avoid their misuse for protectionist intent. A fundamental prerequisite will be a participatory approach to policy making, involving the many actors that have a stake in the debate. Account should be taken of the special needs and constraints of poor countries, which often lack the capacity to meet the preferences of the North, while providing them with sufficient space to follow their legitimate collective preferences in line with their development needs and priorities.

ACKNOWLEDGEMENTS

The author would like to thank Ricardo Meléndez-Ortiz, Lee Ann Jackson, Matthew Stilwell, Tony Bandle, Yvonne Apea, Sarah Mohan and Maria Julia Oliva for their constructive comments and input into this chapter.

NOTES

1   This dichotomy is increasingly being questioned by those who argue that it ignores the importance of the social, economic and historical context in influencing science and risk evaluation.
2   It should be borne in mind that it might not always be valid to blur the difference between consumer preferences and firms' motivations, since assessing the extent to which their interests diverge or converge is crucial to understanding the dynamics that drive ongoing negotiations (Lee Ann Jackson, personal communication, 18 November 2004).
3   One example in this regard could be the continued (and controversial) use of the pesticide DDT to fight malaria. It could be argued that countries using DDT, such as South Africa, are pursuing their collective preference for a cost-effective and efficient means of achieving specific health objectives. In many developed countries, however, DDT has been banned in response to countries' preference for long-term health and environmental protection. While these preferences can co-exist, trade could bring them into conflict if, for instance, DDT residues were found in agricultural exports to developed country markets.
4   The Appellate Body also noted, however, that these criteria should not be regarded as a closed list (WTO, 2001). The ruling implied that the competitive relationship between products is an overarching consideration.
5   In the sardines case, the Panel ruled against an EC regulation prohibiting the use of the term 'sardines' on tins containing the species *Sardinops sagax* which is found outside European waters. While the EU had argued that the use of the word 'sardines' for products other than preserved *Sardina pilchardus* would be mislead European consumers, the Panel concluded that the EC had 'created' consumer expectations which were then used to justify its trade-restrictive measures (WTO, 2002).
6   The social clause would aim to ensure that trade rules respect minimum social standards. The idea goes back to Article 7 of the Havana Charter, which recognized the links between trade and international labour standards. Some industrial nations believe such a clause should be included in multilateral trade rules, an idea generally opposed by developing countries.
7   Men, for instance, have been found to be generally more supportive of biotechnology than women (ABE, 2002).
8   For further information on the consultations, see www.gmnation.org.uk .

REFERENCES

ABE (2002) *Public Attitudes to Agricultural Biotechnology*, Issue Paper 2, Agricultural Biotechnology in Europe

ABE (2003) *European Views on Agricultural Biotechnology: An Overview of Public Opinion*, Issue Paper 7, Agricultural Biotechnology in Europe

Althaus, S L (2003) *Collective Preferences in Democratic Politics: Opinion Surveys and the Will of the People*, Cambridge University Press, Cambridge, UK

Anderson, K, Damania, R and Jackson, L A (2004) *Trade, Standards and the Political Economy of Genetically Modified Food*, World Bank Policy Research Working Paper 3395, Washington, DC

Busch, L, Grove-White, R, Jasanoff, S, Winickoff, D and Wynne, B (2004) *Amicus Curiae Brief*. Submitted to the Dispute Settlement Panel of the World Trade Organization in the case of EC: Measures Affecting the Approval and Marketing of Biotech Products. See www.lancs.ac.uk/fss/ieppp/wtoamicus/amicus.brief.wto.pdf

CEC (2004) *Maize and Biodiversity: The Effects of Transgenic Maize in Mexico – Key Findings and Recommendations*, Commission for Environmental Cooperation of North America, Montreal

Charles, D (2001) *Lords of the Harvest – Biotech, Big Money, and the Future of Food*, Perseus Publishing, Cambridge, US

Chinsembu, K and Kambikambi, T (2001) 'Farmers' perceptions and expectations of genetic engineering in Zambia', *Biotechnology and Development Monitor*, no 47, pp13–14

Dhar, B (2001) 'Regulations, negotiations and campaigns: Introducing biotechnology in India', *Biotechnology and Development Monitor*, no 47, pp19–21

Dye, T R (1990) *Political Economy and Public Policy: The Political Legitimacy of Markets and Governments*, vol 7 (Political Economy and Public Policy), JAI Press, Greenwich, Connecticut

Egziabher, T (2003) 'When elephants fight over GMOs', *Seedling*, October, pp1–3

FAO (2000) *Report of the Panel of Eminent Experts on Ethics in Food and Agriculture*, First Session, 26–28 September, Rome

James, C (2004) 'Preview: Global status of commercialized transgenic crops: 2004', *ISAAA Briefs no 32*, ISAAA, Ithaca, NY

Lamy, P (2004) *The Emergence of Collective Preferences in International Trade: Implications for Regulating Globalisation*. Presented at the conference on 'Collective preferences and global governance: What future for the multilateral trading system?', 15 September. Available at http://trade-info.cec.eu.int/doclib/html/118925.htm

Lamy, P and Laïdi, Z (2002) *Governance or Making Globalisation Meaningful*, prepared for the Conseil d'Analyse Economique, available at www.laidi.com/papiers/governance.pdf

Lewanika, M M (2001) 'Establishing acceptance: Biosafety regulations in Zambia', *Biotechnology and Development Monitor*, no 47, p15

Marceau, G and Trachtman, J P (2002) 'The technical barriers to trade agreement, the Sanitary and Phytosanitary Measures Agreement, and the General Agreement on Tariffs and Trade: A map of the World Trade Organization law of domestic regulation of goods', *Journal of World Trade*, vol 36, no 5, pp811–881.

Marris, C (2001) 'Public perceptions of transgenic products: The influence of the behaviour of laboratory scientists', in Toutant, J-P and Balàzs, E (eds) *Molecular Farming*, INRA editions, pp289–305

Morris, E J and Koch, M (2002) 'Biosafety of genetically modified crops – an African perspective', *AgBiotechNet*, vol 4, ABN 102

Musselli, I and Zarrilli, S (2002) 'Non-trade concerns and the WTO jurisprudence in the Asbestos Case: Possible relevance for international trade in genetically modified organism', *Journal of World Intellectual Property*, vol 5, no 3, pp373–393

Paarlberg, R L (2002) *The US–EU trade conflict over GM foods: Implications for poor countries*, Weatherhead Center for International Affairs, Harvard University

Perdikis, N (2000) 'A conflict of legitimate concerns or pandering to vested interests: Conflicting attitudes towards the regulation of trade in genetically modified goods – The EU and the US', *Estey Centre Journal of International Law and Trade Policy*, vol 1, no 1, pp51–65

Pew Initiative (2003) *Public Sentiment about Genetically Modified Food*, Pew Initiative on Food and Biotechnology, Washington, September

Runge, C F, Bagnara, G-L and Jackson, L A (2001) 'Differing US and European perspectives on GMOs: Political, economic and cultural issues', *Estey Centre Journal of International Law and Trade Policy*, vol 2, no 2, pp221–234

Shiva, V (2004) Full interview with Vandana Shiva on the ills of the world trading system. Via3.net, 6 April

Toni A and von Braun J (2001) 'Poor citizens decide on the introduction of GMOs in Brazil', *Biotechnology and Development Monitor*, no 47, pp7–9

WTO (1998a) *United States – Import Prohibition of Certain Shrimp and Shrimp Products – Report of the Appellate Body*, AB-1998-4. Available at http://docsonline.wto.org/

WTO (1998b) *EC Measures Concerning Meat and Meat Products (Hormones) – Report of the Appellate Body*, WT/DS26/AB/R, WT/DS48/AB/R. Available at http://docsonline.wto.org/

WTO (2001) *European Communities – Measures Affecting Asbestos and Asbestos-Containing Products – Report of the Appellate Body*, WT/DS135/AB/R12. Available at http://docsonline.wto.org/

WTO (2002) *European Communities – Trade Description of Sardines – Report of the Panel*, WT/DS231/R. Available at http://docsonline.wto.org/

5

Benefiting from Agricultural Biotechnology: Challenges for Developing Countries

Padmashree Gehl Sampath

The last decade has seen a rapid increase in the adoption of genetically modified (GM) crops. Whereas only six countries were planting GM crops in 1996 (US, China, Canada, Argentina, Australia and Mexico) and the total area of plantation was only 1.7 million hectares, this had gone up to 81.0 million hectares worldwide in 17 countries by 2004 (James, 2004). More and more developing countries are embracing GM crops due to expected yield increases. GM varieties are also touted to be advantageous for developing countries since they allow for the creation of varieties immune to environmental influences and varieties containing higher vital ingredients, thereby helping to solve problems of food security and nutrition.

Although the kinds of GM crops available may potentially result in higher yields and a reduction of some fixed costs, such as costs of insecticides or other farm inputs, they may impose other costs, such as increased seed costs or costs due to adverse social or environmental impacts (Cuffaro, 2002, p35). The decision to adopt GM crops on a large scale, therefore, is a decision that should be influenced not by the lure of increased yields only, but by the cumulative impact that GM crops can have on the agricultural sector and on society in developing countries. To be able effectively to utilize biotechnology to increase their agricultural productivity and competitiveness, developing countries must address all these factors simultaneously in policy-making efforts.

THE STATE OF PLAY OF GM CROPS IN THE DEVELOPING WORLD

Most GM crops being planted today contain two main traits – herbicide tolerance and insect resistance. Herbicide tolerant crops contain genetic modifications that allow for the use of certain herbicides to target weeds around the farms that would have otherwise killed the crops along with the weeds. As a result, there can be more effective weed prevention in and around farms. Insect resistant crops are derived from the insertion of a gene from a bacterium – *Bacillus thuringiensis* (Bt). This causes the plant to release toxins against certain kinds of insects. Varieties that contain both traits – herbicide tolerance and insect resistance – are the next most common form of GM crops grown, with virus resistant crops coming last (Hayenga, 1998, p48). According to James (2004), since GM crops were first introduced in 1996, the largest market share was taken up by herbicide resistant crops which in 2004 accounted for 72 per cent of the area grown with GM crops. Another 19 per cent of the total land under GM cultivation is taken up by insect resistant crops, with the rest being occupied by crops that had mixed traits and virus resistance.

Twenty-six per cent of total global GM agriculture takes place in developing countries today, with China and Argentina accounting for almost 98 per cent of this total (Nap et al, 2003, p3). The main GM crop that is grown in developing countries continues to be insect resistant cotton (Nuffield Council on Bioethics, 2003, p21). Most developing countries are yet to approve the planting of GM food crops, although GM food crops, such as rice varieties (herbicide resistant, virus resistant, rich in Vitamin A or iron), maize varieties and virus resistant varieties of papaya and sweet potatoes are being planted in the developed countries (Spillane, 2002, p68; CIPR, 2002, p64). The exceptions to this are South Africa and the Philippines where GM maize is being grown and Argentina where GM maize and soybean is being grown (Nuffield Council on Bioethics, 2003, p21).

GM crops and evidence of yield increases for poor farmers

Although the world's poorest farmers account for 60 per cent of total global agriculture and 80 per cent of all agriculture in developing countries, they manage to produce only around 15–20 per cent of the world's food produce (Spillane, 2002, p69). In such a setting, the positive impacts of GM crops in terms of increased yields and decreased fixed costs of farming could very well usher in an era of prosperity for poor farmers in the South.

Preliminary harvest results in South Africa, China and Mexico suggest that insect resistant Bt cotton can result in higher yields for farmers. Ismael et al (2001, p16) show from their study of Bt cotton in 1998–1999 and 1999–2000 in the Makhathini region of South Africa that whereas Bt cotton resulted in an 18 per cent increase of yields for farmers in the first season, it resulted in a 60 per cent increase in the second season. Pray et al (2001, 2002) conclude similarly from their study of Bt cotton plantations in China. They found that Bt cotton varieties not only resulted in higher yields in 1999, 2000 and 2001, but also led to an overall reduction of pesticide costs (Pray et al, 2002, p426). They estimate that it brought down the pesticide spraying from around 12 times a growing season to just about three or four times (Pray et al, 2001, p821).

Although these studies lead us to conclude that there is proof of yield increases in the case of Bt cotton, it is hard to draw concrete conclusions on the precise yield increase as a result of GM crops. This is because GM crops are susceptible to natural factors that also impact conventional farming, such as infestation rates, soil and weather conditions. When yield increases occur, they may vary in different climatic zones, or even within the same climatic zone, in different seasons.

Ismael et al (2001), for instance, attribute the high fluctuations in Bt cotton yields between the two seasons they studied in South Africa to varying rainfall levels. Rainfall levels affect pest infestation rates and may also impact upon the length of a particular growing season (Ismael et al, 2001, p17; McGloughlin, 1999, p166).[1]

Apart from rainfall levels, other extraneous influences, caused by biotic and abiotic stresses, can give rise to particular forms of viruses or enhanced rates of soil erosion, and affect farming and yield rates. As a result, estimates from one country may not always hold true in another. Whereas farmers in some regions experience substantial gains from Bt crops, farmers elsewhere may only have small gains. Also, gains over seasons for the same set of farmers may vary considerably.

Developing countries should take this risk of disparate results into account when estimating the potential of increased productivity due to Bt crops. GM seeds cost much more than conventional seed varieties and usually come with a technology fee that farmers have to pay for the technology they contain. Poor farmers who do not experience any significant increase in yields but pay high seed prices, may find themselves worse off.

Other factors that affect increase in yields of GM crops

Efficiency of agricultural production in developing countries is decided by several factors acting in tandem. Evidence on Bt cotton yields presented above shows that abiotic stresses, such as rainfall levels, can lead to fluctuating yields. Apart from such extraneous influences, lack of resources, equity issues and access to competitive markets are other factors that can affect efficiency of agricultural production.

In *resource-poor farming*, which is defined as farming that uses limited access to production and managerial resources (Spillane, 2002, p68), there are several reasons that cause efficiency losses in agricultural production. Lack of external resources, lack of organization skills in smaller farms and lack of fertility of agricultural lands all contribute to less-than-average crop yields even when traditional varieties of crops are used (Ezumah and Ezumah, 1996, p5).

Restricted access to resources and competitive markets is another important factor that affects farming practices. Even where adequate resources may be present, access to resources may not be designed on rules of equity. Where resources may be adequate and access is available, farmers may completely lack the managerial competence required to handle farming in an efficient way. To add to all this, since small-scale farming is mostly done on a subsistence basis, marketing of agricultural produce is not the general measure of performance. This could mean that even where resources may be available and farmers have managerial competence, the lack of access or poor access to competitive markets, where agricultural produce can be traded, may hinder their potential.

If GM crops are to result in sustained yield increases in developing countries, these factors have to be catered for effectively through national policy making.

Rectifying systemic setbacks in agricultural production systems in developing countries

The term *good management* refers to the ability to manage farming with high resource inputs and good managerial skills so that it results in increased profit margins (Ezumah and Ezumah, 1996, p5). Good management of farms is a precondition to obtain higher yields consistently through the use of GM crops. The potential of GM crops to produce higher yields in developing countries in the mid- or long-term will be critically affected by the presence (or rather the absence) of adequate managerial and production resources at the farm level.

Since farmers in most developing countries are resource-poor and lack access to good agricultural practices (Kuyek, 2002, p11), policy efforts should focus on ensuring better access to production resources and increased information and training on agricultural practices. There are examples where this has been done in the past, in the context of the green revolution. For example, the state of Tamil Nadu in India adopted green revolution seed varieties along with other measures for poverty alleviation that included, among others, better access to resources and information dissemination (Pinstrup-Andersen and Cohen, 2001, p183).

More information too regarding the environmental risks of GM crops and the safeguards that farmers need to take should be provided. For example, governments in developing countries should provide more information about bollworm resistance to Bt cotton and the ways in which this development can be slowed down (Pray et al, 2001, p823; for an explanation of 'insect resistance', see below).

However, in some countries, especially in Africa, providing access to resources and training farmers in better agricultural practices may not be so easy. Around 70 per cent of African agricultural production is handled by women, who farm, sometimes even part-time, while their husbands engage in wage labour (Spillane, 2002, p69; Kuyek, 2002, p3; Ezumah and Ezumah, 1996, p9). Although farm-level evidence shows that women have produced as much as men in South Africa, for instance (Ismael et al, 2001, p17), the uneven access to resources for women in developing countries should be rectified in order to ensure that their potential is exploited to the fullest extent.

In the context of access to markets, smaller farmers in developing countries tend to have poor market access, although this has not been the case for Bt cotton. One of the reasons behind the success of Bt cotton is that intermediaries have facilitated market access for farmers who would otherwise have had little or no access to it. But such an automatic gain may not occur in the case of GM food crops, such as Bt maize or Bt wheat.

In such cases, small-scale farmers may find themselves in a position where they have to rectify this gap themselves (Bunders and Broerse, 1991, p3). Whether they will be able to do so themselves depends on effective policy intervention that facilitates optimal use of markets to such farmers to benefit from increased yields. Such policy intervention should be in the form of governmental programmes that increase information to farmers regarding market prices and practices and improve transportation and processing facilities that encourage farmers to engage in organized production (Bunders and Broerse, 1991, p3).

Moreover, in determining the impact of GM crops on local farmers' profits in developing countries, a distinction has to be made between cases where developing countries are mainly exporters of GM produce and developing countries seeking to produce such crops for improved domestic yields (Pinstrup-Andersen, 1999, p216). In the case of the former set of countries, biosafety policies will affect market access for farmers in developing countries who seek to export their GM produce. The long-term gains for countries such as Argentina, Brazil and Thailand that are planting GM crops with the main aim of exporting the produce will largely depend on international acceptance of GM products, notably, within the EU, and on clarity of rules and regulations regarding mandatory labelling (Pinstrup-Andersen, 1999, p216).

MOBILIZING RESOURCES TO MEET DEVELOPING COUNTRIES' REAL PRIORITIES

The previous section shows that given certain initial endowments, such as access to good managerial and production resources and access to markets, it is possible to imagine sustained yield increases and decreased farming costs as a result of GM crops in developing countries.

But increased productivity is just a very small first step in exploiting the potential of GM technology for developing countries. If GM crops are to address food security in the long term, varieties need to be developed that can cater more effectively to local needs. Ideally, developing countries need GM crops that focus more on *output* traits such as higher nutritional value – while retaining certain input traits such as resistance to abiotic stresses, in addition to the already available herbicide tolerance and insect resistance traits – in order to solve their food and nutrition problems (Hayenga, 1998; Shimoda, 1998, p64; Spillane, 2002, p71). A closer look at only those GM varieties that are in the research and development (R&D) pipeline in Europe (both private and public sector) shows that varieties with mainly input traits are expected to be released in the next five years; varieties that are dominated by input traits but have some output traits will be released from 2007 onwards; and GM varieties that contain abiotic stress factors and a higher content of 'functional' ingredients are likely to be released only after 2011 (Lheureux et al, 2003, pp23–24).

This means that the focus of research has to shift from those crops that are perceived to have a commercial value by the private sector to those that cater more to local needs in developing countries. This shift will not be automatic and in order to be able to steer research in this direction, developing countries have to focus on building local capacity and on fostering public–private partnerships for research. Local capacity building is the key to achieving competitiveness among developing countries and good public–private or public–public research partnerships can help developing countries in building local capacity.

Secondly, developing countries have to take into account the other costs that GM crops can impose in terms of adverse environmental impacts or adverse impacts on organization of labour in their local settings. Minimizing the potential environmental and social impacts of GM crops is a precondition for realizing their advantages.

Issues for agricultural research and capacity building

One factor that has impeded developing countries' ability to cope with the technology divide is intellectual property protection. Apart from this, there are other issues of scientific and technological capacity building that developing countries need to focus on in order to attain long-term competitiveness in biotechnological research.

Intellectual property rights and competition policy in agricultural biotechnology

Article 27.3(b) of the Agreement on Trade-related Aspects of Intellectual Property Rights (TRIPS)[2] and developments in various industrialized nations that also allow for patent protection of plant varieties have strengthened the position of seed companies and intellectual property holders. How Article 27.3(b) of the TRIPS Agreement is interpreted, and what options are available to developing countries as a result, will have a major impact on the potential for bridging the technology divide between countries. Designing the appropriate interface between intellectual property law and other components of national regimes, such as competition policy, is another factor that is decisive for enhancing local technological prospects.

Competition law and intellectual property are inextricably linked in the sense that they both try to promote innovation, albeit in two different ways. Whereas intellectual property rights protect inventors by creating monopoly positions, competition policy seeks to promote innovation through increased, unhindered competition (Dumont and Holmes, 2002, p151).

The combination of an oligopolistic seed industry and very strong intellectual property rights means that market power and R&D prowess are concentrated among a select few globally. This might create barriers to entry for institutes and firms in developing countries, due to abuse of dominant positions by firms that hold intellectual property on seed varieties or on research tools of agricultural biotechnology. Broad patents on biotechnological inventions run the risk of imposing transaction costs of contracting for 'first generation' research tools that are protected through intellectual property rights, but are necessary for 'second generation' innovation (Dumont and Holmes, 2002, p154).

Developing countries should enact appropriate competition policies that make it possible for them to (a) control oligopolistic practices in the seed industry which lead to increased prices of seeds in their countries and (b) promote easy access to inventions and research tools in agricultural biotechnology. They should follow in the footsteps of the developed countries in enacting plant biotechnology laws under which breeders can request compulsory licences to exploit plant varieties for breeding purposes without infringing patents – as is possible under Article 12(1) of the European Biotechnology Directive and also under the UK Plant Breeders Act (see Correa, 1999, p18).

Building local capacity, public–private partnerships and sharing know-how
There are huge disparities even among developing countries in research and scientific capabilities. As noted rightly by Woodward et al (1999), some developing countries like India, Mexico and China have not only competitive universities and trained scientists but also demonstrate reliance on local research. Africa, on the other hand, is a combination of competent research institutes that specialize in agricultural research on local crops – such as the International Institute for Tropical Agriculture (IITA), the Kenyan Agricultural Research Institute (KARI) and the Agricultural Research Council (ARC) in South Africa – and countries with almost no resources to even use agricultural biotechnology (Woodward et al, 1999, p175; Kalaitzandonakes, 1999, p149).

Investment in publicly funded agricultural research is key to exploiting the potential of biotechnology for poor farmers in developing countries (Pardey and Beintema, 2001, p22). Countries that do not have a sound research infrastructure will have to invest in overall capacity building, such as competent educational institutions, universities and research institutes, trained scientists and personnel as well as legal and institutional frameworks which foster research initiatives. Such capacity building activities must be carefully planned and coordinated, lest they end up being unsustainable. Pardey et al, in their survey of African R&D expenditures conclude that, mainly as a result of unplanned spending in the last three decades, the sudden upsurge in research staff was not paralleled by a proportionate increase in financial resources. They propose a dramatic reduction of research staff since the present rate of growth is unsustainable if additional funds are not raised (Pardey et al, 1996, p18).

Developing countries can also look to public–private partnerships that focus on their agricultural priorities. Some public–private research partnerships on crops of importance to developing countries sound very promising indeed. One of these is the collaboration to tackle the maize streak virus (MSV) that plagues farmers in East African nations, causing up to 100 per cent yield losses (Wambugu and Wafula, 2000, p3). The MSV Research Project – an initiative facilitated by the International Service for the Acquisition of Agri-biotech Applications (ISAAA) – raises hopes for similar initiatives for the other major viruses that prey on maize in Africa. It is a public–private consortium that includes the KARI, the International Center for Insect Physiology and Ecology, the John Innes Centre for molecular marker studies and agro-inoculation and the University of Cape Town (Wambugu and Wafula, 2000, p5).

Discounting social and environmental costs from total gains

In addition to building capacity, good regulatory frameworks are required to cater to the potential social and environmental threats that GM technologies pose. The social costs of GM technologies may come in the form of decreased labour demand, whereas the potential environmental costs of GM technologies can be more diverse.

Impacts on farmers' incomes and social organization

A major reason for weak agricultural growth in developing countries is the gender gap in access to and utilization of resources in agriculture (Ezumah and Ezumah, 1996, p9). As discussed above, given that women are mainly responsible for agriculture in several developing countries and only pursue it part-time, enhancing yields by using GM crops seems to be all the more important. Studies regarding the suitability of GM crops under such constraints need to be undertaken and GM crops, where introduced, should be propped up by governmental initiatives to influence shifts to good agricultural practices which promise better gains.

In certain studies conducted on the benefits of Bt cotton, the samples surveyed indicate that around 10 per cent of the farmers were induced to adopt Bt cotton by reduced labour costs (Ismael et al, 2002, p3). This evidence, albeit preliminary in nature, indicates that GM technology could create job losses in the mid- or long term. Therefore, governmental policies should aim at finding ways in which productivity is increased without affecting the job opportunities of farmers in developing countries (Spillane, 2002, p70).

Assessment of potential environmental impacts of GM crops

An ever-increasing body of scientific evidence is being generated on the environmental risks inherent in the use of GM crops. The potential risks imposed by GM crops on the environment can be grouped into four main categories: the creation of invasive weeds, the creation of invasive insect species, loss of agricultural diversity due to monocultures and contamination of wild gene pools of the species in question.

Herbicide resistant crops, in certain cases, can pass on their genes to weeds surrounding the farms, thereby leading to the creation of herbicide resistant weeds. Such weeds, also called invasive weeds, can pose a serious threat to genetic diversity surrounding agricultural fields. In a similar way, Bt crops can lead to creation of gradual resistance to Bt among insect populations, thus creating invasive species of insects (GM Science Review Panel, 2003, pp111–117). These insects can find their way into surrounding ecosystems and pose a threat to genetic diversity therein (GM Science Review Panel, 2003, pp119–131). GM crops can also, by way of large-scale introduction, lead to the neglect of traditional varieties that are an integral part of agriculture in developing countries. Since traditional agricultural varieties do not possess strong survival characteristics on their own, these varieties may only survive for a few agricultural seasons if neglected (Royal Society of Canada, 2001, p121). Lastly, GM crops, when introduced back to tropical countries where wild relatives of the same variety can be found, pose a threat of contamination of wild gene pools (Royal Society of Canada, 2001, p130).

Although these threats are very real, they come with two caveats. Firstly, some of these environmental risks are also present in the use of conventional varieties. Secondly, the impact of GM crops on different ecosystems can differ, depending on the kind of GM crop and the kind of ecosystem in question (Royal Society of Canada, 2001). This renders it hard to generalize about the harmful effects of GM crops.

Thus, laws on biosafety should be based on balanced scientific considerations, and more research needs to be generated on the impact of GM crops on agricultural and non-agricultural genetic diversity to deal with the potential environmental impacts of GM crops. Such research is especially important to avoid excessive legislation that may prevent developing countries from exploiting the true potential of GM technologies.

CONCLUSIONS

Agricultural biotechnology, especially genetic modification techniques, may very well hold much untapped potential for solving food issues in developing countries (Pardey and Beintema, 2001, p19). But if developing countries are to realize this potential to attain local food security and competitiveness, their role has to shift from that of passive users to active participants in both the use and production of agricultural biotechnology.

The impact of GM varieties on increasing yields in developing countries may vary. Ensuring sustained yields from GM crops to enhance overall agricultural productivity requires that the large-scale adoption of GM crops is augmented by governmental policies that create conditions for it to work. In order to secure competitiveness in agricultural biotechnology and to steer research in directions beneficial to them, developing countries need to pursue several strategies in parallel – invest in research infrastructure and capacity building at the local level, foster public–private partnerships and transfer of know-how that boost the local capacity building process, and enact national intellectual property protection regimes as well as sound competition policies that complement their *sui generis* plant variety protection laws. Lastly, developing countries have to enact suitable biosafety regimes that can foresee and counter the potential environmental costs that large-scale planting of GM varieties can impose on their biological resources. The benefits of agricultural biotechnology lie in the optimal design and coordination of all these policies – on agricultural productivity, on biosafety, on *sui generis* protection and intellectual property – at the national levels.

NOTES

1   Similar effects have been observed in developed countries too, in the case of Bt crops. Referring to the United States Department of Agriculture (USDA) report for 1999, Altieri and Rosset note that yields of GM crops were not much higher than those of non-GM crops in 12 out of 18 crop–region combinations and where the GM crops did do better, the productivity gains were between 5 and 30 per cent only (Altieri and Rosset, 1999, p156).

2   'Members may also exclude from patentability . . . (b) plants and animals other than micro-organisms, and essentially biological processes for the production of plants or animals other than non-biological and microbiological processes. However, Members shall provide for the protection of plant varieties either by patents or by an effective sui generis system or by any combination thereof. The provisions of this subparagraph shall be reviewed four years after the date of entry into force of the WTO Agreement' (Article 27.3(b), TRIPS Agreement).

REFERENCES

Altieri, M A and Rosset, P (1999) 'Ten reasons why biotechnology will not ensure food security, protect the environment and reduce poverty in the developing world', *AgBioForum*, vol 2, nos 3–4, pp155–162

Bunders, J F G and Broerse, J E W (1991) 'Introduction', in Bunders, J F G and Broerse, J E W (eds) *Appropriate Biotechnology in Small-scale Agriculture: How to Reorient Research and Development*, Cabi Publishing, Amsterdam, pp1–7

CIPR (2002) *Integrating Intellectual Property Rights and Development Policy – Final Report*, Commission on Intellectual Property Rights, London

Correa, C M (1999) 'Intellectual property rights and the use of compulsory licenses: Options for developing countries', *Trade-Related Agenda, Development and Equity, Working Papers 5*, South Centre, Geneva

Cuffaro, N (2002) 'Population growth and agricultural intensification in developing countries', in Swanson, T M (ed) *Biotechnology, Agriculture and the Developing World: The Distributional Implications of Technological Change*, Edward Elgar, Cheltenham, UK, pp25–43

Dumont, B and Holmes, P (2002), 'The scope of intellectual property rights and their interface with competition law and policy: Divergent paths to the same goal?', *Economics of Innovation and New Technologies*, vol 11, no 2, pp149–162

Ezumah and Ezumah (1996) 'Agricultural development in the age of sustainability', in Benneh, G, Morgan, W B and Uitto, J H (eds) *Sustaining the Future, Economic, Social and Environmental Change in Sub-Saharan Africa*, United Nations University Press, Tokyo

GM Science Review Panel (2003) *An Open Review of the Science Relevant to GM Crops and Food Based on Interests and Concerns of the Public*, GM Science Review Panel, UK

Hayenga, M L (1998) 'Structural change in the biotech seed and chemical industrial complex', *AgBioForum*, vol 1, no 2, pp43–55

Ismael, Y, Bennett, R and Morse, S (2001) 'Farm level impact of Bt cotton in South Africa', *Biotechnology and Development Monitor*, no 48, pp15–19

Ismael, Y, Bennett, R and Morse, S (2002), 'Benefits from Bt cotton use by smallholder farmers in South Africa', *AgBioForum*, vol 5, no 1, pp1–5

James, C (2004) 'Preview: Global status of commercialized transgenic crops: 2004', *ISAAA Briefs No 32*, ISAAA, Ithaca, NY

Kalaitzandonakes, N G (1999) 'Agrobiotechnology in the developing world', *AgBioForum*, vol 2, nos 3–4, pp147–149

Kuyek, D (2002) *Genetically Modified Crops in Africa: Implications for Small Farmers*, Brief for Genetic Resources Action International, Barcelona, Spain

Lheureux, K, Libeau-Dulos, M, Nilsagård, H, Rodriguez Cerezo, E, Menrad, K, Menrad, M and Vorgrimler, D (2003) *Review of GMOs Under Research and Development and in the Pipeline in Europe*, European Science and Technology Observatory, Joint Research Centre, European Commission, Brussels

McGloughlin, M (1999) 'Ten reasons why biotechnology will be important to the developing world', *AgBioForum*, vol 2, nos 3–4, pp163–174

Nap, J-P, Metz, P L J, Escaler, M and Conner, A J (2003) 'The release of genetically modified crops into the environment' *The Plant Journal*, no 33, pp1–18

Nuffield Council on Bioethics (2003) *The Use of Genetically Modified Crops in Developing Countries*, Nuffield Council on Bioethics, London

Pardey, P G, Roseboom, J and Beintema, N M (1996) 'Agricultural research in Africa: Three decades of development', *ISNAR Briefing Paper 19*, pp1–19, The Hague, Netherlands

Pardey, P G and Beintema, N M (2001) *Slow Magic: Agricultural R&D a Century After Mendel*, Agricultural Science and Technology Indicators Initiative, International Food Policy Research Institute, Washington DC

Pinstrup-Andersen, P (1999) 'Agricultural biotechnology, trade and the developing countries', *AgBioForum*, vol 2, nos 3–4, pp215–217

Pinstrup-Andersen, P and Cohen, M J (2001) 'Modern agricultural biotechnology and developing country food security', in Nelson, G C (ed) *Genetically Modified Organisms in Agriculture: Economics and Politics*, Academic Press, New York, pp179–189

Pray, C, Ma, D, Huang, J and Qiao, F (2001) 'Impact of Bt cotton in China' *World Development*, vol 29, no 5, pp813–825

Pray, C E, Huang, J, Hu, R and Rozella, S (2002) 'Five years of Bt cotton in China – the benefits continue' *The Plant Journal*, vol 31, no 4, pp423–430

Royal Society of Canada (2001), *Elements of Precaution: Recommendations for the Regulation of Food Biotechnology in Canada*, An Expert Panel Report on the Future of Food Biotechnology, The Royal Society of Canada, Ottawa, Ontario

Shimoda, S M (1998) 'Agricultural biotechnology – master of the universe', *AgBioForum*, vol 1, no 2, pp62–68

Spillane, C (2002) 'Agricultural biotechnology and developing countries: Proprietary knowledge and diffusion of benefits', in Swanson, T M (ed) *Biotechnology, Agriculture and the Developing World: The Distributional Implications of Technological Change*, Edward Elgar, Cheltenham, UK, pp67–135

Wambugu, F and Wafula, J (2000) 'Advances in maize streak virus disease research in eastern and southern Africa', *ISAAA Briefs No 16*, ISAAA, Ithaca, NY, pp1–7

Woodward, B, Brink, J and Berger, D (1999) 'Can agricultural biotechnology make a difference in Africa?', *AgBioForum*, vol 2, nos 3–4, pp175–181

6

Approaching Biotechnology: Experiences from Brazil and Argentina

BRAZIL

Maurício Antônio Lopes and Maria José Amstalden Moraes Sampaio

Brazil is one of the largest countries in the world, with an area of 851 million ha, a large supply of fresh water, abundant solar energy and a rich biodiversity. Besides the world's largest tropical forest, the country has over 200 million hectares of savannah (known as *cerrado*) with immense agriculture and livestock production potential. The cerrado is the main agricultural frontier in Brazil and one of the largest in the world, not only due to its considerable areas still available for farming expansion, but also its potential for increasing productivity through technology improvements. It has been estimated that Brazil could increase its total cultivated area by approximately 170 million hectares or more if key legal, technical and financial developments occur in the near future (FAS, 2003).

Brazil has used its diversity and resources to successfully become a world leader in many sectors, including agriculture. The strength of Brazilian products in world markets has resulted in a robust demand for its agricultural exports, which topped US$15 billion in 2001, and has led the country to become the world's fourth largest net exporter in this sector (WTO, 2001). Technology development for tropical agriculture has been one of Brazil's main strengths, as illustrated by the evolution of the soybean crop in the country, which has increased from 1.5 million tons in 1970 (Embrapa, 2002) to an estimated volume of 52.2 million tons in 2003. Today, Brazil is the second largest producer in the world, with an estimated volume of 52.2 million tons in 2003, only exceeded by the United States. Technology in breeding and genetics, crop and soil management, developed by the Brazilian Agricultural Research Corporation (Embrapa) and other partner organizations, has resulted in an increase of average soybean yields of approximately 130 per cent over the past 30 years (PECAD, 2003), while seed quality is as high as any produced in the world, including in the United States.

Although there is a large potential for the expansion of the soybean crop in Brazil, part of its competitive advantage – low costs of agricultural land and abundant and cheap labour – will soon run out. New technology developments will be essential to enhance Brazil's competitiveness in world markets. The soybean example also applies to many other agricultural commodities in Brazil and other developing countries, for which competitiveness and sustainability will be dependent on the capacity to incorporate advanced technologies into production, in an effort to overcome challenges of the environment (such as weeds, pests, drought, salinity, aluminium toxicity), add market value, and increase Brazil's competitive advantage in the region and in export markets. The more the country is able to export, the more it can provide services and benefit its population. Poverty alleviation programmes, which have been the forefront strategy of the newly elected government, are always dependent on how well the country can manage its economy.

Agricultural biotechnology has the potential to increase yields, functional qualities and market value for tropical agriculture. It promises to produce plants that will grow in harsh environments with less need for chemical input, therefore protecting the environment, to produce new cultivars with enhanced nutritional composition and to reduce post-harvest storage losses. Some of these promises have already emerged from laboratory benches (Contini et al, 2003). However, questions have been raised on consumer acceptance, environmental impacts, public versus private sector roles, biosafety and intellectual property rights issues related to the first products of biotechnology, in particular genetically modified (GM) plants. These factors have contributed to a general lethargy among developing country governments in promoting adoption of this technology for their agricultural systems.

This subchapter analyses the case of Brazil, one of the countries where GM plants are still not fully approved for commercial planting. GM maize has been used since 2001 for direct animal feeding. The first part of the subchapter analyses the new biosafety legislation the present requirements for research and commercial release of GM crops in the country. An analysis of the potential economic impact of the adoption of transgenic crops in Brazil is presented in the second part of the subchapter, including herbicide tolerant soybeans, Bt cotton and Bt maize, for which transgenic technology is already available and well disseminated around the world, including in developing countries.

BRAZILIAN BIOSAFETY REGULATIONS

In March 2005, after multiple amendments by the two houses of the Brazilian Congress, the Biosafety Law No 11.105 was signed into law. The new bill grants authority over construction, culture, production, manipulation, transportation, transfer, import, export, storage, research, marketing, environmental release and discharge of genetically modified organisms (GMOs) to a national technical biosafety commission (CTNBio) made up of representatives of several federal ministries, independent scientists, and experts in the fields of consumer rights, health, environment, biotechnology, farms and work health. According to the law, CTNBio is the central body on biotech regulations and has the authority, which is binding over other administrative agencies, to make decisions on import, export, environmental release and all other GMO activities by issuing its technical opinion on a case-by-case basis regarding the biosafety of GMOs; authorizing the import of GMOs and their by-products for research; identifying activities that have the potential to damage the environment; and publicizing the details of its activities in a 'biosafety information system' public bulletin. In one of the most controversial parts of the law, which was alleged to be unconstitutional in a case brought to Brazil's Supreme Court by Brazilian Attorney-General Claudio Fonteles in June 2005, CTNBio can decide whether or not it is necessary for a GMO to undergo a risk assessment prior to the approval process. Once approved, actual authorization of particular products, imports for commercial use and implementation of the decision is carried out by registration and inspection agencies in each of the federal ministries. If CTNBio determines that a GM product has the potential to degrade the environment, but nevertheless authorizes it, the Ministry for the Environment is given the authority to inspect and register particular products.

In addition, the law allows the national biosafety council (CNBS) to provide higher advisory assistance in formulating and implementing the National Biosafety Policy, establishing principles and guidelines, and considering 'the socio-economic convenience and opportunities and national interest' entailed in commercial authorization of GMOs. While it is not supposed to participate in each request for a GMO release, it is allowed to do so when requested by CTNBio or by the majority of its members or its chairperson. In this case, CNBS can halt a commercial release despite CTNBio's approval, although in general CNBS approval is not a mandatory step for commercial approval.

Article 17 requires any institution using GM techniques to set up a biosafety internal commission (CIBio) to keep workers and members of the community informed about health, safety, accidents and risk assessments resulting from the technology. Moreover, Article 40 states that all food for human or animal consumption that contains or is produced with GMOs must show this information on their label, in accordance with relevant regulations. Brazilian Decree No 4.680, published in April 2003, requires labelling for all foods or food ingredients containing more than 1 per cent of GMO ingredients. The decree also mandates the labelling of animal products from animals fed with GM grains.

LEGAL BARRIERS FOR THE COMMERCIAL RELEASE OF GMOS IN BRAZIL

For a number of different reasons, Brazil has not seen an organized and scientifically based approval of a transgenic crop for commercial use up to now. The petition for commercialization of Monsanto's Roundup Ready soybean tolerant to glyphosate herbicide, approved by CTNBio in September 1998 with a requirement to perform environmental monitoring over five years, was questioned in the courts by groups opposed to biotechnology, which challenged the authority of CTNBio to grant final approval. These groups also alleged that CTNBio should have required Monsanto to perform a full Environmental Licensing process. In 1999, a lower court issued an injunction suspending the CTNBio approval pending resolution of the case on its merits. Appellate Court rulings in June and September of 2000 denied requests to cancel the injunction. In December 2000, the Federal Government issued a Provisional Measure restating the Biosafety Commission's authority to approve GM products and in early 2001 asked for an expedited Court decision. The case was assigned to a panel of three judges for a decision and in early 2002 the leading judge issued her position indicating that the law giving CTNBio authority to approve the glyphosate tolerant soybean was in accordance with the Brazilian Constitution and voted to cancel the injunction. In September 2004, the Appellate Court publicized the decision, made in June 2004 by a majority of its judges, to cancel the injunction and uphold the authority of CTNBio to grant final approval for the commercial use of transgenic crops.

Widespread illegal use of glyphosate tolerant soybean in the South

The cost savings obtained by soybean farmers in competitor countries from planting GM soybean has contributed to the illicit flow of genetically modified seeds from Argentina into Brazil's southern region (Bonalume Neto, 1999), where the climate is fairly similar. In December 1999, some of the GM soybean illegally planted in the southern state Rio Grande do Sul was destroyed by federal authorities (Lehmann and Pengue, 2000). However, due to Brazil's extensive territory, it became very difficult for the Ministry of Agriculture to go after every farmer who was infringing the law, so the flow continued in the following growing seasons reaching as much as 80 per cent of the total crop area in the State of Rio Grande do Sul in the 2002–2003 season, according to unofficial estimates. Official mapping of the situation in 2003–2004 shows that the intention of using GM soybean has increased in that state. The amount of genetically modified soybean harvested in the South has been estimated by various trade sources at between 7 and 8 million tons in 2003 and should go up to 10 or 12 million tons in 2004. Due to its illegal nature in 2002, this large GM harvest brought significant problems to Brazil's processing and export of southern soybean grain. At the insistence of Chinese authorities, the Brazilian Ministers of Agriculture and Health had to issue safety certificates to the Chinese government in February 2003 confirming the safety of Brazil's soybean exports for human and animal consumption in order for the shipments to be accepted.

In March 2003, the new Federal Government issued a Provisional Measure (No 113/2003) providing amnesty to soybean farmers who had illegally planted GM soybean during the ban. This Provisional Measure, which was converted to

Law No 10.688/2003 in June, states that the provisions of the Biosafety Law do not apply to the 2003 harvest and establishes that the products containing GM soybeans should bear a label informing the consumers of the presence of GM components. The labelling requirements resulted from a new Decree (No 4.680/ 2003), published in April 2003, which established a threshold of 1 per cent for adventitious mixture and required labelling of all GM plant products and derivatives, sold as grains or as manufactured products. The Decree also obliges the labelling of animals, which have been fed with transgenic grains, and the products prepared with these animals. The Decree makes an exception for the 2003 harvest of GM soybeans and derivatives.

The fact that the commercialization of the 2002–2003 transgenic soybeans harvest was made legal above and beyond any other legal requirements has created a precedent for the binding aspects of the existing regulatory framework related to GMOs and has led to an immediate demand for different Ministries to get ready for the certification of 2003–2004 seeds, which would have to be GM-free, according to the same legal instrument. However, as most of the farmers in the South have benefited from the illegal use of the technology without paying any 'technology fee' or usage payments to Monsanto, and are accustomed to keeping their own seeds for three to four years, most of them told the Government and Congress that they intended to plant their own saved seeds in the 2003–2004 cropping season. Without much alternative and still depending on the judges to rule on the GM soybean court case, the Government issued another Provisional Measure (No 131/2003) in September 2003 lifting the ban on the planting of farmer's saved seed from the previous year and, of course, commercialization and export of the product. While under discussion in the Congress, an article was added to allow for public and private legal breeding programmes to be able to register and multiply their own genetic seed in the hope that when the technology finally gets approved, illegal seeds can be substituted by certified seeds, giving the farmers the assurance of higher production and better phytosanitary conditions. This Provisional Measure was approved by Congress with modifications and should be approved by the President without any vetoes. The law took Brazilian soybean farmers and the industry onwards until March 2004, when GM soybean was again deemed illegal – until the Government issued yet another Provisional Measure on 14 October 2004 allowing the sale of GM soybeans until January 2006. These developments led to confusion among many farmers who did not understand why GM soybean was only legal for a few months each year. However, this uncertainty was resolved in what was perhaps the most controversial part of the March 2005 new Biosafety legislation. Law No 11.105 explicitly says in Article 35 and 36 that it is authorized to 'produce and market glyphosate tolerant genetically modified sowing soybean seeds that are registered with the National Seed Registration (RNC) under the Ministry of Agriculture, Cattle-Raising and Supply', and that farmers are allowed to use these seeds for their own crop for the 2004–2005 season, although 'it is forbidden to sell the production as seed'.

Legal hurdles for agro-biotechnological research and commercialization

The legal 'imbroglio' around the release of GMOs in Brazil has also had serious consequences for all organizations dedicated to agricultural biotechnology research and development. If the transgenic plants or their products enter the human food chain, they are also regulated by the food safety rules implemented by ANVISA, the National Agency for Health and Surveillance of the Ministry of Health. In the case of Bt plants or other plants containing any biopesticide characteristics, the Brazilian Pesticide Law also applies. Virus coat protein could not be deregulated as an exception following the US model. For these plants with biopesticide action, authorization for laboratory, greenhouse and field studies must be obtained from the SDA (Plant Protection Secretariat – Ministry of Agriculture), IBAMA (Brazilian Institute of Environment and Renewable Natural Resources – Ministry of Environment) and ANVISA. The proponent of such research must apply for a Special Temporary Registration. These agencies will also grant the consent for final registration of any commercial product, each acting in its own specific area. Unfortunately, most of these rules and requirements have not yet even been written.

Every private company, university or Embrapa laboratory has had to discontinue research on GM biopesticide plants since 2000 because groups opposed to biotechnology made a legal appeal alleging that regulations for the Pesticide Law – specifically for GMO – were not in place. The Court approved the petition and the regulations got published only in November 2002. However, due to the change of Government in January 2003 and the discontinuity of every other process in the ministries, licensing assessments for field research were restarted only in June 2003. This delay was disastrous for Embrapa which lost for the second year the opportunity to set up field experiments with common beans resistant to golden mosaic virus. Also, papaya and potato research have been severely affected.

In addition, the National Environmental Council (CONAMA)'s Resolution 305 was approved in June 2002 and applies to GMOs in general, including pest- or herbicide-resistant plant varieties. It determines the criteria and procedures to be observed for the environmental licensing of activities and undertakes that 'the use of GMOs or products thereof, is (even before experimental data has been collected) an effective or potential pollutant activity'. Therefore, for the Ministry of Environment authorities each and every GMO must go through an elaborate battery of tests for environmental impact. Discussions have been under way to decide whether GMO experimental plots need to collect data on all the environmental parameters such as those required for the licensing of the construction of a new dam or a new nuclear plant. If implementation of this Resolution is taken to unrealistic limits, making it very expensive to produce the data, it will probably become an excellent instrument for a 'white' moratorium, which will only serve to increase the technology gap between Brazil and other nations that have managed to avoid this gridlock.

On 12 August 2003, Judge Selene Maria de Almeida, the same judge that had given her vote in favour of the planting of transgenic soybean more than a year earlier, signed a pro-suspension ruling to Monsanto's petition, arguing that the current confusing situation negatively impacted on agribusiness development and the Brazilian export balance and that so far, in all this time since 1998, she had received no further information regarding the prejudicial effects of the product to human health or the environment. Newspaper headlines on 13 August already stated that IDEC, Brazil's consumers protection institute, would use all legal means available to embargo the decision. They have done so and won, suspending the legal planting, leading to the issuing of the second Provisional Measure No 131/2003 mentioned above. While it seemed like the 'transgenic saga' was a never-ending story, as noted above, the long-awaited new biosafety bill was signed into law by Brazilian President Luiz Inacio 'Lula' de Silva on 24 March 2005. Although it was hoped that the new bill would introduce predictability into the GM regulatory process, a number of challenges to the legitimacy of CTNBio from the Environment and Health Ministries to the new National Biosecurity Council, and also from Brazilian Attorney-General Claudio Fonteles to the Brazilian Supreme Court, have cast doubt on the future of the regulatory process.

POTENTIAL ECONOMIC IMPACT OF ADOPTING TRANSGENIC CROPS IN BRAZIL

Biotechnology – and its applications to produce new plant varieties, new solutions for animal husbandry, different applications in bio-pharming and new methods to mitigate environmental disasters – is something that is bound to be rooted in our future. However, how governments will deal with the establishment of appropriate biosafety regulations and with the accommodation of interests around the very complicated scientific and commercial issues that have arisen over the last years is not easy to foresee. Therefore, any analysis of possible economic, social or environmental costs and benefits of adopting the technology as part of agribusiness depends on the actual crop, specific new traits and the possible market share that the new variety may reach due to the changing aspects of consumer acceptance.

Some recent studies (Contini et al, 2003; Gianessi et al, 2003; Gianessi et al, 2002; Kirsten and Gouse, 2002; PG Economics Ltd, 2003; Whitfield, 2003; Wickel and Rautenberg, 2002) have looked at different aspects (such as weed control by different herbicide mixtures, environmental damage, agricultural management systems, pest control, quality of farmer's life, among others) of the actual and potential economic impact of the major GM commodities already on the market. As expected, the results vary with the country, with the region, with the crop, with the technological fee, with pest infestation per season, with the comparable prior system in use, and with the size of the farming enterprise.

Also, these studies did not take into full consideration the fact that with the European Union's new labelling and traceability requirements, which came into effect in April 2004, the world – with the possible exception of the United States of America – will demand labelling of GM food and feed products. With the need to certify production chains and implement traceability systems, the positive economic impact may be much reduced, although these costs may also be born by the final consumer and not exclusively by the farmer. Moreover, in the case of Brazil, significant differences exist between soybean (an export crop with no wild or weedy relatives in the country, which is in the hands of medium-sized to large farming enterprises), maize (a semi-export crop but very important for internal consumption, planted by small and medium-sized farmers and with many landraces spread in certain areas of the country) and cotton (an industrial crop planted by very small to medium-sized and very large farmers, depending on the region, and with several wild relatives (Freire, 2000) already mapped in the Amazon and Pantanal ecosystems), giving rise to many more variables to consider.

Taking into account the model and the variables used by Contini et al (2003), the potential annual benefit for GM soybean producers, measured in terms of cost reduction, was estimated to amount to US$500 million per year. The simulations performed in this study also include a quantification of the anticipated losses resulting from the continued prohibition of the commercial use of GM soy. In addition to the potential economic benefits of transgenic technology, this technology allows for the maintenance of clean ploughing and the application of herbicide only in the places where there is weed infestation. It also reduces losses during harvesting due to the absence of weeds, economizes costs with machinery and labour, and allows for reduced use of some herbicides, which have a more deleterious environmental impact than glyphosate. Given the potential benefits, Bonalume Neto (2003) estimates that an area of 18.6 million hectares will be planted with soybean, of which approximately 3.5 million hectares will be sown with GM soybean not only in the State of Rio Grande do Sul but also in the States of Mato Grosso, Mato Grosso do Sul and Paraná.

For Bt cotton and Bt maize the estimated potential benefits were much lower. However, as the technology reduces the production costs and appears to reduce the environmental and health effects of pesticide, the adoption of Bt varieties could be important for Brazil from a socio-economic standpoint, if properly managed. Due to the reduction in production costs with transgenic seeds, the Brazilian competitiveness in cotton production could grow, assuming fair competition with other exporters such as China. Of course, other factors such as the change of prices in the international market would have to be taken into consideration as much as the practicality of buffer zones to isolate the regions where wild varieties are found. As soon as research can be resumed in the country, regional experiments will have to show the real potential of the present technology, which lacks the characteristics needed to control one of the biggest cotton pests in Brazil – the boll weevil (*Anthonomus grandis grandis* Boheman). Also, data (Clarke, 2002) obtained in US fields have shown that in crops of Bt maize and Bt cotton, larvae feeding on the different crops for a longer period of time could increase the speed of resistance acquisition by the targeted pests. This is a new variable that will need to be tested under specific Brazilian conditions.

According to the different hypotheses of adoption used by Contini et al (2003), the potential benefits for cotton and maize producers varied. In the hypothesis of an adoption rate similar to the worldwide average for cotton, benefits for the Brazilian producers would be around US$21.5 million per year. In the hypothesis of a faster adoption, as for example observed in China, benefits would amount to approximately US$40 million per year. If all the area presently cultivated with cotton in Brazil were sowed with transgenic varieties, benefits could reach US$179 million per year. The possible increase in planting area in the cerrado region – less affected by boll weevil – if Bt cotton were approved could increase gains.

If the planting of Bt maize were approved in Brazil and the world adoption rate were assumed, the potential area planted with transgenic maize could reach 638,000 hectares in the 2002–2003 season. The cash benefit would be around US$10 million per year. If transgenic maize were adopted for the whole area of maize, the total benefits could reach US$193 million in the 2002–2003 season (Contini et al, 2003). However, since the technology has not yet been tested on Brazilian grounds, and given the many problems already verified in practical field experiments in the US, the numbers estimated for maize have to be taken with great care. Only research and post-commercial monitoring developed in the country itself will allow scientists to verify actual impacts. However, before such experiments can take place, Brazilian authorities and legislators must find a way to avoid the long delays in analysing the extensive package of information required for approval of controlled risk assessment experiments, which continue to prevent the technology from being even rightfully tested.

ARGENTINA

Eduardo Trigo, Daniel Chudnovsky, Eugenio Cap and Andrés López[1]

The intensification of agricultural production in Argentina during the 1990s constitutes, without a doubt, one of the positive impacts of the structural reforms and economic policies implemented at the beginning of that decade. The elimination of taxes and withholdings on agricultural exports; the substantial reduction of import tariffs on inputs and capital goods; and the Convertibility Plan and deregulation of some markets, all created favourable macro-economic conditions and paved the way for a large expansion of production volumes for cereals and oilseeds (from 26 million tonnes in 1988–1989 to over 67 million in 2000–2001), and particularly for soybeans, which soon became Argentina's leading export. The increase in export value occurred within a context of erratic international prices and in the face of competition with other countries, which, unlike Argentina, profit from government subsidies to production and exports.

This growth in agricultural production is a result of both a substantial expansion of the planted area (basically at the expense of livestock), and an incremental increase in physical productivity per unit area, derived from a significant adoption of new technologies, notably the introduction of transgenic crops in Argentine agriculture. Thus, in 1996, the first transgenic crop – Monsanto's Roundup Ready (RR) soybean tolerant to glyphosate herbicide – was commercially released into the Argentine market. Since its release, the rate of expansion of RR soybean in Argentina has increased considerably and has exhibited a growth even higher than the one in the US, which was the first country to introduce this kind of crop. The area planted to herbicide tolerant soybean shot up from less than 1 per cent of the total area planted to soybeans in the 1996–1997 season to more than 90 per cent (around 9 million hectares) in the 2000–2001 season.

Later on, transgenic varieties of maize and cotton tolerant to herbicides and resistant to insects were approved. This included a significant adoption of Lepidoptera resistant maize – albeit lower than soybeans – accounting for 20 per cent of the total cultivated area during the last farming season (the third year since its introduction). The diffusion of Bt cotton has, in turn, been very limited, amounting to 7–8.5 per cent of the total planted area. At present, Argentina ranks second only to the US in terms of agricultural surface cultivated with transgenic crops and is therefore a major player in the international arena.

ENVIRONMENTAL IMPACT OF AGRICULTURAL EXPANSION IN ARGENTINA

The sharp increase of Argentine agricultural production during the last decade has taken place hand in hand with the outstanding increase of no-tillage practices[2] as the main farming management strategy for the Pampas crops. The use of the no-till planting system – facilitated by the introduction of RR soybean, which drastically reduces weed incidence and management requirements – rose from approximately 300,000 hectares in the 1990–1991 season to over 9 million hectares in the 2000–2001 season. This technology constituted an important factor in the expansion of production, as it expanded the area cultivated with double cropping soybean (planted after the wheat harvest) to new production areas. During the 1999–2000 season, for example, this was translated into an increment of 3 million hectares of arable land.

However, the most important aspect of the widespread adoption of no-till techniques, coupled with the introduction of transgenic soybean, is the 'virtuous intensification' or 'environmentally friendly' nature it has bestowed upon the process of technological change. The combination of no-till planting techniques with

herbicide tolerant soybean joins two technological concepts: new mechanical technologies that modify crop interaction with the soil; and the utilization of general-
use, full range herbicides (with glyphosate in first place), which are environmentally
neutral, due to their high effectiveness in controlling any kind of weed as well as
their lack of residual effect. While both factors imply a more intense use of inputs,
this intensification is, nevertheless, deemed 'virtuous', because it has both reduced
tilling and lowered the consumption of herbicides with the highest toxicity level.

It is worth noting that, even after the increase in the use of agrochemicals
throughout the period, the total use per hectare of arable land was still far below
that recorded in other countries. Furthermore, the utilization of agrochemicals
appears to have stabilized after the 1996–1997 season. If we also consider the
favourable externalities generated through the progressive recovery of soil fertility
along with other potential impacts – such as benefits on the greenhouse effect
reaped from this type of practice – there is no doubt that the overall environmental
impact of these transformations has been positive.

From this perspective, Argentina would fit into a win–win model in which
commercial release facilitates the expansion of agricultural production at the same
time that it fosters the adoption of environmentally friendly technologies developed abroad. This technological package also seems to have produced positive
effects from the social point of view, as it has encouraged a dramatic increase in
jobs derived from the agricultural sector. Moreover, the significance of this effect
is reinforced by the fact that it took place simultaneously with an increase in labour
productivity within the sector, and during a period in which the rise in unemployment rate constituted one of Argentina's thorniest social problems.

THE SPECIAL CASE OF RR SOY

Argentina enjoyed favourable conditions for a rapid adoption of genetically modified organisms (GMOs). The Argentine seed industry profited from the active
participation of national companies and subsidiaries of multinational corporations
as well as public institutions; and, to top it off, the country also cherished a long-
standing tradition in the field of germplasm improvement. At the same time,
momentous institutional decisions were made, particularly with regard to biosafety
regulations – the creation of the National Advisory Committee on Agricultural
Biotechnology (CONABIA) in 1991 being one of the most important ones. The
fact that Argentina provides a major area (amounting to 26 million hectares of cultivable land) for the potential use of new technologies outside their country of
origin, combined with the aforementioned elements, provided the proper incentives and a most suitable 'landing field' for the rapid adoption of these biotechnological inputs.

However, public (and private) resources allocated to research and development
(R&D) in Argentine agriculture – especially in the area of biotechnology – are

scarce compared to corresponding efforts at the international level. Beyond their meaningful contribution to R&D activities on some crops (such as alfalfa) and in the area of veterinary science, institutes devoted to agricultural biotechnology research in Argentina have hardly participated in the transformation events approved by the CONABIA. Rather, it has been multinational companies that have taken the lead in releasing new technologies into the environment in Argentina – as well as in many other countries.

It is important to bear in mind that, so far, only RR soybean stands out as an exceptional case in the diffusion of GMOs. The massive adoption of the RR soybean can be accounted for by the reduction in production costs (regardless of the size of the crop farm) and, above all, by the expansion of cultivable area brought about by the RR soybean. These elements are not unique to the Argentine case. What does draw a distinction in this specific case, however, is the instrumental role played by certain idiosyncratic institutional factors in the rapid and effective expansion of RR soybean.

The first factor concerns the way in which the RR gene was originally transferred to Argentina. Initial access to the Roundup Ready gene was achieved through negotiations between Asgrow and Monsanto in the US, whereby Asgrow, including its Argentine branch, was granted the use of the gene. Argentine biotech firm Nidera soon acquired Asgrow Argentina and thereby gained access to the gene, which it disseminated widely in Argentina but could not patent (because it was not the creator). When Monsanto subsequently tried to patent the gene in Argentina, it was unable to do so because the gene had already been released in Argentina and so did not meet the novelty requirement. Nonetheless, Monsanto signed private settlements with other, smaller firms in Argentina to commercialize the Roundup Ready gene. These settlements explicitly identify Monsanto's 'patent' ownership over the gene and agree that the firms will pay Monsanto royalties for each seed sold. While the firms did not necessarily have to sign the agreement with Monsanto, given the fact that the Roundup Ready gene was freely available in Argentina, they did so voluntarily to try and stay on good terms with the company so as to gain access to future innovations. However, because Nidera did not do so, and because it does not have a patent, Monsanto has not been able to charge a per-use technology fee every season nor has it been able to restrict the use of the seed by Argentine farmers, who use Roundup Ready soybeans for approximately 95 per cent of their crop.

The second factor is related to the operational aspects of the seed market and its effect on the price of RR soybean. On the one hand, under the 1978 International Union for the Protection of New Varieties of Plant (UPOV), farmers can legitimately retain seeds for their own use; on the other hand, there are clandestine operations (the so-called 'white bag') through which seed multipliers sell seed without the authorization of the companies holding the corresponding legal production rights. Both factors have driven down the price of RR soybean, thus promoting its rapid adoption. Within this context, the stunted growth of the seed market over recent years should come as no surprise, despite the sharp increase observed in the acreage planted to soybean, which is the leading crop in the market.

Another contributing factor in this context is the fact that soybean seed falls into the category of autogamous species, in which genetic quality can be maintained through seed retained by farmers for their own use or which may be used for clandestine multiplication practices.

The third factor contributing to the wide diffusion of RR soybean in Argentina is the increasing reduction in the price of glyphosate from about US$5.60 per litre in 1996 to about US$2.67 in 2001. This reduction stemmed from a fiercer competition in local markets resulting from the introduction of new agents in the manufacturing and commercialization of glyphosate.

Keeping in mind that so far Argentina has encountered no difficulties in accessing target markets for its RR soybean exports and that, in spite of the perceptions of foreign consumers, price differentials between conventional and RR soybeans in the world market do not penalize the latter, it is hardly surprising that almost all Argentine soybean crop is RR. Neither is it surprising that not only input suppliers but also farmers, the scientific community and government authorities are all in favour of this new technology. Only a few non-governmental organizations, such as Greenpeace, have introduced part of the international debate in Argentina. Yet, Argentine public opinion – overwhelmed by major issues such as unemployment, poverty and corruption, and in the face of anti-globalization campaigns focusing their criticism on banks and privatized companies – has not offered much fertile ground for negative views about these new technologies.

The excessive reliance on this crop, pushed by the high international prices, may affect the fertility of the soil. In this context, a report by the National Institute of Agriculture Technology (INTA, 2003) states that the 'no tillage system + RR soybean' cannot go on as a sustainable strategy without rotating crops in the Pampas. At the same time, the 'agriculturization' process in the northeast and west of the country due to the soybean expansion is not sustainable in these ecologically fragile areas. The two processes could affect both the quantity and quality of the country's natural resources and lead to a fall in agriculture production.

Moreover, although more sustainable production methods (based on rotation with maize and livestock) are available and are being adopted by some farmers despite their higher operating costs, the fact that 50 per cent of the land is leased and the price of the lease is fixed in kilograms of soybeans is a serious constraint for the diffusion of these methods (INTA, 2003).

THE DIFFUSION OF BT MAIZE AND BT COTTON

Unlike RR soybean, the performance of Bt maize and Bt cotton has been much less dynamic. Bt varieties have been released much more recently, and farmers tend to consider Bt crops as some sort of insurance.[3] In contrast to RR soy, a technology fee is charged to Argentine farmers for transgenic maize and cotton varieties – which in some cases is higher than in the US – as both crops are covered by patents. As a result, farmers cannot keep their own seed for planting, and therefore, the relative weight of the certified seed in the corresponding market increases. In the case of cotton, the real issue concerns the commercialization strategy, which is based on formal agreements between the sole supplying company and the farmers, whereby the farmers' right to their 'own use' of the seed is restricted. Consequently, farmers have no choice but to pay for the seeds at four times the price of conventional varieties, which, in turn, hinders the diffusion of this technology in the country.

In addition, some clear and obvious differences arise from the comparison of RR soybean with both Bt maize and Bt cotton. The use of transgenic soybeans is a win–win situation, as the adoption of this new technology is not related to farm size (thus, small and large farmers all benefit more or less the same) and because of the equitable distribution of benefits among input suppliers and farmers (technology providers do not extract a disproportionate share of the proceeds) the Argentine economy as a whole benefits (see Figure 6.1). The evidence available for Bt maize and Bt cotton does not point in the same direction (see Figures 6.2 and 6.3), although the performance observed in these cases does not differ much from the one found in other contexts. It can thus be concluded that the situation depicted is not attributable to country-specific conditions, but to the nature of these technologies and to the way in which this impacts on the performance of the actors in the process of adopting such technologies.

Finally, it is clear from the above discussion that one of the main problems in Argentine agriculture is the illegal trade of seeds, potentially amounting to 35 or even 50 per cent of the market. In addition to the risk of a potential reduction in

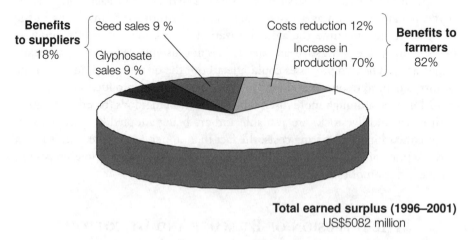

Benefits to suppliers 18% { Seed sales 9 % Glyphosate sales 9 %

Costs reduction 12% Increase in production 70% } **Benefits to farmers** 82%

Total earned surplus (1996–2001)
US$5082 million

Figure 6.1 *RR soybean adoption: Distribution of benefits*
(does not include 'white bag' seed)

Source: Prepared by the authors based on results generated by runs of the SIGMA v2.02 model

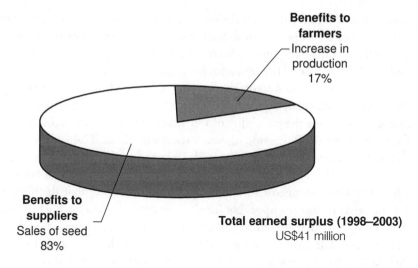

Figure 6.2 *Bt cotton adoption: Distribution of benefits*

Source: Prepared by the authors based on results generated by runs of the SIGMA v2.02 model

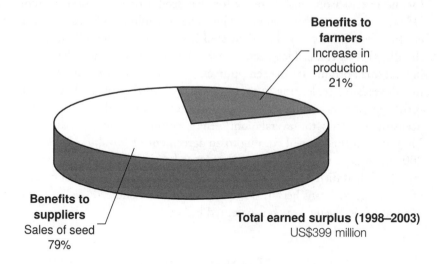

Figure 6.3 *Bt maize adoption: Distribution of benefits*

Source: Prepared by the authors based on results generated by runs of the SIGMA v2.02 model

productivity (seed with lower genetic quality and germinatory power) or with respect to phytosanitary issues, the existence and growth of illegal practices might also mean that many of the breakthroughs in biotechnology – and in other conventional technologies as well – may not be effectively incorporated into production. In other words, the dissemination of new knowledge takes much longer than it actually would if the seed market worked under normal conditions. The dissolution of the National Seed Institute (INASE), which constituted the regulating authority responsible for the enforcement of effective regulations, at the end of 2000 aggravated the situation. In response to the increasing proliferation of illegal sales of unlicensed seeds, the Secretary of Agriculture decided to reopen the Institute four years later. As well, in February 2004, the Ministry of Agriculture said it was studying the possibility of adhering to the 1991 Act of the International Convention for the Protection of New Varieties of Plants. The 1991 version of the Act requires farmers to report how seeds obtained in their harvest were used.

The problem of illegal trade in seeds was made more visible in January 2004 when Monsanto stopped selling RR soybean seeds, saying that the black market for the seeds makes it impossible for the company to earn back its investments. This led to fears that Argentina might lose out on biotech advances and new seed varieties and that farmers who would have wanted to buy the seeds legally might instead not plant them at all, resulting in lost productivity, or buy them on the black market. In late September 2004 Monsanto suggested the government of Argentina create a royalty collection system in which farmers purchasing new seed would be required to sign a sworn statement testifying to how much seed they were saving for the next season, and to repay for that seed a fixed amount of, reportedly, US$1.50 for every 25 kilograms. This system would enable legal seed sellers to ensure a return for every time their seed is planted, and would effectively curtail the illegal seed trade. However, under a 1973 Argentine seed law intended to protect small producers, an exemption exists which recognizes the right of farmers to cull seeds for replanting in the case of self-fertilizing plants like soy or wheat. Although farmers and the Agriculture Ministry responded harshly to Monsanto's licensing proposals, for several months the government continued discussions with Monsanto in the hope of coming to an agreement on royalties. However, in July 2005 the Argentine government suspended talks with Monsanto after the company said that it had filed a patent infringement suit in Denmark against two importers of Argentine soybeans because samples from a vessel showed the beans contained Monsanto's RR gene, which is patented in Denmark.

LOOKING AHEAD

Whereas the foreign debt situation, the lack of international financing and the stagnation of the local financial system aggravated the already critical economic and social situation of the country, the devaluation of the local currency – regardless of withholdings on exports (particularly agricultural and energy exports) being in force once again – should prove beneficial to the performance of agriculture. In view of the impact of exports on farming, changes are likely to be favourable for the primary sector, with quite significant increases in the share of the total income currently received by farmers vis-à-vis their situation prior to devaluation. The new scenario should promote the consolidation of trends observed over the last years, at least in the case of price ratios. Based on the aforementioned findings and the characteristics of Argentine agriculture, it is possible to draw some conclusions and highlight some implications.

In the first place, we cannot fail to single out the exceptional nature of the RR soybean case and the highly unlikely reoccurrence of the set of factors leading to it; therefore, all policies and strategies to be adopted hereafter cannot be a simple 'projection of past situations'. Moreover, it is worth mentioning that there are several sustained positive factors, which should be taken into consideration when developing a strategy in this field.

A review of technologies in the pipeline suggests that, in the next five to ten years, there will be a flow of incremental innovations rather than radical innovations. This process will go hand in hand with a steady increase in the number of species adopted as well as with a diversification of the sources of supply of new technologies, with countries such as China becoming major suppliers of new transgenic events.

This means that, even if the innovative flow that is to come does not have the same radical impact as soybeans, Argentine agriculture will still find it attractive. First, the focus will remain on temperate and subtropical crops, broadening out to encompass a wider range of options in terms of crops and events. Second, the coming second and third generations of innovation will benefit consumers. Third, Argentina still fulfils the required structural conditions to reap the benefits of innovations generated abroad. This refers to the 26 million hectares of commercial crop area, cultivated by farmers used to adopting technological changes, and with a dynamic area of technological services and inputs along with an extensive logistic and territorial network. As already stated, these have been the factors determining the processes that have taken place so far, and they will, no doubt, continue to promote and offer significant incentives in order to ensure a steady expansion of new breakthroughs in Argentine agriculture.

However, foreign innovative processes are likely to mirror the priorities and the biases of the economies of their countries of origin, which may be quite different from Argentina's. This suggests that the encouragement of biotechnological research in the country must always constitute an overriding priority, even in cases when it may be deemed incompatible with the immediate concerns of the country. In the mid- and short term, this issue will most probably require a recognition of the idiosyncratic characteristics of Argentine agriculture.

Other GMOs are likely to feature higher costs of adoption than those of RR soybean – such is the case of Bt cotton, among others. This prospect further highlights the significance of a proactive policy at a national level in terms of research in agricultural biotechnology, not only to ensure that idiosyncratic issues concerning Argentine agriculture are duly addressed, but also as a tool to come up against the competition by promoting alternative sources of 'events' in order to prevent monopolistic behaviours within the seed market.

Argentina has modern legislation on competition defence, approved in 1999 (Act 25156) and in force since 2000. However, the contestability of the genetic inputs market can only be secured if, besides the required legal instruments, the country is in a condition to diversify the supply of innovations.

All the aforementioned aspects – along with: the consensus needed to establish and enforce proper protection standards against risks (effective or perceived); ensuring consistent availability to the public; and the strong possibility of an increasing degree of complexity from scientific, technical and commercial perspectives in terms of issues, crops and events to be dealt with – indicate that it is absolutely necessary that the CONABIA be institutionally vested with the power required, and that its scientific and technical capabilities be reinforced.

The rule applicable to market analyses for the approval of the new transgenic events should be further reviewed. Moreover, all topics related to the labelling and traceability of GMOs and their derivatives should also be addressed.

With regard to market assessment, the rule in force – whether the event has or has not already been approved in the major export markets – proved effective during the relatively quiet decade of the 1990s, but in the face of a scenario of events increasingly diverse and complex, along with those that can be anticipated, it will probably end up adversely affecting investments, particularly in the field of R&D at the national level. In other words, it would not appear profitable to invest in the development of biotechnology solutions to country-specific problems – for instance, the Río IV disease that strikes maize – if knowing in advance that such innovations will not pass market assessment when the time comes for their release. The fact that RR soybean had already been approved in the EU – the main destination of Argentine exports – has definitely been a contributing factor to the dynamism that characterized the diffusion process of the crop. But today's scenarios differ considerably from those of 1996 and it would therefore constitute a mistake to make market access projections on the basis of such data.

The Cartagena Protocol has now entered into force, which will require Parties to implement national biosafety frameworks. In the meantime, there already is an increasing number of countries whose national legislations are adopting higher labelling and traceability requirements concerning GMOs. This will pave the way for the gradual development of differentiated markets for conventional and transgenic products – a process that would be further consolidated as second and third generation GMOs are released into the market.

Unfortunately, Argentina is not in a condition to defray the costs of the aforementioned processes. There is no information, neither in the private nor in the public sectors, that can be used for an assessment of the potential economic implications stemming from the segregation of products, both for the primary sector and the food processing industry. Efforts should be undertaken to generate this information and to attract the investment required to develop the logistics that the new market conditions demand.

Lastly, those issues requiring the formulation of specific policies should be clearly identified. The complexity of the topics addressed in the debate calls for capacity building in terms of follow-up and analysis of ever-changing national and international realities. The release of GMOs in Brazil and the eventual abolition of the European Union moratorium as well as the significant role played by China – and lately by other countries such as India – in this technology should contribute to the redefinition of the international and regional strategy adopted by Argentina on these issues.

Notes

1   The authors adapted this subchapter from a book with the same title which was finalized in October 2002 by Centro de Investigaciónes para la Transformación (CENIT) under the direction of Daniel Chudnovsky and Eduardo Trigo, in collaboration with the Trade Knowledge Network of the International Institute for Sustainable Development and the International Centre for Trade and Sustainable Development with financial support from the Rockefeller Foundation, the International Development Research Centre (Canada) and the Department of Agriculture of Argentina.
2   'No-tillage' maintains a permanent or semi-permanent organic soil cover (usually a growing crop or dead mulch) that protects the soil from sun, rain and wind and allows soil micro-organisms and fauna to take on the task of 'tilling' and soil nutrient balancing – natural processes disturbed by mechanical tillage.
3   Unlike weeds, which are always present, pests may or may not appear in any given year, consequently the effectiveness of the Bt control strategy will vary from year to year, yielding higher or lower profits depending on the level of infestation occurring in that particular year.

References

All the Brazilian legislation cited in this chapter can be found at www.planalto.gov.br/

Bonalume Neto, R (1999) 'Smugglers aim to circumvent GM court ban in Brazil', *Nature*, vol 402, pp344–345
Bonalume Neto, R (2003) 'GM confusion in Brazil', *Nature Biotechnology*, vol 21, no 11, pp1257–1258
Clarke, T (2002) 'Corn could make cotton pests Bt resistant – Insects offered GM-free refuges are eating modified crops further afield', *Nature Science Update*, 4 December
Contini, E, Sampaio, M J and Ávila, A F D (2003) *GM Plants and Biosafety Regulations: Potential Impact on Research and Agribusiness in Brazil.* Paper presented at the Ravello Biotechnology Conference, Italy, July 2003 (to be published by the organizers)
Embrapa (2002) *Tecnologias de Produção de Soja – Região Central do Brasil*, Embrapa Soja, Embrapa Cerrados, Embrapa Agropecuária Oeste, ESALQ/USP, Londrina, PR, p199
FAS (2003) *Brazil: Future Agricultural Expansion Potential Underrated*, Foreign Agriculture Service, US Department of Agriculture, Washington, DC

Freire, E C (2000) *Distribuição, Coleta, uso e Preservação das Espécies Silvestres de Algodão no Brasil*, Campina Grande, Embrapa Algodão, p22

Gianessi, L P, Silvers, C S, Sankula, S and Carpenter, J E (2002) *Plant Biotechnology: Current and Potential Impact for Improving Pest Management in US Agriculture: An Analysis of 40 Case Studies*, The National Center for Food and Agricultural Policy, Washington, DC

Gianessi, L P, Sankula, S and Reigner, N (2003) *Plant Biotechnology: Potential for Improving Pest Management in European Agriculture* (A Summary of Three Case Studies, June), The National Center for Food and Agricultural Policy, Washington, DC

INTA (2003) *El INTA ante la Preocupación por la Sustentabilidad de la Producción Agropecuaria Argentina*, Instituto Nacional de Tecnología Industrial, Buenos Aires

Kirsten, J and Gouse, M (2002) 'Bt cotton in South Africa: Adoption and impact on farm incomes amongst small and large-scale farmers', *ISB News Report*, October, pp7–9

Lehmann, V and Pengue, W A (2000) 'Herbicide tolerant soybean: Just another step in a technology treadmill?', *Biotechnology and Development Monitor*, no 43, pp11–14

PECAD (2003) *Brazil: Future Agricultural Expansion Potential Underrated, Production Estimates and Crop Assessment Division Foreign Agricultural Service*, US Department of Agriculture, Washington, DC

PG Economics Ltd (2003) *Consultancy Support for the Analysis of the Impact of GM Crops on UK Farm Profitability – Final Report*, PG Economics, Dorchester, UK

Wickel, M and Rautenberg, O (2002) 'Bt cotton in South Africa: A success story for small-scale farmers as well', *Bio-scope.org*, 23 October

Whitfield, J (2003) 'Transgenic cotton a winner in India – Insect-resistant varieties show big yield improvements', *Nature Science Update*, 7 February

WTO (2001) *International Trade Statistics*, World Trade Organization Publications, Geneva

7

Addressing Challenges of Tropical Agriculture Through Biotechnology: Colombia's Cassava Case

Paul Chavarriaga-Aguirre, Douglas Pachico and Joe Tohme

Cassava (*Manihot esculenta* Crantz, Euphorbiaceae) is a root crop of southern Amazonian origin that was spread throughout the Old World tropics by Portuguese sailors in the 16th century. Since then cassava has gradually become an economically important crop in developing countries due mainly to its tolerance to drought, poor soil fertility and acid soils. In Africa, fresh roots of cassava are a staple food and constitute a commodity for regional trade. In Thailand, Vietnam and Indonesia, dried cassava is an export commodity, while in Colombia and Brazil cassava is produced mainly for internal consumption. Today cassava ranks fourth among the major sources of carbohydrates in the tropics where it is an indispensable staple for millions of people. The importance of cassava as a low-cost source of carbohydrates in the world merits the application of modern biotechnological techniques to improve germplasm for nutritional quality and biotic and abiotic stress tolerance among other traits. This chapter focuses on the prospects of development and deployment of transgenic cassava, while attempting to examine possible social implications of the endeavour.

INTERNATIONAL TRADE IN CASSAVA

Because physiological and bacterial deterioration of cassava roots starts immediately on harvest, only processed products, such as cassava chips, starch or flour, are at all important for international trade. The value of all international trade in fresh cassava is less than US$1 million annually and occurs almost exclusively in Africa (FAO, 2002). This trade is almost certainly cross-border trade in local markets.

Similarly, some fresh cassava may be shipped occasionally from northern Vietnam into China, but overall international trade in fresh cassava is simply not significant.

Dried cassava has long dominated international cassava trade. In the early 1990s more than 10 million tons of dried cassava, the equivalent of about 25 million tons of fresh cassava, were traded annually. Nearly 80 per cent of this trade was between Southeast Asia (mainly Thailand) and Europe (FAO, 2002). To a large extent, this trade was the artifact of European policy, which had established high internal prices for animal feed and had left open a loophole that permitted the import of dried cassava without the tariffs that limited the import of other animal feed. Over time, European regulations on the import of cassava tightened and, by the late 1990s, this trade had fallen to less than 4 million tons annually. Europe still constitutes over 80 per cent of the world market for dried cassava.

In contrast, international trade in cassava starch has grown from about 400,000 tons in the early 1990s to nearly 800,000 tons in 1999 (FAO, 2002). This latter figure is the equivalent of about 5 million tons of fresh cassava. Most of this trade in cassava starch occurs within Asia, with Thailand being the principal exporter, holding over three-quarters of the market, and China and Japan as the main importers.

SCIENCE, SCIENTISTS AND THE RISKS OF GM CROPS

Transgenic or genetically modified (GM) crops have aroused considerable interest for their potential to make a contribution to world food production and for the possible risks they might present to the environment or to human health. While some see the prospect of great potential benefits from transgenic crops, others see looming environmental catastrophe (Evans, 1998; Oxfam, 1999). Clarifying the actual risks of GM crops is becoming increasingly important as genetically modified crops have seen a growing demand of at least 10 per cent annually since their introduction in 1996. In 2004, the estimated global area grown with transgenic crops was 81.0 million hectares (James, 2004).

The scientific community is keenly aware of the potential of GM crops to cause environmental damage and considerable research is being conducted to assess these issues, although, as yet, little is clear (Wolfenbarger and Phifer, 2000). The same scientific bodies that are aware of the potential benefits of transgenic crops also make clear the need for thorough risk assessment of such crops: 'There is no consensus as to the seriousness, or even the existence, of any potential environmental harm from GM technology. There is therefore, a need for thorough risk assessment of likely consequences at an early stage in the development of all transgenic plant varieties' (Royal Society of London et al, 2000). Consistent with this scientific view, procedures for assessing the risks involved in using these crops are emerging as part of regulatory frameworks in national and international contexts.

These concerns over potential threats to biodiversity from genetically modified organisms (GMOs) led to the adoption of the Cartagena Protocol on Biosafety in January 2001. The Protocol focuses on the transboundary movement of living modified organisms (LMOs) and calls for countries to have a domestic risk assessment procedure for locally developed LMOs, which needs to be scientifically sound and should be carried out in a transparent manner. The assessment should be conducted on a case-by-case basis, depending on the specific LMO, its intended use and the likely receiving environment.

A recommendation from a risk assessment to authorize the international movement of an LMO does not require the demonstration of no possible risks. Rather, authorization can follow if such risks are acceptable or manageable due to the nature of the anticipated adverse consequences, their level of likelihood, or the possibility of remedial action. The Protocol provides no standards or criteria for what might be an acceptable or unacceptable risk, or a manageable or unmanage-able risk. Presumably this is left to the judgement of the importing country. There could be scope for dispute, however, were the judgements on what is acceptable or manageable to differ substantially between an importer and an exporter, possibly requiring international arbitration.

DEVELOPING STEMBORER RESISTANT CASSAVA

Various species of stemborer (lepidopterans and coleopterans) are widespread throughout the American hemisphere and the world generally. One of these, found in Colombia, Venezuela and Brazil (Bellotti, 2000), is the cassava stemborer *Chilomima clarkei*, a lepidopterous insect whose principal and perhaps only host is the cassava plant. The insect spends most of its life inside the stems. The young larvae cause most of the damage by boring tunnels that weaken the plants and cause considerable yield and/or planting material losses, more than 60 per cent in some cases (Vides et al, 1996).

Chilomima clarkei was first detected in Colombia's cassava-growing regions in the 1970s (Lohr, 1983). It probably entered through the Eastern Plains and during the last decade, became a major pest in the Caribbean Coastal Region, Eastern Plains and Magdalena River Valley, affecting up to 85 per cent of the country's cassava crops. Its rapid dispersion in Colombia was facilitated mainly by the exchange of infected stakes, which appear healthy externally, and by the adult moth's capacity for flight.

CIAT and the international effort to develop transgenic cassava

The International Center for Tropical Agriculture (CIAT) is a not-for-profit organization that conducts socially and environmentally progressive research aimed at reducing hunger and poverty and preserving natural resources in developing countries. CIAT is a Future Harvest organization supported by the Consultative Group on International Agricultural Research (CGIAR, www.ciat.cgiar.org). Research with transgenic plants at CIAT includes cassava, Phaseolus beans, rice and Brachiaria grasses. The Center's scientists study, develop, deploy and monitor genetic transformation technology, as well as products developed through it, in partnership with national research programmes and biosafety authorities. This technology is vital for increasing the effectiveness and speeding the pace of practical, problem-solving research that meets the needs of developing country farmers.

Most of CIAT's genetic improvement research currently depends on conventional crossing methods. When these approaches show little promise for solving particular problems, Center scientists test genetic transformation technology (as one component of a broader plant breeding strategy) for its ability to safely improve traits that are clearly relevant to the Center's humanitarian goals.

CIAT assesses the risks of the transgenic plants it develops for the tropics on a case-by-case basis. In its biosafety research, the Center actively collaborates with national partners to determine the potential environmental effects of genetic transformation technologies. CIAT also participates in the dialogue on biosafety issues with national and regional institutions, civil society organizations and the mass media. Finally, CIAT abides by host country legislation governing this work and by the Cartagena Biosafety Protocol.

WHY GENETIC TRANSFORMATION FOR CASSAVA?

Sources of varietal resistance to the cassava stemborer may possibly be found among the more than 6000 cassava accessions maintained at CIAT. However, results of samplings from more than 2000 accessions have been inconclusive (Herrera and Bellotti, 2002, personal communication). Meanwhile, the pest is exerting increasing pressure on the crops, making it necessary to find alternatives for its control such as:

- genes, if any, of varietal resistance;
- biological controls that have been identified (Ospina et al, 2002; Melo, 2002; Ramírez, 2001) but not exploited commercially; and
- genes for insecticidal qualities from bacteria (notably, the Bt gene, see below) that have already been introduced, through genetic transformation, into market crops such as cotton, maize and soybean (James, 2004).

Both the varietal resistance and Bt genes would be integrated in a system of integrated pest management (IPM) for more effective control of the stemborer and other lepidopterans (Bellotti et al, 1999).

Genetic transformation systems for cassava are well established, reproducible and moderately efficient in obtaining transgenic lines (Li et al, 1996; Sarria et al,

2000; Schopke et al, 1996). To introduce a Bt gene (cry 1Ab) in cassava varieties selected by small farmers of the Colombian North Coast, CIAT and the Colombian corporation of agricultural research (CORPOICA) are cooperating on a project with the Colombian agricultural biotechnology programme for small farmers (PBA). The project is financed mainly by the Directorate-General for International Cooperation (DGIS) of The Netherlands (Ladino et al, 2002). Among these varieties, the most important is *La Venezolana* (M Col 2215), which is the best adapted to the area's agricultural conditions and to consumer demands. One of its major drawbacks is high susceptibility to the stemborer.

Obtaining cassava varieties by conventional breeding (crossings and selection) can take up to 15 years. Cassava is a highly heterozygous species, with many different alleles, which means that each variety represents a unique genotype that practically disappears when crossed with another variety. On making a cross, two complete genomes mix and produce a totally different genotype. The process of recovering the original genotype by means of careful selection of progeny is what consumes the time. Genetic transformation can help substantially to reduce the time needed to obtain the desired variety (five to seven years), because most of the original genotype is conserved on introducing only one or few new genes from among the more than 50,000 genes that can compose a cassava genome.

POTENTIAL BENEFITS AND CONCERNS

An important benefit of incorporating genes for resistance to the cassava stemborer via genetic transformation is the considerable reduction of time needed to develop a resistant variety. The gene, or new genes, would not only enrich the species' gene pool but also, theoretically, reduce the number of insecticide applications made to control the stemborer and other lepidopterans such as the cassava hornworm *Erinnyis ello*. Examples of such insecticides are: Profitox®, which is normally used against the hornworm and is applied once to four times during the crop's cycle, depending on the severity of the attack; systemic insecticides to eliminate the stemborer from infected planting material and bio-insecticides containing *Bacillus thuringiensis* such as Thuricide®, which are more unstable and more expensive than chemical insecticides.

Some genes of bacterial origin for insecticidal qualities are more commonly known as *Bt* or *cry* genes and are derived from the soil bacterium *Bacillus thuringiensis*. This bacterium has been known for more than a hundred years and was first used as a biological insecticide more than 40 years ago, with no known adverse effects to human health (Nester et al, 2002). However, the effect of transgenic cassava plants with Bt genes on the entomofauna (insects) associated with the crop is unknown. Small-scale trials should be conducted when the first transgenic plants are taken to the field.

Much of the plant breeder's work concentrates on obtaining plants with resistances to various pests such as viruses, fungi, bacteria and insects. Once incorporated into the plants, these resistances can be lost by poor crop management and/or through the appearance of new strains and resistant individuals. In the US, where transgenic plants with Bt genes are cultivated, regulations are in force to oblige farmers to maintain a proportion of their crops as non-transgenic plants (known as refuges) to reduce the probability of resistant insects appearing. Genes for resistance to Bt are found naturally in insect populations at relatively high frequencies (1.5×10^{-3} in the European corn borer; Gould, 1998), which could be increased if selection pressure on susceptible individuals increases. To reduce this selection pressure and to reduce the possibilities of resistance appearing, the proportion of non-transgenic plants maintained as refuge can reach 20 per cent, depending on the crop and on the severity of pest attacks in each region. For specific cases in maize and other crops, the reader should consult the website www.usda.gov.

In Colombia, the national Agricultural and Livestock Institute (ICA) has regulations for the introduction, production, release and marketing of genetically modified organisms (ICA, 2002). It also authorizes the National Technical Committee, in charge of regulating transgenic organisms, to demand refuges as necessary.

It should be remembered that, for any crop, transgenic or not, regulation per se will not prevent resistance to Bt appearing if the appropriate genes exist in the insect populations and if no IPM programmes, including refuges when transgenic plants are planted, are set up and implemented.

Of constant concern in the production of transgenic plants for the benefit of small and medium-sized farmers in developing countries are the restrictions imposed by intellectual property rights. The Bt gene that is being introduced into cassava was purchased by three CGIAR centres (CIAT, CIP and CIMMYT) from the Plantech Research Institute (part of the Mitsubishi Chemical Corporation), Japan, thus guaranteeing its use in varieties that would eventually be released for marketing. However, all other genes, including regulatory sequences and some molecular and/or cellular technologies used in cassava genetic transformation, may be subject to intellectual property rights. What then would be the alternatives?

One option is to invest heavily in the search and use of one's own genes and regulatory sequences that would be safe for the environment and consumer and not restricted by intellectual property rights. Another option is to follow the example of the 'golden rice' case (Xudong et al, 2000), where a variety of transgenic rice with high β-carotene content in the seed is being made accessible to the small farmers in India. This rice may be cultivated, kept and marketed freely only within the country and provided the farmer's earnings from its marketing do not exceed US$10,000. Golden rice is perhaps the only transgenic plant of mass consumption that belongs to the public domain. Its genes are now being incorporated into other varieties also accessible to small farmers.

Is gene flow a concern in stemborer resistant cassava in Colombia?

The transfer or flow of genes between organisms is a major force of evolution. With the appearance and marketing of transgenic plants, especially those that carry genes for resistance to herbicides, gene flow has become a cause for concern. Transgenes, especially herbicide resistance genes, are assumed to be able to be passed on to weedy relatives, converting them into 'super-weeds' that would be difficult to control. What would be the minimum requirements for this to happen?

One factor is the co-existence of the species, that is, both the transgenic species and its weedy relative must cohabit and must have an effective flow of genes between them. Other factors enabling gene flow are coincidence in flowering; viability, vigour and competitive advantage of the progeny conferred by the transgene and introgression of the transgene into the population. The degree to which all these factors occur determines the possibility of gene transfer.

Although highly possible, cross-breeding between cassava and its closest wild relatives has yet to be confirmed as actually happening in the American continent. By contrast, close examination of gene flow between cassava (*Manihot esculenta* subspecies *esculenta*) and *M. glaziovii*, a *Manihot* species that was introduced into Côte d'Ivoire and Nigeria, reveals that such cross-breeding has taken place in Africa. Natural hybrid swarms have been found and their hybrid nature confirmed through use of DNA-based molecular markers (Beeching et al, 1993). These hybrid individuals are commonly known as tree cassava and form a gene pool that is usually located between those of the two parents.

What can Latin American scientists make of the African case of gene flow between cassava and *Manihot glaziovii*? The answer is not much, because the American continent has a number of different wild relatives of cassava for which a separate risk assessment has to be done on a case-by-case basis. Both the species producing the tree cassava in Nigeria are originally from Brazil, with the Glaziovianae section of *Manihot* living together with cassava in northeast Brazil, where this crop is widely cultivated. This means that the condition of proximity is fulfilled and that the possibility of cross-breeding between a transgenic cassava resistant to stemborer and the wild relative *Manihot Glaziovii* could take place in this part of Brazil. Mapping the distribution of these two cross-compatible species in the Americas will be critical for the general awareness of decision makers on planning and conducting biosafety risk assessment studies with transgenic cassava.

Another candidate for cross-breeding with cassava is its close relative *M. esculenta* subspecies *flabellifolia*. Preliminary studies carried out at CIAT (Roa et al, 1997) demonstrated that the two plants are capable of inter-mixing and producing thousands of seeds that may therefore potentially carry GM traits. Outside the lab, under natural conditions, such cross-breeding has not been confirmed and the existence of *Manihot esculenta* subspecies *flabellifolia* has not been reported in Colombia. Nor is cross-breeding always possible or easy. In contrast to the above, only five seeds were obtained after two crosses of cassava and

M. aesculifolia, a more distantly related species that is also present in Central America. But nature still holds a lot of secrets on the natural exchange of genes between related species of plants. Microsatellites (one form of DNA molecular marker) have shown that Mexican and Guatemalan cassava accessions are a rich source of novel and unique forms of these markers, whose presence may be explained by gene flow from related species (Chavarriaga-Aguirre et al, 1999).

COLOMBIA: BIOSAFETY ISSUES IN CASSAVA TRADE

For Colombian cassava, the issue of international movement of transgenic cassava is unlikely to lead to biosafety issues. First, as far as is known, Colombia does not export fresh cassava and its exports of processed cassava products are modest. During 1995–1999 exports averaged about 200 tons per year, with a total value of about US$100,000 annually (FAO, 2002). Even if exports of fresh cassava were to begin, the risk of exported transgenic cassava from Colombia getting into the environment and reproducing is essentially nil because the roots, the economically valuable part, cannot be conventionally used to propagate cassava. Likewise, even if exports of processed cassava products were to increase substantially in the future, they would not create a risk to biodiversity by their release into the environment because they cannot reproduce.

Human or animal health risks from processed cassava entering international trade cannot be totally ruled out if novel substances generated by transgenes were able to survive processing. These health risks would have to be assessed on a case-by-case basis and would depend on the presence and persistence of compounds in transgenic cassava or its processed products that were damaging to human health, for example novel toxins or allergens. Although no a priori basis exists to assume that all transgenic cassava would hold risks to human health, some risks could indeed occur.

Planting material of transgenic cassava could be moved internationally, particularly to neighbouring countries. As yet, no formal international trade in cassava planting material exists anywhere in the world, but if transgenic cassava had traits that particularly attracted farmers, then perhaps farmers from neighbouring countries might privately bring in cassava planting material, working outside the formal plant quarantine or other regulatory system. Essentially, this represents risk through biopiracy or evasion of and non-compliance with existing regulatory systems.

Even in the absence of international trade, Colombia would have to assess environmental risks according to its own regulatory framework before permitting the release into its environment of a transgenic cassava (CBD, 2000; Royal Society of London et al, 2000). Risks would include gene flow from transgenic cassava to wild cassava species; effects on untargeted organisms, including soil micro-organisms; and effects on human health.

The only obvious international biosafety risk of transgenic or non-transgenic cassava would be through the illegal shipment of cassava planting material aimed at evading standard quarantine procedures. While such biopiracy cannot be ruled out, the most likely biosafety risks from transgenic cassava in Colombia would be national rather than international. The use of GM cassava in Colombia should remain contingent on a scientific risk assessment of the national environmental risks.

CONCLUSIONS

Because of the characteristics of both cassava and international trade in cassava, the likelihood of any conceivable environmental biosafety risks from transgenic cassava deployed in Colombia would appear to be minimal as compared to other crops such as maize, due to the breeding system and mode of propagation of cassava.

Natural hybridization probably occurs between cassava and some of its closest, cross-compatible relatives whenever they are existing together. As stated above, mapping possible contact zones between cassava and its relatives will serve as a guide for Colombian national authorities to implement and/or reinforce programmes to regulate the introduction, release and management of transgenic cassava. The deployment of transgenic cassava will have to take into account the distribution of wild relatives especially in countries rich in *Manihot* species such as Brazil and Mexico.

Gene flow between transgenic and non-transgenic cassava varieties (intra-specific gene flow) could happen, especially if plantations were side by side. This may be considered a cause of concern for environmental biosafety and for international trade. Cassava spreads asexually, which means that farmers do not conserve or use botanical or sexual seed for propagation. The frequency of gene movement from transgenic to non-transgenic plantings and plantations will depend on their isolation by natural or artificial barriers such as plantings of other crops. Again, more studies on gene flow and risk assessment in cassava are crucial for proper decision-making, regarding the use of transgenic cassava, in all cassava-growing countries that wish to deploy the technology.

In considering the introduction of transgenic cassava, Colombian authorities will likely look towards the 2002 decision of Colombia's Institute for Commercial Agriculture (ICA), approval on behalf of the Colombian government to authorize use of Monsanto's GM Bt Cotton for pre-commercial purposes. This decision generated unease amid Colombian civil society groups who feared in particular the effects on native varieties as the country is a centre of diversity for cotton (FOEI, 2004). In February 2003, Colombian non-governmental groups initiated a legal action against the government decision, and in October 2003 a Colombian administrative tribunal suspended Monsanto's authorization to import, grow and test genetically modified cotton. The tribunal ruled that the import and testing of this GM cotton violated the collective rights to a healthy environment and public health, as well as the consumer's right to choose and the right to public participation in decisions that can affect the environment. The tribunal agreed with the plaintiffs that the lack of an environmental licence granted by the Environment Ministry and the absence of the required environmental impact assessment (which Monsanto should have prepared) contravene Colombian environmental laws. Nonetheless, in early 2004 the Colombian government decided to permit full commercial cultivation of GM cotton and indicated that they have plans to allow the planting of other GM crops, such as maize.

ACKNOWLEDGEMENTS

Research on cassava transformation at CIAT is supported by funding from the Directorate-General for International Cooperation (DGIS) of the Netherlands, the Colombian Ministry of Agriculture and Rural Development (MADR) and the Department for International Development (DFID) of the United Kingdom. The authors wish to thank these institutions for their continuous support.

REFERENCES

Beeching, J R, Marmey, P, Gavalda, M-C, Noirot, M, Haysom, H R, Hughes, M A and Charrier, A (1993) 'An assessment of genetic diversity within a collection of cassava germplasm using molecular markers', *Annals of Botany*, vol 72, pp515–520

Bellotti, A C (2000) 'Las plagas principales del cultivo de la yuca: Un panorama global', in Proceedings XXVII Congreso, held in Medellín, Colombia, on 26–28 July 2000, Sociedad Colombiana de Entomología (SOCOLEN), Bogotá, Colombia, pp189–217

Bellotti, A C, Smith, L and Lapointe, S L (1999) 'Recent advances in cassava pest management', *Annual Review Entomology*, vol 44, pp343–370

Chavarriaga-Aguirre, P, Maya, M M, Tohme, J, Duque, M C, Iglesias, C, Bonierbale, M W, Kresovich, S and Kochert, G (1999) 'Using microsatellites, isozymes and AFLPs to evaluate genetic diversity and redundancy in the cassava core collection and to assess the usefulness of DNA-based markers to maintain germplasm collections', *Molecular Breeding*, vol 5, pp263–273

CBD (2000) *Cartagena Protocol on Biosafety*, Convention on Biological Diversity, Montreal

Evans, L T (1998) *Feeding the Ten Billion*, Cambridge University Press

FAO (2002) *FAOSTAT Data Collection*, Food and Agriculture Organization of the United Nations, Rome

FOEI (2004) *Genetically Modified Crops: A Decade of Failure*, Friends of the Earth International, Amsterdam

Gould, F (1998) 'Sustainability of transgenic insecticidal cultivars: Integrating pest genetics and ecology', *Annual Review of Entomology*, vol 43, pp701–726

ICA (2002) Acuerdo No 2, Instituto Colombiano Agropecuario, Bogotá

James, C (2004) 'Preview: Global status of commercialized transgenic crops: 2004', *ISAAA Briefs No 32*, ISAAA, Ithaca, NY

Ladino, J J, Echeverry, M, Mancilla, M I, López, D, Chavarriaga, P, Tohme, J and Roca, W M (2002) 'Genetic transformation of cassava: Confirmation of transgenesis in clone 60444 and analysis of CRY1Ab protein in transgenic lines. Preliminary data on transformation of farmer-preferred cultivars SM1219-9 and CM 3306-4', Annual report SB2 Project, Centro Internacional de Agricultura Tropical (CIAT), Cali, Colombia, pp203–207

Li, H Q, Sautter, C, Potrykus, I and Puonti-Kaerlas, J (1996) 'Genetic transformation of cassava (*Manihot esculenta* Crantz)', *Nature Biotechnology*, vol 14, pp736–740

Lohr, B (1983) 'Biología, ecología, daño económico y control de *Chilomima clarkei* (Ansel) barrenador de la yuca en control integrado de plagas', in Reyes, J A (ed), *Yuca: control integrado de plagas*, CIAT, Cali, Colombia, pp159–161

Melo, E L (2002) 'Potencial del control biológico en el manejo de las plagas de la yuca', in Ceballos, H and Ospina, B (eds), *La Yuca en el Tercer Milenio: Sistemas Modernos de Producción, Procesamiento y Comercialización*, Centro Internacional de Agricultura Tropical (CIAT), Cali, Colombia, pp234–249

Nester, E W, Thomashow, L S, Metz, M and Gordon, M (2002) '100 years of *Bacillus thuringiensis:* A critical scientific assessment', Report, American Academy of Microbiology, Washington, DC

Ospina, P, Ceballos, H, Alvarez, E, Bellotti, A C, Calvert, L A, Arias, V, Cadavid, L, Pineda, L, Llano, R, and Cuervo, M I (eds) (2002) *Guía Práctica para el Manejo de las Enfermedades, las Plagas y las Deficiencias Nutricionales de la Yuca*, CIAT, Cali, Colombia

Oxfam (1999) 'Genetically modified crops, world trade and food security', Policy Department, Oxfam (Great Britain), London

Ramírez, C (2001) *Aportes al Estudio de la Biología, Comportamiento y Distribución del Barrenador del Tallo de la Yuca* Chilomima clarkei *Amsel en el Departamento del Tolima*. Thesis, Facultad de Ingeniería Agronómica, Universidad del Tolima, Ibagué, Colombia

Roa, A C, Maya, M M, Duque, M C, Tohme, J, Allem, A C and Bonierbale, M W (1997) 'AFLP analysis of relationships among cassava and other *Manihot* species', *Theoretical and Applied Genetics*, vol 95, pp741–750

Royal Society of London, US National Academy of Sciences, Brazilian Academy of Sciences, Chinese Academy of Sciences, Indian National Science Academy, Mexican Academy of Sciences, Third World Academy of Sciences (2000) *Transgenic Plants and World Agriculture*, National Academy Press, Washington, DC

Sarria, R, Torres, E, Angel, F, Chavarriaga, P and Roca, W M (2000) 'Transgenic plants of cassava (*Manihot esculenta*) with resistance to Basta® obtained through *Agrobacterium*-mediated transformation', *Plant Cell Reports*, vol 19, pp339–344

Schopke, C, Taylor, N, Carcamo, R, Konan, N K, Marmey, P, Henshaw, G G, Beachy, R N and Fauquet, C (1996) 'Regeneration of transgenic cassava plants (*Manihot esculenta* Crantz) from microbombarded embryogenic suspension cultures', *Nature Biotechnology*, vol 14, pp731–735

Vides, O L, Sierra, O D, Gómez, H S and Palomino, A T (1996) 'El barrenador del tallo de la yuca *Chilomima clarkei* (Lepidoptera: Pyralidae)' en el Creced Provincia del Rio, Bulletin of the Corporación Colombiana de Investigación Agropecuaria (CORPOICA), Produmedios, Colombia

Xudong, Y, Al-Babili, S, Klöti, A, Jing, Z, Lucca, P, Beyer, P and Potrykus, I (2000) 'Engineering the pro-vitamin A (α-carotene) biosynthetic pathway into (carotenoid-free) rice endosperm', *Science*, vol 287, pp303–305

Wolfenbarger, L L and Phifer, P R, (2000) 'The ecological risks and benefits of genetically engineered plants', *Science*, vol 290, pp2088–2093

PART TWO

TRADE IN BIOTECHNOLOGY: NEW CHALLENGES IN AN OLD PLAYGROUND

8

Intellectual Property and Biotechnology: Trade Interests of Developing Countries[1]

Jayashree Watal

Biotechnology has the potential to provide the answers to some of the developing world's most intractable problems. There is scope for developing countries to interpret the provisions of the World Trade Organization's Agreement on Trade-related Aspects of Intellectual Property Rights (TRIPS) on biotechnology at different levels, as evidenced by differing interpretations in the developed world. Equally, however, demands of developing countries on biodiversity-related issues can be countered through the ambiguities in the Convention on Biological Diversity. Instead of attempting to amend the TRIPS Agreement, developing countries should aim to obtain access to the new technologies, at reasonable terms, by collaboration and not confrontation with their owners, with the help of multilateral developmental institutions.

INTRODUCTION

Biotechnology, a modern science less than 30 years old, is revolutionizing production in both industry and agriculture in certain areas. It has the potential to provide the answers to some of the world's most intractable problems concerning agriculture, health, nutrition and the environment. Two sectors where biotechnology has already made significant contributions are pharmaceuticals and agriculture. While it is true that this technology has so far been dominated by corporations based in industrialized countries, mainly the US and Europe, and has tackled mostly problems pertaining to these countries, its potential to solve problems in developing countries cannot be denied.

In particular, developing countries have long possessed capabilities for plant breeding, mainly through public sector research institutions, for which biotechnology now provides new tools. Paradoxically, so far, developing countries have generally been wary that this technology may have adverse effects on health and the environment. Since many of the new biotechnological products and processes are protected by intellectual property rights (IPRs), additional concerns on access to these technologies tend to cloud the debate in developing countries and in international fora such as the World Trade Organization (WTO).

Intellectual property rights for biotechnological inventions also raise related but quite distinct sets of issues concerning equity. Northern firms are accused of pirating and patenting biological material and traditional knowledge from the gene-rich developing world for profit, without fair and equitable sharing of benefits or the appropriate transfer of the new technologies as called for by the Convention on Biological Diversity (CBD). The gene-rich developing countries see the control of access to genetic resources and some form of intellectual property protection for traditional knowledge, including that incorporated in farm-bred varieties, as necessary steps towards bringing about the required transfer of technology and equity. These countries have become increasingly vocal in the WTO on these concerns of 'biopiracy' and its link to the TRIPS Agreement.

This chapter aims to describe the obligations of IPRs on biotechnological inventions under TRIPS and their interpretation so far by developed and developing countries. It also examines the provisions of the CBD and the link between this treaty and the TRIPS Agreement (UNEP, 1999). This chapter is divided into three main sections: The first discusses the relevant provisions in the WTO TRIPS Agreement on biotechnology and some of the interpretation so far by developed and developing countries; the second discusses the link of biodiversity to IPRs and explains the relevant provisions of the CBD; the third outlines the prospects for the review of TRIPS provisions in the WTO on biotechnological inventions and this section is then followed by recommendations for the way forward for developing countries on these complex issues.

TRIPS AND BIOTECHNOLOGY

At the time of the negotiations on TRIPS in the Uruguay Round of multilateral trade negotiations, the US and the EU differed in their approaches to patenting biotechnological inventions. While the US believed that 'anything under the sun made by man', except for human beings, was patentable, the EU was grappling with strong internal resistance to patents on living organisms. Since the debate had not yet been settled in Europe, it was agreed to retain a minimal agreement while committing to revisit this provision within four years from the entry into force of TRIPS, namely by 1999. Article 27.3(b) of TRIPS incorporates this minimal agreement.

Patent protection for biotechnological inventions

Under Article 27, TRIPS obliges patents, for both processes and products, to be granted in all fields of technology. Article 27.3(b), however, allows the exclusion of plants and animals and of essentially biological processes for their production, from patent grant but obliges the protection of micro-organisms and micro-biological or non-biological processes for their production.

This exclusion goes beyond the exclusion of *plant and animal* varieties under the European Patent Convention, adopted in many other national patent laws of developed and developing countries. Thus, the TRIPS obligation is not subject to the definition of a variety, making some of the debate in Europe irrelevant in the interpretation of this provision. However, there is uncertainty over the definitions of certain terms such as *non-biological* or *essentially biological*. But clearly micro-organisms and microbiological processes were not excluded from patent protection, despite resistance from some developing countries. It is important to note that even during the TRIPS negotiations, the East Asian participants, notably Korea, Malaysia and Singapore, had no objections to the patenting of micro-organisms or microbiological processes.

TRIPS, in Article 28.2, extends the rights of process patentees to the product directly obtained from the patented process. Thus, patented microbiological processes would give their owners product-patent-like rights over the products produced directly with the use of these processes. Can WTO Members choose to exclude such rights if the products resulting from microbiological or other technical processes are plants and animals? The answer is not clear. The EU, for instance, does not allow such exclusion while Norway does. Both options, therefore, seem open at present.

TRIPS deals with the ethical, moral aspects of biotechnology (and other technologies) or biosafety by allowing under Article 27.2 patent exclusions of inventions 'the prevention within their territory of the commercial exploitation of which is necessary to protect *ordre public* or morality, including to protect human, animal or plant life or health or to avoid serious prejudice to the environment'. Thus, while such exclusions can be made, the caveat that the prohibition of commercial exploitation was necessary would apply. This also means that countries that choose to exercise this option would then forego the benefits of the new innovations. Clearly, TRIPS does not take away the right of countries to prohibit, restrict or condition the use of any invention even after patents are granted. Article 28 of TRIPS follows the universal principle in all national patent laws by only granting right holders the power to exclude others from using their protected products or processes without authorization. In other words, patent owners have a negative right to exclude others from using, but no positive right to use their inventions.

It is important to note that the three universally recognized criteria of patentability now incorporated into Article 27.1 of TRIPS – novelty, non-obviousness and industrial applicability or utility – also apply to biotechnological inventions. However, the distinction, relevant to patentability, between the *discovery* of something that exists in nature and the *invention* or *creation* of something new involving a pre-determined degree of human effort or intervention, is, in practice, difficult to make in the field of biotechnology. Almost all industrialized countries and some developing ones now allow the patenting of products of nature, if isolated by technical, non-obvious means. Utility is also broadly interpreted so that it is adequate if a future credible use is mentioned in the patent application. These terms are left undefined under TRIPS, leaving countries free to set higher standards to exclude trivial improvements or non-novel products or those whose utility is yet to be clearly determined.

One of the key concerns in the area of IPRs and biotechnology is the patenting of research tools or the grant of over-broad patents that could potentially block further useful research (Eisenberg, 1997). TRIPS provides a way out under Article 30 on exceptions to patent rights and Article 31 on other use without the authorization of the patentee. Article 30 allows limited exceptions to the exclusive rights conferred by a patent, 'provided that such exceptions do not unreasonably conflict with a normal exploitation of the patent and do not unreasonably prejudice the legitimate interests of the patent owner'. Significantly, under this provision TRIPS allows the legitimate interests of third parties to be taken into account. Most legal experts agree that under this provision non-commercial use of a patented product or process for research and experimental purposes would be permitted. Indeed, most patent laws allow this type of exception, the only difference being in how strictly they define *non-commercial*.

Article 31 goes further to vest WTO Members with the power to authorize third parties to use the patented invention even against the will of the patent owner under certain conditions. Significantly, the grounds on which such compulsory licences can be granted are not restricted under TRIPS. It is now widely accepted that, by and large, these conditions are not unduly constraining on developing country governments (Watal, 2001). In the case where the reason for such a grant is stated to be the working of a later patent, which cannot be done without infringing an earlier one, additional restrictive conditions apply. The second or subsequent patent must involve an important technical advance of considerable economic significance relative to the first patent and the owner of the first patent is equally entitled to cross-license the second patent on reasonable terms.

However, a note of caution is warranted: compulsory licences can, by definition, only help where the working of the invention does not require the cooperation of the patent owner. This is the case of *copiable* technologies. Where technologies are difficult to reverse engineer, notwithstanding the full disclosure requirements in patent law, such licences are less useful to developing countries. Biotechnological inventions meet the disclosure requirements by deposit of the starting biological material and there is an international treaty that governs the rules in this regard. Under these rules, the biological material is available to the public under certain conditions. However, even with this and a reading of the technical processes disclosed in a patent, biotechnological inventions may not always be easy to replicate. Indeed, the ability to reverse engineer such processes and products may vary significantly among different developing and least-developed countries, making the policy instrument of compulsory licences less useful than is widely believed.

Many other countries such as Japan, Australia, New Zealand, Korea and Singapore now have laws similar to the US's on the patenting of biotechnological inventions, including the patenting of plant and animal varieties. After a decade of discussion in the highest policy bodies, the European Union passed a new directive on the Legal Protection of Biotechnological Inventions in July 1998. Europe has now gone almost as far as the US on the patenting of biotechnological inventions as plants and animals per se are patentable, although plant and animal varieties are still excluded.

However, farmers' privilege to re-use patented plants or animals has been allowed. On the other hand, Canada and Norway exclude from patentability plants and animals per se, including their varieties, and even define micro-organisms narrowly. Developing countries, such as Argentina, Brazil and the Andean Group, that have implemented TRIPS so far, clearly allow patents only for micro-organisms and microbiological processes, excluding plants, animals, genes and other biological material even if isolated by technical processes. The Brazilian patent law has the clearest enunciation of this exclusion (Law No 9.279, Article 10.IX, May 1996, regulating rights and obligations relating to industrial property). In addition, these Latin American countries have clearly allowed for compulsory licences and research exemptions in their patent laws. Whether these interpretations are TRIPS-compatible or not will only be known if, after the expiry of the grace period allowed for TRIPS implementation to developing countries by January 2000, some of these issues are raised as WTO disputes.

Protection of plant varieties

Under 27.3(b) of TRIPS, if plants are excluded from patent protection, at least an effective *sui generis* system must be put in place for the protection of new plant varieties. In other words, plant breeders' rights (PBRs) are to be protected despite the optional exclusion from the patenting of plants. Countries can also opt to give both choices – patents and PBRs – for the protection of plants.

In contrast to the other subjects under TRIPS, there is no mention of adherence to the pre-existing international convention, UPOV, a French acronym for the International Union for the Protection of New Varieties of Plants, nor of any specific details on scope of coverage, term of protection and limitations to such protection. One possible reason for this is that, at the time of the TRIPS negotiations, a reference to UPOV 1978 was considered inadequate while reference to UPOV 1991 was premature, as it had not entered into force. Another reason for

the brevity of this provision could be that there was no agreement among industrialized countries themselves as to the details of an effective system of protection
for plant varieties. The end result is that countries are free to construct their own
individual regime for such protection, provided it meets the standard of
effectiveness.

Despite this considerable leeway given in TRIPS many read the term *effective*
as meaning UPOV-based legislation, some even going as far as reading a requirement to comply with the latest version of UPOV passed in 1991. This has led to
considerable controversy, with a variety of suggestions on what developing
countries should do in this area. Since it was UPOV 1978 that existed at the time
of the TRIPS negotiations, it could be considered as a model for developing
countries to frame their legislation, provided that they otherwise ensure TRIPS-
compatibility (OECD, 1996). Such a law may contain provisions for the 'breeders'
exemption', allowing the use of the protected variety for breeding purposes and may
also contain the 'farmers' privilege', allowing farmers to retain seed for their own
use or for across-the-fence non-commercial exchange or sales of seeds.

UPOV 1991, on the other hand, disallows some of this flexibility in that the
exchange or sale of seeds by farmers is disallowed and confines the breeders'
exemption to varieties that are not 'essentially derived' from the protected one.
There are other crucial differences, notably that the later version extends to all
genera and species, expands exclusive rights to patent-like rights of reproduction,
importing or stocking, extends exclusive rights to harvested materials such as cut
flowers, timber, fruits and lastly, extends the minimum term of protection from
15 years to 20 years for plants and vines, and from 18 years to 25 years for trees.
Both versions, however, allow restrictions on the free use of exclusive rights for
reasons of public interest, for example, through compulsory licences, subject to the
payment of an equitable remuneration to the right holder. The extension of time
given particularly to encourage developing countries to join UPOV 1978, ended
in April 1999. Only UPOV 1991 is open to Membership now. The differences
explain why developing countries preferred joining the 1978 version, although
some have adopted features in their laws that are close to the 1991 version.

Today several developed and developing countries have plant variety protection
laws that are modelled on UPOV, as evidenced by the 59 Members of UPOV of
which 14 are developing countries (as at September 2005), the latter bound only
to the 1978 version. These are, in the order that they joined during the period
1994–1997: Uruguay, Argentina, Chile, Colombia, Paraguay, Ecuador, Mexico,
Trinidad and Tobago, Kenya, Bolivia, Brazil, Panama, China and Nicaragua. South
Africa had joined as early as 1977 and has not elected to be a developing country
in the WTO. Bolivia, Colombia and Ecuador have PBR laws conforming substantially to UPOV (1991 version) as do other developing countries such as Morocco,
Costa Rica, Venezuela and soon Members of the Organisation Africaine de la
Propriété Intellectuelle (OAPI) in Francophone Africa. Argentina, Chile and
Mexico protect all genera and species even though they follow UPOV 1978. Many

other developing country exporters of cut flowers and ornamental plants like Kenya and Chile see effective PBR protection to be in their long-term interest as it facilitates access to new and better plant varieties.

Clearly, WTO developing country Members do not need to model their *sui generis* legislation on UPOV at all under TRIPS. However, the UPOV is the only international model available so far on PBRs and given the uncertainty on how the term 'effective' will be interpreted in a possible WTO dispute, following UPOV 1978 seems clearly a preferred option for many.

Trade secret protection

In discussions on TRIPS and biotechnology, trade secret protection is often overlooked. Trade secrets have to be protected in all WTO Members under Article 39 of TRIPS. In cases where there is little possibility of independent discovery, trade secret protection can be very useful as it can potentially last forever. Breeders of new plant or animal varieties often keep the parent lines secret. Such protection is usually quite effective for double-cross hybrid plant varieties as their first crossed parent lines can be closely guarded, while the subsequent seeds of such hybrids will not reproduce the same desired characteristics true to type. However, the disadvantage of such protection is that it does not protect the breeder against independent discovery by fair means. Usually, trade secrets are used to supplement and not substitute other IPRs, as sometimes such technological protection may not be as strong as it appears. Newer technologies are being invented to strengthen such *technological protection*, giving rise to widespread protests, particularly in developing countries (Simpson, 1997).

INTELLECTUAL PROPERTY RIGHTS AND BIODIVERSITY CONSERVATION

The link between IPRs and biodiversity emanates from the concept of *bioprospecting*. In searching for new chemical entities or useful characteristics, some research-based industries have found it profitable to screen natural sources such as soil samples, marine waters, insects, tropical plants and genes in developing countries. Some feel that, as compared to the conventional system of screening millions of synthesized chemicals, bioprospecting, especially if further based on traditional knowledge, may even cut costs of pharmaceutical R&D by half. The link to IPRs arises from the fact that in many instances, the bioprospectors or their licensees are granted patent rights over these products, without any acknowledgement of the contribution of countries/regions of origin or of indigenous communities. Developing countries are demanding that when profits are reaped through bioprospecting, benefits and technologies developed should be shared with the original suppliers of genetic resources or traditional knowledge.

Another question linked to this demand is the conceptualization of a new type of IPR or other legal or economic system that recognizes the innovative contributions that farmers and indigenous communities have made over generations using locally available natural resources, so that these are not freely appropriated by others. Many argue that if these measures are not taken, there would be little incentive for people in developing countries to maintain or to enhance Earth's biodiversity, which may, in turn, harm research and development for medicines or useful agricultural products.

However, others believe that with the recent[2] advances in combinatorial chemistry, biological compounds can be synthesized and that this route would be increasingly pursued if access to genetic resources is made more difficult. In addition, recent research by economists has also shown that the value of biodiversity for use in pharmaceutical research may be as low as a few cents per hectare even in the world's biodiversity *hot spots* and that this may not significantly contribute to preserving biodiversity (Roht-Arriaza, 1996). Certainly, to date, few countries have obtained significant financial returns and it is presently not evident that controlling genetic access will be effective or profitable.

It is in the wake of the recent advances in biotechnology and the extension of patent protection to living organisms, that both developed and developing countries realized the importance of access to genetic resources. This was the basis for the conclusion of the Convention on Biological Diversity (CBD) in 1992 at Rio de Janeiro. The CBD reaffirms that countries have sovereign rights over their own biological resources, including genetic resources, and calls for the fair and equitable sharing of the benefits arising out of the utilization of genetic resources. The problem lies in the ambiguous wording of and lack of credible enforcement mechanisms for the provisions of the CBD.

Access to genetic resources is governed by Article 15 of the CBD. Such access has to be on mutually agreed terms (Article 15.4) and subject to prior informed consent (Article 15.5). The results of research and development and the benefits arising from the commercial and other utilization of genetic resources have to be shared in a fair and equitable way with the country providing such resources, on mutually agreed terms (Article 15.7). It is not clear in this context what 'fair and equitable' means as these terms are to be agreed mutually and as there is no effective international arbitration envisaged on this. In addition, botanical gardens and seed banks may have up to one third of the world's plant species collected well before the CBD. The CBD does not require such banks to adopt policies of prior approval by countries holding the original genetic resources for previous collections. This means that these genetic resources can be accessed without any obligation to share benefits with the source countries (Dove, 1998). This is one of the difficult issues in the negotiations in the FAO where there is some support for treating such samples on a par with the post-CBD samples.

Under Article 16 of the CBD, access to genetic resources is juxtaposed against requirements on the transfer of technology, including biotechnology. Article 16 enjoins parties to provide access to and transfer of technology 'under fair and most favourable terms, including on concessional and preferential terms' to the countries providing the genetic resources. For technologies covered by IPRs these terms must be '*consistent with the adequate and effective protection of intellectual property rights*' and '*in accordance with international law*' (emphasis added). Nevertheless, parties are to cooperate, '*subject to national and international law*', to ensure that IPRs are supportive of and do not run counter to the objectives of the CBD. The ambiguous, and sometimes contradictory, wording of this article reflects the difficulties encountered in the negotiations: of reconciling the demand of developing countries to fair access to technologies involving the use of their genetic resources and the position of developed countries on respecting IPRs. In the end, the compromise reached on this provision has given rise to as many contentious issues as it set out to solve. Article 27 and Annex II of the CBD deals with the settlement of disputes between parties on the interpretation of the treaty but this is not subject to the strict time limits and punitive trade sanctions as in the WTO dispute settlement mechanism.

Developing countries and some environmental non-governmental organizations (NGOs) claim that TRIPS needs to be reconciled with the CBD. However, the terms 'adequate and effective protection' of IPRs originate from the US trade law, which envisages unilateral action against countries not according such a level of protection, and similar wording is repeated in the preamble to the TRIPS Agreement. Thus, it would appear that the language in the CBD safeguards the interests of intellectual property right holders in the biotechnology industry, to the extent provided for in TRIPS.

The issue of knowledge, innovations and practices of indigenous and local communities is addressed in Article 8(j). Parties are encouraged to share the benefits arising from the utilization of such knowledge equitably 'as far as possible', 'as appropriate' and subject to national legislation. 'Farmers' rights', or compensation to local farming communities for collective improvements to plant varieties, is not specifically addressed under this article of the CBD but countries are free to frame their legislation on this subject. This concern was first discussed in the FAO's International Undertaking on Plant Genetic Resources in 1989, which recognized that PBRs were not incompatible with its objective of access to and sustainable use of plant genetic resources.

Some point out that at the time of this resolution the prevailing international law on PBRs was UPOV 1978, but do not explain why UPOV 1991 has changed this situation in any fundamental way (Correa, 1999). Presently, negotiations are in progress in the FAO to reconcile the Undertaking with the CBD and define the content of farmers' rights. However, few countries have actually introduced legislation rewarding such rights. Much more work needs to be done in international fora to conceptualize these issues in clearer terms.

Given the unclear and ambiguous language of the CBD and the near absence of national legislation on bioprospecting until recently, the commercialization of biotechnological products and processes, based on genetic resources obtained from developing countries, continues to be based on free market principles of demand and supply. Only a few companies voluntarily share benefits on mutually agreed terms in return for access to genetic resources or traditional knowledge (Otten, 1994). However, more time is required to judge whether legislation will work towards improving or restricting access to genetic resources and whether developing countries would benefit substantively from it.

There is a fear that patents will be granted directly for biological products taken from developing countries. By definition, patents cannot be granted for substances that exist in nature or traditional knowledge taken as it is, as these do not fulfil the criterion of novelty. However, the procedures followed in determining the novelty of patentable inventions differ even among industrialized countries. Developing countries rightly believe that patent systems that are not based on searching both the written and oral prior art for worldwide novelty, such as that of the US, and that do not insist on disclosure of the origin and proof of prior informed consent, as few countries do today, for the use of the biological materials or traditional knowledge on which the invention is based, help in perpetuating the iniquitous system.

In one of the most coherent demands made, India had demanded an amendment to Article 29 of TRIPS in the WTO Committee on Trade and Environment on conditions that can be imposed on patent applicants to incorporate adequate disclosure of country of origin. In recent discussion, developing countries have extended their demand to prior informed consent (PIC). They could argue that without an amendment to TRIPS, there is no legal basis for benefit-sharing, such as those based conceptually on *reach-through* agreements or co-inventorship that are already established patent law practices in developed countries.

Also, without easy access to the knowledge of patent filing, no opposition proceedings can be planned or contracts negotiated on mutually agreed terms. Developed countries argue that disclosure of origin is already required by most patent offices but that PIC, at this initial stage when the commercial value is not clearly known, may be unnecessarily burdensome on patent applicants. In addition, there are problems in correctly identifying the country of origin (International Chamber of Commerce, 1998). It is possible to counter these arguments with more practical solutions, but clearly this is the strategy that should be followed. In the run-up to the 1999 WTO Ministerial Conference, demands relating to biodiversity made by a large number of developing countries dominated the discussions on the review of Article 27.3(b).

REVIEW OF TRIPS ARTICLE 27.3(B)

Built into Article 27.3(b) of TRIPS is a provision for this clause to be reviewed four years after the date of entry into force of the WTO (that is, any time after

1999). At the time of the TRIPS negotiations it was expected that, after the passing of the European Biotechnology Directive, united pressure could be placed on developing countries by the US, Europe and Japan in 1999 for the acceptance of patents on all eligible biotechnological inventions, including plants and animals. Clearly, research-based agricultural biotechnology companies would be particularly interested in plant patents since PBRs, with breeders' exemption and farmers' privilege, may not be sufficient to recoup their investment on R&D. While farmers' privilege may, to some extent, be restricted by the use of hybrids or in the future possibly by using the so-called genetic use restriction technologies (GURTs), breeders cannot legally or technically be excluded under PBRs.

The US had made preliminary proposals on the built-in agenda in the WTO, including on TRIPS, in November 1998 (Watal, 1998, pp281–307). In the context of biotechnology, these proposals call for an examination of the desirability of eliminating the exclusion for plants and animals, and incorporation of the key provisions of UPOV on plant variety protection. The US has, however, not pressed for any immediate modification to TRIPS on biotechnological inventions. On the other hand, United States Trade Representative officials have repeatedly stated in public that the focus for the next few years would be on implementation and dispute settlement rather than on strengthening TRIPS further.

This position reflects that of the international business community, which is reluctant to reopen the debate on Article 27.3(b) (ASSINSEL, 1999). One reason could be that some view this as risky as it would endanger the advances already made in Europe in this area, given the fact that there is not yet complete legal certainty on this issue and that European protection is not yet at the US level. Moreover, as many countries have time up to January 2000 to change their laws to implement this provision of TRIPS, it may be considered premature to review this so early. One more reason for such caution could be the preparations being made by developing countries to demand changes in TRIPS. Paradoxically, in the preparations for the 1999 WTO Ministerial meeting, there were many more proposals for changing the TRIPS text on Article 27.3(b) from developing countries than from developed countries.

In a recent proposal in the WTO an important group of developing countries from Latin America, Africa and Asia have proposed substantive revisions to Article 27.3(b) of TRIPS to incorporate their concerns on biodiversity, equity and transfer of technology (WTO, 1999a). They have demanded that the review of the provision clarify artificial distinctions between biological and microbiological organisms and processes, ensure traditional farming practices and prevent anti-competitive practices.

Some fear that the term 'micro-organism' could be interpreted as extending to genes and even to plants and animals, and call for a clarification in TRIPS that the option to exclude from patentability extends to micro-organisms and micro-biological processes (WTO, 1999b; WTO, 1998). India, supported by other countries, has gone as far as to demand the prohibition of patents inconsistent with

Article 15 of the CBD, although it is not clear what such consistency would entail. Some African countries are also demanding that the period for the implementation of Article 27.3(b) should be extended further and should end five years from the date of the completion of the review.

It is not clear how far these proposals represent negotiating tactics as opposed to real interests. It is also difficult to see how a definition of ambiguous terms favourable to developing countries, even less their exclusion, could be adopted by consensus in the WTO, raising the question whether these countries are better off with the current ambiguity. It is also unclear how much developing countries are willing to trade off to obtain their demands on the biodiversity set of issues. But *demandeurs* for strengthened IPR protection may have reason to fear further weakening of the TRIPS text in any premature review, particularly given the support to developing countries from powerful developed country NGO groups.

THE WAY FORWARD FOR DEVELOPING COUNTRIES

To conclude, the TRIPS provisions on patents for biotechnological inventions already allow considerable leeway to developing countries through exclusions from patent grant, ambiguous wording and exceptions to patent rights. Indeed, these provisions have been implemented in a number of different ways by both developed and developing countries. Ambiguities on these and on plant variety protection will only be resolved if and when these are settled in a future WTO dispute or in future negotiations. Instead of demanding clarifications on these ambiguities in the WTO, a task rendered difficult by the existing process of decision-making by consensus, developing countries are better off interpreting them in reasonable and clearly defensible ways.

Intellectual property rights for biotechnological inventions, however, do pose complex problems relating to access to technologies, unfair exploitation of genetic resources and fair and equitable sharing of the financial benefits. Although steps are necessary to preserve existing biodiversity and enhance equity in international obligations, financial benefits from genetic access legislation may often be exaggerated. Certainly, it would be paradoxical if these countries forego the potential benefits of biotechnology to solve some of their most pressing problems of poverty, disease and malnutrition on account of exaggerated fears or hopes.

Clearly, the more important policy objective should be to develop competitive skills in research in biotechnology. For this, local firms, in both the public and private sector, must be encouraged through the grant of adequate and effective IPR protection, at least up to the level obligatory currently under TRIPS. Some developing countries have already seen the wisdom of going on to the next stage of granting patents for plants, genes and animals and many others may do so, once domestic research capabilities in biotechnology improve. It should be noted that the grant of IPRs does not necessarily preclude the dissemination of these technologies or products by public institutions to certain groups or areas either free or at reasonable prices.

Yet patents should not permit the blocking of research or competition in these areas through over-broad grants, and competition policy instruments should be instituted and used. To safeguard against the adverse effects of restricting competition, liberal use should be made of the flexibility available under TRIPS to grant compulsory licences in cases of egregious anti-competitive behaviour by right holders or for gaining access to essential blocking patents. No further amendments are needed to TRIPS for this purpose.

However, given the existing technological gap between lead developed and developing countries and the capital-intensive nature of product development, the best way forward for developing countries seems to be collaboration and not confrontation. Multilateral developmental institutions should also be encouraged to help developing countries make the transition to a higher level of capability in biotechnology through both financial and technical assistance for R&D projects, including those to obtain and defend IPRs.

Such institutions could even consider playing the role of the *honest broker* in the purchase of core, privately developed IPR-covered biotechnological inventions in essential areas, such as important and unique food crops or medicines, in order to ensure their widest dissemination, at reasonable costs to poorer countries. This could be achieved by, in turn, sub-licensing production to the cheapest possible sources in the world, most likely the larger developing countries and perhaps, even further subsidizing the protected products at the point of consumption. As long as these poorer markets are effectively segregated to prevent arbitrage, this could help resolve the conflict between rewarding private innovations through IPRs for generating such useful technologies and ensuring their widest possible use in and benefit to poorest, least-developed countries.

For private IPR holders the trade-off between volumes and value should make such open licensing beneficial, as they would obtain sales/royalties that were not otherwise possible. Indeed, there are parallels to such trade-offs in the information technology and telecommunications sector, where IPR holders voluntarily submit their IPRs to open licensing at reasonable terms in order to benefit from incorporation of their proprietary technologies into industry-wide standards set by industry associations, governments or international bodies.

None of these options on collaboration with IPR holders are foreclosed by TRIPS and developing countries may see wisdom in not reopening negotiations on the TRIPS text for the present. Proposals on the biodiversity set of issues can and should be raised, in appropriately concrete terms, only to counter developed countries' demands for further protection of biotechnological inventions under TRIPS. Till such time, the present TRIPS text is sufficiently flexible to accommodate solutions to problems raised by developing countries so far.

NOTES

1 The paper which forms the basis of this chapter, was completed before Ms Watal joined the WTO and does not necessarily reflect the views of the WTO Secretariat nor of WTO Members individually or collectively and does not purport to present authoritative interpretations of WTO provisions, which can only be done by WTO Members acting jointly.

2 This paper was written in 1999 and is therefore out of date with respect to developments since then. However, its arguments reflect relevant views in the current debate on biotechnology meriting reproduction in this book. This article first appeared in the *International Journal of Biotechnology*, vol 2, nos 1–3, 2000, Copyright © 2000 Inderscience Enterprises Ltd, and is reproduced with the kind permission of the copyright owners. The *International Journal of Biotechnology* and other relevant journals are available in both hard copy and on-line formats. More information is available at www.inderscience.com.

REFERENCES

ASSINSEL (1999) *Fostering Plant Innovation: ASSINSEL Brief on Review of TRIPS 27.3b*, available at www.worldseed.org

Correa, C M (1999) 'Access to plant genetic resources and intellectual property rights', *Background Study Paper No 8*, Commission on Genetic Resources for Food and Agriculture, FAO, April, available at www.fao.org

Dove, A (1998) 'Botanical gardens cope with bioprospecting loophole', *Science*, vol 283, 28 August, p1273

Eisenberg, R S (1997) *Competition Between Public and Private Research Funding in the Bayh-Dole Era*, working paper, University of Michigan Law School, Michigan, US

International Chamber of Commerce (1998) *Policy Statement: The Review of TRIPS Article 27.3*, 1 July, at www.iccwbo.org

OECD (1996) *Intellectual Property: Technology Transfer and Genetic Resources*, Organisation for Economic Co-operation and Development, Paris

Otten, A (1994) 'The Uruguay Round TRIPS Agreement: Implications for the protection of plant varieties', presentation at the workshop on 'Intellectual property rights in relation to agricultural and microbial biotechnology', Madras, 7 March, photocopy

Roht-Arriaza, N (1996) 'Of seeds and shamans: The appropriation of the scientific and technical knowledge of indigenous and local communities', *Michigan Journal of International Law*, vol 17, summer, pp919–965

Simpson, D R (1997) 'Biodiversity prospecting: Shopping the wilds is not the key to conservation', in *Resources*, vol 126, Resources for the Future, Washington DC, available at www.rff.org

UNEP (1999) 'Consequences of the use of the new technology for the control of plant gene expression for the conservation and sustainable use of biological diversity', *UNEP/CBD/SBSTTA/4/9/Rev1*, dated 17 May 1999, a report to the 4th meeting of the SBSTTA, Montreal, 21–25 June 1999, available at www.biodiv.org

Watal, J (1998) 'The trips agreement and developing countries – strong, weak or balanced protection?', *Journal of World Intellectual Property*, vol 1, no 2, pp281–307

Watal, J (2001) *Intellectual Property Rights in the WTO and Developing Countries*, Kluwer Law International

WTO (1998) WT/GC/W/115, Communication from the United States on General Council discussion on mandated negotiations and the built-in agenda, dated 19 November 1998, available at http://docsonline.wto.org/

WTO (1999a) WT/GC/W/355, Communication from Cuba, Dominican Republic, Egypt, El Salvador, Honduras, India, Indonesia, Malaysia, Nigeria, Pakistan, Sri Lanka and Uganda on implementation issues to be addressed at Seattle, dated 11 October 1999, available at http://docsonline.wto.org/

WTO (1999b) WT/GC/W/302, Communication from Kenya on behalf of the African group, dated 6 August 1999, available at http://docsonline.wto.org/

9

Closing in on Biopiracy: Legal Dilemmas and Opportunities for the South

Jakkrit Kuanpoth

Many complex ecosystems could be mines of green gold – medicines, new crop varieties and other benefits for the entire world. It's only fair that the countries with such resources benefit from their exploitation.

(Pascal Lamy, EU Trade Commissioner, addressing the World Trade Organization Council for Trade-related Aspects of Intellectual Property Rights, September 2002)

Issues of access to genetic resources, the protection of traditional knowledge (TK) and benefit-sharing are of great concern to developing countries. The current system for the protection of intellectual property does not suit the needs of developing countries in this regard. In order to safeguard their interest, developing countries should adopt a *sui generis* system that meets the needs of indigenous people and other local communities and their knowledge and protects the richness of Southern ecosystems. While acknowledging the risks involved in developing archives of TK and genetic resources, I argue for their creation as a step to defend Southern bio-resources from illicit appropriation. The legal dilemmas and options developing countries are faced with are discussed with a view to establishing the means that can facilitate benefit-sharing and equitable use of ethnobiological resources.

MINES OF *GREEN GOLD*

Biological resources of plants and animals are to biotechnology what steam was to the industrial revolution. Ever since two Cambridge scientists, Francis Crick and

James Watson, discovered deoxyribonucleic acid (DNA) in 1953, they opened up vast opportunities to search for new drugs and crops with the help of biotechnological methods, and biotechnological products such as antibiotics, steroids, vitamins and vaccines are estimated to account for nearly 30 per cent of the world drug market (Correa, 1991, p47).

The major difference between inventions of the past and modern biotechnology is that biotechnology products are living organisms capable of replicating and dying (Bent et al, 1987, pp6–7; Cooper, 1985). Bio-inventions are mainly of three types: new varieties of plants, new animal breeds and new micro-organisms. The methods used to produce them are either conventional selective breeding of plants and animals or modern techniques of genetic engineering (WIPO, 1984, p4; Bull et al, 1982, p1). Genetic engineering basically joins up pieces of the DNA of different organisms to produce an organism with new genetic traits.

Southern nations rich in *green gold* see opportunities in the nascent sector of biotechnology. Most of the rare plants and animals containing the 'universal clay' used in biotechnology are found in the South. The origins of the 20 most important food crops and the 20 most important industrial plant species shows that more than 90 per cent of the germplasm of these species originates in developing countries (Crucible Group, 1994).

The opportunities for the South include the possibility of contributing to progress in medical technologies. Evolving biotechnological methods are being used to identify medicinal properties in plants that might result in the discovery of new potent drugs. It is estimated that about two-thirds of the world's plant species possess potential medicinal value (Crucible Group, 1994). And according to the United Nations Development Programme (UNDP), over 7000 medical compounds widely used in modern medicine, from aspirin to birth control pills, are isolated from plants (UNDP, 1999).

Traditional knowledge, which refers to any knowledge, innovation, or collective practice of indigenous peoples or local communities, is significant in biotechnological research. For thousand of years, people in the farming communities have made genetic improvement by selecting crops. Traditional healers have long known the medical properties of plants. This knowledge can be used as a starting point in the discovery and development of useful products. Genetic resources are often used as raw material for product development. There is no doubt that access to the resources and the knowledge associated with those resources can help research-based companies to discover, isolate and/or synthesize useful substances in their laboratories. The companies can save a considerable amount of money and time by using TK to guide the selection of promising species. For example, a pharmaceutical company may search the early literature and collect plants used as medicines by traditional healers and turn them into essential medicines (Blakeney, 1997). Today, as much as 75 per cent of all medical compounds can be linked to knowledge of indigenous people in developing countries (UNDP, 1999). The value of the South's TK is estimated to be as high as US$43 billion (Blakeney, 1997).

PATENTING BIOTECHNOLOGY: THE STORY SO FAR

The debate over patents on life has emerged largely as a response to the booming commerce of bio-inventions over the past 30 years. Initially patents were adopted to protect inanimate inventions in fields such as chemistry and physics. Although biological processes and products have been used in industries for a long time, biotechnological inventions were normally excluded from patentability (Beier et al, 1985, p25). The reasoning for this is that living organisms possess special features such as the ability to replicate, making it difficult to impose strict protection.

The first landmark court ruling that allowed patenting of life came about in 1969. The German *Red Dove* case ruling that an animal-breeding technique was patentable upheld, for the first time in a European court, that a biotechnological method was eligible for patent protection.[1] The second landmark case was a patent awarded in 1980 by the US Supreme Court in *Diamond v Chakrabarty* (United States Patents Quarterly, 1980) on a bacterium in which a plasmid from another strain had been inserted. The Court held that 'anything under the sun made by man' was capable of patenting. What could be patented under US law did not depend on whether the invention was living matter, but on whether it was a result of nature or made by human.

By 1980 two different lines of thought on patenting life emerged. On the one hand, legal thinking had been warming to the growth of the new biotechnology industry. US laws allow the complete patenting of life, to protect the research in the fast growing biotechnology industry. Nonetheless, in other parts of the world society reserves a second thought on the moral and practical dilemmas of patenting life down to humans and animals.

European legislation on patenting life is an example of the more restrictive type of patent system. The European Patent Convention (EPC) Article 53 (b) prohibits the patenting of particular types of biotechnology:

> *European patents shall not be granted in respect of:*
>
> *(b) plant or animal varieties or essentially biological processes for the production of plants or animals; this provision does not apply to microbiological processes or the products thereof.*

The excluded subject matters under European law include plant varieties, animal varieties and essentially biological processes; microbiological processes and the products thereof are still patentable.

Between the two schools of thought there is a set of minimum obligations shared by all countries that constitutes the common legal ground on patent law internationally. Signatories to the World Trade Organization (WTO) Agreement on Trade-related Aspects of Intellectual Property Rights (TRIPS) have been complying with a given set of minimum standards regarding patents, copyrights and intellectual property rights (IPR) instruments since 1995. The TRIPS Agreement leaves it up to a country to adopt additional patent laws on a domestic level over and above these minimum requirements adopted by WTO Members.

According to the TRIPS Agreement, Members commit themselves to provide intellectual property protection in several areas. Article 27.1 stipulates that *'patents shall be available for any inventions, whether products or processes, in all fields of technology'*. Article 27.3(b) allows Member States to exclude plants and animals (other than micro-organisms) from patent protection. The same applies to essentially biological processes for the production of plants or animals other than non-biological and microbiological processes. Countries, however, must provide protection for plant varieties either by patents, by a *sui generis* system (that means *of its own kind*) or by a combination thereof. This provision is currently under review in the TRIPS Council; it could be reworded, deleted, modified in any other way or kept in its current form.

TRIPS: Free-riding on the South's genetic resources and TK

Free trade should not mean free use of developing country resources. However, there are no legal instruments to stop biopiracy of the South's bio-resources and TK. And while Western inventive activity relies on intellectual property law for protection, collective innovation is deemed incapable of patenting under the TRIPS Agreement. [2]

The TRIPS Agreement only acknowledges certain types of innovation that have different *formal* characteristics from traditional innovation. Under the TRIPS Agreement, an invention may be patented if it is new, involves an inventive step and is capable of industrial application. This type of definition fails to provide an interface between the formal IPR system and the customary legal systems that apply to traditional innovation. It does so in a number of ways presented below.

Under the current patent law, patents are granted only for what is new compared to the state of the art and only to the first to invent or file the application, depending on national legislation. Therefore it is almost impossible for TK owners to claim ownership by applying for patent rights. Since TK is basically transferred from one generation to another and its details have always been laid open for public scrutiny, it is not considered a patentable invention. In addition, since no actual inventor can be identified, this raises the question of who is the first inventor of the knowledge that is entitled to patent application.

In addition, under patent law the local community and TK owner are not considered as joint inventors under the concept of joint inventorship. Joint inventorship means that each inventor must have contributed to the inventive thought and to the final result. This condition creates difficulties for the users or owners of TK, who have no demonstrable role in the final conception. In fact, the owners of TK are only the providers of basic knowledge that leads to the invention.

The protection of TK and genetic resources as copyright works has also proved difficult. This is because copyright does not protect the idea itself, but only protects the way the idea is expressed. For TK protection to be meaningful, it is necessary to allow local communities to control the exploitation of the information disclosed in the text, which is not the case under copyright law.

It is also difficult to protect TK under the law of trade secret. TK is characterized as shared information which is often known among several indigenous people, thus making it difficult to fulfil the basic condition of trade secret protection (namely, that the information has been kept secret).[3] Secret information is protected as long as the owner successfully prevents it from falling into the public domain, but the crucial question is how to prove that the knowledge widely used in local communities is still in secrecy.

Trademarks and geographical indications[4] may be used to protect reputation and goodwill of the goods associated with TK. The unfair use of a name, as in the jasmati case (see Box 9.1) can be prevented by these two pieces of law. The laws can deter unfair competition by allowing the TK owners to block marketing of unauthorized products. However, like copyright, trademarks and geographical indications do not provide legal means to protect the ethnobotanical knowledge as such.

From the above it emerges that if intellectual property law is to give efficient protection to Southern genetic resources and TK, it has to be revised substantially. The legal framework of the TRIPS Agreement has to be broadened and has to include a context for benefit-sharing between the Southern providers of genetic resources and Northern biotechnology industry in a fair and equitable manner.

OTHER POSSIBILITIES FOR PROTECTING BIO-RESOURCES AND TK

At present there are no legal instruments or standards that protect indigenous peoples and local communities from the biopiracy of their biological resources and associated knowledge. According to the existing intellectual property law, only the North's industrial model of innovation is recognized. The collective system of innovation of traditional communities is excluded from the legal protection. The only possible course of action for developing countries to protect their genetic resources and associated knowledge from biopiracy is therefore setting up domestic laws that meet local needs for regulation of access to genetic resources and TK. Besides domestic laws, developing countries can look to the Convention on Biological Diversity (CBD) for support in fair access to genetic resources and benefit-sharing. Moreover, Parties to the CBD are required to:

BOX 9.1 THE CASE OF JASMINE RICE

Biopiracy in its many forms continues to threaten developing countries' sovereignty over their genetic resources. TK and genetic resources of the South are often branded and patented as products or intellectual property of foreign companies and individuals. Southern states' already overburdened regulatory mechanisms are not in a position to tackle biopiracy in its various forms. Smuggling of rare plants and animals is but one case of assault on the South's riches. In other cases, such as that of jasmine rice, fending off theft of the resources or attempts to free-ride on their market reputation is more complicated. The crucial question for the South is how to protect its genetic resources and ensure fair and equitable benefit-sharing.

Regarded as the highest quality rice by gourmets both in Thailand and internationally, jasmine is well known for its long, slender and translucent grain. When cooked, jasmine rice is shiny, soft and tender with a strongly aromatic flavour. The variety originates in the eastern part of Thailand, Chachoengsao. A government campaign launched it as a premium national export product and since 1959 jasmine rice has been farmed across Thailand. The Northeast region's saline and sandy soil produces the highest quality grain.

Thailand's exports depend heavily on jasmine rice. The variety accounts for over 25 per cent of Thailand's rice exports. Not only is it vital to the livelihoods of millions of Thailand's small farmers, but the market for jasmine rice has been growing, representing high stakes for Thailand's economy as a whole. Currently, jasmine rice is one of Thailand's most important export products to destinations including Southeast Asian countries, the EU, the US, Africa, the Middle East and China.

However, unfair competition by a US company has exposed Thailand's premium trade to unforeseen dangers. In an effort to capture market share into the jasmine rice market, a US company introduced a brand name that Thailand says attempts to mislead consumers to believe it is jasmine rice. In September 1997, Texas-based Rice Tec Inc sought to register a trademark *jasmati* in several countries. The brand name was moreover claimed to represent a *Texas-grown copy of jasmine rice from Thailand*, which fuelled Thailand's suspicions of unfair play. Rice Tec's jasmati rice has nothing to do with the jasmine or basmati rice (basmati being an Indian and Pakistani variety). In fact, the Texan rice was grown from a parent variety of jasmati originating from the Piedmont area of Italy. Naming its Italian rice *jasmati* misleads the consumer to confuse the Italian variety for Thailand's jasmine rice. Such intentional fraud at the expense of the consumer is a tort under US unfair competition law. The confusion can turn out to harm the market for Thailand's jasmine rice as consumers mistake Thai rice for another, or associate it with fraudulent market behaviour.

Four years after the attack of Rice Tec, an even greater assault on Thailand's jasmine rice was launched. This time, the attempt to develop a local market substitute for Thailand's export rice came from the US Department of Agriculture (USDA). In November 2001, a US researcher, Chris Deren, publicly admitted launching a project to genetically modify the Thai Jasmine rice variety so that it could be farmed in the US. The USDA works through the Everglades Research and Education Center at the University of Florida under the *Stepwise Program for Improvement of Jasmine Rice*. The project aims to develop a new variety of jasmine rice suited to the mechanized farming practices of the US and less sunny weather conditions.

If the US attempt to develop genetically modified jasmine rice goes unchecked, Thailand's trade will receive a great blow. Not only would the US farm for its own market, but it might penetrate other export markets now provided for by Thailand. Thus, a serious chain reaction against Thai-grown rice might be started in the international market place. With Thailand's rice farming sector undermined, the economic livelihoods of millions of poor Thai farmers would be jeopardized.

Source: ETC Group (former RAFI), 2001

respect, preserve and maintain knowledge, innovations and practices of indigenous and local communities embodying traditional lifestyles relevant for the conservation and sustainable use of biological diversity and promote the wider application with the approval and involvement of the holders of such knowledge, innovations and practices and encourage the equitable sharing of the benefits arising from the utilization of such knowledge, innovations and practices. (Article 8j)

Within the TRIPS Agreement, there are substantial opportunities for developing countries to implement intellectual property regulations that meet their own particular needs. The main source of flexibility is that countries may exceed the minimum standards that are mandatory for WTO Member countries and set up additional regulatory mechanisms in the area of intellectual property rights. Plant varieties is one case where countries enjoy significant freedom to choose their own tools of protection, which can be either patents or an effective *sui generis* system or any combination thereof (Leskien and Flitner, 1997, pp26–32).[5] The conventional conditions of plant variety protection, being new, distinct, uniform and stable, can be altered substantially. That is because the TRIPS Agreement does not define the term *effective sui generis system*, its scope or the obligations and standards that would apply under such a system. In addition, the Agreement does not refer to any international convention relating to plant variety protection.

Unlike the economic aim of Western intellectual property law, the objective of domestic IPRs designed by developing countries should also be to protect TK (Blakeney, 1999). Rural communities play a continuing role in creating, maintaining and enhancing knowledge related to bio-inventions, but often none of the commercial gains of bio-inventions trickle down to them. Ideally, IPRs should ensure that economic incentives are working for conservation, development and commercial gain all at once (Reid et al, 1995, pp1–2). One practical means of achieving this is by making the disclosure of origin of bio-inventions mandatory for the award of intellectual property claims (see Box 9.2).

Another concern to be addressed by a *sui generis* law is ensuring prior informed consent (PIC) in access to genetic resources and traditional knowledge. Prior informed consent depends in turn on ensuring that a set of conditions are satisfied. For instance, applicants must seek PIC adequately in advance and consent must be limited to specific uses of the genetic resource. Moreover, PIC must take into account that the value of the commercial application that stands to be invented from bio-resources will remain unknown for some time. Accordingly, PIC must be subject to modification as the value of bio-inventions changes in the future.

In addition, many elements of national *sui generis* systems such as the law to protect TK may be included under the national legislation. The protection of additional subject matter will comply with the TRIPS Agreement's rule of minimum standards, which stipulates that Member States may provide more extensive protection (for example, providing a term of protection longer than

BOX 9.2 CRACKING DOWN ON BIOPIRACY: DISCLOSURE OF ORIGIN GAINS MOMENTUM IN THE WTO

A long-standing proposal developing countries have been pushing for in the TRIPS Council is to require patent applicants to disclose the origin of bio-resources and associated TK used in inventions. Currently, the lack of obligation under the TRIPS Agreement to state a source of origin for the patented product makes it possible for the biotech industry to get away with pirating Southern resources. The South on the other hand does not have the means to verify the origin of genetic material and associated knowledge involved in each and every patent. Clearly, this failure of the TRIPS Agreement helps the biotech industry to free-ride at the expense of the South whose genetic resources are up for grabs.

Several proposals from a group of developing countries, led by Brazil and India and supported by the Africa Group, to require patent applicants to declare the geographical origin of bio-material used in inventions – together with evidence of prior informed consent and benefit-sharing – have gained some momentum in the TRIPS Council.[6] The EC has also agreed to examine and discuss the possible introduction of an obligation for patent applicants to disclose the geographical origin of any genetic resources and TK used in inventions.[7] Switzerland, while favourable to discussing the issue of origin declaration, would prefer an amendment to the World Intellectual Property Organization's Patent Cooperation Treaty that would enable countries to require patent applicants to declare the source of the genetic resources and TK in patent applications.[8]

This effort could broker a fairer deal for developing countries, but its reception by the TRIPS Council is still unknown. The US continues to oppose any discussion on this issue in the TRIPS Council, arguing that disclosure requirements would be incompatible with the TRIPS Agreement. In the end, it might be left to developing countries to take the initiative to protect TK and their genetic resources, as discussed below.

Source: BRIDGES Trade BioRes (undated)

required for patents, trademarks and so on) as long as the additional rights do not contravene the provision of the TRIPS Agreement.[9]

An important legal question developing countries have to address is who should be regarded as the owner of TK. The law may either place ethnobotanical knowledge under the sovereign right of the state, or it may provide rights over such knowledge to an individual. So, for instance, rights over traditional medicine may be conferred on a traditional healer. Alternatively, TK may be subject to the collective rights of the local community and regarded as a community-based property.

In addition, developing countries have to choose between two types of protection: protection through registration and automatic protection. Registration requires TK or bio-resources to be archived by an individual or a community whereas automatic protection allows TK to remain a trade secret. In the case of automatic protection, access to such knowledge can then be negotiated through individual contracts that usually take the form of a material transfer agreement (MTA).

There are costs and benefits in both cases of automatic and registered protection. Like the system of trade secret protection, the automatic protection is easy to obtain, but may cause confusion as to who is the actual owner of the knowledge, especially when two or more persons are claiming rights over the same knowledge. An advantage in the registration of TK is that it limits the possibility of confusion. But the shortcoming of registering TK is in determining who has a right to register it. The situation is even worse if a person who happens to learn of another's knowledge acquires the legal rights to it by being the first to register it.

The registration of TK means that developing countries have to provide archives and administrative support structures. Owners or communities wishing to obtain protection must be registered with a government official and be catalogued and deposited in a restricted access database. Each community will have its own file in the database. The applicant for protection may be the protecting country's national or a foreigner. The TK law may provide legal protection to foreigners on the basis of reciprocity. Since the law is a *sui generis* system, which is not one of the modalities of intellectual property covered by the TRIPS Agreement, the Member States would not be obliged to confer national treatment to foreigners.[10]

Crucial elements of the legal protection developing countries opt for will be the monitoring and enforcement components. Developing countries' protests against cases of biopiracy may end up in victory, but often at all too high a cost. For every patent revoked, developing countries face high costs of litigation and expert advice from highly specialized patent lawyers. So the questions remain: Even if TK were protected under intellectual property law, how will the local communities be able to monitor infringement? Can the communities afford to pay for the litigation if disputes arise?

THE DOWNSIDE OF CATALOGUING TK
AND GENETIC RESOURCES

Cataloguing genetic resources and TK risks playing into the hands of biopirates and therefore requires striking a very fine balance. On the one hand, a policy of narrow publication of indigenous knowledge and resources limits the opportunities for developing its beneficial uses. On the other, cataloguing them makes it easy for bioprospectors to claim bio-resources and TK as their own inventions. The South has received a painful lesson in placing bio-resources in the public domain through past dealings with the Consultative Group on International Agricultural Research (CGIAR). And although the bad precedent has been partly set straight by the moratorium CGIAR placed on intellectual property claims over its bio-resource holdings, legal dilemmas on cataloguing still cloud the horizon.

The CGIAR is the most important and unique collection of plant and genetic material worldwide. Its donors include the United Nations, national governments and the World Bank, which finances 16 research centres across the globe. The

CGIAR evolved in a world without intellectual property rights, aiming to facilitate the flow of scientific information through exchange and conservation of breeders' material. Answering the call of science and conservation, Southern nations donated vast amounts of their genetic and plant resources to these public archives.

In 1997, however, came the wake-up call. It turned out that the CGIAR was used by a few companies based in rich countries as a smokescreen to claim Southern plant varieties as their own. This was despite the fact that the varieties in question were protected under the agreement signed by the CGIAR centres and the UN Food and Agriculture Organization (FAO) in 1994. This agreement specifies that neither the CGIAR centres nor recipients of designated germplasm will seek any intellectual property rights (such as patents) over that germplasm or related information.

The biopiracy scandals that broke out in 1997 revealed gaping loopholes in the Western systems of intellectual property rights. Breeders in Australia for instance were granted monopoly rights over varieties not bred by them but by developing world farmers. In other cases the variety was just pulled from the ground and claimed in Australia. No less than 70 cases of biopiracy were exposed in connection to the CGIAR. The Canadian non-governmental organization Action Group on Erosion, Technology and Concentration (ETC Group, formerly called RAFI) concerned with the social and economic impact of new technologies on rural societies played a key role in uncovering the extent of biopiracy. The ETC Group's Executive Director, Pat Mooney, talked in terms of a 'patent rip-off' affecting developing countries' publicly deposed genetic resources (ETC Group, 1998).

The stir caused by the scandals led the CGIAR to adopt a stopgap policy against biopiracy. In February 1998, the CGIAR placed a moratorium on intellectual property claims on resources under its trusteeship. However, this partial redemption of Southern worries over losing control of national germplasm does not turn the tide. The root concern of the South is the swell of aggressive patenting that accompanies growing privatization of science in the field of biotechnology. In a world where the food supply is increasingly in the hands of a few corporations, the CGIAR and public science have to wrestle with pirating of bio-resources and tricky patenting. That is the case of jasmine rice, for instance (see Box 9.1).

The International Rice Research Institute (IRRI) was directly implicated in the assault on Thailand's jasmine rice. The seeds were under the safekeeping of the Philippines IRRI and the 1994 Agreement committing the IRRI to prevent IPR claims on jasmine rice. Yet in 1995, the USDA received samples of the rice variety without an accompanying MTA, obliging it to step down from IPR claims. Material transfer agreements cover the transfer of genetic resources. They are commonly used as a flexible contracting form in bioprospecting. Normally the MTA issued by the IRRI would have required signatory agreement from the US not to patent the rice variety. As a result of IRRI's negligence, USDA and its researchers are challenging Thailand's premium export trade with the creation of a US jasmine variety.

The main concern of the South over biopiracy is not foregoing monopoly rights over its genetic resources. It is merely to stop others from pursuing monopolistic claims over the use of its resources. The ones who stand to lose out the most from patenting pirated resources are developing country farmers. The absurdity of having to pay royalties upon planting and harvesting a variety that is essentially theirs is flagrant. As poor farmers of the developing world are trying to live on their agricultural trade, predatory corporations are seizing the source of their livelihoods.

The current patenting boom taking place heightens the need to protect Southern germplasm in the trusteeship of gene banks from threats of biopiracy. The numbers of patents in many areas of basic agricultural research reveal a patenting problem. For example, US patents related to rice remained well below 100 per year until 1995. But in 1999 and 2000, more than 600 patents were issued annually. Moreover, these patents are concentrated in the hands of the few who also control Southern food security in this way. About three-quarters of plant DNA patents are in the hands of private firms, with nearly half held by 14 multinational companies; virtually no such patents existed before 1985 (Thomas et al, 1999).

ARCHIVING TK AND GENETIC RESOURCES
TO CURB BIOPIRACY

How can the South respond to the threat of being shut out of its own genetic material? Documenting TK and genetic resources may have opened the way to biopiracy in the past, but it is also a way to stem illicit claims on the resources. Written publication on the knowledge and genetic material would create a tangible reference to its origin, which is now lacking. TK and knowledge of genetic material is often passed on orally. In the case of basmati piracy for instance, Indian civil society groups claimed that documenting could have precluded the US patent. Under US patent law, exemptions from patenting are allowed where the products and processes concerned embody *prior art* or traditional knowledge. A published document or a patent could serve to manifest the existence of *prior art*.

However, systematic sampling, testing and archiving TK and genetic resources challenges the capacities of developing countries. Even a country as biodiverse and as large as India has been laggardly in creating nationwide databases. The People's Biodiversity Registers programme and the Society for Research and Initiatives for Sustainable Technologies and Institutions (SRISTI)'s Honey Bee Network, both of which are located in India, are the only initiatives that exist to date. Both projects have common aims of conserving biodiversity and TK through documentation, as well as setting up databases of information on farmers' innovations and creative practices.

Another serious drawback of compiling a bio-resource database is its current weak international legal status. Under the law of most nations, the compilation of TK will not establish legal claim by a community or individual over the TK included in the database. With the exception of the European Union law, which establishes *sui generis* database rights,[11] the extraction or use of a substantial part of the database's content will not be regarded as infringement of the right over the database under the current law found in most countries (Downes and Laird, 1999, p16). Though the compilation of data is afforded copyright protection, it would not be an infringement to reorganize data in such a compilation. Therefore, the drive for documentation and publication of TK may be nothing but the donation of ethnobotanical knowledge as a common stock or public domain subject matter, which is free for anyone.

Despite the potential drawbacks of creating databases, they are key for developing countries to monitor and scrutinize cases of biopiracy.[12] Therefore the stepping up of the creation of TK and genetic resources database systems must be urged. However, the relevant questions of whether the database system should be laid open to the public, how the use of such a database could be supervised, how the benefits derived from applications of the database would be shared and what legal rights for the protection of databases should be conferred, are left with each nation to answer, depending on their specific needs and circumstances.

CONCLUSION

Biotechnology has now become an important technology, in line with the increasing recognition of the significance of TK and genetic resources. While it was considered necessary for TK and genetic resources to be regarded as the common heritage of humankind so that everyone could have more or less equal access to resources provided by nature to sustain their lives, it is rather unfortunate that, in the highly competitive world of trade, things do not operate on that basis. Free trade, however, should not mean the free use of the developing world's resources. Although developed countries claim that the system will encourage biotechnological innovation, it is still *their* technology. Little benefit trickles down to developing countries.

The current system for the protection of intellectual property is not designed to acknowledge the importance of TK. The absence of such acknowledgement has led to the unquestioned and unchallenged appropriation of such resources from the developing world. Developing countries should deal with the perceived inadequacies of existing legal systems by supplementary legislation. The *sui generis* law may provide for registration of TK and confer exclusive rights on the owner of such knowledge. In another option, the law may regard all kinds of TK as belonging to the state and its utilization requires state authorization. State approval for the use of TK should be granted only when the applicant fulfils all required obligations, such as prior informed consent and equitable benefit-sharing. The law has to lay down criteria for determining who represents a community and how prior informed consent can be obtained. A system of benefit-sharing and TK documentation should also be established to complement the *sui generis* legislation.

NOTES

1 However, the Court finally denied the grant of patent because the claimed invention did not fulfil the particular condition of a written description, as it lacked the repeatable feature. See *International Review of Industrial Property and Copyright Law*, 1970, vol 1, p136.

2 As pointed out by Bowman and Redgwell (1996, p65), 'existing types of IPRs, such as patents or plant variety rights, which require some element of novelty, cannot be used to establish ownership over wild species nor landraces used in traditional societies, nor for that matter for the knowledge of local and indigenous peoples'.

3 See US Supreme Court decision, *Kewanee v Bicron*, 416 US 470, 1973.

4 Geographical indications identify goods as originating in the territory of a Member country, or a specific region within it, where a given quality, reputation or other characteristic of the goods is essentially attributable to its geographical origin. Champagne, to take a famous example, properly comes only from the Champagne region in France.

5 There is no restriction on the scope, obligations or standards of such a system, nor an obligation for the *sui generis* systems to conform to any international convention relating to the plant variety protection. Also, the TRIPS Agreement does not suggest either the adoption of a UPOV (International Union for the Protection of New Varieties of Plants) standard or UPOV itself.

6 See for instance IP/C/W/356, IP/C/W/400, IP/C/W/404, IP/C/W/420, IP/C/W/429, IP/C/W/438 and IP/C/W/442, searchable at http://docsonline.wto.org.

7 EC, Communication to the TRIPS Council, IP/C/W/383.

8 Switzerland, Communication to the TRIPS Council, IP/C/W/400.

9 TRIPS Agreement, Article 1.1, see also Correa, 1997.

10 According to Article 3 of the TRIPS Agreement: 'Each Member shall, with regard to the protection of IPR, accord to the nationals of other Members treatment no less favourable than it accords to its own nationals.' See Correa, 1997.

11 EU Directive 96/9/EC on the Legal Protection of Databases, effective on 1 January 1998.

12 The World Intellectual Property Organization (WIPO) is continuing discussions on possible ways of providing legal protection for traditional knowledge and folklore, including through the use of databases, a multilateral *sui generis* system and disclosure requirements for country of origin, benefit-sharing and prior informed consent in patent application. However, given the lack of mandate to move from study to negotiations mode, the outcome of the discussions is unlikely to impact countries' IPR systems in the near future.

REFERENCES

Beier, F K, Crespi, R S and Straus, J (1985) *Biotechnology and Patent Protection: An International Review*, Organisation for Economic Co-operation and Development, Paris

Bent, S A, Schwaab, R, Conlin, D and Jeffery, D (1987) *Intellectual Property Rights in Biotechnology Worldwide*, Stockton Press, New York

Blakeney, M (1997) 'Bioprospecting and the protection of traditional medical knowledge of indigenous peoples: An Australian perspective' 1997, *European Intellectual Property Review*, vol 6, pp298–303

Blakeney, M (1999) *Intellectual Property in the Dreamtime – Protecting the Cultural Creativity of Indigenous Peoples*, Oxford Intellectual Property Research Centre, Research Seminar, 9 November 1999

Bowman, M and Redgwell, C (1996) *International Law and the Conservation of Biological Diversity*, Kluwer Law, London

BRIDGES Trade BioRes (undated) electronic newsletter produced by the International Centre for Trade and Sustainable Development, Geneva, Switzerland, available at http://www.ictsd.org/biores/.

Bull, A T, Holt, G and Lilly, M D (1982) *Biotechnology: International Trends and Perspectives*, Organisation For Economic Co-operation and Development, Paris

Cooper, I P (1985) *Biotechnology and the Law*, Clark Boardman, New York

Correa, C M (1991) 'The pharmaceutical industry and biotechnology: Opportunities and constraints for developing countries', *World Competition*, vol 15, no 2, pp43–63

Correa, C M (1997) 'TRIPs and the protection of community rights', in Grain and Biothai, *Signposts to Sui Generis Rights*, Bangkok, pp59–60

Crucible Group (1994) *People, Plants and Patents: The Impact of Intellectual Property on Biodiversity, Conservation, Trade and Rural Society*, International Development Research Centre, Canada

Downes, D R and Laird, S A (1999) *Community Registries of Biodiversity-related Knowledge: The Role of Intellectual Property in Managing Access and Benefit*, Paper prepared for UNCTAD Biotrade Initiative, Geneva

ETC Group (former RAFI) (2001) 'US acquisition of aromatic Thai rice breaks trust', Action Group on Erosion, Technology and Concentration, communiqué, 30 October

ETC Group (former RAFI) (1998) 'Toward a global moratorium on plant monopolies', Action Group on Erosion, Technology and Concentration, communiqué, 9 February

Leskien, D and Flitner, M (1997) *Intellectual Property Rights and Plant Genetic Resources: Options for a Sui Generis System*, International Plant Genetic Resources Institute, Rome

Reid, W V, Barber, C V and La Viña, A (1995) 'Translating genetic resource rights into sustainable development', *Plant Genetic Resource Newsletter*, vol 102, pp1–17

Thomas S, Brady, M and Burke J F (1999) 'Plant DNA patents in the hands of a few', *Nature*, vol 399, pp405–406

UNDP (1999) *Human Development Report*, United Nations Development Programme, New York

United States Patents Quarterly (1980) Vol 206, no 193. SIBL reference KF2975.A2.U5

WIPO (1984) *Industrial Property Protection of Biotechnological Inventions*, Publication Biot/CE/I/2, World Intellectual Property Organization

10

Balancing Biosafety and Trade: The Negotiating History of the Cartagena Protocol[1]

Juan Mayr and Adriana Soto

With the development and commercialization of living modified organisms (LMOs)[2] around the world, an intense debate arose concerning the risks associated with their use. In the early 1990s, national regulation to govern the safe use of LMOs was relatively advanced in Organisation for Economic Co-operation and Development (OECD) countries and practically non-existent in the developing countries. At the international level, some codes of conduct and guidelines existed establishing common procedures for ensuring and evaluating safety in biotechnology, such as those from the OECD, the United Nations Industrial Development Organization (UNIDO) and the United Nations Environment Programme (UNEP). While these initiatives constituted an important effort to achieve a degree of international coherence in evaluating and managing the risks associated with LMOs, their terms were not legally binding and therefore their application remained voluntary.

What follows is the history of the hard but heartening negotiating process of the first legally binding multilateral framework that seeks to minimize the risks from LMOs to biodiversity and human health, now known as the Cartagena Protocol on Biosafety. This process is a good example of how different perceptions of biodiversity conservation, technology, trade and development have reached an understanding to address the risk of damage resulting from the release of LMOs into the environment.

EARTH SUMMIT 1992: LAYING THE FOUNDATIONS FOR THE BIOSAFETY PROTOCOL

During the preparations for the 1992 Earth Summit in Rio de Janeiro, the issue of biotechnology and biosafety surfaced in a number of the working groups, especially those responsible for negotiating and drafting Agenda 21 and the Convention on Biological Diversity (CBD). The arguments for and against biotechnology products as a tool for sustainable growth, and the need to explore the possibility of international regulation, were addressed in several chapters of Agenda 21 as well as in the text of the CBD, specifically in Articles 8(g) (In-situ Conservation)[3] and 19 (Handling of Biotechnology and Distribution of its Benefits).

During the negotiations of Articles 8(g) and 19, the developing countries, with the support of Nordic countries and several non-governmental organizations (NGOs), argued that LMOs carried new risks and thus potentially negative effects on the environment; and that the magnitude of those effects could vary with geographical context and the characteristics of the ecosystems where they were produced. The developing countries felt particularly vulnerable in this regard, given their limited institutional and financial capacity to evaluate risks and handle any negative impact of LMOs on their ecosystems. Moreover, they feared that the lack of national biotechnology regulations would encourage field trials of LMOs in their territories, which had not been authorized for release in countries which did have such regulations.

Countries with a relatively advanced biotechnology sector and a good share of the international market for biotechnology products perceived the use of LMOs, especially in agriculture, as the answer to present and future problems of the global population by increasing productivity and serving as basic tools for the conservation and sustainable use of biodiversity. In response to the safety concerns, the proponents of biotechnology argued that there was no scientific evidence to show that biotechnology products could have more or different effects on the environment or human health than the applications of conventional selection and reproduction techniques. Rather, since biotechnology products came from advanced DNA recombination, LMO-associated risks could be minimized and controlled more effectively than products obtained from conventional genetic modification. Therefore, these countries saw the risk assessment procedures to decide whether a given LMO could enter a given country as a restriction on trade and an obstacle to the advancement of biotechnological research.

There was also disagreement over whether the CBD provided the adequate framework for discussing the safety of LMOs. Some thought this would give the terms of any biotechnology regulations to be agreed an environmental flavour, taking precedence over principles considered equally valid, such as free trade. Developing and Nordic countries, however, considered the CBD as the appropriate context, given LMOs' possible effect on the conservation and sustainable use of biodiversity – two of the three objectives of the Convention. They also argued that humans were inherently part of biodiversity, and therefore the effects of LMOs on human health should be an issue for biosafety regulation.

Although the negotiation of Articles 8(g) and 19 of the CBD did not reach a consensus on these issues, there was progress on two other fronts: first, the measures to be adopted by individual countries, at their discretion, in the area of biosafety; and second, the framework for future multilateral discussions on LMOs. Article 8(g) leaves it to individual countries to set national regulations to manage or control risks associated with the use and release of LMOs. It also reduces the scope of application of those regulations to LMOs which might have an adverse effect on the environment and thus threaten biodiversity. One substantive advance was the inclusion of adverse effects on human health as a factor to be taken into account by countries at the national level. It was thereby acknowledged that LMOs may represent a risk not only to biodiversity but also to humans.

While Article 8(g) is an important initiative, it does not deal with the risks of organisms that move, accidentally or otherwise, between one country and another. Article 19.3 of the Convention[4] offers a response to the need to manage and control LMO-associated risks across borders by raising the possibility of drawing up a legal instrument – the first at international level – that would include procedures to enable countries to take an informed decision as to whether or not an LMO could enter their territory for handling and use purposes. As with Article 8(g), this type of approval procedure would only apply to LMOs which may have an adverse effect on biodiversity, thus leaving open the option of excluding those LMOs from the legal instrument, which do not imply such risks, and thereby removing a legal constraint to their free trade. The instrument would be developed within the framework of the CBD as its first Protocol, which would ensure that the Protocol's objectives and principles – including the principle of precaution – would be the same as those of the Convention.

One of the major legacies of the CBD negotiations was that the discussion on biosafety acquired an international dimension. Articles 8(g) and 19.3 of the CBD showed that even if there was no consensus on the fundamental biotechnology-related issues, parameters were set for subsequent negotiations of the Biosafety Protocol and the development of national regulations, based on the assumptions that biotechnology products might present risks to the environment; that activities such as cross-border movement, or the use or handling of LMOs might increase risks; and that by agreeing to proceed with the negotiations for a Protocol, Parties would effectively agree on the Convention as the framework for the legal inter-national agreement on biosafety. It would also be understood that advance informed agreement (AIA) would be one of the mechanisms to be considered as part of the Protocol.

TO BE OR NOT TO BE: LAUNCHING THE NEGOTIATIONS

During the first meeting of the CBD's Conference of the Parties (COP) in Nassau in 1994, discussions on Article 19.3 focused on how an intergovernmental process could be set in motion to define the Biosafety Protocol. The views on the potential risk of biotechnology and the need for an international instrument remained largely the same as during the CBD negotiations. Developing countries, supported by Nordic countries and the NGOs, continued to insist that existing international legislation did not take into account cross-border movements of LMOs and their possible effect on biodiversity. Many of the developed countries, however, held that the Protocol would create barriers to trade, since there was no scientific evidence to show conclusively that LMOs were dangerous to the environment and human health. They also believed that the Protocol would hamper the transfer of biotech-nology and all related benefits from developed to developing countries – casting doubt on one of the tools of the Convention for achieving its objectives. Instead, they regarded the development of strong national legislation on biosafety as sufficient to minimize LMO-associated threats. Others, such as the EU, thought that the first step should be to produce some international technical guidelines on biosafety before evaluating the need for a Biosafety Protocol.

As a compromise, COP-1 set up an *Open-ended Ad Hoc Group of Experts on Biosafety* to consider the need and modalities of a Protocol, including an AIA procedure, and to review existing legislation, knowledge and experience in the field of biosafety. On the basis of the Group's report, COP-2 would reach a decision as to the need for and modalities of a Biosafety Protocol. The report of the Group would take account of a *Panel of 15 Governmental Experts on Biosafety* who would make a series of technical and scientific recommendations. To a certain extent, this COP decision responded to the interests of those countries that wished to postpone the negotiation of the Protocol until new and sufficient technical and scientific evidence became available. For the developing countries, this proposal was a step backwards in the negotiations since it focused the discussion again on whether LMOs did or did not constitute a risk, and therefore whether or not there was a need for a Biosafety Protocol. With this, some feared that the preparation of a draft Protocol risked being postponed indefinitely. The developing countries therefore included a second point in the decision of COP-1, in which the Panel of 15 Experts would also include in their background document the consideration of the modalities of a Biosafety Protocol as mentioned in Article 19.3 of the Convention.

The Panel of 15 Experts on Biosafety,[5] which met in Cairo in May 1995, recognized, among other things, that commercial imports and exports and the inadvertent dissemination of LMOs across political boundaries may raise special concerns which would require international cooperation and coordination. The Panel added that the lack of harmonization among national regulatory systems could create non-tariff barriers to international trade. Despite these conclusions and the mandate given by COP-1, the Panel did not produce a specific recommendation on the need to adopt a legally binding international instrument on biosafety, instead suggesting a range of options, including directives, regulations, codes of conduct or a Protocol.

The meeting of the Open-ended Ad Hoc Group of Experts on Biosafety was held in Madrid in July 1995. The Group's discussions repeated many of the arguments offered at previous meetings and negotiations. Significantly, disagreements began to emerge within the Group of 77 – which up to that point had pursued a coherent position – when the Latin-American and the Caribbean Group could not reach an internal consensus on the need for a Protocol and its components. Brazil, Argentina and Uruguay adopted a view similar to that of some developed countries in favour of strong national biosafety legislation, in particular for the handling and use of LMOs, which they argued were usually undertaken within countries. This reaction is not surprising given that, in Brazil and Argentina, research and development of biotechnology products were becoming increasingly important. These countries would therefore reject any regulation which could imply controls over the production or marketing of such products.

The Group's final document reached a consensus with regard to the elements to be considered in an international framework on biosafety,[6] and several issues, though not enjoying consensus, were supported by many delegations for inclusion in the list of components, namely social and economic considerations, liability and compensation and financial issues. However, like the Panel of 15 Experts, the Group made no recommendation as to whether a Biosafety Protocol should be negotiated, thus leaving the possibility for COP-2 to reopen the debate on the most appropriate instrument.

It was on this point that the G-77 played a decisive role, in particular countries such as Colombia, Ethiopia, India and Malaysia. Despite the rift within the G-77, these delegations with the support of the Nordic countries noted that the great majority of the Group's members were in favour of developing a Biosafety Protocol under the CBD and demanded that their view be properly reflected in the report. As a complement to this, Colombia proposed that COP-2 should consider the formation of an Open-ended Working Group on Biosafety (BSWG) under the COP to draft the Protocol. The majority of countries attending supported this proposal, and it was included in the final recommendations of the Madrid Report. As a result, the Madrid meeting was undoubtedly a very important link in the chain of events prior to the approval of the Biosafety Protocol. Madrid's recommendations avoided long hours of discussion at COP-2 as to whether the Protocol was necessary or not. With the full validity of a process supported by a majority of countries, COP-2 could then give a specific mandate to the Parties to the CBD to formally start the long-awaited negotiations for the first legally-binding multilateral instrument on biosafety and biotechnology.

As the final and decisive step towards launching negotiations of the Biosafety Protocol, COP-2, held in Jakarta in 1995, drafted the terms of reference for the BSWG, which would start the negotiations. Despite a vigorous debate on the type and scope of the BSWG, Decision II/5 of the COP included most of the key recommendations and principles of the Madrid Report. The Decision also stressed that the process of developing a Protocol should be considered as a matter of urgency by the BSWG, which should endeavour to complete its work by 1998. This mandate left behind the argument as to whether the CBD should be the framework for an international action on biosafety, and whether the AIA procedure should be one of the procedures to be considered in the provisions of the Protocol.

PRELIMINARY NEGOTIATIONS:
A CONFIDENCE-BUILDING PROCESS

The first meeting of the BSWG was held in Aarhus, Denmark, in July 1996. In order to push the process along more effectively, the BSWG compiled a general list to include all the elements proposed by delegations. This produced a slightly confused structure for the Protocol, but it also gained an atmosphere of confidence between delegations. The second meeting of the BSWG was held in May 1997 in Montreal. Delegates focused on the content of each of the possible articles of the Protocol. Although no article was actually drafted, the simple fact of structuring the Protocol little by little without generating any major controversy created the feeling that progress was being made in a process which until recently had seemed difficult to achieve. Countries previously opposed to the start of negotiations were seen to be making contributions and discussing concrete proposals. With hindsight, the second meeting of the BSWG was the most productive of the six meetings held. It managed to produce a consolidated text which provided a clearer view of the Protocol's structure and made it possible to see which issues under negotiation would form the core of the Protocol and therefore the object of the most intensive discussions during the final stages of negotiation.

The third and fourth meetings of the BSWG were held in late 1997 and early 1998. Although the second meeting had consolidated proposals for each article, the next step was not an easy one. The differences in often numerous proposals for each article had to be reduced to a minimum in order to move from the consolidated text to the simplification of options. This required a more sophisticated and more controversial process of negotiation. Discussions were moved to two subworking groups – one for the AIA procedure, another for the remaining articles – and two contact groups charged with structuring a legal text with definitions, annexes, institutional matters and the final clauses of the Protocol. The results of the third and fourth meetings of the BSWG were not encouraging, since a simplified version of the Protocol was not achieved. The number of proposals had been reduced for most of the articles, but the language was complex and the text sometimes contained more brackets than words. In international negotiations text in square brackets signifies dissent.

At the fifth (and penultimate) meeting of the BSWG, held in August 1998, delegations made significant progress on the structure and content of the Protocol. Some articles related to administrative matters or procedures were approved, and a single option remained for the rest of the articles, although numerous brackets were still included. At first sight, the text produced by this meeting was relatively coherent in structure and content, but the picture was not so encouraging in the detail: the lack of consensus for the vital articles was apparent from almost 600 sets of brackets and they reflected differences of substance which were not easy to resolve in the couple of weeks of the sixth and final meeting of the BSWG, to be held in February 1999 in Cartagena, Colombia.

CARTAGENA: CRISIS IN THE FORMAT OF NEGOTIATIONS

During regional consultations prior to the final BSWG meeting, divisions within the traditional groups in the UN began to emerge, including within the G-77, when Argentina, Uruguay and Chile stopped a consensus within the Latin America and Caribbean Group and the G-77/China. For these countries, interest in the production and export of transgenic goods were closer to those of the US and Canada than to G-77. The EU and the members of the JUSSCANNZ bloc (Japan, the United States, Switzerland, Canada, Australia, Norway and New Zealand) also failed to make much progress on issues such as the precautionary approach and the relationship of the Protocol with other international agreements, specifically the World Trade Organization (WTO).

As the final BSWG meeting drew to a close, the scheme of work and participation proposed at the start of the BSWG in 1996, which had given good results up to that point, began to show signs of collapse. This was partly because the articles of the Protocol were all closely related to each other and the negotiation of one article involved negotiation of another. The scheme of the two subgroups with their contact groups, with parallel discussion of the same topics in other groups, made the process of negotiation enormously difficult. There were even times when the number of contact groups, drafting groups and consultation groups exceeded the number of delegates available to be present at each at the same time.

The lack of clarity regarding the format of the negotiations, and the complexity of each of the issues to be resolved led to still more radical positions, and the chance of a consensus at Cartagena was receding. In addition, the time available to complete the Protocol was running out. This seemed to confirm the worst fears – that if the Protocol was not approved now it probably never would be. In a last attempt to save the negotiations, BSWG Chair Veit Koester put forward a Chairman's Text with a proposal for the Protocol, which had been initially discussed with the *Friends of the Chair*, a group formed by representatives of the G-77/China, JUSSCANNZ, the EU, and Central and Eastern Europe. No brackets could be added, and only texts agreed by consensus could be considered in the text.

This approach was not very well received, since many delegations felt that the text did not properly represent their views. Moreover, given their complexity, the issues could not be resolved by a group with limited participation and problems of representation, such as the Friends of the Chair, which many saw as inappropriate since it was formed by spokespersons from the traditional UN regional groups. As mentioned earlier, this scheme of representation had previously caused crises within the BSWG, since the interests associated with biosafety did not necessarily correspond to the regional groupings. Further, and in accordance with UN procedures, decisions were taken by consensus in the regional groups; if one country did not agree, it used a veto and blocked the group position on a given subject.

In the case of the Protocol, the positions of the different countries corresponded to the level of development of their biotechnology industries, their capacity to produce and sell LMOs, their capacity to handle LMOs safely, and national legislation on the subject. Thus the traditional system of North–South blocs, which usually form in the UN on discussions of environmental matters and which follow the pattern of developing and developed countries, was completely broken down on the subject of LMOs. This context makes it easier to understand how a country like Argentina could become the dissenting voice in G-77 from the start of negotiations.

The Chairman's Text presented a forced agreement between interest groups which did not reflect the individual positions expressed on biosafety. This impaired the content of the Protocol since the Text had to be sufficiently vague to reflect all group members' positions, but also left most of them unsatisfied. And now at the final session of the BSWG, when more concrete results were being expected, countries tried to protect their positions on basic issues by veto, thus blocking the process. As a result, the sixth BSWG meeting ended without an agreement on the Protocol, leading many to conclude that the process had failed. Others thought that all hope was not lost and that the Chairman's Text had been extremely useful since it had helped to point out the progress which had been made and the remaining gaps in the Protocol.

ExCOP: A NEW FORMAT TO ACCOMMODATE
COMMERCIAL REALITIES

It had became apparent that the negotiating process employed up to that time had to change in order to restore confidence among the negotiators, which was by then at a low point. It was therefore necessary for interest groups to reorganize in such a way that they represented each country's interest and that positions could be clarified. Three definite interest groups emerged. One was composed of the G-77 countries and China, which had formed a 'like-minded Group' (LMG). Argentina, Chile and Uruguay left the G-77 to join the 'Miami Group', composed of the US,

Canada and Australia. The third group was the EU and its member states. Other countries included the SIDS (Small Island Developing States), some Central American countries and the Central and Eastern European countries.

The Extraordinary COP (ExCOP) immediately followed the BSWG meeting. At the start of the meeting, Juan Mayr, as the Chairman on behalf of the host country, set up a scheme of work so that the process would be more open and above all, more representative. The interest groups were asked to identify spokespersons and some adviser-countries. Other countries could also be present. Spokespersons included two for the Miami Group (one from the North and one from the South), five for the LMG (of which one was from the Central America and SIDS); one for Central and Eastern Europe; and one for the EU. The 'Compromise Group' (CG) emerged as another group, consisting of Switzerland, Norway, Mexico, Japan and South Korea, which had not taken extreme positions at any time in the process. This apparently neutral group made it possible for ingenious solutions to be proposed at difficult moments in meetings held after Cartagena.

This new scheme of work proved valuable, and at one point it almost seemed that consensus was close on the basic issues. There was a superb effort among delegations to bring positions into line and push the Protocol forward. If indeed the Protocol was not approved in Cartagena, it was because the solutions went beyond questions of format and goodwill on the part of the negotiators of the LMG, the EU, the CG or Central and Eastern Europe. These groups had come to a unified position which in the end was not shared by the Miami Group. Since it was not possible to gain a consensus with the Miami Group, it was decided in the early morning of the last day of the ExCOP to suspend the negotiations temporarily and for a defined time.

Although the proceedings ended with disappointment, Cartagena set off a chain of events which were to work for the benefit of the Protocol. Cartagena – in addition to producing the new format for negotiation, the Chairman's Text and the commitment to finalize the Protocol within a year – drew the world's attention to what lay behind the fact that no agreement had been reached on an instrument which at the end of the day sought to minimize the risk of possible damage to the environment. The general public began to ask itself why the Miami Group had resisted an agreement at any price, carrying the entire weight of the political decision not to reach any agreement. The media and public opinion also asked questions concerning the risks associated with biotechnology products and the need to take precautions with their use and commercialization. This gave even greater force to the *domino effect* of Cartagena, leading to such events as Monsanto's decision to suspend the production and sale of its 'terminator' seed in the world market, Japan's decision to require the labelling of transgenic products in Japan, and Gerber's decision not to use transgenic ingredients in its baby foods any longer. In 1999, a survey showed that over 80 per cent of Americans wanted genetically modified products to be labelled, while ever more massive demonstrations in Europe led to a drastic reduction in GM food imports into the region.

With hindsight, the Cartagena meeting was a step without which today's Protocol could not have been achieved. Most of the basic issues had not been clearly defined, and the haste to obtain approval would probably have led to a vague result, producing an empty instrument with little practical application.

FROM CARTAGENA TO VIENNA: THE KEY ISSUES

The next meeting after Cartagena was held in Vienna in November 1999, focusing on the AIA procedure and LMOs for use as food or feed, or for processing (LMO-FFP), the scope of application of the Protocol, and the relationship of the Protocol to other international agreements. Using a refined version of the ExCOP format, later known as the Cartagena/Vienna Setting, the Vienna consultations sought mutually agreed concepts instead of proposed texts for these articles. Countries appeared willing to finalize the Protocol in no more than a year. Government negotiations were opened for the first time to NGO representatives, industry and the media.

In Vienna there was also a new format for calling on spokespersons of each of the five interest groups. It was now several months after Cartagena and although there had been attempts to bring the LMG and the Miami Group together, there was a certain evident tension among the participants. No one seemed to want to start the dialogue with a proposal, and in this type of scenario it can make a difference whether one speaks first or last. In this situation, it was something of a surprise to see coloured lottery balls being used in the Vienna conference centre: they were placed in a bag and drawn by the spokespersons for each group. The colour of the ball set the order of presentation. This was not merely democratic, it also added transparency to the presentations and allowed the debate to flow smoothly.

Commodities (LMO-FFP)

The positions of the five groups on the issue of commodities (LMO-FFP) were especially clear in Vienna. The positions of the LMG, the EU and Central and Eastern Europe coincided on several points, among them the need to include import procedures for commodities. The LMG warned that a vague or weak AIA procedure could have disastrous consequences, since decisions made on that basis could be challenged by other international accords such as the WTO agreements. Moreover, the groups thought that the principle of precaution should be one of the elements which an importer could take into account when making decisions on imports. This was particularly important for countries with high biodiversity and diverse farming systems which regarded most of the scientific information available on the effects of LMOs on biodiversity as insufficient to take responsible decisions, as it came from risk assessments made by LMO-producing countries, which also happened to be temperate-zone countries with homogenous farming systems.

The Miami Group regarded domestic legislation as the only viable solution to deal with all these concerns, and that the Protocol should therefore be limited to the specification of the information to be supplied by the exporter so that national regulatory systems could be strengthened. They said that the Protocol could not include obligations regarding trade in agricultural commodities and proposed that there should be a clear demarcation of responsibilities of exporters and importers in the decision-making process for commodities. They also thought it necessary to change the text of the principle of precaution in order to avoid serious contradictions with the rights and obligations of countries under other international accords such as the WTO. They feared that a subjective interpretation of the principle could allow trade restrictions to be implemented – voluntarily or not – with harmful effects on the economy of the country and the international community.

The CG restated the right of countries to take their own decisions on the admission of LMOs to their territories, and stressed the importance of including commodities in AIA procedures as well as appropriate identification or labelling for them. They proposed a set of criteria to be included in the AIA procedure, such as:

- the identification of commodities;
- the right of the importing country to take a decision on the importation of a commodity based on the precautionary approach and a risk assessment;
- a time limit for notification of a decision of import; and
- the possibility that an importing country might change its decision.

Article 31: The Protocol's relationship with other international agreements

The debate on Article 31 concentrated on consistency, mutual supportiveness and non-hierarchical relations with existing obligations under other international accords. Some provisions of the Protocol, such as the principle of precaution, could be openly contradictory to the WTO accords. If the Protocol were subordinated to other international agreements and its terms conflicted with the WTO, the WTO would prevail.

The Miami Group stressed that Article 31 should recognize the rights and obligations of countries under other international accords and the need for the Protocol to be mutually supportive. The Group also stressed the need to avoid building artificial barriers to trade for LMOs which had no adverse effects. For the CG, negotiations for the Biosafety Protocol should concentrate on environmental issues and not on trade, since the WTO was already the forum for trade. The EU stressed the importance of appropriate definitions of the rights and obligations of importers which should be consistent with other accords and without unjustified discrimination in the case of LMOs imported or produced domestically. They also thought it vitally important that importers' decisions on LMOs should be based on obligations in the Protocol, taking account of WTO exceptions on certain environmental matters.

SEATTLE: THE BREAKING POINT

While the Vienna meeting had clarified the positions of the interest groups and provided key concepts for the controversial articles, a final agreement on the Protocol was not yet in sight. The WTO Ministerial Meeting in Seattle was held shortly after Vienna, in December 1999. One of the issues on the agenda was the relationship between biosafety and the WTO, raising the possibility that the WTO could play an active part in discussing trade in LMOs. Among the issues debated was a proposal to form a working group on biotechnology within the framework of the WTO Committee on Trade and Environment. This proposal was strongly supported by some members of the Miami Group in what seemed to be a response to the possible failure of the Biosafety Protocol negotiations to fill a gap in multilateral biosafety legislation. If the working group were formed, the Committee would then be able to recommend developments in legislation within the WTO accords, thus also ensuring that there would be consistency with the interests, principles and obligations of the WTO.

The demonstrations on the streets that surrounded the Seattle meeting – when protesters, among other demands, called for greater transparency in multilateral discussions and more caution in dealing with biotechnology products – penetrated the solid walls of the convention centre. The EU Environment Ministers publicly contradicted their own trade spokespersons and prevented the issue of LMO regulation from forming any part of the WTO framework and thus strengthened the terms of the Biosafety Protocol within the CBD. By then it was obvious that the EU was interested in giving a multilateral character, preferably under the CBD, to measures that were internally still under discussion and would later be adopted as EU directives (particularly, compulsory labelling for LMOs approved the following year).

Following the failure to place biosafety under the control of the WTO, the ExCOP in Montreal, held in January 2000, became the place were the crucial differences between the EU and the United States on trade and LMOs would be decided. It is hardly surprising that the scenario was different by the time the Montreal meeting took place. The Vienna meeting had further clarified the basic points of the Protocol and Seattle undoubtedly helped to make an issue that had previously been thought to be of concern only to the environmentalists into a subject of discussion in other spheres of opinion. By the end of the WTO meeting, it was evident that Montreal was the last chance to settle any disagreements and approve the Protocol. In this regard, Seattle had direct implications for the outcome of discussions on the several key points of the Protocol: the precautionary approach (implemented through the AIA procedure), the relationship of the Protocol with other international agreements, and the simplified procedure for commodities.

MONTREAL: ADDING THE FINISHING TOUCHES

Among the major factors contributing to the successful conclusion of the Protocol's negotiation was the scenario for the negotiations. If the Cartagena/Vienna Setting were to fulfil its function of bringing positions closer, encouraging dialogue and fostering transparency, it would be essential to hold the meeting somewhere which was flexible enough to adapt the venue and set up arrangements in a way that supported this. The organization of the meeting rooms and the UN rules of procedure did not normally allow representatives of civil society, industry or the media to be present. This makes the proceedings less transparent and inclusive; if interests excluded from the process are not able to follow the evolution of the discussions, they immediately become suspicious and mistrustful. This had already been apparent in Seattle where suspicion and mistrust were the decisive factors in blocking the accords. The more restricted the participation in any negotiating process, the greater the risk that any agreement reached will be extremely difficult to validate and implement.

Thus, the Cartagena/Vienna Setting negotiations were transferred to a hotel that provided a more flexible place to ensure greater transparency. The formal setting of the convention centre was used for the opening and closing sessions only. The negotiating room was laid out with a hexagonal negotiating table in the centre for the interest groups. With this layout people could enter and leave the room freely, and there were no line-of-sight obstacles on the negotiating table. It was also vital to ensure that the time allotted to each group should be seen to be fair, and for this purpose five teddy bears made their appearance on the stage. Aside from being a humourous ingredient, the bears served the same purpose as the lottery balls in Vienna, namely to democratize, organize and dynamize each group's interventions.

Last-minute trade-offs

The *Cartagena Protocol on Biosafety* was agreed in Montreal in January 2000 as the first multilateral environmental instrument to regulate the transboundary movement of LMOs. The arguments of the different interest groups regarding the key issues of the Protocol had remained almost unchanged throughout the entire negotiating process and some important trade-offs became necessary during the Montreal meeting for these issues to be resolved.

The precautionary approach had proven to be one of the most controversial issues. In the end, the LMG together with the EU and the CG, succeeded in including the precautionary principle – as set out in the Rio Declaration adopted at the Earth Summit more than 11 years earlier – in the objectives of the Protocol. Moreover, the inclusion of the principle as part of the AIA procedure meant that it became mandatory for all ratifying the Protocol. This outcome marked an important step in the legal recognition of this principle at the multilateral level.

Another accomplishment of this group of countries was the acknowledgement reflected in the Protocol that LMOs might react differently in different ecosystems and different receiving environments, and that countries have the right to decide, on the basis of their own environmental circumstances and available scientific and technical information, whether a given LMO could be safely released in their territory. As a result, in the AIA procedure the Party taking the decision on the admission of an LMO is the importing country. This decision should be based on risk assessment or in some cases on domestic legislation, which must be as stringent as the Protocol or more so. This issue, however, which was of particular importance to the LMG and the EU, was not achieved without a trade-off with the Miami Group.

The Miami Group secured a simplified AIA procedure and with this a limited scope of the Protocol and a reduced trade impact. The AIA procedure does not cover LMOs for contained use or in transit, is restricted to LMOs for intentional introduction into the environment of the Party of import, and is only required for the first transboundary movement of an LMO. Moreover, a Party of import may apply a simplified AIA procedure, under which the transboundary movement of an LMO may occur at the same time as the movement is notified to the Party of import. The Party of import may also exempt imports of LMOs from the AIA procedure altogether. The only requirements imposed by the Protocol are that adequate measures are taken to ensure the safe transboundary movement of the LMO and that the application of the procedure is notified to the Biosafety Clearing House Mechanism in advance.

The Miami Group also succeeded in limiting the scope of the Protocol, including the applicability of the AIA procedure, to a list of LMOs to be defined by the COP. In the future, the COP can assess which LMOs have no probable effects on the conservation and sustainable use of biodiversity – including risks to human health – and decide accordingly what LMOs will not require AIA. Quite possibly, this could lead to a reopening of the debate about the fact that an LMO may be considered safe in one country and unsafe in another, and about the role of available scientific information in decision-making.

Finally, with respect to LMO commodities, both the LMG and the Miami Group achieved their objectives. While the LMG, the EU and the CG succeeded in including commodities in the Protocol, they had to accept that commodities would be exempt from the AIA procedure. In this regard, the Miami Group not only obtained a special approval procedure for commodities, but also managed to safeguard the responsibility of the exporters. These exceptions to the AIA procedure may be considered in two ways. On the one hand, they could be seen as a legal way of side-stepping the Protocol, especially for countries which have domestic legislation on biosafety. On the other, the exceptions allow a greater consistency with existing legal systems on biotechnology and biosafety, thus ensuring that most countries will ratify the Protocol. Finally, although the AIA may not guarantee that there will be no risk arising from the use of LMOs, its implementation can help to reduce any possible risks.

Some unresolved trade issues

While many of the trade issues were addressed in the course of the Protocol's negotiation, some are likely to resurface during its implementation. For instance, the Protocol allows imports to be refused if a Party lacks sufficient scientific certainty regarding possible adverse effects of the LMO in question. However, if there is a gap in scientific information, countries will have to resort to other types of criterion in risk assessment in order to take a precautionary decision. Since these criteria will be outside the scope of science, there could be confusion in interpretations, especially in the framework of the WTO, since decisions taken under the Protocol will have commercial implications. Here, one of the major concerns about the future of the Protocol is how the CBD mechanism for the settlement of disputes between the Parties would work in practice. Even when a decision is based on scientific evidence, it is difficult to foresee what would happen if the exporting country appealed against a refusal to admit an LMO.

The Protocol's final result on the relationship between the Protocol and other international agreements, particularly the WTO, is not entirely clear and sometimes contradicts itself. This reflects the lack of consensus on this issue among countries at the end of the Montreal meeting. Questions have been raised as to what will happen in the event of a contradiction between the Protocol and agreements such as the WTO. Which would be the organ of appeal and the dispute settlement to be used – the CBD or the WTO? What happens if one of the Parties has been acting in accordance with one of the agreements, but counter to the other? Which of the agreements will prevail? And what happens if one of the parties to the dispute is not a Party to the Protocol?

CONCLUDING REMARKS

Despite the moments of despair in the early hours of the last morning of negotiations, what was achieved in Montreal was the product of the trust and belief that we shared in our involvement with the Protocol, and to the Protocol's ultimate benefit. The final result is not perfect, but the Protocol's content is a balanced reflection of all that we were sure of and not so sure of at that time. The implementation of the Protocol will undoubtedly be the best test of whether we were right.

The successful completion of the negotiations was due to a number of different circumstances and events. One of them was the change away from the traditional United Nations scheme of negotiation to a format that matched the realities better. The Cartagena/Vienna Setting has already been adopted in some UN negotiations such as the Rio+10 preparatory process in Bali and the Johannesburg World Summit on Sustainable Development. However, for the Cartagena/Vienna Setting to work, it is essential to recognize that the dynamics of discussions revolving around the basic issues of today's world, such as technology, trade, biosafety, food or climate change, do not necessarily follow the North–South split or the UN traditional regional groups. If we continue to force through agreements along the lines of rigid interest groups, the resulting accords will not be very representative, and therefore they will be weak and have no future. Interests vary, often very widely, depending on the issue and the dynamics that are generated in the groups that form around them. Negotiations that take such things into account, and offer a scheme of participation that is open and transparent start with part of their success already guaranteed.

NOTES

1   The authors adapted this chapter from the paper 'The Cartagena Protocol on Biosafety: A brief history' (2003), produced with the financial support of the World Resources Institute and ICTSD. All references are included in the paper.
2   The Biosafety Protocol of the Convention defines a living modified organism as 'Any living organism that possesses a novel combination of genetic material obtained through the use of modern biotechnology'. Also, 'modern biotechnology' refers to 'the application of a) In vitro nucleic acid techniques, including recombinant deoxyribonucleic acid (DNA) and direct injection of nucleic acid into cells or organelles, or b) Fusion of cells beyond the taxonomic family, that overcome natural physiological reproductive or recombination barriers and that are not techniques used in traditional breeding and selection'.
3   Article 8(g) states that 'Each contracting party shall, to the extent possible and as relevant, establish or maintain means to regulate, manage or control the risks associated with the use and release of living modified organisms resulting from biotechnology, which are likely to have adverse environmental impacts that could affect the conservation and sustainable use of biological diversity, taking also into account the risks to human health'.
4   Article 19.3 states that 'The Parties shall consider the need for and modalities of a protocol setting out appropriate procedures, including, in particular, advance informed agreement, in the field of the safe transfer, handling and use of any living modified organism resulting from biotechnology that may have adverse effect on the conservation and sustainable use of biological diversity.'
5   The Panel was composed of Albania, Argentina, Belarus, Burkina Faso, China, Colombia, Costa Rica, Denmark, Egypt, Hungary, India, Japan, South Africa, the United Kingdom and the United States.

6   Specifically, all activities related to LMOs resulting from modern biotechnology including research and development, handling, transfer, use and disposal; transboundary movement of LMOs, including unintended movement across national boundaries and their potential adverse effects; the release of LMOs in centres of origin and genetic diversity; mechanisms for risk assessment and risk management; procedures for the advance informed agreement; facilitation of exchange of information; definition of terms and capacity building.

11

The Cartagena Protocol on Biosafety: A New Hot Spot in the Trade–Environment Conflict?[1]

Veit Koester

The Cartagena Protocol on Biosafety to the Convention on Biological Diversity (CBD) regulates international trade in living modified organisms (LMOs). As the Protocol concerns trade in commodities, for example, genetically modified seeds and vegetables, it concerns a trade which is of major importance to the world's economy. The relationship between the Protocol and the World Trade Organization (WTO) is therefore of primary importance. The central point in the Protocol is the precautionary principle. This principle is in itself of crucial importance when discussing the relationship between the Protocol and the WTO. Therefore the Protocol must, in more than one sense, be considered a milestone in the discussion about the relationship between trade and environment. The issue of the extent to which the provisions of the Protocol will be respected by the WTO's Dispute Settlement Mechanism might therefore be regarded as decisive for whether it is at all possible to unite trade and environmental interests under the present WTO system. The purpose of this chapter is to discuss this problem and, based upon all the facts, to seek some conclusions.

NEGOTIATIONS FOR THE BIOSAFETY PROTOCOL

Intricate negotiations from the CBD to the Cartagena Protocol on Biosafety

The 1992 Convention on Biological Diversity is the first international legally binding instrument containing provisions on biotechnology. The Convention, which entered into force on 29 December 1993, counts 188 Parties as of September 2003. These provisions reflect the potential benefits and risks that modern biotechnology entails.

One of the provisions, Article 19.3, contains an obligation for the Parties to the Convention:

> *to consider the need for and modalities of a Protocol setting out appropriate procedures, including, in particular, advance informed agreement, in the field of the safe transfer, handling and use of any living modified organism resulting from biotechnology that may have adverse effects on the conservation and sustainable use of biological diversity.*[2]

The term *transfer* is meant to cover transboundary movements, that is export and import, including non-deliberate movements,[3] while the notion *transboundary movement* was introduced in the Jakarta Mandate.

This provision was the result of a compromise that was only made during the last hours of negotiation (Koester, 1997). The history of the negotiation reflects the fact that modern biotechnology was a topical issue some ten years ago. This also appears in Agenda 21, the global action plan for environment and development, which was adopted at the United Nations Conference on Environment and Development (UNCED) in 1992. A whole chapter in this action plan is devoted to the 'environmentally sound management of biotechnology' (Chapter 16).

Article 19.3 in the Convention on Biological Diversity resulted, on 29 January 2000, in the adoption in Montreal of the Cartagena Protocol on Biosafety, the first global environmental agreement in the new millennium.

Many deadlines slipped before negotiators put together a Protocol on Biosafety acceptable to all sides. The lowest point in the four years of negotiations (1996–2000) was resounding failure at Cartagena in February 1999 to carve out a Protocol. At that point it was doubtful whether it would ever be possible to come to an agreement.[4]

The main cause of failure was US resistance to regulation on LMOs that might harm the interests of a fast growing US biotechnology industry. Obstruction carried the day despite the mandate given to the Working Group on Biosafety by the CBD to work out a Protocol.[5] The 'Jakarta' Mandate, named after the capital city of Indonesia that hosted the second CBD Conference of the Parties (COP-2) in 1995, promised a difficult start to the negotiations. The Mandate was detailed and marked by subtleties and items for clarification reflecting the disagreement on the necessity and content of a Protocol on Biosafety.[6]

Five meetings of the Working Group on Biosafety went by in the space of three years (1996–1999) and the Protocol still seemed like a remote prospect. The 1999 meeting in Cartagena intended to conclude and adopt a Protocol that was based on a negotiating text still marked by over 600 pairs of square brackets. In international negotiations text in square brackets signifies dissent. The meeting of the

Working Group finished with a compromise text (UNEP, 1999) elaborated by the Chair, on which the Working Group did not succeed in reaching agreement. The Extraordinary COP that followed immediately thereafter was also unable to agree and was suspended (UNEP, 2000).

The Protocol was finally hammered out after four days of informal consultations in January 2000. Following meetings in July and September 1999,[7] the Extraordinary COP met again in January and concluded at around 5.00am on the morning of 29 January with the adoption of the Protocol.[8]

The most contentious point from the outset of the negotiations of the Protocol on Biosafety was the precautionary principle (PP). In the course of the negotiations, the EU and the like-minded Group, consisting of the G-77 and China, argued that a Protocol on Biosafety should enshrine the PP as a safeguard against the unique risks of LMOs. The PP stipulates that given lack of scientific evidence on the risks of LMOs to human health and the environment, a country should not be prevented from taking measures to mitigate these risks.

Reflecting the PP explicitly in the Protocol would mean that Parties have the sovereign right to refuse LMO imports as long as their impact on human health and the environment remain uncertain. This goes right to the heart of trade interests[9] of LMO exporting countries which, as expected, argued there was no need to include the PP explicitly in the Protocol and also that a Protocol on Biosafety in itself was an application of the PP. The so-called 'Miami Group', consisting of Argentina, Australia, Canada, Chile, the US and Uruguay, consistently blocked the advancement of a Protocol on Biosafety up to 1999.

It is possible to guess why the negotiations failed in 1999, but succeeded in 2000. At the WTO meeting in Seattle in 1999 the Miami Group proposed the establishment of a working group on biotechnology, thereby putting biosafety on the WTO agenda. This move, however, which was regarded by a number of other countries as an attempt to 'kill' the suspended negotiations on the Biosafety Protocol, ultimately failed due to resistance by EU countries. The European stance was supported by a rising tide of activism against LMOs in 1999. Across the globe, activist organizations destroyed genetically modified crops in the fields while the concerned public staged street protests against genetically engineered food.

In the end the industry, under the glare of bad publicity, yielded to adopting a Protocol on Biosafety. Putting a lid on the debate on LMOs by setting rules to the game favoured business stability. The Protocol was thus partly accepted because it would benefit trade in LMOs by strengthening business confidence.

A MAP TO THE PROTOCOL

The scope of the Protocol

The provisions in Articles 1, 2, 3 and 4 contain the objective, general provisions, use of terms and the scope of the Protocol.

The formal scope of the Protocol Article 4[10] is 'trans-boundary movement, transit, handling and use of all modified organisms that may have adverse effects on the conservation and sustainable use of biological diversity, taking into account risks to human health.'

An LMO is defined as 'any living organism that possesses a new combination of genetic material obtained through the use of modern biotechnology'. Article 3 also includes definitions of 'living organism' and 'modern biotechnology'. The definition is not much different from the concept of a (living) 'genetically modified organism' in the EC legislation.[11]

To a lesser extent the Protocol deals with domestic concerns connected to LMOs as well as their international movement. The scope of the Protocol in Article 2.2 contains a general obligation that covers domestic LMOs 'to ensure that the development, handling, transport, use and release of any living modified organism are undertaken in a manner that prevents or reduces the risks to biological diversity, taking also into account risks to human health'. Article 16 on risk assessment also contains a reference to domestic LMOs. In fact, the issue of regulating LMOs domestically is taken up at various places, with Article 20 dealing with information sharing and the Biosafety Clearing House, Article 22, with capacity building and Article 23, with public awareness and participation. Taken together, these provisions add up to the full scope of the Protocol, which thus in practice covers the domestic regulation of LMOs as well as their transboundary movement.

Pharmaceuticals for humans are covered by the Protocol in so far as they are not regulated by other international agreements or organizations. The Parties have the right to subject such LMOs to risk assessment prior to the making of decisions on import (Article 5). Furthermore, transit and contained use are not included in the provisions of the Protocol on the advance informed agreement (AIA) procedure, but other measures are permissible (Article 6).

Procedures: Advance Informed Agreement and the Biosafety Clearing House

Articles 7–13 contain provisions on procedures. Articles 7–10 deal with LMOs for intentional introduction into the environment. They ensure that the Party of import will be notified (Article 8 and Annex I) in order to be in a position to make an informed decision on import prior to the intentional transboundary movement. The Protocol allows some flexibility for Parties to deviate from the procedure, for example, for certain categories of LMOs (Article 13) or for subsequent imports (Article 12.4). This procedure is known as the AIA procedure ('advance informed agreement').

With regard to LMOs intended for direct use as food or feed, or for processing (FFP), the provisions on the AIA procedure do not apply. These LMOs are covered by Article 11, according to which potential exporting countries shall provide, within 15 days after their final decision regarding domestic use, all relevant information to potential importing countries via the Biosafety Clearing House. Alternatively, they may communicate with Parties, having informed the Secretariat in advance that they do not have access to the Clearing House.

A Party taking a decision on import may take such a decision under its national legislation, which should be consistent with the objective of the Protocol (Article 11.4). Or, if the Party is a developing country or a country with an economy in transition without a domestic regulatory framework, the import decision may be taken according to a risk assessment (under Annex III of the Protocol) within a time limit of 270 days (Article 11.6).

Contrary to what applies under the AIA procedure (Articles 15.1 and 2), the Party of import cannot demand that the Party of export undertakes a risk assessment (other than that included in its submission to the Clearing House) or pays the costs of such an assessment (Articles 15.2 and 3). With regard to industrialized countries and other countries with a domestic regulatory framework, the provisions do not include an explicit obligation for the Party of export to wait for the decision of the Party of import.

Both sets of rules explicitly accept the application of the PP as a basis for the decision on import (see 'The precautionary principle in the Protocol', below).

Risk assessment and risk management

The main principle of Article 15 is that risk assessment shall be carried out in a 'scientifically sound manner' and that risk assessment is obligatory with regard to LMOs destined for introduction into the environment. The Parties shall, according to Article 16.1, regulate, manage and control risks that are identified under the Protocol. Article 16.4 includes a provision applicable for both imported and for domestically produced LMOs, namely that these must undergo 'an appropriate period of observation . . . before [they are] put to use'. Risk assessment is also dealt with in Article 16 and in Annex III on risk assessment, attached to Articles 15 and 16.

Illegal transboundary movements of LMOs

Article 17 sets out the ways in which a government should act to protect other countries from the effects of illegal or unintentional movement of LMOs it is responsible for.

Article 25 contains obligations for the Parties to adopt domestic measures aimed at preventing and penalizing transboundary movements of LMOs carried out in contravention of domestic measures in order to implement the Protocol.

Identification

Article 18 contains provisions on handling, transport, packaging and identification. The identification obligations, which do not concern purely domestic identification, vary according to the character of LMOs. While for LMOs destined for introduction into the environment there is an obligation for the accompanying documentation to identify them clearly as LMOs (Article 18.2c), the obligation concerning LMOs for food, feed or processing is restricted to a requirement that the accompanying documentation 'clearly identifies that they "may contain" living modified organisms and are not intended for intentional introduction into the environment' (Article 18.2a). However, no later than two years after the date of entry into force of the Protocol, the Conference of the Parties serving as a Meeting of the Parties to the Protocol (MOP) shall take a decision 'on the detailed requirements for this purpose including specification of their identity and any unique identification' (Article 18.2c).

At the first MOP (MOP-1) in February 2004, Parties made some progress towards operationalizing Article 18.2a by requesting Parties and urging other governments to require all shipments of LMOs for food and feed or for processing to use the commercial invoice or other documents to specify that the shipment 'may contain' LMOs and as not intended for introduction into the environment. Governments were also asked to include a contact point and the name of the importer, exporter or other appropriate authority. In addition, the Decision expands on existing requirements by 'urging' Parties and other governments to require information on the name of the organism and the transformation event or unique identifier code. MOP-1 also established a technical expert group, open to all governments, which was charged with elaborating the documentation requirements for LMO commodities further, including additional information, the use of unique identifiers and if possible labelling thresholds and a review of sampling techniques.

Trade with non-Parties

According to Article 24, Parties to the Biosafety Protocol may trade LMOs with non-Parties. The Protocol envisages that this trade will not defeat the safety standards of the Biosafety Protocol, by stating that such trade 'shall be consistent with the objective of the Protocol'. During the negotiations, several countries insisted on a prohibition of trade with non-Parties, more or less in accordance with the principle of the Montreal Protocol. Such a provision would especially have affected the US, which is one of the very few big countries to be a non-Party to the CBD and therefore – at least for the time being – cannot become a Party to the Protocol. On the other hand, the Miami Group advocated for the weaker provision, that trade with non-Parties should be 'compatible with' instead of what became the final result, 'consistent with' the objectives of the Protocol.

Under Article 14, Parties to the Protocol on Biosafety may form trade area agreements for the trade of LMOs provided that such agreements do not result in a lower level of protection.

Liability, redress and socio-economic considerations

Article 27 on liability and redress is limited to an obligation to time-restrict talks on creating rules fixing responsibility for LMO damage that may arise from international trade. This obligation is so lax that it practically means no rules may emerge for four years after the Protocol comes into force. MOP-1 set up a technical group of experts and a working group. The working group, which was charged with elaborating options for elements of rules and procedures, will complete its work by 2007.

Despite the controversy that surrounds socio-economic considerations, they have managed to permeate the Protocol on Biosafety in Article 26. The article allows countries' trade policies with respect to LMOs to take into account conservation and sustainable use of biological diversity, including indigenous groups' interest in sustaining biodiversity. The Protocol also asserts that socio-economic considerations should not lead a country to overlook its international obligations.

Other provisions

Article 23 is strikingly bold, in that it paves the way to unprecedented levels of public participation in decision-making processes regarding LMOs. In fact, the Protocol on Biosafety goes even further than the Aarhus Convention protecting civil rights with regard to environmental matters (Koester, 1999, p88).

Articles 19–23 and 28 designate competent national authorities, national focal point(s) and the international Biosafety Clearing House. It sets out guidelines dealing with confidential information, capacity building and public participation as well as financial resources for the implementation of the Protocol to developing Parties and Parties with economies in transitions.

Traditional provisions

Articles 29–40 mainly contain traditional provisions on Meetings of the Parties, the Secretariat, reporting and entry into force.

UNPICKING THE DISPUTE BETWEEN THE WTO AND MULTILATERAL ENVIRONMENTAL AGREEMENTS

Using environmental justifications to enforce trade sanctions has been the hotbed of trade disputes for several years now. Disputes over *dolphin-safe tuna*, or *turtle-*

friendly shrimp have riddled the WTO with a back-breaking load of disputes. In these cases, one country invokes higher domestic environmental standards to justify trade sanctions against a country with lower environmental standards. Environmental circles reacted by questioning whether international environmental agreements including trade regulatory measures would be respected in a conflict between trade and the environment (Charnovitz, 1997, p105).[12] Is it greenery or growth?

The WTO has been reticent and anti-confrontational towards multilateral environmental agreements (MEAs) and so the question of a dispute between the two has been mostly academic.[13] But while it brews, the dispute also grows. The debate now ponders over whether trade liberalization can ever be environment friendly (Hunter et al, 1998, p1167) as well as whether it is legitimate or desirable that MEAs utilize trade regulatory measures[14] and, if so, what one should demand from agreements of this nature or from the WTO (Lennard, 1996, p314; Ewing and Tarasofsky, 1997, p13).

Hot spots in the WTO–MEA relationship

In theory trade disputes arising from MEAs should rarely be solved in the WTO. In practice, the opposite might happen. Even as MEAs and the WTO aspire to mutual supportiveness, room for conflict remains. Measures emanating implicitly from, but not directly required by, MEAs may challenge the free trade regime of the WTO. From the WTO perspective, General Agreement on Tariffs and Trade (GATT) Article XX allows some flexibility in interpreting how much 'bending' of rules is legitimate to achieve environmental objectives.

On the face of it, a clash between MEAs and the WTO appears like a remote prospect. Although the WTO Agreement of 1994 neither focuses on environmental matters nor accords special status to MEAs, it is nevertheless founded on the crucial Article XX of its predecessor, the GATT. Article XX contains exceptions for measures 'necessary to protect human, animal and plant life and health' and for measures 'relating to the conservation of exhaustible natural resources'. This article of the GATT suggests that MEAs and WTO aims coincide.

Besides, it would be unreasonable to draft an MEA that clashes with the WTO. This is because countries that have participated in the negotiations of such an MEA would have considered the trade regulatory measures of the agreement to be in accordance with GATT 1994, if the MEA was created after 1994. Otherwise, it would have been inconsistent to adopt the agreement and run into trouble when adhering to it later. With regard to relevant MEAs originating before GATT 1994, conflicts are unlikely because the majority of the world's countries are Parties to both sets of rules (OECD, 1999, p202) and very few of the countries that trade extensively are not Parties to both regimes. Notable exceptions are the Biosafety Protocol, which does not and is not likely to enrol the membership of the US in the near future, and the Basel Convention that also does not include the US in its ranks (OECD, 1999, p127). Speaking in practical terms, such a conflict is hypothetical and should therefore not be subject to further analysis in this article.

If, in spite of this, a conflict occurs involving MEAs originating before 1994, where a country maintains that measures applied are in conflict with GATT 1994, the Dispute Settlement Mechanism (DSM) of the WTO from a theoretical point of view would be competent.[15] Considering the interest shown by the DSM in MEAs and in the light of recent developments, it is likely that the WTO mechanism would consider it important that the measures were applied in accordance with an MEA, perhaps even as measures being necessary under or demanded by the MEA.

A case of dispute that would definitely end up in the WTO is one where the parties embroiled are Members of the WTO, but only one of them is member to the MEA. Then the WTO DSM is the only possible arbiter.

This may be the case with MEAs that came into being relatively recently. That is simply because they are *younger* and will have far fewer parties than the WTO for a time period. This is for instance the case for the Biosafety Protocol and the Rotterdam Convention on Prior Informed Consent Procedure (PIC) for Certain Hazardous Chemicals and Pesticides in International Trade, the only other existing international agreement in a similar position.

Even this sort of problem should not be over-exaggerated however. The fact that a younger MEA may temporarily have a far more limited number of Parties than the WTO is probably not significant as long as it is clear that the period is likely to be transitional. This is because the clout of the MEA depends less on whether it is young than on the basis of international support it enjoys. On these lines, the important factors deciding where an MEA stands against the WTO in a dispute are:

- whether the MEA is adopted by consensus;[16]
- whether it is adopted by a considerable number of countries;[17]
- whether it represents an international consensus (Hunter et al, 1998, p1207) based on an international scientific, technical, economic and political assessment of what is needed to achieve the environmental goal in question;
- whether it reflects global (*erga omnes*) interests, at least if its aims are of a global nature; and
- whether a considerable number of ratifications is demanded for the MEA to enter into force.

An important element is probably also whether the agreement has been signed by many states, or at least, that there is no evident disproportion between the number of countries having signed the agreement and the number of countries participating in the consensus adoption of the agreement.

If these conditions are fulfilled and the measures under consideration are applied in accordance with the MEA it is unlikely that the WTO will dominate in the dispute settlement. However, this applies if the MEA allows trade with non-Parties in accordance with its provisions and if it is possible to enter into bilateral or regional agreements with non-Parties. This implies that the WTO DSM probably will accept measures applied within the broad framework of Article XX of GATT 1994.

The above would seem to indicate that clashes between the WTO and MEAs are an academic question. But this is not so. For a start, MEAs with trade regulatory measures are thought of as equal to the WTO as far as they contain no explicit subordination to existing agreements. If they are not subordinate, by implication an overlapping regime will have to be established between the MEA and the WTO.

This is where things can start to go wrong. A conflict may arise concerning measures which are not demanded by the MEA but are permissible under the agreement, because it permits the application of stricter domestic measures than those reflected in the agreement. It is probable that measures will undergo a stricter examination by the WTO DSM, on the basis that they are implicitly allowed but not required by the MEA. This is particularly true if the basis for stricter measures, as is often the case, demands that those measures be applied in accordance with existing international obligations.

Another source of potential conflict is found in GATT Article III, which prohibits discrimination against foreign and domestic 'like products'.[18] But what constitutes a 'like' product is open to interpretation and in fact, some of the hottest disputes on trade and the environment are framed on what 'like' means.

Moreover, GATT Article XX has been at the centre of the most debated environment-related trade disputes. The sticking point is the condition that any measures taken to protect human health and the environment must not imply 'arbitrary or unjustified discrimination between countries where the same conditions prevail or there is a disguised restriction on international trade' (Hunter et al, 1998, p1182; OECD, 1999, p193; and on 'like' products Lennard, 1996, p312).[19, 20] This was the basis of the *Tuna–Dolphin* and the *Shrimp–Turtle* disputes, for example. The US embargoes against certain tuna and shrimp imports were found to violate GATT/WTO provisions by the GATT Panel decisions (1991 and 1994) and the Appellate Body decision (1998) respectively. With regard to the *Tuna–Dolphin* dispute, see Ewing and Tarasofsky, 1997, p9; Trachtman, 1999, p356; Charnovitz, 1999, p105; and Hunter et al, 1998, p1184; and for the *Shrimp–Turtle* dispute, see Trachtman, 1999, p356 and Cameron, 1998, pp19–21.

WTO DISPUTE SETTLEMENT

If trade measures taken under an MEA are adjudicated in the WTO, the crucial question is to what extent they will be found to be consistent with Article XX of GATT 1994. This is done purely on a case-by-case basis, because the WTO has still to address the issue in a general context (Trachtman, 1999, pp364, 367).

Therefore opinions vary widely on whether the DSM would legitimize trade measures taken under an MEA, particularly an earlier one (Lennard, 1996, p308), and to what extent it would do so. The DSM after all has the power to subordinate MEA measures claiming they are not at all relevant under Article XX (OECD, 1999, p159).

Moreover, the dispute settlement mechanism of an MEA is seen as the poor relative of the WTO DSM. Many consider the WTO as where real power lies. Its DSM is efficient, because it is relatively fast, its decisions are respected and to a certain extent there are possibilities for sanctions in the case of non-compliance. However, this does not mean that the system is beyond criticism (Hunter et al, 1998, p1212).

In spite of the fact that the Mechanism is obligatory for WTO Parties (Cameron, 1998, p18) the WTO has recommended that an effort be made to resolve disputes within the framework of the MEA (Trachtman, 1999, p366; OECD, 1999, p193). However, owing to the weakness of the dispute settlement mechanisms under MEAs, countries might be tempted to use the WTO mechanism, although this is contentious from a political point of view.[21]

An important supplement to the WTO in case there is a clash between international agreements is the Vienna Convention. The Convention on the Law of Treaties deals with overlap between international agreements and its Article 30 stipulates that in the case where provisions of two agreements are found to be in conflict, the most recent of the two agreements rules. However, that applies only if the countries embroiled in the dispute are parties to both agreements.[22] By contrast, there is no rule to cover the case when one country is party to one agreement only.

THE BIOSAFETY PROTOCOL AND THE PRECAUTIONARY PRINCIPLE

The precautionary principle in general

The issue of the precautionary principle was one of the most problematic during the negotiations. It was therefore, as was the case with the Protocol's relationship with the WTO, only resolved at the very last moment. Likewise, the solution is as remarkable as the solution to the WTO problem (which is discussed below).

The most important element of the PP is that uncertainty about the potential risks to the environment and/or human health of a product or an activity does not prevent the authorities from taking a decision.[23] The decision may be to interfere and how to interfere (in the format of a prohibition or a licence under certain conditions or long-term measures such as strategies, programmes, action plans and the like). The decision, which is of a political nature, should normally be based on several different factors, but always – and foremost – on a scientific assessment of the possible risks involved, their character, size and the implications for the environment. The PP, which is closely connected with both the Principle of Prevention and AIA and also includes public participation aspects, is therefore action- or decision-oriented, which is often overlooked in the debate.

The PP has, in the same way as the relationship between trade and environment, caused an extensive debate. Proponents of the principle invoke it to adopt pre-emptive environmental measures against harm that might potentially occur. Its critics claim that the PP leads to over-regulation and might be used as a disguised barrier to trade.

However, the PP has also been the reason for vast numbers of provisions in national law, EC legislation and MEAs as well as soft law instruments on global environmental problems and instruments regulating environmental problems in a transboundary context.[24] Finally, the PP has also been addressed in some international judicial decisions, including decisions from the Permanent International Court of Justice and decisions by the WTO DSM.[25] The principle has also resulted in rules for international institutions, such as the World Bank.

The principle appears, when it is defined or described (which is not the case in the EC Treaty, Article 174), in many different formulations. This is especially the case with regard to MEAs, meaning that the precise content of the notion differs, for instance with regard to the extent to which cost–benefit considerations are acceptable and who carries the burden of proof. That has also influenced the interpretation of the principle. The opinions here vary with regard to the content, both *de lege lata* ('what the law is') and *de lege ferenda* ('what the law ought to be').

In the literature on international environmental law, there is disagreement on whether the PP can be considered as customary international law. Some authors maintain that this is the case,[26] while others refute this.[27] Due to the arguments launched by the last-mentioned group, it is probably doubtful whether the PP can be considered as customary international law yet. The incorporation of the principle in the Biosafety Protocol has probably advanced or will advance considerably the recognition of the principle as part of customary international law because the principle is a central element of the Protocol and has already been applied with regard to major international trades where products play a considerable economic role.

The precautionary principle in the Protocol

The Cartagena Protocol on Biosafety stands out among international agreements for adopting the strongest and most unequivocal formulation of the PP up to now. In its Article 10.6 and 10.8 on provisions and procedures, the relevant wording is as follows:

> *Lack of scientific certainty due to insufficient information and know-*
> *ledge regarding the extent of the potential adverse effects of a living*
> *modified organism on the conservation and sustainable use of biological*

diversity in the Party of import, taking also into account risks to human health, shall not prevent that Party from taking a decision, as appropriate, with regard to the import of the living modified organism in question as referred to in . . . above, in order to avoid or minimize such potential adverse effects.

Moreover, the Preamble confirms the 'precautionary approach contained in Rio Declaration Principle 15'.[28] The provision on the objective of the Protocol is introduced by the words 'In accordance with the precautionary approach in Principle 15 of the Rio Declaration, the objective of this Protocol is . . .'[29]

Finally, Annex II of the Protocol, the section dealing with general principles (3) contains the provision to the effect that 'lack of scientific knowledge or scientific consensus should not necessarily be interpreted as indicating a particular level of risk and absence of risk, or an acceptable risk'. The PP is also reflected more indirectly in other sections of the Annex.

THE PRECAUTIONARY PRINCIPLE IN THE WTO

GATT 1994 and the Agreement on Technical Barriers to Trade

Although GATT and the Agreement on Technical Barriers to Trade (TBT) do not mention the precautionary principle as such, they may be called to judge it. The TBT Agreement deals with standards and technical regulations, such as mandatory labelling, that might impede trade and asserts that they should not be excessively restrictive. The link of the TBT Agreement to the Biosafety Protocol is that they may both govern claims on trade in LMOs.[30]

The question is, therefore, whether the WTO DSM would challenge a decision taken under the Protocol on the basis of the PP. This is not likely to happen because, speaking in practical terms, it would undermine the Biosafety Protocol and void the preambular statement that the Protocol and the WTO are mutually supportive.[31]

It is therefore not entirely necessary to build on the assumption that the PP now belongs to international customary law and that the GATT 1994/TBT Agreement will have to be interpreted in accordance with that assumption. However, it has to be acknowledged that such an assumption has its merit and that it would be reasonable to use this argument when dealing with a concrete dispute.

It would of course be different if a case of misuse of the PP gave rise to a dispute in the WTO DSM. If this were the case and the provisions of the Biosafety Protocol were violated, those provisions would have to be interpreted and applied in accordance with the provisions of the Vienna Convention, at the least, those based on international customary law.

Between the two extremes, there exists a grey zone. The future will decide the precise demarcation of this zone.

The Agreement on the Application
of Sanitary and Phytosanitary Measures

This Agreement on the Application of Sanitary and Phytosanitary Measures (SPS) contains certain provisions reflecting a sort of PP. However, the scope of the Agreement is limited,[32] although a clear common field for the Protocol and the SPS Agreement is that the Protocol also concerns food and that human health should be taken into account in decision-making under the Protocol. This implies that decisions under the PP in the Protocol might be made which, at the same time, would fall under the PP in the SPS Agreement.

Article 5.7 of the SPS Agreement includes circumstances where 'relevant scientific evidence is insufficient', but at the same time contains the precondition that the uncertainty can be cleared up within 'a reasonable period of time'. However, the key term for the SPS Agreement is *objectivity* which relies on scientific evidence of harm. Any restriction on trade of LMOs would be regarded as temporary until a country manages to produce scientific evidence on which to base its concerns. As a result, under the SPS Agreement a country's decision to take trade measures against LMOs would have a temporary and not a permanent character. Contrary to the SPS Agreement, under the Protocol on Biosafety, a country has the sovereign right to restrict trade in LMOs as long as uncertainty on their potential harmful impact lingers on.

In accordance with the 1998 decision of the WTO Appellate Body with regard to meat treated with hormones (USA/Canada versus EU) (Cameron, 1998, p20; Spiermann, 1998, p345 and Cosbey, 2000, p11), the PP is reflected, inter alia, in the SPS Agreement's Article 3.3. However, in this case, the Appellate Body refused to apply the PP outside the framework of provisions explicitly referring to the PP, irrespective of whether the PP might be considered as belonging to international customary law and, therefore, theoretically speaking, could be applied when interpreting the SPS Agreement. The Appellate Body noted furthermore that it was 'less than clear' whether WTO Members had accepted the principle as 'general or customary law', but noted also that 'the principle is regarded by some . . . as having crystallized into a general principle of customary international law'.[33]

This differentiation, mildly speaking, seems to be bizarre and the question is whether it has a basis in the literature. It is one matter that there might be doubts about the precise content of the principle and doubts about the extent to which it can be applied, whether it is applicable, for example, in connection with human health. But if one reaches the conclusion that a principle with a reasonable, clearly defined content and extension belongs to international *environmental* customary law, then it must of course also belong to international customary law. It is international customary law that is the general notion, and the part of international customary law applicable to environmental protection that is the sub-notion.

It is, however, possible to argue that the PP of the Protocol is not conflicting with Article 5.7 of the SPS Agreement, but is supplementing this provision. That means that the Protocol fills in some of the gaps. Cosbey and Burgiel as well as Smith argue that there is a conflict between the science-based SPS provisions and the Protocol that represents a 'movement away from science-based decisions', noting also that there 'is no guarantee that the WTO and Codex policies relating to the use of scientific principles in resolving trade disputes relating to food safety and human health will remain sacrosanct' (Cosbey and Burgiel, 2000; Smith, 2000, p22). The author of this chapter agrees with the conclusion, but certainly not with its premises. The PP is also science-based and science within the framework of the PP cannot and should not be distinguished from science within the framework of the SPS.

Outside the area where the SPS Agreement itself is referring to the PP and where the Appellate Body as mentioned above has refused to utilize the principle, even if it was considered to belong to international customary law, it will be difficult for the WTO DSM to disregard decisions made in good faith in accordance with the objectives of the Protocol, although the DSM in such cases will be forced to make *a tactical withdrawal* (see the conclusions in 'GATT 1994 and the Agreement on Technical Barriers to Trade' above). It will be interesting to see whether, and when this happens.

THE WTO AND THE BIOSAFETY PROTOCOL

If both the Cartagena Protocol on Biosafety and the WTO govern trade in LMOs, the question arises what would happen in the case of a conflict. Most negotiators felt that this point had to be addressed, but there was disagreement on how to resolve it.

During the negotiations, three different proposals were considered:

- a provision subordinating the Protocol to existing agreements, including GATT 1994, referred to as a saving's clause because it 'saves' previous agreements;
- a modified saving's clause which, to a limited extent, did not respect existing agreements; and
- a 'ranging on the same level' clause, which was adopted.[34]

The fourth theoretical possibility, namely no provision at all, was seen as the favourite solution of only a small minority of countries and therefore was not given serious consideration. This option might either have subordinated GATT 1994 to the Protocol or created a dubious legal precedent, as Article 30 of the Vienna Convention does not always provide clear and unambiguous solutions for all cases of conflict between provisions of different treaties. All industrialized and developing countries would hence dismiss this option because of trade considerations.

The chosen clause strikes a fine balance between the Protocol and the WTO. In the preamble of the Protocol its relationship with the WTO is described by the last three paragraphs:

> Recognizing *that trade and environment agreements should be mutually supportive with a view to achieving sustainable development,*
> Emphasizing *that this Protocol shall not be interpreted as implying a change in the rights and obligations of a Party under any existing international agreements,*
> Understanding *the above recital* is not *intended to subordinate this Protocol to other international agreements . . .* [emphasis added][35]

The first recital[36] does not differ from what is typical in a Preamble, while the two other clauses differ from normal preamble language by using the words 'shall not be interpreted' and 'is not intended' respectively. Because of that and the provisions in the Vienna Convention on the interpretation of treaties (Sands, 1995, p118), it is possible that GATT 1994 and the Biosafety Protocol will be considered as ranging at the same level. An effort has been made to establish a *co-habitation*[37] because the third preambular clause neutralizes the effect of the second one. The purpose is to interpret, in a conflict situation, what is in conflict with rights or obligations under the Protocol (or under WTO).

Of course it is possible to envisage conflicts where WTO provisions have been violated by the application of measures which *stricto sensu* ('in the strictest sense') are not violating provisions of the Protocol, if, for example, the import of LMOs identical to those being produced and marketed in a country is refused by the same particular country. On the other hand, it is also possible to violate Protocol provisions without this violation being in conflict with WTO provisions, for instance, if the notification procedures of the Protocol are not complied with. However, if a breach of the obligations in the Protocol results in a real obstacle to trade, this might contribute to a violation of WTO provisions and thereby a temptation to use the WTO DSM, especially if there is no efficient Protocol compliance mechanism available. In this connection, Articles 10.5 and 11.7 of the Protocol are particularly interesting. Article 10.5 states that a failure by the Party of import to communicate its decision within the period of time prescribed (270 days) 'shall not imply its consent' and Article 11.7 that it 'shall not imply its consent or refusal'. However, this problem falls outside the scope of the present analysis.

The WTO DSM is, as mentioned above, only entitled to apply GATT 1994 and not substantive provisions of other international agreements (Trachtman, 1999, p342). Due to the reference in the mandate of the DSM to 'customary rules of public international law', the DSM should, under all circumstances, seek to interpret GATT 1994 in a manner avoiding as far as possible conflicts with other international agreements. The provisions of the DSM mandate are not in themselves modified because of the preamble of the Biosafety Protocol (Article 3.2 in 'Understanding on Rules and Procedures Governing the Settlement of Dispute'). However, due to the preambular provisions of the Biosafety Protocol, the discretion involved in deciding that there is a conflict will be narrower.[38]

Considering that the rule of exception in GATT 1994 Article XX refers to measures being 'necessary to protect', under the TBT Agreement (Article 2.2.2), exceptions for 'protection of human health . . . or the environment' are legitimate. The SPS Agreement contains provisions of a similar nature. It is therefore likely to be assumed that the measures being taken under the Biosafety Protocol without further consideration must be respected as conforming with these exceptions and are therefore not in conflict with WTO rules. On the other hand, trade measures could be found inconsistent with the WTO if they were seen as being means of *unjustifiable discrimination.*

The measures that might be taken under national legislation in accordance with Article 11 of the Protocol on 'FFP (food, feed and processing) commodities' (see 'Procedures: Advance Informed Agreement and the Biosafety Clearing House' above) will probably constitute such an integral element of the Protocol that they also are covered by the above-mentioned conclusion. This applies regardless of the fact that the provisions of the Protocol to a large degree are built on precautionary considerations.

Other relevant provisions

On the other hand, regardless of the co-habitation clause and the fact that Article 2(4) of the Protocol permits 'action that is more protective of the conservation . . . of biological diversity than that called for in this Protocol', stricter national measures would likely be examined in detail by the WTO DSM, given that Article 2(4) explicitly indicates that such actions must be in accordance with that country's other obligations under international law.

This is probably also true with regard to Article 26, which allows Parties in reaching a decision on import under the Protocol to 'take into account consistent with their international obligations, socio-economic considerations arising from' the impact of LMOs on the conservation and sustainable use of biodiversity. Socio-economic considerations are broadly speaking[39] not legitimate under the WTO rules, the aim of which is more or less to get rid of such considerations. On the other hand, the scope of the provision and of its probable application is so narrow that it is not likely to cause many conflicts.

The DSM of the Protocol and compliance

As mentioned above, the DSM of the Protocol is also relevant with regard to the WTO, because the WTO DSM should only be utilized when both Parties to the dispute are Members of WTO but only one of them is a Party to the Protocol.

The DSM of the Protocol is not worse nor better than similar systems in other MEAs. Because of the general reference made in Article 32 of the Protocol to the CBD, the mechanism is the same as that in that Convention. This implies, in case of failure to reach peaceful settlement and dependent on what the Parties to the dispute have accepted in connection with their adherence to the CBD, either arbitration in accordance with Annex II of the Convention or the use of the Permanent International Court of Justice, or action according to Annex II, Part 2.

The compliance mechanism of the Protocol was considered at the MOP-1 (pursuant to Article 34), which established a 15-member Compliance Committee that will receive submissions from any Party with respect to itself and from 'any Party, which is affected or likely to be affected, with respect to another Party'. In cases of non-compliance, the MOP can decide to provide technical assistance, caution the concerned Party and/or publish the case in the Biosafety Clearing House.

CONCLUDING REMARKS

There is no doubt that the adoption of the Biosafety Protocol is to be considered as a success in the political and juridical sense. In spite of the fact that the Protocol had all the odds stacked against it, the end result was a reality and a reasonably strong result seen from an environmental perspective, which might also influence the development of international environmental law in other fields.

At the same time, there is little reason to fear that the trade-regulating measures of the Protocol combined with the PP in themselves will cause conflicts with WTO rules, or that these measures will be disregarded in the case of a dispute.[40] Perhaps the Biosafety Protocol together with the Rotterdam Convention can contribute to the establishment of a reasonable balance between international trade interests and environmental considerations.

Implementing the Biosafety Protocol in practice will not be easy.[41] A huge effort has to be made at the international level. Also with regard to the national system, a lot will be demanded. Many developing countries lack the most elementary rules and, even in most industrialized countries, new enactments will probably be necessary because most of the current legislation in these countries only provides protection for the countries themselves, that is, legislation governing the importation, the domestic production and marketing of LMOs. This also applies to EU legislation. This is why it will take some time before the Protocol will enter into force and even more time before the Protocol will function as a well-oiled mechanism.

NOTES

1   This chapter was originally written in Danish and an abridged version was published in *Juristen* (The Lawyer) in November 2000 under the title 'Cartagena-protokollen om biosafety – en international aftale i braendpunktet mellem handel og miljoe', pp335–348. The article was translated from Danish and updated by the author, edited by Yaw

Osafo and published as 'A new hot spot in trade–environment conflict' in *Environmental Policy and Law*, vol 31, no 2, pp82–94 (Koester, 2001). The author chaired the Open-Ended Ad Hoc Group on Biosafety to elaborate the Protocol, which is mentioned in the article. For a more detailed personal account of the negotiations see Koester, 2002, pp44–61.

2   The Convention uses the notion of 'living modified organism resulting from biotech-nology' (LMO) which is a wider notion than 'genetically modified organisms' (GMO). This is mainly a result of opposition from the US, which did not wish to expose GMOs because they, according to the US, did not differ from organisms modified by the means of traditional biotechnology. See also Sands, 1995, p479, about the American statement on biotechnology in connection with Agenda 21 and the section in this chapter on 'The scope of the Protocol' on how the notion is formulated by the Biosafety Protocol.

3   Neither the CBD nor the Biosafety Protocol covers the transfer of LMOs to areas outside national jurisdiction, especially the high seas. Setting aside that transfers of this nature will hardly be relevant, it is therefore in this connection necessary to rely on the obligations of the Law of the Sea, to protect and preserve the marine environment (Article 192) and to prevent, reduce or control pollution resulting from the introduction of alien or new species which may cause significant and harmful changes thereto (Article 196). Other relevant provisions are found in the CBD, Article 14.1c, for example, on notification, exchange of information and consultation with regard to activities that may have major negative impacts on biodiversity in areas outside national jurisdiction

4   For a more complete account of the negotiation process, including the meeting in Cartagena, the informal consultations thereafter and the final meeting in Montreal in January 2000, see Burhenne-Guilmin, 2000, p46 and Bail et al, 2002. The last work was published after the manuscript of Koester (2001) was finished. On the Protocol, see also Gale, 2000, p7; Smith, 2000, p8; Falkner, 2000, p302; Eggers and Mackenzie, 2000, p252; Chasek, 2001, p206; and Stoekl, 2001, pp327–357. The three last-mentioned references were also published after the manuscript of the present article was finished.

5   In the period between the adoption of the CBD and the first Conference of the Parties, a panel consisting of 15–20 countries and international organizations, set up by the Executive Director of the UN Environment Programme (UNEP) with a view to preparing for the entry into force of the CBD, had examined the problems with regard to Article 19.3. The panel almost unanimously (the Organisation for Economic Co-operation and Development (OECD) and the United States dissenting) concluded that a Protocol should be developed and indicated the rough content of such a Protocol.

The Executive Director at that time was Dr M Tolba. It is probably not a coinci-dence that the Panel's report UNEP/Bio.Div/Panels/Inf.4 (1993) was never officially distributed, neither at the first COP of the CBD during autumn 1994, nor at the intergovernmental meeting in June 1994, which prepared the COP (Secretariat Paper on Article 19(3) and UNEP/CBD/IC/12 of 29 April 1994 does not mention the Panel Report). Nor was it officially distributed at the meeting of the Open-Ended Expert Group mentioned in Note 6. In the meantime UNEP, which was responsible for the Secretariat of the CBD, had a new Executive Director, Elizabeth Dowdeswell of Canada.

The first Conference of the Parties (COP-1) in November/December 1994 decided to establish an Open-Ended Ad-Hoc Group of Experts on Biosafety which on the basis of input from the Cairo panel (which consisted of 15 experts designated by governments) was to recommend whether or not a Protocol should be elaborated and if so, the possible content of such a Protocol. Most countries participating in the working group backed calls for a Protocol although there was disagreement on whether this should contain provisions on liability and redress and social economic considerations.

6   On the Cairo Panel, the Open-Ended Expert Group and the two COPs references are made to the documents UNEP/CBD/COP/2/7/; UNEP/CBD/COP/1/I/9 and UNEP/CBD/COP/2/Dec./II/5 as well as to Bragdon, 1995, p275 and to Ivars, 1998, p88. The COP reconsidered the modalities relating to the Working Group at COP-3 (November 1996). In its decision, UNEP/CBD/COP/3/III/20, COP-3 authorized additional meetings of the Working Group and welcomed 'UNEP International Technical Guidelines for Safety in Biotechnology' which had been adopted in December 1995. At COP4 (in May 1998), after four meetings of the Working Group, it was decided to hold two further meetings of the Working Group. The last meeting in 1999 was followed by an Extraordinary COP with a view to adopting the Protocol (decision UNEP/CBD/COP/4/IV/3).

7   UNEP/CBD/ExCop/1/INF/3. See also Burhenne-Guilmin, 2000, p 46.

8   The Protocol came into force on 11 September 2003. As of July 2005, there are 124 Parties.

9   Important examples of instruments which are comparable to the Protocol are the Convention on International Trade in Endangered Species of Wild Flora and Fauna (1973), the Montreal Protocol (1987) on Substances that Deplete the Ozone Layer, the Basel Convention (1989) on the Control of Transboundary Movements of Hazardous Wastes and Their Disposal, the Rotterdam Convention (1998) on Prior Informed Consent Procedure for Certain Hazardous Chemicals and Pesticides in International Trade, and the Convention on Persistent Organic Pollutants (POPs), adopted in Stockholm in May 2001. There are, however, more multilateral environmental agreements (MEAs), among them the Climate Change Framework Convention (1992), containing possibilities for utilizing trade-related measures. Seventeen MEAs appear in the compilation of relevant MEAs in Fauchald, 1997, p116. With regard to the different types of trade regulatory instruments, see Fauchald, 1997, p74.

10 The title of the Protocol is wider than its content because the Protocol only contains a few provisions dealing with purely domestic affairs (see the section in this chapter on 'Risk assessment and risk management'). The Protocol can be found at www.biodiv.org. See Burhenne-Guilmin, 2000, p47 for a more detailed discussion of the scope of the Protocol, as well as Mackenzie, 2000, pp1, 4; and Falkner, 2000, p306.

11 The definitions are in line with the content of the notion of GMO in Article 3 in the Lugano Convention (1993) on Civil Liability for Damage Resulting from Activities Dangerous to the Environment which, for other reasons, in spite of the fact that only three ratifications are needed, has not yet entered into force. For references to this Convention and on liability and redress for damage resulting from GMOs, see the European Commission (9 February 2000) *White Paper on Environmental Liability* (COM (2000) 66 final), sections 4.2 and 5.1, as well as Ascencio, 1997, p293 and Nijar, 2000.

12 Under Article XVI(1) in the Marrakech Agreement establishing the World Trade Organization, the WTO shall be guided by former decisions and practices. Decisions

of the WTO Dispute Settlement Mechanism (DSM) are made on a case-by-case basis and thus are not binding outside the framework of the concrete dispute; see Ewing and Tarasofsky, 1997, p7.

13   While the issue of the relationship between the WTO and MEAs has been on the WTO agenda, among others in ministerial conferences (See Charnovitz, 1997, p106; Hunter et al, 1998, p1216), there is no indication that a general solution is foreseeable. According to the OECD, the difficulties are centred around the elaboration of provisions which 'precisely qualify the conditions under which trade provisions in MEAs and the multilateral trading system can comfortably co-exist' (1999, p197) as well as political reasons to oppose 'calling into question a multilateral treaty signed by many national Governments' (1999, p192). An effort to draw out the terms of WTO–MEA co-existence is seen in Fauchald, 1997, p83. About 'the relative infrequency, indeed the speculative nature of possible conflict between MEA obligations and WTO Law' see Trachtman, 1999, p368.

14   Hunter et al, 1998, pp1124 and Fauchald, 1997, p77, both advocate such agreements, as does the OECD, 1999, p1198. It is more important than the WTO system itself and has both directly and indirectly recommended such environmental agreements. See OECD, 1999, p192 and Trachtman, 1999, p363 and p367 about the recommendation from the Appellate Body of WTO in the *Shrimp–Turtle* dispute, Trachtman, 1999, p359 on environmental measures which are not unilateral and the support from the WTO Committee on Trade and Environment on multilateral solutions and cooperation with regard to transboundary environmental problems.

15   International Public Law does not include a general rule about which dispute settlement mechanism should be applied in order to resolve the dispute if the dispute concerns several international agreements, each of them having their own dispute settlement mechanism; see Cameron, 1998, p17.

16   The tradition has existed for such a long time that it might be relevant to raise the question of whether it would be correct to rely on Article 9 of the Vienna Convention (setting out that international agreements are to be adopted with a two-thirds majority) in a situation where no rule on how to adopt the result of the negotiation process exists and where it has not been possible to achieve a consensus in this respect. This observation applies irrespective of whether Article 9 of the Vienna Convention is considered to be international customary law, and is thereby also applicable to countries that are not Parties to the Vienna Convention. Françoise Burhenne-Guilmin is the author of this observation. See also Széll, 1996, p211.

17   In the final round of the negotiations of the Biosafety Protocol more than 130 states participated.

18   A provision in the Draft Negotiating Text of the Biosafety Protocol on its application with a view to avoiding unjustifiable discrimination between foreign and domestic products was deleted at the last negotiation meeting as part of the solution of the issue of the relationship between the Protocol and other international agreements (see the section on 'WTO and the Biosafety Protocol').

19   The Agreement on Technical Barriers to Trade (TBT) also contains (in the format of preambular provisions) exemptions similar to the character of Article XX of GATT 1994. Furthermore, Article 2.2(2) of the Agreement acknowledges that legitimate objectives of rules and standards of a technical nature include considerations

corresponding to Article XX in GATT 1994. Article 2.2 of the Agreement on the Application of Sanitary and Phytosanitary Measures (SPS) contains an obligation for Member countries to ensure that any SPS measure being applied to the extent necessary to protect human, animal or plant life or health 'is based on scientific principles [and] sufficient scientific evidence'.

20 What is essential for Article XX of GATT, and what can probably be concluded on the basis of rules, decisions and theory on trade measures is that:

- there is probably no disagreement as to the notion that the objectives and the subjects of MEAs include considerations that can be taken into account under Article XX of GATT 1994;

- the nucleus of the problem is to what extent the measures of MEAs are or will be assessed as being legitimate within the framework of Article XX by the WTO DSM if a conflict occurs on the application of such measures and this conflict is being brought before a panel and thereafter perhaps before the Appellate Body;

- the DSM as a consequence of the provisions governing the mechanism must interpret WTO rules in accordance with 'customary rules of interpretation of public international law', which in accordance with practice is also assumed to include customary rules of public international law;

- Article 30 of the Vienna Convention on the Law of Treaties (which reflects customary international law) is applicable, including its provision that if two international agreements dealing with the same subject do not include provisions regulating this problem and there is a conflict then the conflict shall, generally speaking, be decided on the basis of the latest agreement if the concerned countries are Parties to both agreements, while there is no rule provided if one country only is a Party to one of the agreements;

- the DSM in principle only has to clarify rights and obligations under WTO rules and is not competent to apply all international rules which are theoretically applicable under the circumstances;

- the mechanism up to now has carefully avoided any expression of opinion about how it will react in the case where environmental measures have been taken in accordance with an MEA, although it has included this question in its considerations;

- the mechanism has to seek to interpret the WTO rules in a way that will prevent them from being in conflict with an MEA.

21 Cameron, 1998, p19; Fauchald, 1997, p75 is of the opinion that the risk of a country giving in to this temptation is not totally unrealistic. See also the section on 'The precautionary principle in the Protocol'.

22 On the problems connected with the application of this provision of the Vienna Convention, see Lennard, 1996, p308, whose conclusion is that there is 'ultimately no rule giving a clear precedence to either MEAs or the GATT even where the Vienna Convention applies as a treaty, much less where the issue remains one of customary law'. Suikkari, 1996, p108, has the interesting viewpoint that agreements 'made in the global public interest, so-called *erga omnes* agreements, seem to have priority over other agreements'.

23 Rio Principle 15:

> *Where there are threats of serious or irreversible damage, lack of full*
> *scientific certainty shall not be used as a reason for postponing cost-effective*
> *measures to prevent environmental degradation.*

24 Overviews of MEAs incorporating the PP and discussions of the content, implications and status of the principle in public international law are found in Sands, 1995, p208; Hunter et al, 1998, p360; McIntyre and Mosedale, 1997, p221; Backes and Verschuren, 1998, p43; and in Martin-Bidou, 1999, p631; as well as in the Annex to the European Commission Communication on the precautionary principle of 2 February 2000 (COM 2000 1 final). To this can now be added, first, the reflection on the precautionary principle in the Convention on POPs (Note 9 above) where the PP is referred to in the preambular paragraph 'that precaution underlies the concerns of all Parties to this Convention and is embedded within it' (that is to say neither as a principle nor as an approach, corresponding to the reference to the PP in Annex C, Part II A(2) as 'consideration of precaution') and second, the objective of the Convention with its reference to the 'precautionary approach as set forth in Principle 15 of the Rio Declaration'.

25 Jurisprudence, especially of the Permanent International Court of Justice in the Dispute on the French Nuclear Tests in the Pacific and in the Danube Dams Dispute is examined in McIntyre and Mosedale, 1997, p231. With regard to the Appellate Body's decision in the *Beef–Hormone* dispute, see the section on 'The precautionary principle in the WTO'.

26 Sands, 1995, p212 is doubtful about whether a PP based on a reversed burden of proof – that the state wishing to carry out a certain activity either has to prove that the activity will not result in serious damage or has to take preventive action if there is a possibility of causing serious damage – can be regarded as a rule of general application. However at the same time, he concludes with regard to the PP that there is 'a good argument to be made that it reflects a principle of customary law'. McIntyre and Mosedale, 1997, p235 observe that it 'would appear to conclusively endorse the principle status as a norm of customary international law'. The Commission Communication, Note 24 above, refers to the PP as a 'full-fledged and general principle of international law' (The Commission has almost bitten off more that it can chew, quite natural perhaps in the light of the *Beef–Hormone* dispute!) About the Commission Communication, see also Smith, 2000, p23. Backes and Verschuren, 1998, p57, conclude that the principle 'seems to have gradually evolved into a legal norm', which corresponds more or less to operative paragraph 3 in the European Council Resolution (Nice, 7–9 December 2000) which 'notes that the precautionary principle is gradually asserting itself as a principle of international law in the fields of environmental and health protection'.

27 Martin-Bidou, 1999, p664 refers to the lack of precision and clarity with regard to the extent of the obligations as well as doubt about whether the application of the principle has a basis in an *opinio juris* ('practice following from a sense of legal obligation'). Dupuy, 1997, p889 has by and large the same opinion. It looks almost as if there is an Anglo-Saxon and a French school, the former being for and the latter being against! See also Cosbey, 2000, p10.

28 Quoted in the Annex to the Commission Communication, note 24 above.

29 It is difficult to imagine that the fact that the notion of 'approach' is utilized instead of 'principle' has a major importance (see Mickwitz, 1998, p74). The formulation can be

regarded as a minor concession to the Miami Group, which advocated 'noting' instead of 'in accordance with' as a means of weakening the impact of the PP in the Protocol.

30   See Downes, 1999, p11 and OECD, 1999, p89 about the Montreal Protocol. According to Downes, 1999, it is, because of the definition of the SPS Agreement of the measures it concerns, more likely that the TBT Agreement will be relevant with regard to the Protocol, in spite of the fact that the objective of the SPS Agreement corresponds with the objective of the Protocol. This might be true. However, the Interim Commission for Phytosanitary Measures under the International Plant Protection Convention (IPPC) is a standard-setting body vis-à-vis the SPS Agreement. So the role of SPS vis-à-vis the Protocol will to a large degree depend on the division of competence between the Protocol and the IPPC. See Cosbey and Burgiel, 2000, for an analysis of the relationship between WTO rules and the Biosafety Protocol on the SPS Agreement.

31   In this respect, the conclusions in 'WTO and the Biosafety Protocol' and 'The DSM of the Protocol and compliance' above are therefore still valid without modifications in the situation discussed here.

32   Note 30 above.

33   The conclusions of the Appellate Body with regard to the status of PP in international law are to some extent similar to the vocabulary used by Sands, 1995, and could therefore build on a misinterpretation of what this author is saying. I have not read the whole literature about the PP, but in the latest literature (see Notes 24, 26 and 27) there are no authors applying the same differentiation as the Appellate Body although, as mentioned in Note 27, Francophone authors are generally sceptical with regard to the PP having the status of international customary law.

34   The first-mentioned clause had the following content:

> *The provisions of this Protocol shall not affect the rights and obligations of any Party to the Protocol deriving from any existing international agreement to which it is also a Party except where the exercise of those rights and obligations would cause serious damage or threat to biological diversity,*

similarly to Article 22.1 in the CBD.

35   Compared with the Rotterdam Convention on Prior Informed Consent Procedure (PIC) for Certain Hazardous Chemicals and Pesticides in International Trade, the preamble to the Protocol of Biosafety shows some similarity while also being quite different. The first part of the Preamble is fully in line with the Rotterdam Convention. The second consideration is at the same time both stronger and weaker than the corresponding preambular provision of the Rotterdam Convention. It is stronger because the Protocol uses the wording 'a change' while the Rotterdam Convention refers to 'in any way a change' and weaker because the Protocol refers to 'any existing international agreements' while the Rotterdam Convention only refers to 'any existing international agreement applying to chemicals in international trade and to environmental protection'. With regard to the third consideration the difference between the wording of the Protocol 'subordinate . . . to other' and the wording of the Convention 'create a hierarchy between this . . . and other' is probably only semantic. The Convention on POPs (Note 9 above) only contains one preambular paragraph on the issue of trade and environment, namely: 'Recognizing that this Convention and other

agreements in the field of trade and the environment are mutually supportive' – the 'should' in the Biosafety Protocol has been replaced by *are*: a statement of fact. The Doha Ministerial Declaration (2001) reflects the idea of trade and MEAs being mutually supportive thus supporting the first of the preambular paragraphs of the Protocol dealing with the relationship between the Protocol and the WTO. The Doha Declaration was adopted after Koester, 2001, was published in April 2001 (see Note 1).

36   About 'mutually supportive' see OECD, 1999, p192, translating the idea into 'due respect must be afforded to both'.

37   Lennard, 1996, p314 utilizes the notion of a *co-habitation clause* as an *ideal clause* in order to resolve conflicts between GATT 1994 and MEAs. In the Note for the attention of the 113 Committee of 13 June 2000 (MD 248/00), the European Commission observes that the effect of neutralizing the second consideration is that it 'is now assumed that interpreters should normally fall back on the "later in time" rule in Article 30(3) of the Vienna Convention, allowing the Protocol to have full legal effect'. Depending to a certain degree on what the Commission understands by 'normally', the conclusion of the Commission seems to be (at least at a first glance) too wide. Among other things, the conclusion seems to overlook the importance of the first clause. Smith, 2000, p22, concludes that 'the three statements taken as a whole are open to the inference that the . . . Protocol should take precedence in the future'. This conclusion is based on the argument that the absence in the first clause of a phrase such as 'and facilitating trade . . . seem to point to the precedence of the biodiversity goal over the trade goal'. However, this interpretation seems to overlook the fact that the notion of 'sustainable development', although nobody knows definitively what it should mean, includes economic, that is, trade, considerations, as well as environmental considerations.

38   In Trachtman, 1999, p364, the conclusion of the examination of the *Shrimp–Turtle* dispute, referred to above, is that 'the Appellate Body has retained jurisdiction to address [the relationships between international environmental law and international trade law] and has articulated a standard, balancing test that gives the Appellate Body itself wide flexibility in responding to these problems'.

39   On provisions in the SPS Agreements and GATT 1999 on permissible socio-economic considerations that might be relevant with regard to the Biosafety Protocol, see the analysis *Relationship of the Biosafety Protocol with WTO Agreements* prepared by the Australian Department of Foreign Affaires and Trade, with the assistance of advice from the Australian Government Solicitor. The analysis was published by the *BioSafety Working Group, Policy and Science Updates* No 40, Part 1 and 2, 20 November 2000, after Koester, 2001, was finished (see Note 1). However, many of the conclusions and observations in this chapter correspond with those in the Australian paper.

40   Falkner (2000) holds a somewhat different view, arguing that the 'agreement is unlikely to prevent future tension over some important issues that remain unresolved', PP is 'defined only insufficiently' and provisions on trade and the environment leave considerable room in interpretation' (p300) and the Protocol 'does not prevent GMO-exporting countries from using WTO . . . to clarify existing obligations under the trade regime' (p317).

41   See also Yongo, 2000, p12 and Falkner, 2000, p311. An Intergovernmental Committee for the Cartagena Protocol on Biosafety (ICCP) met in Montpellier 11–15 December

2000 in order to prepare for the first Meeting of the Parties (MOP) to the Protocol focusing, among other things, on capacity building and compliance as well as the Clearing House Mechanism for facilitating the exchange of technical and scientific information (see IISD, 2000). The two following meetings took place in Nairobi (October 2001) and The Hague (April 2002), after Koester, 2001 (see Note 1). It was rather predictable that negotiations on, among other things, the Compliance Mechanism were difficult. While some of these issues have been addressed at the first Meeting of the Parties in February 2004, discussions on the more contentious issues, such as liability and finalizing the compliance measures and documentation requirements for LMO commodities, remain to be settled at subsequent MOPs. Further information on the meetings of the ICCP and the MOP can be found on the CBD website (www.biodiv.org).

REFERENCES

Ascencio, A (1997) 'The transboundary movement of Living Modified Organisms: Issues relating to liability and compensation', *Review of European Community International Environmental Law*, vol 6, no 3, pp293–303

Backes, C W and Verschuren, J M (1998) 'The precautionary principle in International, European and Dutch wildlife law', *Colorado Journal of International Environmental Law and Policy*, vol 9, no 1, pp43–70

Bail, C, Falkner, R and Marquard, H (2002) *The Cartagena Protocol on Biosafety: Reconciling Trade in Biotechnology with Environment and Development*, Earthscan in association with the Royal Institute of International Affairs, London

Bragdon, S (1995) 'International hazard management other than nuclear', *Yearbook of International Environmental Law*, vol 6, Oxford University Press

Burhenne-Guilmin, F (2000) 'The Biosafety Protocol is adopted in Montreal', *Environmental Policy and Law*, vol 30, no 1/2, pp46–48

Cameron, J (1998) 'Dispute settlement and conflicting trade and environment regimes', in Cameron, J and Fijalkowski, A (eds) *Trade and the Environment: Bridging the Gap*, Cameron May, London

Charnovitz, S (1997) 'The World Trade Organization and the environment', *Yearbook of International Environmental Law*, vol 8, Oxford University Press

Chasek, P S (2001) *Earth Negotiations: Analyzing Thirty Years of Environmental Diplomacy*, United Nations University Press

Cosbey, A (2000) *A Forced Evolution? The Codex Alimentarius Commission, Scientific Uncertainty and the Precautionary Principle*, International Institute for Sustainable Development, Canada

Cosbey, A and Burgiel, S (2000) 'The Cartagena Protocol on Biosafety: An analysis of results', *Briefing Note*, International Institute for Sustainable Development, Canada

Downes, D R (1999) *Integrating Implementation of the Convention of Biological Diversity and the Rules of the World Trade Organization*, International Union for the Conservation of Nature and Natural Resources, Switzerland

Dupuy, P-M (1997) 'Où en est le droit international de l'environnement à la fin du siècle?', *Revue général du droit international public*, vol 101, no 4, pp873–904

Eggers, B and Mackenzie, R (2000) 'The Cartagena Protocol on Biosafety, *Journal of International Economic Law*', vol 3, no 3, pp525–543

Ewing, K P and Tarasofsky, R G (1997) 'The "trade and environment" agenda', *Environmental Policy and Law Paper Series*, no 33, International Union for the Conservation of Nature and Natural Resources, Switzerland

Falkner, R (2000) 'Regulating biotech trade: The Cartagena Protocol on Biosafety', *International Affairs*, vol 76, no 2, Royal Institute of International Affairs, pp288–313

Fauchald, O K (1997) 'The World Trade Organization and Multilateral Environment Agreements', in Basse, E M (ed) *Environmental Law – From International to National Law*, GadJura, Copenhagen

Gale, L (2000), 'Application of the precautionary principle to biosafety', *IUCN Newsletter*, January–April, International Union for the Conservation of Nature and Natural Resources, Switzerland

Hunter, D, Salzman, J and Zaelke, D (1998) *International Environmental Law and Policy*, Foundation Press, New York

IISD (2000) *Earth Negotiations Bulletin*, vol 9, no 173, International Institute for Sustainable Development, Canada

Ivars, B (1998) 'Observations related to a Biosafety Protocol under the Convention on Biological Diversity', in Cameron, J and Fijalkowski, A (eds) *Trade and the Environment: Bridging the Gap*, Cameron May, London

Koester, V (1997) 'The Biodiversity Convention negotiation process and some comments on the outcome', in Basse, E M (ed) *Environmental Law – From International to National Law*, GadJura, Copenhagen

Koester, V (1999) 'Aarhus konventionen om "borgerlige rettigheder" på miljøområdet' (The Aarhus Convention on 'civil rights' with regard to environmental matters), *Juristen*, no 3, pp87–102

Koester, V (2001) 'A new hot spot in trade–environment conflict' *Environmental Policy and Law*, vol 31, no 2, pp82–94

Koester, V (2002) 'The Biosafety Group (BSWG) process: A personal account of the negotiations', in Bail, C, Falkner, R and Marquard, H *The Cartagena Protocol on Biosafety: Reconciling Trade in Biotechnology with Environment and Development*, Earthscan in association with the Royal Institute of International Affairs, London

Lennard, M (1996) 'The World Trade Organization and disputes involving Multilateral Environment Agreements', *European Environmental Law Review*, no 5, pp306–314

Mackenzie, R (2000) 'Cartagena Protocol on Biosafety: Overview', *IUCN Newsletter*, January–April, International Union for the Conservation of Nature and Natural Resources, Switzerland

Martin-Bidou, P (1999) 'Le Principe de précaution en droit international public', in *Revue général du droit international public*, vol 103, no 3, pp631–666

McIntyre, O and Mosedale, T (1997) 'The precautionary principle as a norm of customary international law', *Journal of Environmental Law*, vol 9, pp221–242

Mickwitz, P (1998) *Implementation of Key Environmental Principles: Experiences from the Protection of the Baltic Sea*, Nordic Council of Ministers, Copenhagen

Nijar, G S (2000) *Developing a Liability and Redress Regime under the Cartagena Protocol on Biosafety*, Institute for Agriculture and Trade Policy, US

OECD (1999) *Trade Measures in Multilateral Environmental Agreements*, Organisation for Economic Co-operation and Development, Paris

Sands, P (1995) *Principles of International Environmental Law*, Manchester University, Manchester, UK

Smith, F B (2000) 'The Biosafety Protocol: The real losers are developing countries', *Monographs*, vol 4, no 3, National Legal Center for the Public Interest, Washington, DC

Spiermann, O (1998) 'WTO og verdenshandlens nye vilkår – om folkeretten, en ny bilæggelsesmekanisme og traktatfortolkninger' (WTO and new conditions for the World Trade: on international public law, a new dispute settlement mechanism and interpretation of treaties), *Juristen*, vol 80, no 8, pp312–328

Stoekl, L (2001) 'Das Verhaeltnis multilateraler Umweltschutzabkommen zum WTO-Recht, dargestellt am Beispiel des Biosafety Protocol', *Aussenwirtschaft: schweizerische Zeitschrift fuer internationale Wirtschaftsbeziehungen*, Bd 56 Heft 3

Széll, P (1996) 'Decision-making under Multilateral Environmental Agreements', *Environmental Policy and Law*, vol 26, no 5

Suikkari, S (1996) 'The GATT/WTO system and trade provisions in multilateral environmental treaties', in Tema Nord, *The Effectiveness of Environmental Agreements*, Nordic Council of Ministers, Copenhagen

Trachtman, J P (1999) 'The Domain of WTO Dispute Resolution', *Harvard International Law Journal*, vol 40, no 333, pp338–344

UNEP (1999) *Report of the Sixth Meeting of the Open-Ended Ad Hoc Working Group on Biosafety*, UNEP/CBD/ExCOP/1/2, United Nations Environment Programme, available at www.biodiv.org/doc/meetings/cop/excop-01/official/excop-01-02-en.pdf

UNEP (2000) *Report of the Extraordinary Meeting of the Conference of the Parties for the Adoption of the Protocol on Biosafety to the Convention on Biological Diversity*, UNEP/CBD/ExCOP/1/3, United Nations Environment Programme, available at www.biodiv.org/doc/meetings/cop/excop-01/official/excop-01-03-en.doc

Yongo, T (2000) 'Towards implementation of the Biosafety Protocol', *IUCN Newsletter*, January–April, p12

12

Building Sound Governance Structures for the Safe Application of Biotechnology

Arturo Martinez and Kakoli Ghosh

From China to South Africa to Argentina, developing countries are faced with a genetic revolution that has the potential to help combat problems ranging from human diseases to environmental degradation. Within biotechnology, the rapid innovations in genetic engineering and genomics are expanding the horizons of healthcare, industry, environment and agriculture. To fully reap the benefits of these developments, it is important to ensure that advancements in biotechnology are managed efficiently to minimize any potential risks to biodiversity and human health. Thus, to make biosafety an effective management tool for the sustainable use of biotechnology, developing required capabilities is an essential step. This is true for all practitioners of biotechnology and particularly so for developing countries. Due to a variety of internal and external reasons, developing countries lack adequate capacity for ensuring biosafety – or indeed for accessing and adapting new and useful biotechnologies for local priorities – and there is an urgent need to strengthen their endogenous capacities. To be effective, however, capacity building has to be considered in the context of overall technological development and not as an isolated event. Cooperative arrangements and partnerships offer a way, but first developing a critical mass of biotechnology expertise is crucial. The main thrust of the initiatives must be sustainable development of biotechnology through policies and practice.

A LOOK ACROSS INTERNATIONAL STANDARD-SETTING ACTIVITY IN BIOSAFETY

Biotechnology and its safe use attracted global attention in Agenda 21 (UNEP, 1992a), which was adopted by the United Nations Conference on Environment and Development (UNCED) in 1992. Chapter 16 on 'Environmentally Sound Management of Biotechnology' acknowledges that biotechnology offers new opportunities for global partnerships and can contribute to sustainable development. It further states that:

> There is a need for further development of internationally agreed principles on risk assessment and management of all aspects of biotechnology, which should build upon those developed at the national level. Only when adequate and transparent safety and border-control procedures are in place will the community at large be able to derive maximum benefit from and be in a much better position to accept the potential benefits and risks of, biotechnology. (Agenda 21, 16.29)

The Convention on Biological Diversity (CBD) adopted in 1992 recognizes the twin aspects of biotechnology and addresses them through Article 19 of the Convention (UNEP, 1992b). Article 19 deals with the distribution of benefits from biotechnology and at the same time recognizes the need for establishing provisions for reducing potential risks to the environment and human health. It calls for measures to promote 'on a fair and equitable basis' access to the results and benefits arising from biotechnology and to develop a protocol with appropriate procedures to enhance the safe transfer, handling and use of biotechnology. The need to regulate the risks of biotechnology within the framework of the CBD led to the adoption of the Cartagena Protocol on Biosafety (CPB) in January 2000 (UNEP, 2000). The Protocol covers the transboundary movement, transit, handling and use of all living modified organisms (LMOs), except pharmaceuticals for human use, which may have adverse effects on the conservation and sustainable use of biological diversity.

Within biosafety in general, there is a subset of questions that relate to the applications of the new biotechnologies to food and agriculture. The Conference of the Parties to the CBD, in its Decision II/15, recognized 'the special nature of agricultural biodiversity, its distinctive features and problems needing distinctive solutions'. The Food and Agriculture Organization (FAO) deals with environmental and food risk-assessment questions (directly and indirectly) through a series of instruments in the field of food and agriculture under a more general concept of *biosecurity*, namely the application of sanitary and phytosanitary measures (SPS) and a methodology of risk analysis for food and agriculture, including fisheries and forestry. The SPS Agreement of the WTO explicitly recognizes the standards set by the joint FAO/WHO Codex Alimentarius Commission in the area of food safety. The Commission adopted risk analysis standards for foods derived from biotechnology in July 2003, and is currently working on standards for labelling and for several other food safety aspects of LMOs.

As regards plant health, the SPS Agreement recognizes the standards set by the International Plant Protection Convention (IPPC). In April 2004, the Interim

Commission on Phytosanitary Measures, the governing body of the IPPC, adopted guidelines for assessing the potential risk to plants and plant products posed by LMOs. The guidelines were developed to protect the plant and crop ecosystems from potential risks arising from the introduction of LMOs. The guidelines also cover LMOs that may be harmful to plants, such as insects, fungi and bacteria. The guidelines stress that measures to manage pest risks caused by LMOs should be cost-effective, feasible, not more trade-restrictive than necessary and non-discriminatory.

In the area of animal health, the SPS recognizes the World Organisation for Animal Health (OIE) as the standard-setting body. The OIE has recently launched a database and information exchange mechanism on its partner institutions' capacity building programmes that are intended to help strengthen the capacity, particularly of developing countries, to detect and control animal diseases, including those transmissible to humans (OIE, 2003).

The key steps to capacity building for biosafety in the Cartagena Protocol

The objective of the CPB is to:

> *contribute to ensuring an adequate level of protection in the field of the safe transfer, handling and use of living modified organisms resulting from modern biotechnology that may have adverse effects on the conservation and sustainable use of biological diversity, taking also into account risks to human health and specifically focusing on transboundary movements.* (Article 1)

For the implementation of the Protocol countries have to meet a number of targets. They have to:

- ensure that the development, handling, transport, use, transfer and release of LMOs are undertaken in a manner that prevents or reduces the risks to biological diversity, taking into account human health (Article 2.2);
- establish and maintain appropriate mechanisms, measures and strategies to regulate, manage and control risks identified in the risk assessment provisions of the Protocol associated with use, handling and transboundary movements (Article 16.4);
- endeavour to ensure that imported or nationally developed LMOs have undergone an appropriate observation before being put to use (Article 16.4);
- fulfil obligations relating to the effective administration of the Protocol (Article 19 and others); and
- promote and facilitate public awareness, education and participation including access to information on LMOs (Article 23).

All this requires human and financial resources, both of which need to be long-term commitments so that biotechnology products can be used routinely and safely within the framework of the Protocol. More importantly, there is a need for continuous availability of competent human resources so that as biotechnology advances, the tools for its safe use are constantly evaluated, upgraded and applied. In other words, biosafety regulations should be a dynamic management tool for biotechnology.

Article 22 of the CPB deals with capacity building (Box 12.1). It calls for developing and strengthening both human resources and institutional capacities in biosafety, in particular, in developing countries so that they may effectively implement the Protocol. The Article also sets a limit on capacity building activities to the extent needed to serve the purposes of biosafety. At first glance this appears to be a curious limit set out in the Article, when the very focus of the Protocol is to ensure biosafety in matters related to biotechnology. However, it is understandable when one considers the enormous task of capacity building a country faces with respect to the Protocol within limited financial resources.

BOX 12.1 CAPACITY BUILDING (ARTICLE 22 OF THE CARTAGENA PROTOCOL ON BIOSAFETY)

1   The Parties shall cooperate in the development and/or strengthening of human resources and institutional capacities in biosafety, including biotechnology to the extent that it is required for biosafety, for the purpose of the effective implementation of this Protocol, in developing country Parties, in particular the least developed and small island developing States among them and in Parties with economies in transition, including through existing global, regional, sub-regional and national institutions and organizations and, as appropriate, through facilitating private sector involvement.

2   For the purposes of implementing paragraph 1 above, in relation to cooperation, the needs of developing country Parties, in particular the least developed and small island developing States among them, for financial resources and access to and transfer of technology and know-how in accordance with the relevant provisions of the Convention, shall be taken fully into account for capacity-building in biosafety. Cooperation in capacity building shall, subject to the different situation, capabilities and requirements of each Party, include scientific and technical training in the proper and safe management of biotechnology and in the use of risk assessment and risk management for biosafety and the enhancement of technological and institutional capacities in biosafety. The needs of Parties with economies in transition shall also be taken fully into account for such capacity building in biosafety.

Source: Convention on Biological Diversity (Cartagena Protocol)

The Article, however, does point out that for the full realization of capacity building, developing countries, in addition to financial resources, need access to and transfer of technology in accordance with the conditions outlined in the Convention.

BOX 12.2 ACCESS TO AND TRANSFER OF TECHNOLOGY (ARTICLE 16 OF CONVENTION ON BIOLOGICAL DIVERSITY)

1   Each Contracting Party, recognizing that technology includes biotechnology and that both access to and transfer of technology among Contracting Parties are essential elements for the attainment of the objectives of this Convention, undertakes subject to the provisions of this Article to provide and/or facilitate access for and transfer to other Contracting Parties of technologies that are relevant to the conservation and sustainable use of biological diversity or make use of genetic resources and do not cause significant damage to the environment.

2   Access to and transfer of technology referred to in paragraph 1 above to developing countries shall be provided and/or facilitated under fair and most favourable terms, including on concessional and preferential terms where mutually agreed and, where necessary, in accordance with the financial mechanism established by Articles 20 and 21. In the case of technology subject to patents and other intellectual property rights, such access and transfer shall be provided on terms which recognize and are consistent with the adequate and effective protection of intellectual property rights. The application of this paragraph shall be consistent with paragraphs 3, 4 and 5 below.

3   Each Contracting Party shall take legislative, administrative or policy measures, as appropriate, with the aim that Contracting Parties, in particular those that are developing countries, which provide genetic resources, are provided access to and transfer of technology which makes use of those resources, on mutually agreed terms, including technology protected by patents and other intellectual property rights, where necessary, through the provisions of Articles 20 and 21 and in accordance with international law and consistent with paragraphs 4 and 5 below.

4   Each Contracting Party shall take legislative, administrative or policy measures, as appropriate, with the aim that the private sector facilitates access to, joint development and transfer of technology referred to in paragraph 1 above for the benefit of both governmental institutions and the private sector of developing countries and in this regard shall abide by the obligations included in paragraphs 1, 2 and 3 above.

5   The Contracting Parties, recognizing that patents and other intellectual property rights may have an influence on the implementation of this Convention, shall cooperate in this regard subject to national legislation and international law in order to ensure that such rights are supportive of and do not run counter to its objectives.

Source: Convention on Biological Diversity

Article 16 of the CBD explicitly recognizes that access to and transfer of technology, including biotechnology, are important in meeting the objectives of the Convention (Box 12.2). A number of conditions are set out for access to and transfer of technology. These include that:

- access to and transfers of technology to developing countries be on fair and most favourable terms, including on concessional and preferential terms;
- patents and other intellectual property rights of such technologies are respected;

- countries take appropriate legislative, administrative and policy measures to provide access to and transfer of technology, including proprietary technologies, on mutually agreed terms to developing countries, in particular to those that provide genetic resources; and
- the private sector facilitates the transfer of technology for the benefits of both public and private institutions in developing countries.

These conditions have a number of policy implications (UNEP, 1996). They establish mechanisms for international technology transfer and call for a process of negotiation between relevant parties to agree on the terms of access to genetic resources and transfer of technologies including biotechnology. Furthermore, they point to the need for building competence in administrative and legislative aspects connected with technology transfer in addition to enhancing capabilities that would be required for the use of the technology itself.

An important conclusion emerging from Articles 16 of the CBD and 22 of the CPB is that access to technology through transfer of technology must go hand in hand with investing in capacity building for managing the potential risk of the technology. Otherwise building capacity for biosafety is perhaps meaningless. Taken together, Articles 16 and 22 aim to ensure that capacity building for biosafety is undertaken in conjunction with developing adequate competence in biotechnology.

THE NEED FOR BROAD-SPECTRUM CAPACITY BUILDING IN BIOSAFETY

To ensure that biotechnology is applied safely across a wide range of sectors, capacity building has to take place on an equally broad level encompassing scientific, technological, organizational and institutional aspects to ensure effective development and safe deployment of biotechnology, especially in developing countries (UNEP, 2002). With respect to the implementation of the CPB in particular, developing countries have to strengthen training in scientific and technical aspects of biotechnology, including risk management, information structures and decision-making. As trade of genetically modified food crops grows, adequate technical capacity would be required to monitor imported food in emergency situations as well as routine trade in seeds and crops. Competence also needs to be developed for policy and regulatory oversight while adopting the precautionary approach, and consideration should be given to the need to develop public participation to reflect socio-economic issues in decision-making. In other words, biosafety has to be made an all-round tool for the management of biotechnology.

The current state of biotechnology and related regulatory capacity is shown in Box 12.3. In intergovernmental meetings on biosafety and related areas, developing countries from all over the world have identified a wide range of items that need to be addressed through capacity building initiatives. Their focus has not been limited to a few specific aspects of biosafety; rather they have stressed the need for broader initiatives which include:

- enhancement of technical capacity for the safe use of biotechnology;
- institution building and development of related management capacity;
- strengthening information capacity that helps policy makers and public to make informed choices;
- development of legal capacity and legislation to enable access to international markets; and
- development of negotiating capacity among decision makers for effective participation in international fora.

BOX 12.3 GLOBAL CAPABILITIES IN BIOTECHNOLOGY AND ASSOCIATED REGULATORY MECHANISMS

Type I: Highly developed biotech research and regulatory capacity within universities, companies and public and private research institutions; these have predictable laws, regulations and enforcement of statutory protection and biosafety regulations. Examples: The European Community, Japan, the United States.

Type II: Early stage biotech research and regulatory capacity primarily within parastatal and international research centres and a limited number of universities; recently enacted and unpredictably enforced laws and regulations regarding statutory protection of discoveries and biosafety.
Examples: Brazil, India, South Africa, Mexico, China.

Type III: Very little or no biotechnology research and regulatory capacity; historical heavy dependence on improved agricultural seed products from the international research centres; very newly enacted statutory and biosafety legislation and no predictable experience in enforcement.
Examples: Kenya, Syria, most of Eastern Europe, Vietnam, Colombia.

Source: Adapted from Krattiger, 2002

For compliance with the CPB, technical expertise is needed for a number of areas of safety assessment, namely risk identification, assessment and management as well as implementing labelling provisions and applying the precautionary approach. Furthermore, all assessment procedures need to give due consideration to socio-economic considerations, maintaining and developing agro-biodiversity, and protecting farm- and landraces and regionally adapted varieties for sustainable food security. Labelling, especially in the food safety and consumer protection areas, is

being increasingly addressed at international and national levels (Codex Alimentarius Commission, 2001). Capacity building initiatives need to have a multidisciplinary nature and sound investments need to be made in basic training through
universities and education curricula. In developing countries, capacity building
initiatives need this kind of focus so that a team of local personnel can be built for
sustained maintenance of biotechnology and biosafety.

Institutional development becomes a very important factor in this strategy.
Institutions offer ways for creating and mobilizing financial, human and technological resources, and directing these to the solution of specific problems. Although
a number of institutions in several developing countries have taken important steps
to bolster human capacity in various aspects of biotechnology, they are still only a
few (Cohen, 1999). When they are public sector ventures, they often lack a
sustained financial capacity and infrastructure to continue research and related
activities. Biosafety, including monitoring and evaluation, is also being neglected.
The limited institutional capacity deprives developing countries of the benefits of
biotechnology. Often trained personnel choose to carry on research activity outside
their own countries for a variety of reasons, including the lack of infrastructure,
funding and encouragement. This needs to be rectified and it is important that the
public sector retains enough capacity, resources and flexibility to provide the
regulatory and support services on which the national private sectors can build. As
biotechnology is usually carried out in the private sector, its investment in building
strong institutional capacity within the country needs to be encouraged. A multi-
stakeholder approach could be considered for ensuring capacity building for the
safe use of biotechnology. The challenge is to develop institutional arrangements
that incorporate public–private partnerships in a win–win strategy.

Access to information is a basic condition for public participation and is one
tool that could help to realize the benefits and avoid the risks of modern biotechnology. Open discourse with civil society, including non-governmental organizations working in the field of environment and consumer policy, facilitates policy
work and diffuses tension. Developing countries have stressed the need to build
capacities for using advanced information systems, internet and networking that
could bring research communities and decision makers, entrepreneurs and users
from industrialized and developing countries closer together. It could also foster
public participation and promote dialogue at the national and sub-regional levels
through cooperation, exchange of information and experience.

In addition, requisite legal capacities will have to be strengthened. Laws provide
enabling mechanisms through which countries can avoid the risks of modern
biotechnology, but many developing countries at present do not have any national
biosafety laws, despite being signatories to the international CPB. When formulating national biosafety legislation, developing countries have to consider how
benefits of biotechnology can be reaped without compromising safety concerns or
the proper consideration and evaluation of risks. A concerted focus is required to
address the capacity needs of several developing countries (Box 12.3) to rectify the

lack of legislation and institutions necessary for implementing the CPB. However, building a regulatory framework in itself is not enough and ways and means of making regulations work, and ensuring that they are properly resourced, have to be devised. This is crucial to ensure that economic activity, trade and access to international markets is not hampered. Capacity building has to be integrated with the needs of the economic sector so that the biotechnology products can reach markets and ensure economic benefits. Most developing countries also have limited capacities for negotiating effectively for technology transfer or on trade-related issues.

As biosafety regulatory oversight includes environmental protection and food safety, capacity building has to be closely associated with policy development or strategic planning for realizing the benefits of biotechnology. The challenge to the national policy makers is to prioritize needs for biotechnology capacity building and allocate resources wisely to meet the most pressing of those needs. Policy measures could include incentives and other economic measures to stimulate the growth as well as review how existing intellectual property rights might be used to support the local biotechnology industry and national economy. Within negotiating strategies, provisions can be geared to emphasize the development and utilization of local resources, including human resources, in technology transfer contracts. Specific measures to promote small enterprises specializing in biotechnology could be encouraged. The twin benefit of such a drive could make biotechnology self-sustaining by stimulating the national capacity of the biotechnology sector. Policy measures and strategic planning would also need to be focused on building a strong environment for biotechnology as well as realizing the goal of conservation and sustainable use of biodiversity.

In sum, strengthening institutional, technical, legislative and informational platforms needs to be given priority in the process of human resource development for the safe use of biotechnology. It takes time and money to establish and maintain an effective system (Cohen, 1999). Therefore, an integrated approach to capacity building for biotechnology and biosafety must be the hallmark for fulfilling the aspirations of developing countries. The approach has to be multi-sectoral and would require institutional linkages at the national and international levels. An important condition for capacity building to succeed is the development of mechanisms to ensure greater accountability. Success would also depend on the right combination of economic incentives and regulatory mechanisms backed by adequate monitoring and surveillance and supported by the capacity to address biosafety issues at the local level.

ONGOING PROGRAMMES ON CAPACITY BUILDING FOR THE SAFE USE OF BIOTECHNOLOGY

A brief assessment of biosafety capacity building programmes shows that a number of public, private, government, non-governmental and intergovernmental organizations are involved in one way or another in such initiatives. More than one hundred project activities are listed in the Biosafety Capacity Building database of the Cartagena Protocol on Biosafety. Agencies involved in such initiatives are the International Service for National Agricultural Research (ISNAR), the ISNAR Biotechnology Service (IBS), the International Centre for Genetic Engineering and Biotechnology (ICGEB), the International Service for the Acquisition of Agri-biotech Applications (ISAAA), the Global Environment Facility (GEF), the United Nations Industrial Development Organization (UNIDO), the US Agency for International Development (USAID) and many more. They are involved in a range of activities for building capacity in developing countries, and focus areas include research, institutional development, technology transfer, biosafety measures and related regulatory oversight. Another popular area is policy support. Although there is some overlap between the services offered by these organizations, each fulfils a certain function different to others, or places more emphasis on certain areas.

ISAAA focuses on brokering transfers between the private sector in the North and the public sector in the South and operates mostly in Africa and Southeast Asia. Under its *Biosafety Initiative* it assists client countries to build their institutional capacity in biosafety field trials and associated regulations for enabling the safe and effective transfer of biotechnology applications. The Biotechnology Service of ISNAR places emphasis on policy, addressing the need to create regulatory capacity particularly in agricultural research (UNEP, 1998). ICGEB on the other hand concentrates on providing institutional services, including scientific training in risk assessment and information dissemination on the release of LMOs into the environment through its Biosafety Clearing House. The Consultative Group on International Agricultural Research (CGIAR) centres have a significant biotech-nology capacity building component aimed at setting practical standards for biotechnology transfer. Besides developing regulatory capacity, each centre specializes in a select range of crops.

Some private funding agencies and a few industries are also active in capacity building initiatives. For instance, a focus of the Rockefeller Foundation is on development of research capacity in biotechnology, including capacity building on biosafety through partnerships with government agencies and the seed industry. Several projects on the transfer of technology are currently being carried out by the private sector. The focus is primarily on the development and release of crops for commercial planting, including transfer of technology for transgenic cassava, banana, sweet potato and papaya. Often their initiatives focus on training selected personnel who are directly responsible for biosafety regulation within the country. They are also involved in the development of human resources through fellowships and internships.

Short and long term training courses aim at enhancing competence and confidence of scientists, regulators and reviewers in a specific area of biosafety. The main strategies adopted for human resource development are running technical training courses, organizing workshops, providing internships and fellowships and disseminating information through the internet. Normally training includes general informative sessions on biotechnology and is useful in raising awareness and broadening the perspectives of senior policy makers who manage research or communicate with the public. Long term training programmes focus on more intensive technical training and are usually targeted at members of national biosafety committees and those reviewing field-test proposals or analysing biosafety guidelines.

Workshops are considered an effective way for building capacities through shared resources and experiences. The workshops are a combination of plenary presentations, working group sessions and joint follow-up discussions. They may be based on a case-study approach to allow participants to receive hands-on experience relevant to implementing biosafety measures. Workshop groups are generally small in size and mostly made up of those who have been assigned the creation of regulatory mechanisms. A mix of individuals from regulatory agencies that have been implementing biosafety regulations, companies that have used the regulations, ecologists, specialists on intellectual property rights and civil society representatives are usually invited to deliver lectures in these training courses and workshops.

Internships and scholarships are provided to a selected few for a relatively longer term. These fellowships could be for personnel responsible for developing oversight structures for biosafety or for carrying out research. Government agencies and seed companies, often in collaboration with private organizations, provide these kinds of training programmes.

Growth in the use of the internet has made distance learning and internet-based information dissemination a very appealing way of building capacity. Biosafety-related information, discussion and sharing of experiences are conducted through electronic publishing, e-conference and e-discussions. A number of organizations are involved in disseminating biosafety information and publishing biosafety documents for wide distribution, including ICGEB, UNIDO's Biosafety Information Network and Advisory Service (BINAS) and the Organisation for Economic Co-operation and Development (OECD) to name a prominent few.

The projects listed in Table 12.1 are being carried out at the regional level in Africa, which attracts a lesser number of initiatives compared to Asia, Latin America and the Caribbean (LAC). The Southeast Asian region is one of the prime focuses of activity of IBS, ISAAA and the Asian Development Bank. In Latin America, regional organizations active in biotechnology include the Inter-American Institute for Cooperation on Agriculture (IICA), CamBioTech and the Technical Cooperation Network on Plant Biotechnology in Latin America and the Caribbean, under the sponsorship of FAO (REDBIO/FAO). There are fewer African capacity building initiatives that are mostly coordinated and conducted by organizations, including the United Nations Environmental Program Global Environment Facility (UNEP-GEF), AfricaBio, South Africa Regional Biosafety Program (SARB), the East African Regional Programme and Research Network

Table 12.1 *Examples of capacity building initiatives on biotechnology and biosafety in Africa*

Status	Name	Coordinating Agencies	Collaborating Agencies/Corporations/Foundations	Goals and Type of Project
CO	Training Programme on Biosafety	United Nations Institute for Training and Research (UNITAR)	Proposed involvement of IUCN, UNEP, and the South Centre	Training, biosafety awareness and legal assistance to enable selected countries to meet the requirements of the Cartagena Protocol
ON	Biosafety Initiative	International Service for the Acquisition of Agri-biotech Applications (ISAAA)	Rockefeller Foundation; Agway; Monsanto; Centre for Research and Further Studies of the National Polytechnic Institute (Mexico) (CINVESTAV); National Institute for Research in Forestry Agriculture and Livestock Development (Mexico) (INIFAP); Fox Group; Animal and Plant Health Inspection Service of the United States Department of Agriculture (USDA/APHIS); the William Brown Fellowship	Information and resource sharing and provision of cumulative hands-on experience on biosafety that allow countries to formulate their own biosafety systems
ON	Plant Biotechnology Programme	African Agency of Biotechnology (AAB)		1) Reinforcement of national capabilities of African states in: (a) biotechnology and priority of biotechnological applications (b) production, distribution and commercialization of biotechnological products 2) reinforcement of infrastructures through training activities, research, equipment and infrastructures
ON	Capacity-Building Efforts of Individual Biotechnology Companies	Global Industry Coalition	Developing country research institutions, regulatory officials, biotechnology industry, OECD country universities, Agribiotechnologia de Costa Rica, AgrEvo GmbH, ANPROS (Chile), Asgrow Seed, Cargill, Dupont, ELM/Seminis, Monsanto, Mitsubishi Chemicals, Novartis, Pioneer Hi-Bred International, ProAgro (India), Schering, Zeneca Plant Sciences, ICI	Human-resources development and training, information exchange and data management (including the Biosafety Clearing House) and Institutional capacity building (including national regulatory frameworks)

ON	Research Capacity-Building on Agricultural Biotechnology	Rockefeller Foundation	A wide range of developing country research institutions; CGIAR-system international research institutions; developed countries agencies; private companies	Human-resources development and training and institutional capacity building (including national regulatory frameworks) in order to develop plant biotechnology research and develop capacities in developing countries, including biosafety procedures
ON	Demonstration projects on Implementation of National Biosafety Frameworks	UNEP/GEF	Relevant ministries and agencies in the participating countries	Strengthening national capacities for the implementation of the National Biosafety Frameworks in order to realize the objective of the Cartagena Protocol on Biosafety, through a variety of projects including institutional capacity building, risk management and scientific and technical collaboration
ON	Southern Africa Regional Biosafety Program (SARB)	South African Agricultural Council; Vegetable and Ornamental Plant Institute (VOPI)	Several national institutions	Building regional policy and technical capacity to support science-based regulation of the development, commercial application and trade in agricultural products derived from modern biotechnology through human-resources development and training, risk assessment and other scientific and technical expertise, public awareness, education and participation and scientific, technical and institutional collaboration
PL	Africa-wide Capacity Building Programme in Biosafety	Commission of the African Union	United Nations Environment Programme (UNEP) and Ethiopian Environmental Protection Authority	Strengthening the capacity of the African Union Member States to deal with biosafety issues through institutional capacity building, risk management, technical assistance and assitance in formulating national biosafety laws

Table 12.1 *Examples of capacity building initiatives on biotechnology and biosafety in Africa (continued)*

Status	Name	Coordinating Agencies	Collaborating Agencies/Corporations/Foundations	Goals and Type of Project
ON	Biotechnology and Biosafety programme	Association for Strengthening Agricultural Research in Eastern and Central Africa (ASARECA)	Institut des Sciences Agronomiques du Burundi (ISABU); Institut National Pour l'Etude et la Recherche Agronomiques (INERA) – DR Congo; Department of Agricultural Research and Human Resource Development (DARHRD) – Eritrea; Ethiopian Agricultural Research Organization (EARO); Kenya Agricultural Research Institute (KARI); Centre National de la Recherche Appliqué au Développement Rural (FOFIFA) – Madagascar; Institut Des Sciences Agronomiques du Rwanda (ISAR); Agricultural Research Corporation (ARC) – Sudan; Division of Research and Development (DRD), Ministry of Agriculture and Cooperatives – Tanzania; National Agricultural Research Organisation (NARO) – Uganda	The strategic goal of the programme is 'safe application of biotechnology for enhanced and sustainable productivity, competitiveness and value added agricultural systems'. The purpose is to promote the development and dissemination of relevant demand-driven biotechnologies for resource poor farmers as well as appropriate policies and regulations in the areas of biosafety and intellectual property rights
ON	USAID Program for Biosafety Systems (PBS)	International Service for National Agricultural Research (ISNAR)	International Food Policy Research Institute (IFPRI); Donald Danforth Plant Science Center; Agriculture and Biotechnology Strategies (AGBIOS) – Canada; Michigan State University (MSU); Western Michigan University (WMU); University of the Philippines (BIOTECH); National Agricultural Research Organization – Uganda	PBS is being implemented to enhance the ability of developing countries in Africa and Asia to address more effectively the impacts of modern biotechnology on the environment and human health. It seeks to address biosafety effectively within a sustainable development strategy anchored by agriculture-led economic growth, trade, and environment objectives of the partner countries and of the US

ON	East African Regional Programme and Research Network for Biotechnology, Biosafety and Biotechnology Policy Development (BIO-EARN)	Biotechnology Advisory Center (BAC) of the Stockholm Environment Institute (SEI)	Building national human resources, institutional and public capacity and competence in biotechnology, biosafety and biotechnology policy in Ethiopia, Kenya, Tanzania and Uganda
ON	AfricaBio	AfricaBio	AfricaBio is a non-political, non-profit biotechnology association for the safe, ethical and responsible research, development and application of biotechnology and its products. The Association also serves as a forum for informed dialogue on biotechnological issues in Africa. Activities include informing and lobbying key stakeholders, providing accurate information on biotechnology to the media and the general public, and providing international organizations lobbying for or against biotechnology with information on the need for this technology in South Africa and Africa

Note: CO = Project completed
ON = Project ongoing
NK = Status not specified
PL = Planned
Source: Biosafety Capacity Building database of the Cartagena Protocol on Biosafety, November 2004.

for Biotechnology, Biosafety and Biotechnology Policy Development (BIO-EARN), ISAAA, the Swedish International Development Cooperation Agency (Sida) and USAID. With most projects it is hoped that the partnerships thus developed would lead to the sharing of experiences and exchange of information within the region. However, the number of projects listed in Table 12.1 is not exhaustive and can only be considered indicative of the variety of capacity building activities going on in different regions of the world.

Workshops appear to be the most popular capacity building activity. Projects on diverse themes have been listed in the Biosafety Capacity Building database of the Cartagena Protocol of which an overwhelming number have already been completed. In recent years, a significant number of them have been organized by government agencies and intergovernmental and non-governmental organizations mainly for policy support and regulatory oversight. They are mostly short duration courses lasting on average three or four days. It is not possible to analyse the impact of these courses without analysing the feedback of the participants in some detail. Although fellowships provide long-term training, it is evident from Table 12.1 that they are but few in number and provided by government agencies only for selected research projects.

Since biosafety requires protection of the environment, human health and agricultural production and equitable distribution of the benefits for the welfare of its inhabitants, capacity building to fulfil these needs of developing countries is a heavy responsibility. On the one hand, there are the projects undertaken by various public, private, governmental and intergovernmental organizations, and on the other, there are the needs and legitimate demands of developing countries as outlined in the previous section that remain to be addressed. Only some developing countries have biosafety regulations and the majority do not. What is even more critical is that many do not have the personnel with interdisciplinary training needed to carry out risk analyses and risk management as required by current regulations. Therefore, despite considerable financial commitment by the donors and executing agencies through the numerous projects that have been undertaken, much still needs to be done. An assessment of capacity building needs in the critical areas is being conducted by GEF through its Capacity Development Initiative. It has recently launched a comprehensive, long-term strategy and action plan with the assistance of regional and national experts to address these pertinent problems (UNEP, 2002).

TRANSFER OF TECHNOLOGY AND BIOSAFETY CAPACITY BUILDING – TWIN GOALS

Biotechnology uses a wide range of disciplines and its safe application draws on various scientific and technical skills combined with effective policy, regulatory and institutional frameworks that can facilitate its sustainable use and safe deployment.

The international agreements on regulatory frameworks for the conservation of biodiversity (CBD) and the safe use of biotechnology (CPB) endorse the need to improve developing countries' access to biotechnology and to develop their capacity in biosafety. Along with Agenda 21, these agreements emphasize the equitable distribution of the benefits of biotechnology and the minimizing of risks of the new technology.

The need for capacity building in biosafety arises particularly when the country has an operating biotechnology sector. Capacity is then needed for everything from ensuring safety in laboratory research to addressing long-term environmental and food safety concerns. The main prerequisite, however, is that there is the necessary workforce and infrastructure for biotechnology itself. Many developing countries lack both, although they are eager to access and use biotechnologies which can alleviate some of the problems. Their capacity building needs cannot be considered in the narrow context of *biosafety*, which only deals with risks and hazards posed by the spread of LMOs. Besides, it cannot be overlooked that the CPB's Article 22 on capacity building is linked to the conditions of access to and transfer of technology. It clearly indicates the desire of the international community to ensure that benefits of biotechnology are fully accessed while managing any potential risks. Therefore, all capacity building strategies have to be integrated with the overall management of biotechnology so that they are mutually supportive and complementary. Negotiators and lawmakers may wish to consider this broader approach in their work.

A variety of projects and programmes are listed in the capacity building database. They do address some of the critical and necessary aspects of human resource development, but seem to lack a focused and comprehensive strategy. One-off training programmes targeted at building competence for the implementation of the CPB cannot be of much assistance. Feedback mechanisms also have to be strengthened. Developing countries for their part need to retain capacity and open ways of channelling capacity to the local level. This calls for visionary policies in decision-making and infrastructure development. They also need effective negotiating strategies for technology transfer and for creating favourable conditions for trade and sustainable development. A broad-based multi-stakeholder approach to capacity building with effective information dissemination that promotes communication in all aspects of risk and benefits of biotechnology could be a step in that direction.

References

Codex Alimentarius Commission (2001) *Summary and Conclusions*, Twenty-fourth Session, Geneva, 2–7 July 2001, ALINORM 01/41, paras 99–207, Rome

Cohen, J (1999) *Managing Agricultural Biotechnology; Addressing Research Program Needs and Policy Implications*, CABI Publishing, Wallingford, UK

Krattiger, A (2002) 'Public-private partnerships for efficient proprietary biotech management and transfer, and increased private sector investments', *IP Strategy Today*, no 4, bioDevelopments International Institute Inc., Ithaca, NY

OIE (2003) 'A good start by the OIE on the implementation of Doha Declaration and its commitment to assist developing countries, including strengthening infrastructures on their veterinary services', Office International des Epizooties Press Release, 8 January, Paris

UNEP (1992a) *Agenda 21*, United Nations Environment Programme, Geneva

UNEP (1992b) *Convention of Biological Diversity*, United Nations Environment Programme, Geneva

UNEP (1996) *Promoting and Facilitating Access to, and Transfer and Development of Technology*, UNEP/CBD/COP/3/21, United Nations Environment Programme, Geneva

UNEP (1998) *Measures to Promote and Advance the Distribution of Benefits from Biotechnology in Accordance with Article 19*, UNEP/CBD/COP/4/21, United Nations Environment Programme, Geneva

UNEP (2000) *Cartagena Protocol on Biosafety*, United Nations Environment Programme/ Convention on Biological Diversity, Geneva

UNEP (2002) 'Largest ever project to promote biosafety launched by UNEP', United Nations Environment Programme Press Release, January, Geneva

13

Regulating Trade in GMOs: Biotechnology and the WTO[1]

Christiane Wolff

The World Trade Organization (WTO)'s Agreements on Sanitary and Phyto-sanitary Measures (SPS) and Technical Barriers to Trade (TBT) establish rules that give countries the right to restrict trade to protect health and the environment, while aiming to prevent the use of technical regulations and sanitary and phyto-sanitary measures for protectionist purposes. WTO Members have the obligation to notify all new or changed SPS and TBT regulations that are not based on international standards if they have a significant effect on trade. An increasing number of TBT and SPS measures that do have such a significant impact on trade are related to the trade of genetically modified organisms (GMOs). As of November 2004, more than 140 SPS notifications related to GMOs have been circulated concerning diverse topics including genetically modified food and feed additives, risk assessments of GMO products and labelling. Under the TBT Agreement, more than 90 GMO-related notifications have been circulated, often related to labelling requirements. Many governments have notified GMO regulations under both Agreements, while others have only notified under one. The purpose of these measures is to ensure that GMOs do not pose an unacceptable risk to human health or the environment, or to provide information to consumers through labelling requirements. The measures are taken under increasing pressure from consumer groups, industry and the media. Whether all of these measures are in conformity with the TBT and SPS Agreements is an open question.

THE ORIGINS OF THE SPS AND TBT AGREEMENTS

Prior to the establishment of the WTO, its predecessor, the General Agreement on Tariffs and Trade (GATT), recognized the right of governments to take the measures necessary to protect human, animal or plant life or health, or the environment. They had to ensure that these measures did not arbitrarily or unjustifiably discriminate between countries where the same conditions prevailed, or constituted a disguised restriction on international trade.

During the Uruguay Round, countries wished to make the rules that applied to this area more operational and to increase transparency. They revised the TBT Agreement, also known as the Standards Code, which had been developed during the Tokyo Round of trade negotiations. This Agreement deals with technical requirements in general, requiring that they are not more trade-restrictive than required to achieve a legitimate objective. In addition, the SPS Agreement was negotiated to establish rules for measures that are taken to ensure food safety, animal and plant health in trade. These Agreements also address the concern that reductions in subsidies and tariffs could increase the pressure to use technical regulations, including sanitary and phytosanitary measures, as disguised trade barriers.

The SPS and TBT Agreements do not contain rules that deal explicitly with biosafety and biotechnology, but since they cover all goods traded between WTO Members, they also apply to products of biotechnology. Which Agreement applies to a national regulation on GMOs depends both on the type of measure and on its objective (see below).

FUNDAMENTALS OF THE SPS AGREEMENT

The SPS Agreement makes it clear that each country has the right to decide what level of health risk it considers acceptable, or in other words, what level of protection is desirable.[2] While free to choose what level of protection they deem appropriate, WTO Members have to avoid arbitrary or unjustifiable distinctions in the levels that are considered appropriate in different situations, if these distinctions result in discrimination or a disguised restriction on international trade (Article 5.5).

The Agreement recognizes that it is sometimes unavoidable to restrict trade in order to protect human, animal or plant life or health. It allows governments to take the sanitary (human and animal health) and phytosanitary (plant health) measures that are necessary to protect health, but seeks to prevent unnecessary trade obstacles. One of the basic obligations contained in the SPS Agreement is that SPS measures must be based on scientific principles and may not be maintained without sufficient scientific evidence (Article 2.2). This last provision means that even measures taken prior to the entry into force of the SPS Agreement require a scientific foundation. In cases where scientific evidence is insufficient, Article 5.7 allows countries to adopt provisional measures (see Box 13.1).

BOX 13.1 SPS AGREEMENT ARTICLE 5.7

In cases where relevant scientific evidence is insufficient, a Member may provisionally adopt sanitary or phytosanitary measures on the basis of available pertinent information, including that from the relevant international organizations as well as from sanitary and phytosanitary measures applied by other Members. In such circumstances, Members shall seek to obtain the additional information necessary for a more objective assessment of risk and review the sanitary or phytosanitary measure accordingly within a reasonable period of time.

Source: World Trade Organization

There are two alternative ways of ensuring that an SPS measure has a scientific basis. The first option is to base measures on a relevant international standard, guideline or recommendation. This alternative has the advantage that measures conforming to an international standard are presumed to be consistent with the SPS Agreement (Article 3.2). The Agreement explicitly recognizes the international standards, guidelines and recommendations of three international organizations. In the area of food safety, the relevant standards are those established by the joint Food and Agriculture Organization (FAO)/World Health Organization (WHO) Codex Alimentarius Commission. For animal health and diseases passed from animals to humans the Agreement recognizes the standards developed by the World Organisation for Animal Health (OIE). In the area of plant health, the relevant standards are those of the FAO International Plant Protection Convention (IPPC). Additionally, for matters not covered by these organizations, the SPS Committee may identify standards, guidelines and recommendations promulgated by other organizations.

In cases where no relevant international standard exists, or where a WTO Member decides not to adopt an existing international standard, an SPS measure must be based on a risk assessment (Articles 3.3, 5.1–5.3). These risk assessments have to take into account available scientific evidence, relevant processes and production methods, inspection, sampling and testing methods, pest and disease prevalence, relevant ecological conditions and quarantine or other treatment. In assessing risks to animal or plant life or health, WTO Members also have to take into account relevant economic factors, including potential damage in terms of loss of production or sales, the cost of control or eradication programmes, and the relative cost-effectiveness of alternative approaches to limiting risks. WTO Members do not necessarily have to carry out their own risk assessments; measures can be based on risk assessments carried out by another country, or by a regional or international body.

The SPS Agreement requires WTO Members to ensure that measures are not more trade-restrictive than required to achieve the appropriate level of sanitary or phytosanitary protection (Article 5.6). The Agreement makes it clear that a measure is not more trade-restrictive than required unless another measure is reasonably available, taking into account technical and economic feasibility, that achieves the appropriate level of protection and is significantly less restrictive to trade. Thus, if a less trade-restrictive measure exists, but a country is technically or economically unable to implement it, this in itself does not constitute a violation of the Agreement.

FUNDAMENTALS OF THE TBT AGREEMENT

The TBT Agreement applies to product requirements that are mandatory (technical regulations) as well as voluntary (standards) and to conformity assessment procedures. Technical regulations must not be more trade-restrictive than necessary to achieve a legitimate objective. These legitimate objectives include health and environmental protection. Although the TBT Agreement does not require that all measures be based on science, scientific and technical information may be considered a relevant element to take into account when assessing risks (see Box 13.2). In addition, the TBT Agreement does not allow for discrimination between like products (Article 2.1).

BOX 13.2 TBT AGREEMENT ARTICLE 2.2

Members shall ensure that technical regulations are not prepared, adopted or applied with a view to or with the effect of creating unnecessary obstacles to international trade. For this purpose, technical regulations shall not be more trade-restrictive than necessary to fulfil a legitimate objective, taking account of the risks non-fulfilment would create. Such legitimate objectives are, inter alia: national security requirements; the prevention of deceptive practices; protection of human health or safety, animal or plant life or health, or the environment. In assessing such risks, relevant elements of consideration are, inter alia: available scientific and technical information, related processing technology or intended end-uses of products.

Source: World Trade Organization

Like the SPS Agreement, the TBT Agreement encourages governments to use international standards (Article 2.4). However, the TBT Agreement does not explicitly recognize the standards developed by certain international organizations; it is up to WTO Members to decide which international standards are relevant. Under the TBT Agreement, WTO Members may deviate from international standards if they are thought to be ineffective at or inappropriate to achieving the legitimate objective pursued, for example because of climatic or geographical factors, or because of fundamental technological problems. In addition, the TBT Agreement recognizes that developing countries may adopt measures aimed at preserving indigenous technology and production methods compatible with their development needs and that developing countries therefore should not be expected to use international standards, including test methods, that are not appropriate to their development, financial and trade needs (Article 12.4).

ARTICLE XX OF GATT

The GATT 1994 lays down the basic rules for trade in goods. It contains provisions on non-discrimination, for example, that are relevant to trade in GMOs, including national treatment on internal taxation and regulation. In particular, products from other WTO Member countries must not receive less favourable treatment than that accorded to like products of national origin.[3]

Article XX permits Members to derogate from general GATT obligations in certain circumstances. Among other things, WTO Members are allowed to take measures that would otherwise violate GATT rules to protect public morals, human, animal or plant life or health and to conserve exhaustible natural resources (Article XX(a), (b) and (g)). The Member invoking Article XX in defence of a measure carries the burden of proving that the measure meets the criteria for an Article XX exception and that it is not an abuse of an exception under the introductory clause of Article XX. In the case of measures taken to protect human, animal or plant life or health, a WTO Member would first have to show that the measure was *necessary* and that no alternative measure to achieve the same end was consistent with GATT nor reasonably available.[4] In addition, measures taken under Article XX must not be applied in a manner that would constitute a means of arbitrary or unjustifiable discrimination between countries where the same conditions prevail, nor be a disguised restriction on international trade.

TRADE IN GMOs: WHICH WTO AGREEMENT APPLIES?

Under what circumstances do the SPS and TBT Agreements or GATT apply to GMO regulations? The SPS Agreement has a very limited scope. The definition of an SPS measure contained in Annex A of the Agreement is described in Table 13.1.

In the discussion of biosafety and biotechnology, the first and last parts of this definition seem particularly relevant, namely, protection from food safety risks and from damage caused by pests. In the case of food safety, the SPS Agreement applies to risks from additives, contaminants, toxins or disease-causing organisms. Any measure addressing a risk arising from the possible presence of toxins in GM food or GM additives would thus be covered. On the other hand, a regulation with the objective of protecting the environment to avoid the spread of GMOs, their

Table 13.1 *Applications of the SPS Agreement*

The SPS Agreement applies to all measures taken by governments	
to protect:	from:
Human health and life	risks arising from additives, contaminants, toxins or disease-causing organisms in foods and beverages; or risks arising from disease carried by animals, plants or their products, or from the entry and spread of pests
Animal health and life	risks arising from the entry, establishment or spread of pests, diseases, disease-causing or disease-carrying organisms; or risks arising from additives, contaminants, toxins or disease-causing organisms in feedstuffs
Plant life and health	risks arising from the entry, establishment or spread of pests, diseases, disease-causing or disease-carrying organisms
The territory of the country	other damage from the entry, establishment or spread of pests

Source: World Trade Organization

breeding with wild relatives, or negative effects on wild animals, for example, might be considered a measure taken to prevent or limit damage from the entry, establishment or spread of pests. It is important to note that in this definition of SPS measures, 'animal' includes fish and wild fauna; 'plant' includes forests and wild flora; 'pests' include weeds and 'contaminants' include pesticide and veterinary drug residues and extraneous matter.

The TBT Agreement addresses technical regulations and conformity assessment procedures. In addition, in an annex it contains the Code of Good Practice for the Preparation, Adoption and Application of Standards. For the purposes of the TBT Agreement, a technical regulation is a document that lays down mandatory product characteristics or their related processes and production methods. It may include terminology, symbols, packaging, marking or labelling requirements that apply to a product, process or production method. A standard, as defined by the TBT Agreement, lays down similar requirements to a technical regulation, but compliance with standards is not mandatory. A conformity assessment procedure is any procedure that is used to determine that relevant requirements in technical regulations or standards are fulfilled.

The TBT Agreement explicitly excludes SPS measures, so that there can be no overlap in coverage. However, sometimes a government might adopt a regulation that contains some elements covered by the TBT Agreement and other aspects that fall under the SPS Agreement. Thus, regulations on pesticides might contain quality requirements and safe handling instructions, which would be covered by the TBT Agreement and maximum residue levels for pesticides in food, which would be covered by the SPS Agreement.

Both the SPS Agreement and Article XX of the GATT 1994 contain provisions concerning measures taken to protect human, animal and plant life or health. In the preamble of the SPS Agreement, WTO Members state that they are elaborating 'rules for the application of the provisions of GATT 1994 which relate to the use of sanitary and phytosanitary measures, in particular the provisions of Article XX(b)'. Article 2.4 of the SPS Agreement further clarifies that SPS measures which conform to the SPS Agreement shall be presumed to comply with the relevant obligations under GATT 1994, in particular the provisions of Article XX(b).[5]

The relationship between the TBT Agreement and the GATT 1994 is less clear. In the preamble, WTO Members state their desire to further the objective of GATT 1994, but there is no presumption of consistency with GATT for measures that comply with the TBT Agreement. In the *Asbestos* dispute, the panel found that an import ban did not constitute a technical regulation and thus was not covered by the TBT Agreement, but by the GATT 1994. The Appellate Body reversed this finding and added that the TBT Agreement was a specialized legal regime for a limited class of measures that imposed obligations that are *different* from and *additional* to the obligations imposed on WTO Members under the GATT 1994.[6]

So far no trade dispute over GMOs has been examined by a WTO dispute settlement panel and it is not entirely clear how the rules would be applied. The following section looks at areas where governments are developing different types of regulation and some of the relevant provisions that might be applied. Many GMO-related regulations, test requirements before field trials are permitted, for example, might not have a big impact on trade. The SPS and TBT Agreements and GATT are relevant only when a regulation has a direct or indirect impact on international trade between WTO Members.

NATIONAL POLICY LINKAGES TO THE TBT AND SPS AGREEMENTS

Health-related requirements

Food safety regulations are generally covered by the SPS Agreement but other health concerns are covered by the TBT Agreement. Depending on which Agreement applies to a particular regulation, it would have to fulfil different requirements to be in conformity with WTO rules. Which Agreement applies depends on the precise nature of the risk the regulation is addressing. In the case of GMOs, the most common health concerns are related to toxic substances or allergenicity. Regulations might also address new substances that could potentially be present in the food, or nutritional changes. Another concern is possible development of antibiotic resistance due to the presence of antibiotic marker genes in GMOs.[7]

Any regulation concerned with toxic substances that might be present in GM food or feed would be covered by the definition of an SPS measure contained in the SPS Agreement (see Table 13.1). Such measures therefore need to have a scientific foundation and be based either on an international standard, or on a risk assessment. Since plants naturally produce toxins, it is imaginable that through breeding or genetic modification these toxins could be produced at higher levels. On the other hand, if genetic modification reduces damage to the product, by reducing insect feeding, for example, this could lead to lower levels of toxins such as aflatoxins. A requirement to test GM foods for toxins before they can be placed on the market thus would be scientifically justifiable (depending on how it is done).

It is less clear whether regulations to require testing for allergens in food, or labelling of foods containing allergens, would be covered by the SPS Agreement. The question is whether an allergen would be considered a toxin or a disease-causing organism within the definition of an SPS measure. Since it is well known that certain proteins trigger allergies in some people, it would probably not be controversial scientifically to require labelling to protect consumers from this risk. Many countries already require labelling for common allergens. New proteins present in GM food could potentially trigger allergies and might require testing.[8] Thus, regardless of whether the SPS or TBT Agreement applies, testing for and labelling of allergens are likely to be in conformity with the relevant provisions.

Other measures might be concerned with changed nutritional values of genetically modified foods necessitating labelling, or might deal with safe handling of GMOs. Although these measures address health concerns, they are not related to food safety and would thus be covered by the TBT Agreement. Health protection is a legitimate objective under the TBT Agreement. As long as such a measure complies with the other provisions of the TBT Agreement, such as being the least trade-restrictive way to achieve the legitimate objective, it should be acceptable to WTO Members. A measure addressing risks associated with antibiotic resistance might be covered by the SPS or TBT Agreements, depending on its precise objective.

In July 2003, the Codex Alimentarius Commission adopted three risk analysis standards for food derived from biotechnology, including general principles for the risk analysis of such foods and more detailed draft guidelines for the food safety assessment of foods derived from recombinant DNA plants and micro-organisms. The standards contain references to the 'tracing of products' and food labelling as risk management tools, and an annex on the assessment of possible allergenicity. In addition, the Codex Committee on Food Labelling is working on recommendations for labelling of foods derived from biotechnology.

Some of the standards developed by the OIE deal with animal diseases that have human health and biosafety implications. These standards are approved by the OIE Member countries and published in the OIE International Animal Health Code. The OIE also publishes the Manual of Standards for Diagnostic Tests and Vaccines and a few of the tests and vaccines use GMOs. The OIE has had a working group on biotechnology since 1996. Standards developed by Codex and the OIE can become reference points for WTO Members' SPS and TBT measures, although deviations from international standards under the circumstances described above are permitted.

Environmental regulations

Depending on their objective, environmental regulations on GMOs could be covered by different agreements. Some of the main concerns that environmental regulations might address are pesticide resistance, genetic flow and weediness of crops. Measures taken in response to some of these risks would be covered by the SPS Agreement. Thus, a measure that is taken to protect animals or plants from harmful effects of GMOs would fall under the SPS Agreement if the GMO could be considered a disease-causing organism or a pest, or if the GMO is used as a food or feedstuff and contains toxins. An example of such a risk is harm to non-target species feeding on a genetically modified plant that contains a pesticide.

If GMOs that are engineered to facilitate pest management cause pesticide resistance, this might lead to problems if a target species, an insect, say, becomes more difficult to manage. It could be argued that a measure dealing with such a risk was taken to protect a country from damage associated with pests and thus covered by the SPS Agreement. Likewise, if crops engineered to be herbicide resistant become a weed, or if such a trait gets transferred to wild relatives of a crop plant through gene flow, they could be considered a pest and thus covered by the SPS Agreement.

Environmental measures that fall under the SPS Agreement would have to comply with the provisions of the Agreement, including scientific justification. WTO Members would have to choose the least trade-restrictive alternative available to them. If a GMO-related environmental measure did not fit into the definition of an SPS measure, it would probably be covered by the TBT Agreement. Under the TBT Agreement, scientific and technical information are relevant elements to be considered when assessing risks. A TBT measure would have to be the least trade-restrictive way of achieving the measure's objective of environmental protection and comply with the other provisions of the TBT Agreement.

The IPPC has formed an open-ended working group on phytosanitary aspects of GMOs, biosafety and invasive species. It will develop standards for pest risk assessment of living modified organisms, in close cooperation with the Secretariat of the Cartagena Protocol on Biosafety. Standards developed by the IPPC will be relevant for WTO Members that are defining their policies in these areas. Like standards developed by Codex and the OIE, IPPC standards provide a safe haven for countries developing their national GMO policies, although deviations are possible where there is a scientific justification under the SPS Agreement, or for the reasons contained in the TBT Agreement.

CURRENT DEBATES IN THE TBT AND SPS COMMITTEES

Labelling

Labelling of GM products may be desirable for several reasons, including both health and environmental concerns. Labels can provide information about allergens, changed cooking characteristics or nutritional content of food, ethical or environmental concerns, and can help to prevent deceptive practices. As mentioned above, where there is a food safety concern related to toxins, a labelling requirement would be covered by the SPS Agreement. Labelling requirements to do with nutritional characteristics or other concerns not related to food safety would be covered by the TBT Agreement.

Labelling of genetically modified organisms has been hotly debated in the TBT Committee. The discussion has focused on the question of whether providing consumer information through labelling of GMOs is a legitimate objective that justifies a trade restriction. The list of legitimate objectives in the TBT Agreement is an open list, but it does not explicitly include informing consumers. Some WTO Members, including the EU and Norway, argue that consumers have the right to know what they are purchasing and that a label allows them to make informed choices. From their point of view, labelling is a less trade-restrictive alternative to an import ban. Other WTO Members, such as Canada and the United States, are of the view that labelling GMOs would mislead consumers into thinking that there is something wrong with the product even if there is no health risk and the product has the same characteristics as a non-modified product. There is also a broader discussion in the TBT Committee whether the Agreement covers labelling requirements related to processes and production methods that do not alter the characteristics of the final product.

Much of the debate on GMO labelling was sparked by a European Union requirement for labelling of GMO foods under the Regulation on novel foods and novel food ingredients (EC 258/97) that was notified under the TBT Agreement in 1997. This regulation did not clarify the threshold for GMO content above which labelling would be required and thus led to insecurity on the part of the EU's trading partners. Since testing for GMOs is in many cases costly and difficult, many WTO Members expressed concern regarding the difficulties of ensuring and enforcing compliance with the regulation. Many Members also argued that mandatory labelling for GMOs would require keeping GMOs separate from non-modified products, which would be very costly. According to these countries, even in the absence of a government-mandated labelling scheme, voluntary labelling schemes and niche markets would develop if there was demand from consumers, comparable to the market for organically grown foods.

Another reason for labelling might be to give consumers who are morally opposed to genetic modification the option of avoiding GM foods. One example might be people who, for religious reasons, do not wish to consume products containing pig genes. Such a regulation might fall under Article XX(a) of the GATT, which covers measures that are necessary to protect public morals.

Some WTO Members are developing or implementing regulations that would require traceability of genetically modified foodstuffs. For example, new EU regulations, which came into effect in April 2004, require traceability as well as labelling of genetically modified food and feed, not only for GMOs as or in products including seeds, but also for products derived from GMOs, such as oil or flour produced from genetically modified soybeans. The stated objectives of the traceability requirement are: facilitation of withdrawal of products should an unforeseen risk to human health or the environment be established; targeted monitoring of potential effects on human health or the environment, where appropriate; and control and verification of labelling claims.[9] In addition, the new regulations set a threshold of 0.9 per cent, below which GM products would be exempt from labelling, and 0.5 per cent for the adventitious presence of GMOs that are unauthorized but have nevertheless been assessed as risk-free.

The EU initially only notified the new EU regulations under the TBT Agreement, but after questions from several WTO Members in the TBT and SPS Committees, the EU notified them under the SPS Agreement as well. At TBT Committee meetings, one WTO Member expressed concern that the regulations could impede trade, that they were not commensurate with the risks which might arise and were inconsistent with the EU policies concerning similar risks in other situations. At the SPS Committee meeting, a few WTO Members expressed concern that the measure was not scientifically justified and that it was more trade-restrictive than necessary.[10]

Import bans

A general ban on imports of genetically modified products would probably be hard to justify under WTO rules. In the absence of scientific evidence of health or environmental risks, a ban with the objective of ensuring food safety would not be consistent with the SPS Agreement's requirement for scientific justification. However, if a WTO Member considered that in a particular situation scientific evidence was insufficient, it could adopt a provisional measure based on available pertinent information if it fulfilled the conditions described in Box 13.1.

In the SPS Committee, Thailand has raised concern regarding Egypt's restrictions on canned tuna imports, allegedly because of concerns that the tuna was canned in genetically modified soy oil. In September 2000, Thailand requested official consultations with Egypt under the WTO Dispute Settlement Procedure. Although officially the procedure remains open, the two parties reportedly have agreed on a solution involving certification that Thai tuna is not canned in oil produced from genetically modified soybeans.

There is some debate over whether import bans are covered by the TBT Agreement at all, whether they can be considered technical regulations. In the

Asbestos case, the panel found that the French prohibition on the importation of asbestos fibres and products that contain asbestos fibres was not a technical regulation and thus was not covered by the TBT Agreement. The Appellate Body reversed this finding, arguing that the measure lays down product characteristics and can thus be considered a technical regulation as defined in the TBT Agreement. However, the Appellate Body emphasized that it did not mean that *all* import prohibitions were to be considered technical regulations under the TBT Agreement.[11]

Assuming that an import restriction on GM products is covered by the TBT Agreement, its consistency with the Agreement depends on whether GMOs and their products on one hand and their non-modified counterparts on the other hand are considered *like* products, that is, whether they are substantially the same products. According to established practices under the GATT, likeness is determined on a case-by-case basis according to four criteria, the products' physical properties, end-uses, tariff classification and consumers' tastes and habits (Musselli and Zarrilli, 2002). This is another rather contentious issue in the WTO and one whose outcome remains uncertain. In the case of processed foods a decision might have to be made, for example, on whether mayonnaise containing oil from modified soybeans and mayonnaise containing oil from non-modified soybeans are like products.

Both the SPS and TBT Agreements require measures to be no more trade-restrictive than necessary. Unless there is evidence of health or environmental risks, an import ban would probably be considered more trade-restrictive than necessary under both Agreements. As noted before, under the SPS Agreement such a measure might be acceptable if less trade-restrictive alternatives were not economically or technically feasible.

WHOSE SCIENCE IS RIGHT UNDER THE SPS AGREEMENT?

Scientific justification is of crucial importance in deciding whether GMO regulations are consistent with WTO rules, especially with the SPS Agreement. The examination of the scientific basis for SPS measures invariably raises the question: what is acceptable scientific evidence? And, since scientists have been known to disagree, whose scientific opinion will be taken into account? In dispute settlement, a panel usually consists of specialists in trade law, but not of scientific experts. The SPS Agreement thus states that in cases involving scientific or technical issues, a panel should seek expert advice. The panel itself chooses these experts in consultation with the parties to the dispute. The panel may decide to consult individual experts, or to establish an advisory group of technical experts. Under the TBT Agreement, panels may establish a technical expert group to assist in questions of a technical nature.

Experts were consulted in all SPS disputes, either at the request of the parties or at the panel's own initiative.[12] The experts were selected from lists provided by the relevant international organizations of experts in fields related to the cases and the parties submitted further names of experts. The panels, again in consultation with the parties, submitted written questions to each expert. The experts provided their responses in writing to those questions they felt qualified to address. They also participated in a meeting with the panel and the parties to discuss their written answers and to respond to additional questions. Verbatim transcripts of these meetings are annexed to the panel reports.

However, even the experts consulted by a panel might disagree. It is important to note that in one of the SPS cases, the Appellate Body found that risk assessments could set out both the mainstream scientific opinion on a matter, as well as the opinions of scientists taking a divergent view.[13] The Appellate Body thought that the very fact that qualified scientists had divergent views might indicate a state of scientific uncertainty. In some cases governments may act in good faith on the basis of what, at a given time, might be a divergent scientific opinion coming from qualified and respected sources. If a risk assessment was based on such divergent opinions, according to the Appellate Body this did not necessarily signal the absence of a reasonable relationship between an SPS measure and the risk assessment, especially where there was a serious risk to public health.

Scientific knowledge evolves; a measure that at one time seemed justified might not be considered necessary as science evolves. On the other hand, in light of new scientific evidence a measure that at one point was thought to achieve the desired level of health protection might no longer appear to be sufficient. WTO Members thus have to ensure that their measures are adapted based on new evidence and that they are not maintained where the science no longer supports them. Comparing measures with past decisions, or with measures taken by other WTO Members in similar situations could also be helpful. Of course, nothing prevents Members from adopting provisional SPS measures to ensure that health is protected even in cases where scientific evidence is insufficient, as described in Box 13.1.

NO SINGLE APPROACH TO BIOSAFETY AMONG WTO MEMBERS

In preparations for the Ministerial Conference in Seattle in 1999, several WTO Members proposed the establishment of a working group in the WTO to study GMOs. This group might have examined GMOs and their relationship with the different WTO Agreements and evaluated the need for further action. However, no such working group has been established and the issue has not been discussed since the Seattle Ministerial.

In accordance with Article 20 of the Agreement on Agriculture, negotiations to continue the agricultural reform process that started with the implementation of the results of the Uruguay Round began in 2000. In this context, the United States has submitted a proposal that calls for disciplines to ensure that processes covering trade in products developed through new technologies are transparent, predictable and timely.[14] Korea's proposal calls for appropriate measures to address consumers' concern on food safety and quality and potential risks of GMOs to human health and the environment.[15] However, these aspects of the two proposals have not been discussed in any detail.

In the context of these negotiations and although the Agriculture Agreement does not directly address health issues, the European Union and Japan have also submitted informal proposals on food safety. In Japan's view it is necessary to evaluate, in the light of new consumer concerns, including those about genetically modified organisms, whether the existing agreements are sufficient to ensure food safety. The European Union has proposed to clarify the application of the *precautionary principle* in the WTO. In particular, the EU has proposed a series of criteria for the application of *precaution* that it believes to be fully consistent with relevant provisions of the SPS Agreement as interpreted by the Appellate Body in, for example, the *Hormones* case (see Box 13.3). The EU wants WTO Members to reach an agreed understanding on such criteria.

In the discussions of these proposals, WTO Members generally stressed the importance they attach to food safety. However, although a number of Members supported the EU proposal, other countries were opposed to the specific ideas put on the table. They feared that an understanding along the lines proposed might weaken the importance of science as a basis for SPS measures and thus lead to protectionism. In any event, they considered that food safety issues should be addressed in the SPS and TBT Committees and/or in the relevant international standard-setting organizations. It is unclear how these diverging views might be reconciled. Other subjects to be addressed in the agriculture negotiations are consumer information and labelling, and developing country aspects.

At the Ministerial Conference held in Doha, Qatar, in November 2001, WTO Members agreed to negotiations on the relationship between existing WTO rules and specific trade obligations set out in multilateral environmental agreements (MEAs); procedures for regular information exchange between MEA secretariats and the relevant WTO committees; and reduction or elimination of tariff and non-tariff barriers to environmental goods and services.[16]

The Ministerial Declaration also instructs the Committee on Trade and Environment to give particular attention to: the effect of environmental measures on market access, especially in relation to developing and least-developed countries and those situations in which the elimination of trade restrictions and distortions would benefit trade, the environment and development; the relevant provisions of the Agreement on Trade-related Aspects of Intellectual Property Rights; and labelling requirements for environmental purposes. WTO Members explicitly state that neither the negotiations on environmental issues nor the work of the Committee on Trade and Environment shall add to or diminish the rights and obligations of WTO Members under existing WTO agreements, in particular the SPS Agreement.

Although GMOs or biotechnology are not specifically mentioned in the Doha Ministerial Declaration, the new work programme launched at this meeting is quite relevant to the subject, especially regarding trade and the environment. The clarification of the relationship between WTO rules and MEAs might have implications for trade in GMOs, for example through the Cartagena Protocol. The discussions of the Committee on Trade and Environment on the trade effect of environmental measures and on environmental labelling are also potentially very pertinent. The negotiations and discussions are an opportunity for WTO Members to discuss whether greater clarity is needed in the applicability of WTO rules to biosafety and biotechnology.

BOX 13.3 PRECAUTION AND THE SPS AND TBT AGREEMENTS

In the *Hormones* dispute, the EC did not invoke Article 5.7 of the SPS Agreement (see Box 13.1). It stated explicitly that its measure was not provisional. Instead, the EC invoked the *precautionary principle* as a customary rule of international law or, at least, a general principle of law, and argued that the obligation to base SPS measures on risk assessment did not prevent WTO Members from being cautious when setting health standards in the face of conflicting scientific evidence and uncertainty.

The Appellate Body did not take a position on the status of the *precautionary principle* in international law, but it noted that it 'finds reflection in Article 5.7 of the SPS Agreement'. The Appellate Body agreed with the finding of the panel that the *precautionary principle* – to the extent that it is not explicitly incorporated in Article 5.7 – does not override the provisions regarding risk assessment contained in Article 5.1 and 5.2 of the SPS Agreement. In the *fire blight* dispute, the Appellate Body clarified that Article 5.7 was triggered by the insufficiency of scientific evidence, and not by the existence of scientific uncertainty.

The preamble of the TBT Agreement recognizes that no country should be prevented from taking measures necessary to protect human, animal or plant life or health or the environment, at levels it considers appropriate, subject to the requirement that they are not applied in a discriminatory manner and are otherwise in accordance with the TBT Agreement. The application of the TBT Agreement to precautionary measures has not been tested in a dispute, but it is likely that invoking the precautionary principle in general would not allow WTO Members to violate provisions of the TBT Agreement, much as the Appellate Body found in the *Hormones* case.

Sources: WTO Dispute Settlement Documents WT/DS/48 and WT/DS/245; SPS Agreement; TBT Agreement

---

CONCLUSION

At the time of publishing, a panel is considering a dispute settlement case brought by Argentina, Canada and the United States against the European Communities' measures affecting the approval and marketing of biotech products. It is too early to predict how the dispute will be resolved; the publication date of the panel report has been delayed to allow, among other reasons, the panel to seek scientific and technical expert advice. With progress in the current negotiations slow, it is not at all clear which path – negotiations or dispute settlement – might lead to an end more quickly. Since at this point it does not seem likely that even a successful outcome of the negotiations would bring any clarity to the GMO issue, some WTO Members may think that a decision by the dispute settlement system is better than no decision at all.

NOTES

1   The views expressed in this chapter are those of the author only and do not necessarily reflect the views of the World Trade Organization.

2   The text of WTO Agreements, as well as related documents and information, can be downloaded from the WTO website at http://www.wto.org .

3   GATT 1994, Article III.4. In one dispute, 'European Communities, Measures Affecting Asbestos and Asbestos Containing Products', the Appellate Body stated an important general principle relating to *likeness* under Article III.4: 'a determination of *likeness* under Article III.4 is, fundamentally, a determination about the nature and extent of a competitive relationship between and among products' (WTO Document WT/DS135/AB/R (12/03/2001) paragraph 99). In this context, the Appellate Body considered that a known health risk associated with a product would have an influence on consumers' tastes and habits regarding that product (paragraph 145). Consumers' tastes and habits are one of the criteria that have been examined in past reports to determine *likeness* (see Report of the Working Party on Border Tax Adjustments, BISD 18S/97, para. 18. 1970). An overview of the state of play of WTO disputes and all panel and Appellate Body reports are available on the WTO website.

4   See the Appellate Body report in 'European Communities, Measures Affecting Asbestos and Asbestos-containing Products', WTO Document WT/DS135/AB/R, 12/03/2001, pp60–65.

5   See also the panel report on 'EC Measures Concerning Meat and Meat Products (Hormones)', WTO Document WT/DS48/R/CAN. The panel discussed which Agreement to examine first. If it had decided to examine GATT first, it would still have had to examine the SPS Agreement, whether or not a violation of GATT had been found. Therefore, it decided to begin with the SPS Agreement (pp169–171).

6   See the panel and Appellate Body reports on 'European Communities, Measures Affecting Asbestos and Asbestos Containing Products', WTO Document WT/DS135/ R and WT/DS135/AB/R.

7   For a discussion of possible side effects from genetically modified products, see Nelson et al, 1999.

8   In 1995, a soybean was developed that included a Brazil nut gene. Testing showed that this gene could trigger allergic reactions in people with allergies to Brazil nuts and the soybean was never commercially produced.

9 *Regulation (EC) No 1829/2003* of the European Parliament and of the Council of 22 September 2003 on genetically modified food and feed; *Regulation (EC) No 1830/2003* of the European Parliament and of the Council of 22 September 2003 concerning the traceability and labelling of genetically modified organisms and the traceability of food and feed products produced from genetically modified organisms and amending Directive 2001/18/EC.

10 The European Commission's responses to comments on the proposed regulations are available from the WTO website (G/SPS/GEN/33, G/TBT/W/179 and G/SPS/GEN/338, G/TBT/W/180).

11 Appellate Body report 'European Communities, Measures Affecting Asbestos and Asbestos Containing Products', WTO Document WT/DS135/AB/R (12/03/2001), pp23–31.

12 The SPS cases are: 'EC, Measures Concerning Meat and Meat Products (Hormones)', WT/DS26 (United States complaint) and WT/DS48 (Canadian complaint); 'Australia, Measures Affecting Importation of Salmon', WT/DS18; and 'Japan, Measures Affecting Agricultural Products', WT/DS76. In addition, a panel was established in June 2002 to examine Japan's restrictions on apple imports due to fire blight, a bacterium-generated disease particularly destructive for apples and pears, WT/DS/245.

13 See the panel and Appellate Body reports in 'EC Measures Concerning Meat and Meat Products (Hormones)', WTO documents WT/DS48/R/CAN and WT/DS48/AB/R.

14 WTO (2000) Proposal for Comprehensive Long-Term Agricultural Trade Reform, submission from the United States, WTO Document G/AG/NG/W/15, 23 June 2000. Proposals are available on the WTO website at www.wto.org.

15 WTO (2001) Proposal for WTO Negotiations on Agriculture, Submitted by the Republic of Korea, WTO Document G/AG/NG/W/98, 9 January 2001.

16 WTO Ministerial Declaration, WTO Document WT/MIN(01)/DEC/1, 20 November 2001.

REFERENCES

Musselli, I and Zarrilli, S (2002) 'Non-trade concerns and the WTO jurisprudence in the Asbestos Case – Possible relevance for international trade in genetically modified organism' *The Journal of World Intellectual Property*, vol 5, no 3, pp373–393

Nelson, G C, Josling, T, Bullock, D, Unnevehr, L, Rosegrant, A and Hill, L (1999) 'The economics and politics of genetically modified organisms in agriculture: Implications for WTO 2000', Bulletin 809 (November), College of Agricultural, Consumer and Environmental Sciences, University of Illinois at Urbana-Champaign

14

The Emerging Global Biotech Trade Regime: A Developing Country Perspective[1]

Atul Kaushik

The Cartagena Protocol on Biosafety covering trade in living modified organisms (LMOs) is certainly an important step in protecting human health and the environment from unknown risks of biotechnology. However, disciplining the new trade will take much more. Countries need to balance their international commitments to free trade against the concerns of a sceptical public that may want to restrain trade in LMOs. These concerns stem partly from the inability to ensure that genetically modified (GM) goods can be produced and sold in a traceable, transparent and predictable manner. The creation of regulatory mechanisms for GM trade is a daunting task for developing countries in particular, as they lack the resources to carry out controls, labelling and other standard-compliance procedures. Besides managing compliance, developing countries need to participate in the crafting of the rules of biotechnology trade. The World Trade Organization (WTO) with its strong dispute settlement mechanism is for many countries the preferred arbiter for global disputes. At the same time, trade in biotechnology is not explicitly covered by WTO rules as yet. In order to protect their interests, it is imperative for developing countries to identify their biotechnology and biosafety trade concerns that impact the debate in the WTO and to participate in the forging of rules in the future.

With this in view, this chapter deals with the topic in three parts. While the first part looks at the main set of developing country trade concerns, the next one discusses where the WTO stands on these biotechnology-related issues that are likely to arise. The third part examines which WTO body would most appropriately address biotechnology and biosafety issues in the future and draws some conclusions on the desirable strategy for developing countries in the transition to a new trade regime.

DEVELOPING COUNTRIES LOOK TOWARDS BIOTECH BUT CONCERNS STAND IN THE WAY

The *gene revolution* is expected to bring sweeping changes in the 21st century just as the *green revolution* did in the 20th century. In the aftermath of the green revolution, world food production has been outstripping population growth (Aziz, 1990; Mitchell et al, 1997) and there has been a long-term trend of declining food prices in real terms (ABARE, 2000). Without the green revolution, the agricultural technology of the 1940s could not have met the food demand of today's population. Similarly, it is difficult to assume that the food requirement of the people of 2020 will be sustained by the technology of today (Ghosh et al, 2001). Therefore, the advancement in agriculture through biotechnology is expected to play a major role in farm production. While major food biotechnology research initiatives have been seen in the developed world and in multinational corporations (MNCs), many developing countries have also invested in this area with a view to finding succour from hunger in a cost-effective manner. The perceived benefits of genetically modified crops, namely better weed and insect control, higher productivity and more flexible crop management, are adding more countries to the biotechnology bandwagon.

At the same time, developing countries fear they may be highly prone to risks of biotechnology. Impacts of loss in biodiversity are more severe in developing countries where most of the world's biodiversity hot spots are found. With culture as well as the economy being dependent on biodiversity, developing countries are concerned that biotechnology may undermine their interests as it threatens to wipe out variety of life. The predominance of the private sector in biotechnology research is another source of concern. Developing countries see the concentration of corporate power as a threat to food security. They are concerned that they might lose control over genes or plants native to their territories without any benefit-sharing on the one hand and end up faced with unaffordably expensive biotech-inventions such as GM seeds on the other.

The aim of developing countries in light of the above is to ensure access to biotechnology as a means for increasing food production, while reducing and controlling risks to human health and the environment.

Access concerns

Access to biotechnology is a challenge for developing countries; a challenge that they must meet to relieve hunger. Biotechnology is the key to the development of marginal ecological zones – left behind by the green revolution, but home to more than half of the world's poorest people (UNDP, 2001, p35).

However, among the biggest problems for developing countries is that biotechnology research is not geared to the needs of poor subsistence farmers. As the technology is increasingly under the monopolistic control of MNCs, holding up-to-20-year-long patents on inventions, the price of GM crops may be too high for developing countries. Also, MNCs invest more in research in those crops that are grown by farmers in rich countries, as poor subsistence farmers in tropical countries are less attractive as commercial customers. As a result, developing-country subsistence crops such as cassava, millet and cowpeas are not among the first crops transformed with GM techniques (Paarlberg, 2000).

Weak intellectual property rights (IPR) policies have often been deployed by developing countries to ensure availability of research results at affordable costs. Perhaps no direct conflict exists between promotional public investment policies and precautionary IPR policies in the GM crop area, since one can help make up for the other (Paarlberg, 2000). Hence the concern here is to direct more public funds towards research and development of biotechnology, following the examples of a few developing countries, including India, China and Brazil. While enhancing the scope for South–South cooperation, developing the public biotech research sector will increase the capacity to absorb the technology locally. Extensive work experience in both developing and industrialized countries indicates that the higher the level of infrastructure for a technology, the higher the benefit derived from the technology (Mitchell, 2001).

Biosafety concerns

Ensuring the safe use of biotechnology is an additional concern of developing countries. While many developing countries have established detailed legislation and rules in the area of biosafety,[2] the implementation of these rules is often slow (Kaushik, 2000, pp79–81). The ability to implement biosafety regulations depends on the quality of risk assessment and risk management, which is generally poor in the developing world. Not only is biosafety a concern for imported biotechnology goods, but it is also needed to meet the requirements of export markets and thereby ensure market access for Southern products. Developing countries need to create the *infrastructure* necessary to implement biosafety regulations, such as for example import regulation and quarantine, efficient testing and monitoring facilities, state-of-the-art virus diagnosis and quality control for tissue culture.

Faced with lack of means, developing countries require technical and financial assistance for institution building, risk assessment and risk management (UNEP, 2001). This call for technical assistance enjoys wide international support and is recorded in relevant provisions of the Biosafety Protocol. One way of making such assistance available is on a South-to-South basis from frontline developing countries close to the ground reality and the need for appropriate technology of other developing countries. For example, in October 2001, India established a national facility for plant virus diagnosis and quality control for tissue-culture-raised plants and another facility for the containment-cum-quarantine of transgenic plant material in the National Bureau of Plant Genetic Resources.

CONCERNS OF EXPORTERS, IMPORTERS AND PRODUCERS

From another perspective, the concerns outlined above can be looked at from the point of view of the exporters, importers and producers of biotech products, who have common interests at times but contradictory ones at others.

Concerns of developing countries as exporters of biotech products

A free or at least predictable trade regime is what exporters aim for, yet in the case of exports of biotech products from developing countries these aims may prove hard to achieve. Cumbersome industrialized country import restrictions may be a major cause of developing country exporters' frustration. The WTO Agreements on the Application of Sanitary and Phytosanitary Measures (SPS) and of Technical Barriers to Trade (TBT) could be used as veiled means of protection, while many developing country exporters would have little capacity to determine whether industrialized importers are bending their TBT/SPS rules to keep foreign competition out.

Cases of dubious import standards, in the area of food trade for instance, go unquestioned due to lack of developing countries' capacity to challenge the measure in legal terms. Developing country exporters would have little means to determine whether a measure were used for protectionist purposes or to ask the importer to justify regulation that exceeds international standards. Not only are developing countries unable to detect unfair play, but they are concerned over further tightening of product standard rules, such as non-product-related processes and production methods (PPMs) that would place additional costs of compliance on them.

Import restrictions may also be raised on account of Article XX of the General Agreement on Tariffs and Trade (GATT), the provision allowing countries to restrict trade to protect human health and the environment. The WTO *Asbestos* decision (WT/DS135/12) that allowed France to ban imports of asbestos for causing cancer and other health damage has established a strong precedent for trade restrictions on environmental and public health grounds. In time, this ruling could make it feasible for more exceptions to WTO rules to be granted because of concerns over the health of animals, plants and humans.

Apart from the GATT provisions on environmental and health protection, a restriction against biotechnological goods would most likely be based on the precautionary principle (PP) championed by the Convention on Biological

Diversity (CBD). Nonetheless, the validity of the PP is yet to be established in the TBT or SPS Agreements and it may be difficult for developing country exporters to fight a battle based on the use of this exception.

Yet the biggest trade barrier to developing countries' biotech exports stems from within developing countries themselves, that is, the inability to carry out GM risk assessments domestically. This could add to the compliance cost burdens on exporters as they may be required to go through risk assessment in the country of import if their own governments do not have the capacities to establish such procedures.

In the future, exports of LMOs may encounter an additional obstacle resulting from the further elaboration of identification requirements imposed on such exports under the Biosafety Protocol. So far, the basic requirement for LMOs sold as food, feed or for use in processing is that accompanying documentation states that they *may contain* LMOs and gives a point of contact for further information. However, it is not until the Protocol completes two years in force (September 2005) that more detailed rules will be carved out under the Biosafety Protocol (Article 18). For developing world Parties to the Protocol, once the procedures for *may contain* LMOs labels are finalized, their market competitiveness will rely on setting up fast and legally sound procedures of certification and labelling. This may prove to be a hurdle for the South, as industrialized countries are likely to have an edge in complying with meticulous identification requirements.

Lack of protection for biotech inventions could also trouble developing country exporters of biotech goods. Not only is compliance with the Agreement on Trade-related Aspects of Intellectual Property Rights (TRIPS) wanting in the South, but the TRIPS Agreement fails to address clearly the problem of differing national legislations, which may lead to a product being in line with laws in the country of export but not so in the country of import. For example, India's plant variety protection law provides farmers' exemptions and farmers' right to a greater extent than some of India's trading partners. As a result, Indian crop exports to these countries may be challenged by the proprietors of IPRs of the varieties imported although such IPRs could not be claimed within India.

Concerns of importers

Standing by their international commitment to free trade while addressing public concerns on the safety of LMOs is a balancing act that may prove challenging for developing countries. In developing as well as in industrialized countries, the concerned public is increasingly pushing for a go-slow approach on the acceptance of biotechnology. Public scepticism is reinforced by the stance of stakeholders such as domestic seed industries that have business interests in deterring imports of bio-engineered seeds. Developing countries have to identify which of these concerns are genuine, concerns such as a threat to public health from the allergenic effects of GM products. Another important concern stems from difficulties that developing countries might face when implementing labelling regulations, raising fears that harmful material might be released into the environment inadvertently.

Moreover, developing countries often face difficulty in meeting procedural requirements. For example, developing countries may fail to notify their regulations under the TBT or SPS Agreements of the WTO and risk assessment procedures are frequently inadequate. Capacities required for coordination between customs authorities on the one hand and quarantine authorities on the other are simply not available in many cases. A further problem is expected once the Protocol becomes operational and compliance with the Advance Informed Agreement (AIA) procedures and participation in the Biosafety Clearing House Mechanism become necessary to ensure safe imports. These procedures are likely to be quite cumbersome for developing countries, particularly for those that do not yet have the necessary scientific or institutional infrastructure.

Another set of concerns is linked to developing countries' efforts to defend their own restrictions for GM imports. This could be difficult for developing countries if such restrictions impact on the trade interests of a rich country. Exporters to developing countries may invoke GATT provisions on national treatment (Article III) or quantitative restrictions (Article IX). Of course, developing countries could make use of the general exception in Article XX, but their capacity to fight such costly and time-consuming battles in the WTO is doubtful.

More important, such battles would be winnable on the ground of availability of sound science or the effort being made to pursue scientific data to establish possible harm to health or the environment (Article 5.7 of SPS allows imposition of restrictions on the basis of incomplete science, but enjoins that pursuit of full science should continue and the measure be reviewed on that basis within a reasonable period of time). It is unlikely that developing countries would have the capacity to establish sound science behind their trade measures or to pursue the scientific inquiry to its logical conclusion. For example, the Genetic Engineering Approval Committee of the Ministry of Environment and Forests of India fought a see-saw battle with the environmentalists over the release of Bt cotton into India's environment despite years of systematic trials, and the commercial release of Bt cotton was only possible as late as 2002.

Concerns of producers

Similar but more serious problems exist for biotechnology production in developing countries. Producers who may have invested a lot in manufacturing biotech goods may not know whether their products would be allowed into the market or what help is available to make them market-worthy.

Lack of domestic policy coherence is the foremost source of troubles for producers of biotech goods. Different ministries dealing with the subject may not have a common understanding of the issues, leading to the Trade, Agriculture and Science Ministries each having a different approach to a producer. Mechanisms to distinguish between GM and non-GM products remain limited even in developed countries; implementation of such mechanisms in developing countries would take even longer and may be impossible where uncontrolled sprawl of GM products has already taken place. The issue of traceability of GM products will pose further problems. The existence of Bt cotton in some fields in the Indian state of Gujarat was, for example, detected thanks to the alertness of non-governmental organizations that brought the matter forward. This may not happen in many other countries where the existence of GM farming may go unnoticed while claims to being GM-free are nonetheless asserted.

Lack of rules in the market for LMOs would have serious business consequences for producers of GM and non-GM alike. Supplying a market for particular GM characteristics, such as disease-free seeds or high productivity seeds, would not be possible without guarantees to consumers of the quality of the product. Similarly producers of GM-free produce would be crippled by the same lack of transparency, which would mean that their goods would not be able to be guaranteed as GM-free.

The important question from the point of view of the scope of this chapter is which of these concerns can be addressed through the WTO. While specific WTO provisions that can play a role are discussed in the next part, a word of caution would be in place here in the light of the experience of developing countries in the WTO. Being a trade body, the WTO's principle function is facilitating free (or freer) trade and not development. Although a whole Part (Part IV, entitled Trade and Development) of GATT is devoted to development, developing countries have found little use for it so far. The 'special and differential treatment' provisions of the WTO Agreements have been couched in 'best endeavour' language, without any contractual obligation on the part of the developed countries to implement them in letter and spirit. For this reason, since the start of the preparations for the Seattle Ministerial Conference of the WTO up to the present, developing countries have been seeking effective implementation of these provisions, but largely in vain.

OPPORTUNITIES AND CONCERNS FOR DEVELOPING COUNTRIES IN THE WTO

GATT – General Agreement on Tariffs and Trade

The key international trade rules that would be evoked against GM import restriction are GATT rules requesting that the same treatment be given to imported and domestic goods (Article III) as well as GATT rules banning quantitative import restrictions. Such a challenge could be met with use of Article XX(b) allowing exceptions to GATT rules based on health considerations, Article XX(g) based on biodiversity conservation and Article XX(d) where the restrictive measure is in compliance with laws or regulations (such as those relating to customs enforcement) that are otherwise not incompatible with GATT/WTO provisions.

A key issue for developing countries in the WTO is the discussion on homogeneous product-specification standards, in other words applying the same standards on production across economies. This cannot but harm poorer countries that are at a very different stage of development from industrialized economies and will be burdened excessively by complying with their production standards.

To address this issue, developing countries can turn to GATT/WTO provisions meant to provide them with a differential treatment and increased market access. The phrase 'discrimination between countries where the same conditions prevail' in the chapeau of Article XX, read with the preamble of the WTO Agreement (referring to the 'need for positive efforts designed to ensure that developing countries . . . secure a share in the growth in international trade') need to be operationalized to create an easier regime for developing countries. The same conditions cannot be said to prevail, for example, in poor countries with respect to the testing procedures that should reflect the appropriate technology for each country's stage of development.

The SPS Agreement

Membership of the WTO affords developing countries the benefit of being eligible for technical and financial assistance through various Agreements. Article 9 of the SPS Agreement for instance can be used to seek both technical and financial assistance so that competition from GM goods does not worsen developing countries' global market position. This provision can be used, for example, to seek grants from importing developed countries for establishing national regulatory bodies or testing houses required to fulfil the sanitary or phytosanitary requirements in the export market. Longer time frames for compliance with such requirements in developed countries, time-limited exceptions from obligations and assistance in participating in the work of the standard-setting bodies can be sought under Article 10 and paragraph 2 of Annex B. If a trade restriction in the developed country is based on the precautionary principle, for example, exception from the obligation until sound science is available could be sought.

Developing countries should seek to participate in the standard-setting activity taking place in three specific organizations that are endorsed by the SPS Agreement. Of particular importance are the food labelling guidelines being developed by the Codex Alimentarius Commission, where developing countries' interests need to be reflected.[3] Apart from the Codex Alimentarius, the remaining two organizations explicitly recognized by the SPS Agreement are the World Organisation for Animal Health (OIE), for animal health and diseases transmitted from animals to humans, and the International Plant Protection Convention (IPPC) on the area of plant health. Standards adopted by these three bodies form part of the WTO *acquis* and enjoy virtually the same status as WTO rules.[4]

Most important, Article 4 of the SPS Agreement states that national health standards of one Member are equivalent to those of another under specific circumstances. Based on this Article, the use of different testing equipment or a different measure should not preclude GM goods produced in the developing world from being compliant with WTO rules for health certification.

In addition, Article 10 of the SPS Agreement obliges developed countries to take into account special needs of developing countries in the preparation and application of their SPS regulations. It also allows time extensions for application of these regulations to products from developing countries and assists them in participating in the work of bodies such as Codex, OIE and IPPC. Through these provisions, developing countries should either acquire testing equipment needed to access developed country markets, or get assistance to create equivalence agreements based on their home-grown testing equipment or procedures.

As they stand, Articles 9 and 10 of the SPS Agreement are potent provisions, but are rarely used by developing countries. The reason is that developing countries have to actively seek to take advantage of the provisions that are favourable to them. That involves identifying specific forms of assistance and taking them up bilaterally and multilaterally with the developed countries. Developed countries are obliged to hear these demands within the respective WTO committees. Moreover, Articles 9 and 10 can be made more operational by providing for assistance to developing countries whose market access is likely to be eroded by the introduction of new and complex trade measures *before* these measures kick in. The potential for market access erosion could be evaluated based on the present exports.

The TBT Agreement

With respect to import bans on GM products, the TBT Agreement is relevant, more so after the WTO Appellate Body in the *Asbestos* dispute held that the ban on imports of asbestos and asbestos-containing products was covered under Article 2.2 of the Agreement.[5] This Article states that trade regulations should not be more trade-restrictive than necessary to fulfil legitimate objectives, such as national security or health and environmental objectives. The *Asbestos* decision establishes a strong precedent in favour of import bans within the WTO under certain conditions, which may have relevance for similar decisions against trade in LMOs in the future.

As under the SPS Agreement, developing countries can turn to the TBT Agreement to lever assistance in establishing institutional mechanisms that address the issues of technical regulations and standards in trade. Article 11 of the TBT Agreement obliges developed countries, on request from developing countries, to provide technical assistance for establishing, among other things, national standard-setting bodies or setting up conformity assessment procedures.

Since a request has to precede the grant of assistance, developing countries are well advised to seek specific assistance where required and can even seek assistance to identify what assistance would be helpful in retaining or increasing their market access to respond to emerging technical barriers.

Moreover, Article 12 asks developed countries not to insist that developing countries adopt their technologies and testing procedures and to recognize different procedures that meet the same legitimate objectives. It further exhorts them to assist developing countries in participating in international standard-setting bodies, as well as asking these bodies to prepare standards for products in which developing countries have specific trade (export) interests. It further encourages them to give more time to developing countries to meet regulations. Thus, Article 12 of the TBT Agreement helps developing countries in getting friendly regulations installed in their export markets. None of this, however, is possible unless developing countries ask for particular assistance and ask to participate in the standard-setting process. The thrust of the recommendation on both Articles 11 and 12 of the TBT Agreement as well as Article 10 of the SPS Agreement is that developing countries have to identify their needs, ask for help and take it up in WTO committees if the help is not forthcoming. The help will not come automatically, as developed countries would not know what help was needed and would not care to identify it, as that falls beyond their obligation.

On the basis of provisions of Article 12, developing countries could insist on information with respect to the special consideration given to their trade, development and financial needs in standard setting, time-limited exceptions from obligations and assistance in participation in the international standard-setting bodies. There is a need to further strengthen this Article, however, to create a contractual obligation on developed countries to ensure that unnecessary barriers to trade of developing countries are not created. For example, Article 12.3 could be clarified to mean that special development, financial and trade needs of developing countries would be met before applying technical regulations or conformity assessment procedures to their exports. This last sentence has come from demands of developing countries as stated in their so-called 'implementation issues and concerns', on which negotiations have been mandated in the Doha Declaration.

Although the TBT Agreement to some extent encourages standards that best reflect each country's stage of development provided they meet legitimate objectives, this could be strengthened. The concept of equivalence has been built into the TBT Agreement through Article 2.7 and for developing countries particularly through Article 12.4. Some of the provisions are, however, merely 'best endeavour' clauses and do not oblige developed countries in any way to make sure that standards developed by them do not adversely affect market access of developing countries. Instead, developing countries should aim to convert the provisions into more specific and contractual obligations.

Controversy persists on whether GM and non-GM products are 'like products' in the context of the WTO (Zarrilli, 2000). While this controversy may be resolved only after a panel or Appellate Body of the WTO decision, the concept may be more relevant in the context of the TBT than the SPS Agreement (where processes and production methods are valid ground for a distinction) or Article XX of GATT (which is an exception to the entire GATT/WTO and hence also to the concept of 'like products'). In the TBT Agreement, on the other hand, it is still not clear whether non-product-related PPMs can be considered relevant for technical regulations[6] and this debate is at the root of the long-standing controversy in the TBT Committee and the Committee on Trade and Environment (CTE) over the applicability of TBT disciplines to eco-labels. However, GM products can be considered to have a different product characteristic from non-GM products (as the new gene changes the character of the product), resulting in their being considered product-related PPMs and hence covered under the disciplines of the TBT Agreement.

The TRIPS Agreement

The TRIPS Agreement is controversial for developing countries' biotechnology research interests. Article 27.3(b) enjoins WTO Members to grant patents for micro-organisms but leaves it up to the discretion of Member countries to decide what qualifies as a micro-organism. On the one hand, MNCs currently dominating biotechnology research may use their patents to make it difficult for developing country farmers to access the benefits. On the other hand, experts have held that the flexibility allowed by the TRIPS Agreement for different interpretations of micro-organism means that Members can effectively adopt the level of patent protection that best meets their interests (Reichman, 1997). In fact, developments in the area of public health in recent times have shown that even developed countries are not averse to the use of flexibilities available in the TRIPS Agreement. Hence, developing countries' policy options may not be constrained by the TRIPS Agreement. MNCs, through some developed country Members, may attempt to further strengthen and restrict patenting of GM products as a part of the review of Article 27.3(b) or the review of the implementation of the TRIPS Agreement (as mandated by Article 71.1); developing countries have to be on guard to protect their interests in these reviews.

WTO BODIES THAT MAY HOST A DEBATE ON BIOTECH TRADE

Various Committees provide a possible forum for discussing biotechnology and biosafety issues in the WTO. Before choosing the preferable forum, it is important to note that WTO Members are free to raise any issue in any forum; it is for the forum to decide whether to accept a discussion on the issue or not. Such a decision is taken by consensus as per WTO practice (although voting is theoretically possible, it has never been practiced in WTO, nor is it likely to be). Hence, the Member raising the issue has to think through the consequences of the issue coming on the table, given the provisions of the relevant agreement and the possibility of a future decision impacting on other aspects of the functioning of the agreement, such as on market access.

For developing countries, it may be more important to protect against possible erosion of their existing market access than to seek clarification on GM products or biosafety issues. Indeed, most developing countries are at present GM-free and even if they start to use biotechnology, they could also simultaneously start creating adequate market differentiation between GM and non-GM products in order to satisfy their buyers of the content of their produce. Provisions such as Article XX already make it possible for Members to pursue a policy most suited to their specific circumstances and to defend trade restrictions based on health and environmental objectives, so long as these are not unjustified, arbitrary or disguised restrictions. Thus, the best way for developing countries to protect their biotech trade interests in the WTO might not be through a review of the WTO agreements, but rather by negotiating exceptions on a one-off basis to meet particular trade needs. The recent victory of developing countries in negotiating access to generic drugs on account of public health interests, to fight diseases such as HIV, demonstrates the advantages this negotiating route has to offer.

The Committee on Agriculture, the SPS Committee, the TBT Committee, the CTE, the Committee on Trade and Development (CTD) and the Working Group on Trade and Transfer of Technology are the possible fora in the WTO where these issues can be discussed, although a decision of the WTO would be possible only if there were consensus around a particular course of action. If a Member wishes to force the issue, and there is a trade measure involved in the access regime for the biotech product, that Member can raise it in the Dispute Settlement Mechanism (DSM) and get a decision.

The Committee on Agriculture

It is unlikely that biosafety will be raised within the context of the agriculture negotiations, as net food-importing countries and agricultural exporting countries (such as those in the Cairns Group) would likely prefer to keep these negotiations free from further complications. For developing countries the thrust in the agricultural negotiations is to achieve fair play according to the principles of comparative economic advantage, which would be enough on its own to ensure food security and increased export trade for their farmers. With such a strong case on their side, developing countries prefer to avoid the complicated issue of biotechnology that could cloud negotiations and lead them to unfavourable *give-and-take* in the endgame.

The SPS and TBT Committees

The SPS and TBT Committees have a narrow scope for discussions on biotechnology and biosafety and may not be able to fully address the concerns of the WTO Membership. The SPS Committee would be restricted to examining measures that are applied for the protection of animal or plant life or health against risks arising from pests, diseases, additives, contaminants, toxins, among others, and may not cover the gamut of issues involved in examining risks posed by GM products. The limited focus of developing countries in this area should be to participate in and closely follow developments in the Codex Alimentarius Commission, the OIE and the IPPC. Similarly, the TBT Committee would restrict the examination to protection of health or life or the environment, but based on sound science, which is not fully available for GM products, at least not yet.

Also, concerns that may be more important from the perspective of developing countries or even the civil society of the developed world, such as the ethical and developmental issues, may not be addressed in these Committees. Canada and Japan had, during the run-up to the Seattle Ministerial Conference, proposed the establishment of a Working Group on Biotechnology to discuss all issues related to trade in biotechnology products. This idea was supported by the US, with the intention perhaps to ensure that no distinction between GM and non-GM products is agreed to in the WTO.[7] This was not supported by developing countries, and now that the US has, under civil society pressure, established a plan for differentiation between GM and non-GM products in their domestic market and is coordinating efforts in this regard with the EU, they are likely to push for acceptance of rules based on their emerging domestic policy rather than on developing country interests. It is not, therefore, likely that such a Working Group would be helpful for developing countries.

The Working Group on Trade and Transfer of Technology

The Doha Ministerial Conference has set up the Working Group on Trade and Transfer of Technology, but judging from the interventions in the Group up to now, not much scope appears to be emerging for a discussion on biotechnology. Even if developing countries were to become *demandeurs* of such a role for this Working Group, there is the problem that the Group will lose its present focus on transfer of technology, which is a much more important demand of developing countries and needs to be pursued in a focused manner by them.

The Committee on Trade and Environment

The CTE has been discussing an elaborate ten-item agenda since 1995, where issues of interest to both developed and developing countries are on the table. For example, clarification of rules on trade measures in MEAs, the precautionary principle and eco-labelling are of interest to developed countries, while market access, TRIPS-related issues and domestically prohibited goods are of interest to developing countries. Were there to be a resolution of the issues in the CTE, it may perhaps present a more balanced result for both developed and developing countries. Moreover, the CTE is not a negotiating forum yet, but it has the mandate as per the Marrakech Decision on Trade and Environment to recommend modifications to WTO rules for resolution of environmental issues. It also has a strong development dimension in the discussions that have taken place so far. Furthermore, it has a stronger civil society involvement than any other forum in the WTO.

Moreover, the Doha Declaration (adopted in November 2001), while not explicitly mentioning biotechnology, has instructed the CTE to launch negotiations on the relationship between WTO rules and multilateral environmental agreements (paragraph 31.1); these negotiations are likely to be of relevance with the regard to the Biosafety Protocol. The CTE was also mandated to discuss other potentially relevant issues that did not graduate to negotiations, including eco-labelling and the relationship between the TRIPS Agreement and the CBD. Current indications are that many WTO Members are keen to revive the work in the CTE post-Doha to determine the final tally of issues arising therefrom for future negotiations, as perhaps they feel it provides the right balance to move the environmental agenda forward. All these factors would recommend the CTE as the most suitable body for resolving biotechnology and biosafety issues.

The Committee on Trade and Development

The CTD is a body meant primarily to discuss and coordinate work on development in the WTO and its relationship to development-related activities in other multilateral agencies. A discussion on biotech here would more likely focus on the broader developmental and ethical issues, which are most important for the developing countries. However, it may be that developed countries would not find much use focusing on the issue in the CTD because the issue of ensuring a 'predictable trading regime' (vis-à-vis the impact of standards and so on) and other technical issues receive little attention there. Furthermore, the CTD does not have an explicit negotiating mandate based on a Ministerial text to recommend changes in related rules – unlike the CTE.

In the pre- and post-Doha environment, the CTD has attracted increased attention with attempts by developing countries to strengthen and operationalize provisions for special and differential treatment. However, most developed countries, and many developing countries, do not see the biotechnology issue as purely a development issue, but rather a specific trade issue requiring further clarification and/or application of trade rules. Hence, even though the CTD is the most favourable forum for highlighting the development dimension of biotechnology, the WTO Membership may not be comfortable in addressing it in a forum often referred to as a 'talk shop'.

The Dispute Settlement Mechanism

The DSM of the WTO is usually considered the most effective means of clarifying the application of trade rules; it is the fastest and most precise way of doing so. That is partly due to the rule of reverse consensus governing WTO arbitration, whereby a decision stands unless all WTO Members agree to reject it. However, the DSM tends to vacillate between what is judicially acceptable and what is politically enforceable. Developing countries lacking political clout therefore risk seeing their interests superseded by those of the more powerful WTO Members. In the case of trade in biotechnology, where international consensus on the relevant trade rules is still emerging, developing countries risk all the more by turning to the DSM.

Thus, seeking resolution of these issues in the context of the DSM may perhaps be the most harmful route for developing countries, as WTO panels and the Appellate Body are not known to necessarily base their decisions on development concerns. For example, although both the Panel and the Appellate Body in the *Shrimp–Turtle* dispute had argued that the US did not take the desirable step of entering into a multilateral environmental agreement on the protection of turtles, this favourable pronouncement did not swing the decision to the interests of developing countries.[8] In the end, the decision was based only on the compatibility of the disputed US measure with trade rules, while the inability of the US to pursue turtle protection through an MEA slipped into the background.

Inability to make space for the development dimension is another disadvantage of the DSM from a developing country's perspective. Panels and the Appellate Body are constrained by the Understanding on Rules and Procedures Governing the Settlement of Disputes (DSU) which states in Article 3.2 that the DSM serves to clarify the existing provisions of WTO agreements only and that the Dispute Settlement Body cannot add to or diminish the rights and obligations provided in those agreements. This rule is very beneficial to developing countries in retaining the predictability negotiated into the agreements, but does not help them in pursuing the preambular language on the development dimension in all agreements.

Looking beyond the WTO

Ultimately, developing countries may find the existing WTO rules more suitable to their trade and safety interests than elaborate rules that would oblige them to build further capacities regarding notifications and compliance and subject them to a stricter dispute settlement mechanism. Instead, it may be more beneficial to focus on ongoing work in fora other than the WTO. The Biosafety Protocol is the most important such forum, where the Intergovernmental Committee for the Cartagena Protocol (ICCP) – and as of February 2004 the Meeting of the Parties (MOP) – has been undertaking an elaborate exercise to build capacities of Parties to start using the provisions of the Protocol and has sufficient mandate to help developing countries build capacities in this area.

The Codex Alimentarius Commission, in addition to risk analysis standards for biotech food adopted in July 2003, is working on labelling guidelines for GM foods, while the IPPC is developing standards for pest risk assessment of living modified organisms. Developing countries need to participate strongly in these fora and protect their interests.

Another relevant forum is the UN Food and Agriculture Organization (FAO) which has undertaken a revision of its International Undertaking on Plant Genetic Resources for Food and Agriculture to align it with the CBD, integrating trade and IPR-related rules in the new International Treaty (adopted in November 2001, but not yet in force). Developing countries need to focus there too, to ensure availability of germplasm for plant improvement in the future.

CONCLUSION

Developing countries as producers of agricultural goods have a pressing need to increase agricultural productivity, and biotechnology may provide the much-needed solution. As exporters, they have concerns that industrialized countries could increasingly use health- and environment-related standards to restrict market access for their produce. Thus, they have to remain alert to the possible development of rules relevant for trade in biotechnology products. They also have to build capacities, particularly infrastructure, to meet legitimate standards for biotechnology products in their markets. As importers, developing countries have to protect themselves from undesirable biotechnology imports, both from health and biodiversity angles. They need to participate closely in the ongoing work in the MOP relating to the operationalization of the Biosafety Protocol. This work would also enable them to incorporate the development dimension of biosafety, as the Protocol's provisions enable them to access technical and financial assistance for this purpose. Developing countries also need more time to adjust to the regulatory and scientific environment required to benefit from biotechnology. Finally, they need to be careful in agreeing to a discussion on the issue in the WTO, given that it is a trade body and is not known to have served development interests fully.

NOTES

1   The views given here are the author's own and do not necessarily reflect the views of the government of India.
2   Documents available on www.biodiv.org show, on the basis of responses to questionnaires, that many developing countries have put in place laws regulating LMOs and some, Mexico, South Korea, Sri Lanka and Thailand among them, have even implemented labelling regulations. See also Appendix II.
3   Testing products for GM content is a costly exercise. Tests can cost from US$10 to US$700 and take from five minutes to ten days, depending on the test. See Kaushik, 2000.
4   Standards developed by International Organization for Standardization (ISO) or any other standard-setting organization have not been specifically adopted in the TBT Agreement, although ISO definitions appear in Annex I of the TBT Agreement. On the other hand, standards developed by the three organizations recognized by the SPS Agreement have been accepted as international standards in the SPS Agreement.

5 Paragraphs 75 and 76, Appellate Body Report in the Asbestos case, WT/DS135/AB/R, 12 March 2001, are available on www.wto.org. It is important to note that the Appellate Body ruling only applies to the particular measure in question and does not mean that 'all internal measures covered by Article III:4 of the GATT 1994 "affecting" the "sale, offering for sale, purchase, transportation, distribution or use" of a product are, necessarily, "technical regulations" under the TBT Agreement' (paragraph 77).

6 Annex 1 to the TBT Agreement defines a technical regulation as a document that lays down product characteristics or *their* related processes and production methods. Also see Article 2.8, which emphasizes that Members 'shall specify technical regulations based on product requirements in terms of *performance rather than design or descriptive characteristics*' (emphasis added).

7 The US, in their proposal entitled 'Measures Affecting Trade in Agricultural Biotechnology Products' (WT/GC/W/288, 4 August 1999), had proposed that the objectives for the negotiations include rules to ensure that trade in agricultural biotechnology products is based on transparent, predictable and timely processes. Although this proposal was submitted as a part of agriculture negotiations, it is assumed that were such a Group to be constituted, the US would focus on free trade whereas safety issues are equally important from the EU's perspective and are also important for developing countries.

8 WTO Panel Report: United States – Import Prohibition of Certain Shrimp and Shrimp Products, AB-1998-4, WT/DS58/AB/R; WTO Appellate Body Report: United States – Import Prohibition of Certain Shrimp and Shrimp Products, AB-1998-4, WT/DS58/AB/R.

REFERENCES

ABARE (2000) 'The impact of agricultural trade liberalization on developing countries', *ABARE Research Report 2000.6*, Canberra

Aziz, S (1990) *Agricultural Policies for the 1990s*, Development Centre Studies, OECD, Paris

Ghosh, S K, Guhasarkar, C K and Prathiba, R (2001) 'GM crops and biosafety concerns', *The Hindu Businessline* at www.thehindubusinessline.com, 13 March 2001

Kaushik, A (2000) 'India and the Biosafety Protocol', *RIS Biotechnology and Development Review*, vol 3, no 2, pp79–81

Mitchell, B (2001) 'Developing infrastructure for biotechnology', *Viewpoints*, Center for International Development, Harvard University, Massachusetts, www.cid.harvard.edu/cidbiotech/comments/comments111.htm

Mitchell, D O, Ingco, M D and Duncan, R (1997) *The World Food Outlook*, Cambridge University Press

Paarlberg, R L (2000) 'Governing the GM revolution: Policy choices for developing countries', *Food, Agriculture and the Environment Discussion Paper 33*, International Food Policy Research Institute, Washington, DC

Reichman, J H (1997) 'From free riders to fair followers: Global competition under the TRIPS Agreement', *New York University Journal of International Law and Politics*, vol 29, nos 1–2, pp11–93

UNDP (2001) *Human Development Report 2001*, Oxford University Press

UNEP (2001) *Report of the Executive Secretary Summarizing Information Received in Response to the Questionnaire on Capacity-Building*, UNEP/CBD/BS/EM-CB/1/2, United Nations Environment Programme

Zarrilli, S (2000) *International Trade in Genetically Modified Organisms and Multilateral Negotiations: A New Dilemma for Developing Countries*, UNCTAD/DITC/TNC/1, United Nations Conference on Trade and Development, paragraphs 87–89

Appendix I: International Legal Frameworks for Biotechnology, Biosafety and Trade

BINDING INTERNATIONAL LEGAL INSTRUMENTS

Table I.1 *Multilateral trade agreements under the WTO*

General Agreement on Tariffs and Trade (GATT)	• Lays down the basic rules for trade in goods • Articles of particular relevance: 　– Article I (most-favoured-nation treatment) 　– Article III (national treatment, including non-discrimination for like products in Article III 4) 　– Article XX (general exceptions, including to protect public morals, human, animal or plant life or health and to conserve exhaustible natural resources in Article XX(a), (b) and (g))
Agreement on the Application of Sanitary and Phytosanitary Measures (SPS)	• Recognizes the sovereign right of Members to provide the level of protection of human, animal or plant life or health they deem appropriate • Aims to ensure that SPS measures do not represent unnecessary, arbitrary, scientifically unjustifiable, or disguised restrictions on international trade • Articles of particular relevance: 　– Article 3 (harmonization of SPS measures, including through the use of international standards, guidelines or recommendations, or of risk assessment) 　– Article 5.7 (precautionary approach)
Agreement on Technical Barriers to Trade (TBT)	• Aims to ensure that technical regulations and standards, as well as testing and certification procedures, do not create unnecessary obstacles to trade • Articles of particular relevance: 　– Article 2.1 (non-discrimination for like products) 　– Article 2.2 (legitimate objectives)
Agreement on Trade-related Aspects of Intellectual Property Rights (TRIPS)	• Establishes the minimum standards of intellectual property protection to be provided by each WTO Member, including the subject matter to be protected, the rights to be conferred and permissible exceptions to those rights, and the minimum duration of protection • Sets out domestic procedures and remedies for the enforcement of intellectual property rights • Articles of particular relevance: 　– Article 27.1 (criteria of patentability)

       – Article 27.2 (exclusion from patentability to protect *ordre public* or morality, including to protect human, animal or plant life or health or to avoid serious prejudice to the environment)
       – Article 27.3(b) (patentability of life forms)

Table I.2 *Other multilateral agreements*

Convention on Biological Diversity (CBD) 1992	• Aims to ensure the 'conservation of biological diversity, the sustainable use of its components and the fair and equitable sharing of the benefits arising out of the utilization of genetic resources, including by appropriate access to genetic resources and by appropriate transfer of relevant technologies'
	• Articles of particular relevance:
	  – Article 8(j) (traditional knowledge, prior informed consent, benefit-sharing)
	  – Article 16 (access to and transfer of technology, including biotechnology)
	  – Article 19 (handling of biotechnology and distribution of its benefits)

Cartagena Protocol on Biosafety (CPB) 2000	• Protocol to the CBD (pursuant to Article19) • Aims to ensure 'an adequate level of protection in the field of the safe transfer, handling and use of living modified organisms resulting from modern biotechnology that may have adverse effects on the conservation and sustainable use of biological diversity, taking also into account risks to human health, and specifically focusing on transboundary movements' • Deals with living modified organisms intended for environmental release, and for use as food, feed or for processing • Seen by many as the first operationalization of the precautionary principle (Articles 1, 10.6 and 10.8) • In force since 11 September 2003

International Treaty on Plant Genetic Resources for Food and Agriculture (PGRFA) 2001	• Objectives: conservation and sustainable use of plant genetic resources for food and agriculture and the fair and equitable sharing of the benefits arising out of their use, in harmony with the CBD, for sustainable agriculture and food security
	• Instructs governments to protect farmers' rights
	• Establishes a multilateral system that aims to facilitate access and benefit-sharing for PGRFA
	• Articles of particular relevance:
	  – Article 9 (farmers' rights)
	  – Article 13.2(b) (access to and transfer of technology, including technologies for the use of PGRFA which are under the Multilateral System)
	  – Part IV (benefit-sharing)
	• In force since 29 June 2004

International Union for the Protection of New Varieties of Plants (UPOV) 1961	• Provides a framework for intellectual property protection of plant varieties (plant variety or plant breeders' rights) • Revised in 1972, 1978 and 1991 • Protection for plant varieties is granted independently of the technology used (traditional breeding or transgenic)

NON-BINDING INTERNATIONAL INSTRUMENTS

Table I.3 *Declarations and action plans*

Rio Principles	• Contained in the Declaration of the UN Conference on Environment and Development (1992)
	• Adopted by consensus of 178 states
	• Principles of particular relevance:
	  – Principle 2 (states' sovereignty over their natural resources)
	  – Principle 9 (technology transfer)
	  – Principle 15 (precautionary approach)
	  – Principle 17 (environmental impact assessment)

Agenda 21	• Action plan for sustainable development adopted at UNCED 1992 by 178 governments
	• Chapters of particular relevance:
	  – Chapter 2 (trade, financial resources and economic policies)
	  – Chapter 15 (conservation of biological diversity)
	  – Chapter 16 (environmentally sound management of biotechnology)
	  – Chapter 34 (transfer of environmentally sound technology, cooperation and capacity building)

World Summit on Sustainable Development (WSSD) – Plan of Implementation	• Adopted at the World Summit on Sustainable Development (2002)
	• Articles of particular relevance:
	  – Article 42 (biodiversity), including biotechnology (42(q)) and a mandate for negotiations of an international benefit-sharing regime (42(o))
	  – Section V (sustainable development in a globalizing world)
	  – Articles 84–94 (trade)

Universal Declaration on the Human Genome and Human Rights (UNESCO) 1997	• Aims to protect the human genome by setting out basic principles bearing on research in genetics and biology and the application of its results • Endorsed by UNESCO's General Conference in November 1997 and in the following year by the UN General Assembly

Table I.4 *International standard-setting bodies recognized under the SPS Agreement**

Secretariat of the International Plant Protection Convention (IPPC)	• In the process of formulating a draft standard to provide guidance on the conduct of pest risk analyses for living modified organisms
	• IPPC (1952):
	  – legally binding
	  – aims to secure common and effective action to prevent the spread and introduction of pests of plants and plant products and to promote measures for their control
	• Amended in 1979 (entered into force in 1991); revised in 1997 (but not yet in force) to reflect contemporary phytosanitary concepts and the role of the IPPC in relation to WTO Agreements, especially the SPS Agreement

Codex Alimentarius Commission (created jointly by the FAO and WHO in 1963)	• Adopted by the Commission in July 2003: – Principles for the risk analysis of foods derived from modern biotechnology – Guideline for the conduct of food safety assessment of foods derived from recombinant-DNA plants – Guideline for the conduct of food safety assessment of foods produced using recombinant-DNA micro-organisms • Committee on general principles: – Working principles for risk analysis for application in the framework of the Codex Alimentarius (adopted in July 2003) – Proposed draft working principles for risk analysis for food safety • Committee on food labelling: – Draft recommendations for the labelling of foods obtained through certain techniques of genetic modification/genetic engineering
Office International des Épizooties (OIE)	• Manual of standards for diagnostic tests and vaccines

* *Note:* Under the SPS Agreement, WTO Members are encouraged to 'base' their sanitary and phytosanitary measures on international standards, guidelines and recommendations where they exist. Three international standard-setting bodies are explicitly recognized under the Agreement: the Secretariat of the International Plant Protection Convention (plant health), the Codex Alimentarius Commission (food safety) and the Office International des Épizooties (animal health). Standards set by these three bodies are 'presumed to be consistent' with the SPS Agreement. Where no standards exist or a Member chooses to adopt a stricter standard, an SPS measure must be based on a risk assessment.

Table I.5 *Other international standards, guidelines and recommendations*

Voluntary Code of Conduct for the Release of Organisms into the Environment (UNIDO) 1991	• Outlines the general principles governing standards of practice for all parties involved in the introduction of organisms or their products/metabolites to the environment (including genetically modified plants, animals, and micro-organisms, their products and by-products) • Prepared by the UNIDO/UNEP/WHO/FAO Working Group on Biosafety
International Code of Conduct for Plant Germplasm Collecting and Transfer of Germplasm (FAO) 1993	• Aims to promote the rational collection and sustainable use of genetic resources, to prevent genetic erosion, and to protect the interests of both donors and collectors of germplasm • Proposes procedures to request and/or to issue licences for collecting missions, provides guidelines for collectors themselves, and extends responsibilities and obligations to the sponsors of missions, the curators of gene banks and the users of genetic material
International Technical Guidelines for Safety in Biotechnology (UNEP) 1995	• Aim to provide a common framework for safety in biotechnology at national, regional and international levels • Address the human health and environmental safety of all types of applications of biotechnology, from research and development to commercialization of biotechnological products containing or consisting of organisms with novel trait(s)

Code of Conduct for Responsible Fisheries (FAO) 1995	• Provides principles and standards applicable to the conservation, management and development of all fisheries • Covers the capture, processing and trade of fish and fishery products, fishing operations, aquaculture, fisheries research and the integration of fisheries into coastal area management • Provides for a precautionary approach to conservation, management and exploitation of living aquatic resources
Draft Code of Conduct on Biotechnology as it relates to Genetic Resources for Food and Agriculture (CGRFA)	• Aims to maximize the positive effects, and minimize the possible negative effects, of biotechnology • Currently under negotiation
Organisation for Economic Co-operation and Development (OECD)	• Recombinant-DNA Safety Considerations, 1986 • Safety Considerations for Biotechnology, 1992 • Safety Evaluation of Foods Derived by Modern Biotechnology: Concepts and Principles, 1993 • Safety Considerations for Biotechnology: Scale-up of Crop Plants, 1993

REGIONAL INITIATIVES

Table I.6 *Regional initiatives*

European Union	• 'Council Directive on the deliberate release into the environment of genetically modified organisms' (*2001/18/EC*; revision of *90/220/EEC*) adopted in March 2001, entry into force on 17 October 2002 • *Regulation (EC) 258/97* on novel foods and novel food ingredients • *Regulation (EC) 50/2000* on additives and flavourings • *Regulation (EC) 49/2000* on adventitious contamination of GM material in conventional food • *Regulation (EC) 1829/2003* of the European Parliament and of the Council of 22 September 2003 on genetically modified food and feed • *Regulation (EC)* 1830/2003 of the European Parliament and of the Council of 22 September 2003 concerning the traceability and labelling of genetically modified organisms and the traceability of food and feed products produced from genetically modified organisms and amending *Directive 2001/18/EC* • Commission Recommendation of 23 July 2003 on guidelines for the development of national strategies and best practices to ensure the co-existence of genetically modified crops with conventional and organic farming (*Recommendation 2003/556/EC*)
Andean Community, Decision 391: Common Regime on Access to Genetic	• Regulates access to the genetic resources of the member countries and their by-products • Recognizes the importance of access to and transfer of biotechnology

Resources	• Instructs member countries to adopt a common regime on biosecurity and to conduct respective studies, in particular with regard to cross-border movement of living modified organisms
Draft African *Model Law on Safety in Biotechnology*	• Developed by the Organization of African Unity (now 'African Union'), in collaboration with the Ethiopian Environmental Protection Agency, and endorsed by the Organization of African Unity Assembly of the Heads of State in July 2001
	• Aims to serve as a basis for formulating national biosafety laws
	• Covers the import, contained use, release or placing on the market of any GMO or GMO product, and includes detailed provisions for institutional arrangements, decision-making procedures, risk management and labelling
	• Not yet implemented by any country

Appendix II: National Legal Frameworks for Biotechnology, Biosafety and Trade[1]

STATUS OF APPROVAL OF BIOTECH PRODUCTS IN KEY INTERNATIONAL MARKETS

While the estimated global area of transgenic or genetically modified (GM) crops continues to grow, the vast majority of acreage remains confined to just five countries, namely the US (59 per cent), followed by Argentina (20 per cent), Canada (6 per cent), Brazil (6 per cent) and China (5 per cent), with minor plantings found in Paraguay, India, South Africa, Uruguay, Australia, Romania, Mexico, Spain, the Philippines, Colombia, Bulgaria, Honduras, Germany, and Indonesia (James, 2004). In most developing countries it is still not legal to plant GM crops on a commercial basis, largely due to hold-ups in the approval. Even countries that have in the past moved rapidly on the adoption of genetically modified organisms (GMOs), including China and Argentina, are now slowing down the approval processes.

The United States has moved most rapidly on the approval of GMOs. The first GM food product went on sale in the US in 1994. Since then 96 bioengineered foods have been approved as of 11 October 2004.

The EU has been considerably more cautious in this regard with just 20 GM products authorized, including several food crops authorized for farming on a commercial basis such as maize and soy. The year 1998 saw an end to all approvals of new GMO products for the EU market. A de facto moratorium was placed on approvals as a result of calls by Denmark, Greece, France, Italy and Luxembourg for strengthened regulations on labelling and traceability of GM goods. The EU has crafted such new rules and they came into effect in November 2003. Regarding GM food products, the new EU rules cover both foods containing GMOs and those derived from GMOs such as oils or flour. Only one variety of soybean and six varieties of maize have so far been assessed as suitable for human consumption and thirteen food products derived from GMOs, which, qualifying as 'substantially equivalent' to non-GM food, have been released into the market.[2]

For its part, Australia is carrying out 34 field trials of GM plants, but has so far only approved four plants for commercial release, namely a violet carnation, a carnation with improved vase life, Bt cotton and transgenic canola. A number of GM food products are also being imported to Australia for sale, including soybeans, canola oil, maize, cotton, potatoes and sugar beet. Several Australian states, however, have instituted moratoria on the commercial release of certain GMOs, including GM canola, which has been blocked from commercial release in South Australia, Victoria, Western Australia and New South Wales. In New Zealand, the moratorium on approvals for environmental release ended on 31 October 2003 and conditional release and contained field research were enabled by amendments to the Hazardous Substances and New Organisms Act, which came into force on 30 October 2003. In December 2003, the Environmental Risk Management Authority approved contained field tests of onions modified to be resistant to the herbicide glyphosate, but the country has not yet approved any commercial production of GM crops.

In Asia, the only major GM crops approved for commercial growing are GM cotton, which is grown commercially in China, India and Indonesia, and GM maize, recently approved in the Philippines in December 2002. To date, no Asian government has given official permission to plant GM soybeans or rice. India had not approved the commercial planting of any GM crops until March 2002, when India's Genetic Engineering Approval Committee (GEAC) finally approved the commercial production of three varieties of GM cotton amid widespread protests by anti-GMO activists. China had initially moved quickly on the approval of GM crops for commercial release, with a total cultivation area of GM crops exceeding 2.1 million hectares and 31 approvals between 1997 and 2000 of which insect resistant GM cotton is the only crop to be widely adopted. The approval process, however, has slowed considerably since 2000 and strict regulations have been implemented for GMO imports. While Japan has approved 61 crops for planting in open field, and has approved more than 43 varieties of six crops – maize, soybean, sugar beet, potato, rapeseed and cotton – for human consumption, the country does not contain even 1 per cent of worldwide GM crop acreage.

Large differences exist among approvals and commercial releases of GM crops in Latin American countries. Argentina, the world's second largest producer of GM crops, approved 495 licences for farmers to grow GM crops, including food crops such as maize, soy and alfalfa, over the decade 1991–2001 (see also Chapter 6). The most popular GM crop among Argentina's farmers is Monsanto's Roundup Ready soybean, modified to tolerate the herbicide Roundup. Adoption of this soybean variety in Argentina has risen from a few per cent of the six million hectares planted in 1996 to almost 100 per cent of the 10.5 million hectares of soy grown in 2002.

In contrast, Brazil has been traditionally hesitant to approve the commercialization of GM crops. A number of GM maize varieties can be legally imported into Brazil for use in feed, but no GM foods have been approved for sale so far. Only one GM crop – Monsanto's Roundup Ready soybeans – has been approved for commercial release by Comissão Técnica Nacional de Biossegurança (CTNBio, the agency responsible for setting GMO-related regulations and approving GMOs in Brazil) and widely adopted in the country. However, in 1999, a lower court issued an injunction on the commercial planting of the soybeans in Brazil, following opposition by Brazilian consumer groups. In September 2004, the Appellate Court made public the decision, made in June 2004 by a majority of its judges, to cancel the injunction and uphold the authority of CTNBio to grant final approval for the commercial use of transgenic crops. As a result of the 'judicial moratorium', government approval of the commercial release of GMOs was on hold. However, despite the moratorium, illegally planted GM soy is becoming increasingly widespread, in particular in Brazil's South, due to smuggling of seeds from Argentina. The share of GM soy is now thought to amount to as much as half of the total crop in some areas. In order to legalize this phenomenon and enable biotechnology companies to legally demand payment for the usage of GM seeds, the government has issued Provisional Measures in 2002, 2003 and 2004 allowing the sale of GM crops for a limited amount of time (see also Chapter 6).

In Africa, approval of GM crops for commercial growing and import of GM-containing goods continues to be extremely slow. South Africa remains the only African country that allows commercial growing of GM crops, including soybeans, cotton and maize. Nearly 90 per cent of its cotton, 20 per cent of its yellow maize, and 20 per cent of its soybean is genetically modified. Kenya is regarded as one of the most promising sources of locally engineered GM crops that address the needs of sub-Saharan farmers. After successfully launching the first field trials of virus resistant sweet potatoes in 2001, Kenya plans to launch Bt maize resistant to local diseases. In Zimbabwe, the only country other than South Africa that has adopted a biosafety law, no GMO crop has so far been approved for commercial release.

SELECTED NATIONAL IMPORT REGIMES FOR BIOTECH GOODS

Overview

The scope of import regulations for GMOs varies greatly from country to country and is in most cases closely related to the status of the domestic biotech industry and export interests in GM products. Thus, while the US and Argentina – the two biggest producers of GM crops – have comparatively lenient regulatory systems where labelling is not mandatory, other key markets, such as the EU, Japan and Korea, are busy tightening their import regulations. This correlation is not necessarily true for all countries, however. Australia, for instance, while investing heavily in biotechnology, has one of the best-developed biotechnology regulatory frameworks and one of the most stringent labelling schemes in the world. Similarly, China, which is developing the largest plant biotechnology research capacity outside North America, has implemented its Regulations on Safety of Import of Agricultural GMOs, which requires the imported GMOs to obtain a safety certificate. When the regulations were issued in 2002, GMO exporters such as the US had criticized the lengthy approval process. To address these concerns, one-year

'Interim Safety Certificates' were issued from 2002 to April 2004, after which a three- to five-year safety certificate system was introduced to replace the interim system.

The EU is clearly the most advanced region when it comes to biotech regulations. East and Southeast Asia are also seeing increasing use of import regulations, which are now in place or being developed in Japan, Korea, Thailand, China, India and the Philippines. The status of biotech regulations in Latin America varies greatly. Some countries, in particular many in Central America, have yet to implement adequate regulatory systems, while others, such as Argentina, Brazil and Mexico, have made significant progress, albeit with varying levels of stringency.

In Africa, only South Africa, Kenya, Nigeria and Zimbabwe have put in place a biosafety law, while the existing laws are left to cater for the needs of biosafety in the remaining continent. Cameroon, Algeria, Namibia and Ethiopia are in the final phases of developing a bill regarding biosafety. In addition to efforts at the national level, the continent is also pursuing a regional approach to establishing biotechnology-related policies. In October 2002, the Southern African Development Community (SADC) set up an Advisory Committee on GMOs to develop guidelines that would assist member states guard against potential risks in food safety and contamination of genetic resources, and deal with ethical issues, trade-related issues and consumer concerns. Shortly afterwards, in November 2002, member states of the Common Market for Eastern and Southern Africa (COMESA) agreed to create a regional GMO policy, thereby responding to recent concerns throughout the area regarding GMOs, in particular GM food aid. In 2003, the New Partnership for Africa's Development (NEPAD) and the International Food Policy Research Institute (IFPRI) established a regional platform, the African Policy Dialogues on Biotechnology, through which African countries will be able to engage in dialogue and develop a common biotechnology strategy across the continent.

Bolivia and Sri Lanka have both bowed to pressures to abandon ambitious plans for GM regulation. On 1 May 2001, Sri Lanka's Health Ministry imposed import restrictions requiring 21 categories of food imports to be free of GM products. The ban was later suspended following a World Trade Organization (WTO) request that the country give its trading partners 60 days to prepare for the restrictions. The ban was finally postponed indefinitely. Bolivia imposed a ban on the imports of GMOs in January 2001, which was revoked in October 2001, allegedly due to pressure by the Argentine soy corporate sector, despite assurances by the Bolivian government in August that it would not lift the ban. The EU also effectively ended its de facto moratorium on GMO approvals when it authorized the first GM product in May 2003, which some civil society groups allege was a result of the 2003 WTO challenge launched by the US, Canada and Argentina against the de facto moratorium.

With regard to the scope of organisms targeted under GMO import regulations, a controversial type of product is one that is derived from, but no longer contains GMOs, and is 'substantially equivalent' to its conventional counterpart. One example of a derived product is soy oil that is made from GM soy, but so highly refined that the DNA carrying altered genetic traits is entirely broken down, making the oil 'equivalent' to non-modified soy oil. While laws in some countries, such as Argentina, Australia and Japan, explicitly exclude such products from their legislation, others, notable the EU and China, require such foods to be labelled as derived from GMOs, although under Chinese regulations only for certain agricultural GMOs, including: soybeans and maize (including their seeds, powder, oil and meal); rapeseed, oil and meal; cotton seed; and tomatoes, tomato seed and tomato paste.

Labelling requirements also vary widely in terms of labelling thresholds. The EU proposals again are the most stringent, requiring all GM products with GM content greater than 0.9 per cent to be labelled as containing GMOs. The threshold for the accidental presence of GMOs is 0.5 per cent for GMOs that are unauthorized but have nevertheless been assessed as risk-free. Australia and New Zealand have adopted a 1 per cent threshold for such accidental presence of GMOs, while Brazil requires labelling for all foods or food ingredients with a labelling threshold of 1 per cent as well as the labelling of animals fed with GM grains and products prepared with these animals. Korea is more lenient in this regard with a 3 per cent threshold and only requires labelling for certain genetically modified 'raw materials', including GM soybean, maize and bean sprouts and GM potatoes. Japan also requires only a subset of GMOs to be labelled on the condition that the GM material is still detectable. Several other countries are developing labelling regulations, including Brazil, Mexico, Zimbabwe, South Africa and Thailand.

National legislation in selected countries

Argentina
Resolutions no 656 (1992) and no 289 (1997) regulate research and environmental release of GMOs. They are administered by the National Advisory Commission on Agricultural Biotechnology (CONABIA) under the Secretary of Agriculture, Livestock, Fisheries and Foods (SAGPyA). GM food and feed are regulated by Resolutions no 412 (2002), no 511 (1998) and no 289 (1997), administered by the National Service of Health and Agrofood Quality (SENASA). The regulations apply to GMOs that are not substantially equivalent to their conventional counterparts. There are currently no requirements for mandatory labelling of GMOs.

Australia
The *Gene Technology Act* (2000) and associated Acts regulate all 'dealings' with GMOs, experimental use, breeding, propagation, manufacture, growing, import, possession, supply, use, transport or disposal. For the purpose of the Act, GMOs

are defined as (a) an organism that has been modified by gene technology; or (b) an organism that has inherited particular traits from an organism (the initial organism), which occurred in the initial organism through the application of gene technology; or (c) anything declared by the regulations to be a genetically modified organism, or that belongs to a class of items declared by the regulations to be genetically modified organisms. The Act is administered by the Gene Technology Regulator (plus three advisory committees).

The sale of food produced using gene technology is regulated by *Standard A18 Foods Produced using Gene Technology* (1999) in the Australian Food Standards Code. The Standard, which covers GM food and food with GM ingredient(s) that contains novel DNA and/or novel protein or has altered characteristics, is administered by the Australia–New Zealand Food Authority (ANZFA) and the Australia–New Zealand Food Standards Council (ANZFSC). It requires mandatory labelling of GM foods with a threshold of 1 per cent for the accidental presence of GM material. Exempted from labelling are foods derived from GMOs where the GM material is no longer detectable, most processing aids and food additives, flavours present in a concentration less than or equal to 0.1 per cent, and food prepared at the point of sale. While not explicitly including traceability requirements, compliance with the Standard is likely to require verifiable documentation regarding the GM status of the food to be transmitted from growers, processors, suppliers and importers to manufacturers and retailers along the supply chain.

Brazil

The *Brazilian Biosafety Law (Lei No 11.105)* (24 March 2005) regulates the use of genetic engineering techniques in the construction, culture, production, manipulation, transportation, transfer, import, export, storage, research, marketing, environmental release and discharge of genetically modified organisms (defined as an organism whose genetic material (DNA/rDNA) has been modified by any technique of genetic engineering). The law is administered by the national technical biosafety committee (CTNBio), which has the binding authority to make decisions on import, export, environmental release and all other GMO activities by issuing its technical opinion on a case-by-case basis regarding the biosafety of GMOs; authorizing the import of GMOs and their by-products for research; deciding if a GMO has to undergo a risk assessment prior to release or not; and identifying activities which have the potential to damage the environment. In addition, the law establishes the national biosafety council (CNBS) to provide higher advisory assistance in formulating and implementing the national biosafety policy, establishing principles and guidelines, and considering 'the socio-economic convenience and opportunities and national interest' entailed in commercial authorization of GMOs. While it is not supposed to participate in each request for a GMO release, it is allowed to do so when requested by CTNBio or by the majority of its members or its chairperson. In this case, CNBS can halt a commercial release despite

CTNBio's approval, although in general CNBS approval is not a mandatory step for commercial approval. Decree No 4.680, published in April 2003, requires labelling for all foods or food ingredients with a labelling threshold of 1 per cent. The decree also mandates the labelling of animals fed with GM grains and products prepared with these animals.

China

Agricultural GMOs (animals, plants, micro-organisms and their products whose genetic structures have been modified by genetic engineering technology for the use of agricultural production or processing) are regulated by the *Implementation Regulations on Safety Assessment of Agricultural GMOs, Implementation Regulations on Safety of Import of Agricultural GMOs* and the *Implementation Regulations on Labelling of Agricultural GMOs*.[3] These regulations were issued on 5 January 2002 and were scheduled to enter into force on 20 March 2002, but were again temporarily waived. The regulations are administered by the Agricultural GMO Committee responsible for safety evaluations and the Agricultural GMO Safety Administration Office responsible for safety administration of agricultural GMO imports. Final approval is granted by the Ministry of Agriculture. The regulations require labelling of certain agricultural GMOs, including those derived from but no longer containing GMOs, as set out in the labelling regulations (currently soybeans and maize including their seeds, powder, oil and meal; rapeseed, oil and meal; cotton seed; and tomatoes, tomato seed and tomato paste).

The *Administrative Measures on Hygiene of GMO Foodstuffs* (2001) regulates foods and food additives made from the animals, plants and micro-organisms whose genome composition is modified through biotechnology. They are administered by the GMO Food Expert Commission under the Ministry of Health. Labelling is required for all food products, including raw and processed foods.

European Union

The 'Council Directive on the deliberate release into the environment of genetically modified organisms' (*2001/18/EC*) was adopted in March 2001 and entered into force on 17 October 2002. The Directive covers any GMO or product consisting of or containing GMOs, including products derived from but not containing GMOs. Applications for the release of GMOs into the environment are assessed by the member state where the product is first placed onto the market. If approved and if no objections are raised by other member states, the product can be marketed throughout the EU. If objections are raised, the decision will be taken at the Community level. GM foods are covered by Regulation (*EC*) *258/97* on novel foods and novel food ingredients, Regulation (*EC*) *50/2000* on additives and flavourings and Regulation (*EC*) *49/2000* on adventitious contamination of GM material in conventional food. The authorization process is similar to that under Directive *2001/18/EC*.

On 25 July 2001, the European Commission put forward two legislative proposals on GMOs, a Regulation on GM food and feed (*COM 2001 – 425 final*) and a Regulation on traceability and labelling of GMOs and products produced from GMOs (*COM 2001 – 1821 final*). The regulations were adopted by the European Parliament and the European Council of Ministers in July 2003 with certain amendments.[4] Under the new regulations, the authorization process for GMOs for release into the environment and GM food or feed has been simplified with a 'one door one key' procedure: a single risk assessment and a single application are required to obtain approval for the deliberate release of GMOs into the environment and for use in food or feed. Scientific risk assessments will be conducted by the newly established European Food Authority. The Commission will then draft a proposal for granting or refusing authorization, which will be submitted for approval by member states within a Regulatory Committee. The new regulations entered into force in October 2003 with a six-month compliance period.

While traceability requirements were already included in general terms in the 2001 Directive, the new regulations further elaborate on these provisions. In particular, the 2001 Directive requires operators to transmit and retain specified information for GMOs, including their unique codes, at all stages of the placing on the market. With regard to labelling, the new regulations extend the current labelling requirements to all GM food or feed, irrespective of whether the GM material can still be detected. Thus, all pre-packaged products consisting of or containing GMOs on the market must be labelled as 'containing GMOs', while products, including bulk quantities that are not packaged and the use of a label is not possible, must be accompanied by the relevant information. The labelling threshold is 0.9 per cent, below which GM products are exempt from labelling. The threshold for the accidental presence of unauthorized GM material is 0.5 per cent, provided that the GMOs have been judged as safe for human health and the environment by the relevant Scientific Committees or the European Food Authority.

India

Biotechnology is regulated by the *Rules for the Manufacture, Use, Import, Export and Storage of Hazardous Micro-organisms, Genetically Engineered Organisms or Cells (1989)* and the *Guidelines for Toxicity and Allergenicity Evaluation of Transgenic Seeds, Plants and Plant Parts* (1994, revised in 1998). The rules apply to genetically engineered organisms, micro-organisms and cells; and substances and products and foodstuffs, among others, of which these form part. The rules are administered by the Department of Biotechnology under the Ministry of Science and Technology and various competent authorities including the Review Committee on Genetic Manipulation (RCGM) which approves the import of transgenic material. Approvals for environmental release are given by the Genetic Engineering Approval

Committee (GEAC) under the Department of Environment, Forests and Wildlife. No mandatory labelling is required.

Japan
The *Law Concerning the Conservation and Sustainable Use of Biological Diversity through Regulations on the Use of Living Modified Organisms (Law No 97 of 2003)*, which entered into force in February 2004, applies to all uses, import and export of living modified organisms in Japan and explicitly sets out to implement the Cartagena Protocol on Biosafety. Under the law, anyone interested in making use of or importing LMOs must submit an application to the Ministry of the Environment that includes the name and address of the applicant; the name, type and intended method of use of the LMO; a Biological Diversity Risk Assessment Report; and a document detailing measures for efficiently preventing adverse effect on biological diversity. GM foods are also regulated by the *Labelling Standard for Genetically Modified Foods and the Specifications and Standards for Foods, Food Additives and Other Related Products*, which are administered by the Ministry of Health, Labour and Welfare (MHLW). Labelling is required for GM agricultural products and foods processed as listed in the Standard (currently soybeans, including green soybeans and soybean sprouts, maize, potato, rapeseed and cotton-seed). Exempt from labelling are foods derived from but no longer containing GMOs and processed food where the GM ingredient is not a main ingredient.

Mexico
The *Draft Official Mexican Standard NOM–056–FITO–1995* covers organisms manipulated by genetic engineering for agricultural use. It is administered by the Directorate-General of Plant Health (DGSV) under the Secretariat of Agriculture, Livestock, and Rural Development (SAGARPA). The Directorate bases its decisions to grant permits on the opinion of the national Biosafety Committee on Agriculture, set up in 1989 as a consulting body to the DGSV. In addition, the Intersectoral Commission for Biosafety and Genetically Modified Organisms (CIBIOGEM) was established in 1999 to develop GMO-related policies.

In February 2005, the Mexican Senate passed new legislation which allows for the sale and cultivation of GM crops. The law requires GM products to be labelled according to guidelines to be developed by the Ministry of Health, designed to implement the Cartagena Protocol on Biosafety. The law also calls for the development of a special protection regime for native maize varieties.

Regarding GM foods, the Mexican *Health Act* requires all biotechnology products or their derivatives that are intended for human consumption, to be notified to the Secretariat of Health. In March 2000, the Mexican Senate passed an amendment to the Act that would require all genetically modified or transgenic foods to be labelled.

Philippines

The *Rules and Regulations on the Importation and Release into the Environment of Plants and Plant Products Derived from the use of Modern Biotechnology* (entry into force on 1 July 2003) covers plants or plant products altered or produced through the use of modern biotechnology. The main regulatory agency is the Bureau of Plant Industry (BPI) under the Department of Agriculture. Risk assessment, which is based on 'substantial equivalence', is carried out by a Scientific Technical Review Panel, which was set up by the BPI. The rules do not cover labelling.

South Africa

The South African Executive Council for Genetically Modified Organisms was set up in 1997 under the *Genetically Modified Organisms Act* (1997) as the responsible agency for authorizing imports and release of GMOs. The Act covers the development, production, use, application or environmental release of GMOs. The (*Draft*) *Regulations Governing the Labelling of Foodstuffs obtained through Certain Techniques of Genetic Modification*, released on 4 May 2001 by the Ministry of Health, would require GM foods to be labelled if they were significantly different with regard to the composition, nutritional value and mode of storage, preparation or cooking; or contained allergens from any of the products listed in the draft Regulation. The threshold for accidental presence would be 1 per cent. In January 2004 the Health Ministry published the regulations to the Foods, Cosmetics and Disinfectants Act, which state that food with GM ingredients requires labelling only if its composition, nutritional value, or mode of storage or cooking is significantly different from conventional food.

US

In the United States, GMOs are regulated through existing legislation, which is implemented by three federal agencies, namely USDA – Department of Agriculture's Animal and Plant Health Inspection Service (development and field testing on most GMOs); EPA – Environmental Protection Agency (development and release of GM plants with pest control properties); and FDA – Food and Drug Administration (safety of food and feeds). There are no mandatory risk assessment requirements and labelling is voluntary. The FDA has released several guidance documents for bioengineered foods, including the *Statement of Policy: Foods Derived from New Plant Varieties* (1992), the draft *Premarket Notice Concerning Bioengineered Foods* (2001) and the *Draft Guidance for Industry Voluntary Labelling Indicating Whether Foods Have or Have Not Been Developed Using Bioengineering* (2001).

Zimbabwe

The statutory instrument dealing with biosafety in Zimbabwe is the *Research (Biosafety) Regulations* (2000), which focuses on biosafety considerations in the context of research and field testing of GM crops. The Act establishes the Biosafety Board under the Research Council of Zimbabwe. Non-binding standards for GM food labelling are currently being developed by the Standards Association of Zimbabwe.

NOTES

1   This appendix is based on the paper: Baumüller, H (2003) *Domestic Import Regulations for Genetically Modified Organisms and their Compatibility with WTO Rules – Some key issues*, IISD–ICTSD Trade Knowledge Network, available at www.tradeknowledge network.org/. Full references are included in the paper. The information provided in this appendix is current as of February 2005.
2   These include food derived from but no longer containing GMOs, which are 'substantially equivalent' to existing foods in terms of composition, nutritional value, metabolism, intended use and the level of undesirable substances.
3   Note that the following outline of China's GMO regulations is based on unofficial translations of the relevant regulations. Consequently, names of agencies and regulations might differ from other translations.
4   Amendments include language to allow EU member states to impose 'appropriate measures' to avoid the unintended presence of GMOs in other products (co-existence). The European Commission has released guidelines for the development of national strategies and best practices to ensure the co-existence of GM crops with conventional and organic farming.

REFERENCES

James, C (2004) 'Preview: Global status of commercialized transgenic crops: 2004', *ISAAA Briefs No 32*, ISAAA, Ithaca, NY
This appendix also draws on information from the following sources:
   AgBiotechNet, CAB International, www.agbiotechnet.com/
   Checkbiotech, www.checkbiotech.org
   FAO-BioDeC, UN Food and Agriculture Organization,
   www.fao.org/biotech/inventory_admin/dep/default.asp
   Global Knowledge Center on Crop Biotechnology, www.isaaa.org/kc/
Additional references for this Appendix can be found in the full-length paper available at
   www.tradeknowledgenetwork.net/publication.aspx?id=587

Appendix III: Participants at the ICTSD dialogue on 'Biotechnology, Biosafety and Trade: Issues for Developing Countries'

The dialogue took place in Bellevue, Switzerland, on 18–20 July 2001.

PARTICIPANTS

Mr Julio G. Alvarado
Permanent Mission of Bolivia

Mr Martin Barugahare
UNCTAD

Mr Victor Batanin
Permanent Mission of the Russian
Federation

Ms Betty Berendson
Permanent Mission of Peru

HE Nguyen Quy Binh
Permanent Mission of Vietnam
to the UN

HE B M Bowa
Permanent Mission of Zambia
to the UN

Mr William Bradnee Chambers
UN University

Mr Cristian Espinosa
Permanent Mission of Ecuador

Mr Michail Faleev
Permanent Mission of the Russian
Federation

Mr B Guritno
Permanent Mission of Indonesia

Ms Mariko Hara
UNEP, Economics and Trade Branch

Ms Libertina Kautwima
Embassy of the Republic of Namibia

Ms Susanna Köhler
Bolivian Association of Political
Economy of Globalisation

Ms Martha Lara
Permanent Mission of Mexico
to the WTO

Mr Pisan Luetongcharg
Permanent Mission of Thailand
to the WTO

Mr Felix Maonera
Permanent Mission of Zimbabwe
to the UN

Ms Constanza Martinez
Consultant

Ms Isabelle Padilla
Permanent Mission of the
Dominican Republic

Mr Leo Palma
Permanent Mission of the Philippines

Mr Rafael Paredes
Permanent Mission of Ecuador

Ms Virginia Perez
Permanent Mission of Venezuela

Mr Marcoflavio Rigada
Permanent Mission of Mexico
to the WTO

Mr Pedro Roffe
UNCTAD

Mr Gary Sampson
Institute of Advanced Studies,
UN University

Mr Someshwar Singh
South Centre

Ms Salimatta Touray
Embassy of the Republic
of The Gambia

Mr Santiago Urbina
Permanent Mission of Nicaragua

Mr Alexey Vikhlyaev
UNCTAD

Ms Lai Peng Yap
Permanent Mission of Malaysia
to the WTO

Mr Yüksel Yücekal
Permanent Mission of Turkey
to the WTO

SPEAKERS AND DISCUSSERS

Mr Paolo Bifani
Consultant

Mr Joseph Gopo
Biotechnology Research Institute,
Scientific & Industrial Research and
Development Centre, Zimbabwe

Mr Calestous Juma
Science, Technology and Innovation
Programme, Centre for International
Development, Harvard University

Mr Atul Kaushik
Cabinet Secretariat,
Government of India

Mr Arturo Martinez
Department of Environmental Affairs,
Ministry of Foreign Affairs, Argentina

Ms Jayashree Watal
WTO Intellectual Property Division

Ms Christiane Wolff
WTO Agriculture and Commodities
Division

Mr A H Zakri
Institute of Advanced Studies,
UN University

ICTSD STAFF

Ms Heike Baumüller
Programme Manager, Natural
Resources

Mr Ricardo Meléndez-Ortiz
Executive Director

Ms Jennifer Ngai
Programme Associate

Mr Vicente Sanchez
Senior Fellow

Ms Jeanette Tantillo
Programme Officer

Selected Readings on Biotechnology, Biosafety and Trade

Agriculture

ActionAid (2003) *GM Crops: Going Against The Grain*, ActionAid, London

ERS (2001) *Economic issues in agricultural biotechnology*, Economic Research Service, US Department of Agriculture, Washington, DC

Evenson, R E, Santaniello, V and Zilberman, D (2002) *Economic and Social Issues in Agricultural Biotechnology*, CABI Publishing, Wallingford, UK

Gould, F and Cohen, M B (2000) 'Sustainable use of genetically modified crops in developing countries', in Persley, G J and Lantin, M M (eds), *Agricultural Biotechnology and the Poor*, conference proceedings, 21–22 October 1999, Washington, DC

Marra, M C, Pardey, P C and Alston, J M (2002) 'The payoffs to agricultural biotechnology: An assessment of the evidence', *Environment and Production Technology Division Discussion Paper No 87*, International Food Policy Research Institute, Washington, DC

Moschini, G (2001) ' Biotech – who wins? Economic benefits and costs of biotechnology innovations in agriculture', *The Estey Centre Journal of International Law and Trade Policy*, vol 2, no 1, pp93–117

Murray, D A (2003) *Seeds of Concern: The Genetic Manipulation of Plants*, CABI Publishing, Wallingford, UK

Paarlberg, R L (2001) 'Governing the GM crop revolution: Policy choices for developing countries', in Pinstrup-Andersen, P and Pandya-Lorch, R (eds), *The Unfinished Agenda Perspectives on Overcoming Hunger, Poverty and Environmental Degradation*, International Food Policy Research Institute, Washington, DC

Persley, G J and Lantin, M M (2000) *Agricultural biotechnology and the poor*, Proceedings of an international conference, 21–22 October 1999, Washington, DC

Qaim, M, Krattinger, A and von Braun, J (2000) *Agricultural biotechnology in developing countries: Towards optimizing the benefits for the poor*, Kluwer, Boston/Dordrecht

Royal Society of London, US National Academy of Sciences, Brazilian Academy of Sciences, Chinese Academy of Sciences, Indian National Science Academy, Mexican Academy of Sciences, Third World Academy of Sciences (2000) *Transgenic Plants and World Agriculture*, National Academy Press, Washington, DC

Scoones, I (2002) 'Science, policy and regulation: Challenges for agricultural biotechnology in developing countries', *IDS Working Paper 147*, Institute of Development Studies, Brighton, UK

BIODIVERSITY AND ENVIRONMENT

Batie, S and Ervin, D E (2001) 'Transgenic crops and the environment: Missing markets and public roles', *Environment and Development Economics*, vol 6, no 4, pp435–457

Benbrook, C (2003) 'Impacts of genetically engineered crops on pesticide use in the United States: The first eight years', *BioTech InfoNet Technical Paper No 6*, Benbrook Consulting Services, Sandpoint, Idaho

Conner, A J, Glare, T R and Nap, J P (2003) 'The release of genetically modified crops into the environment Part II – overview of ecological risk assessment', *The Plant Journal*, vol 33, pp19–46

FAO (2001) *Genetically Modified Organisms, Consumers, Food Safety and the Environment*, UN Food and Agriculture Organization, Rome

Ervin, D E, Batie, S S, Welsh, R, Carpentier, C L, Fern, J I, Richman, N J and Schulz, M A (2000) *Transgenic Crops: An Environmental Assessment*, Henry A. Wallace Center for Agricultural & Environmental Policy at Winrock International, Little Rock, Arkansas

National Research Council (2004) *Biological Confinement of Genetically Engineered Organisms*, Committee on the Biological Confinement of Genetically Engineered Organisms, The National Academies Press, Washington, DC

Nap, J P, Metz, P L J, Escaler, M, Conner, A J (2003) 'The release of genetically modified crops into the environment Part I – overview of current status and regulations', *The Plant Journal*, vol 33, pp1–18

Pardey, P and Koo, B (2003) 'Biotechnology and genetic resource policies', *Research at a Glance Briefs 1–6*, International Food Policy Research Institute, Washington, DC

Royal Society (1999) *GMOs and the Environment*, Royal Society, London

Ulph, A and O'Shea, L (2002) 'Biodiversity and optimal policies towards R&D and the growth of genetically modified crops', *Environmental and Resource Economics*, vol 22, no 4, pp505–520

Wolfenbarger L L and Phifer, P R (2000) 'The ecological risks and benefits of genetically engineered plants', Science, vol 290, pp2088–2093

THE BIOSAFETY PROTOCOL AND THE WTO

Bail, C, Falkner, R and Marquard, H (2002) *The Cartagena Protocol on Biosafety: Reconciling Trade in Biotechnology with Environment and Development*, Earthscan Publishing and the Royal Institute of International Affairs, London

Brack, D, Falkner, R and Goll, J (2003) 'The Next Trade War? GM Products, the Cartagena Protocol and the WTO', *RIIA Briefing Paper No 8*, London

Boisson de Chazournes, L and Thomas, U P (2000) 'The Biosafety Protocol: Regulatory innovation and emerging trends', *Schweizerische Zeitschrift für internationales und europäisches Recht*, vol 4, pp512–557

Cors, T A (2000) 'Biosafety and international trade: Conflict or convergence?', *International Journal of Biotechnology*, vol 2, nos 1/2/3, pp27–43

Cosbey, A and Burgiel, S (2000) 'The Cartagena Protocol on Biosafety: An analysis of results', *IISD Briefing Note*, Winnipeg, Manitoba, Canada

Eggers, B and Mackenzie, R (2000) 'The Cartagena Protocol on Biosafety', *Journal of International Economic Law*, vol 3, no 3, pp525–543

Gupta, A (2000) 'Governing trade in genetically modified organisms – The Cartagena Protocol on Biosafety', *Environment*, vol 42, no 4, pp22–33

Hobbs, A L, Hobbs, J E and Kerr, W A (2005) 'The Biosafety Protocol: Multilateral agreement on protecting the environment or protectionist club?', *Journal of World Trade*, vol 39, no 2, pp281–300

Isaac, E (2003) 'The WTO and the Cartagena Protocol: International Policy Coordination or Conflict?', *Current Agriculture, Food and Resources Issues*, vol 4, pp116–123

Mackenzie, R, Burhenne-Guilmin, F, La Viña, A G M and Werksman, J D (2003) 'An explanatory guide to the Cartagena Protocol on Biosafety', *Environmental Policy & Law Paper No 46*, IUCN Environmental Law Programme, Cambridge, UK

McLean, M A, Frederick, R J, Traynor, P L, Cohen, J I and Komen, J (2002) 'A conceptual framework for implementing biosafety: Linking policy, capacity and regulation', *Briefing Paper 47*, International Service for National Agricultural Research (ISNAR), The Hague

Newell, P and Mackenzie, R (2000) 'The 2000 Cartagena Protocol on Biosafety: Legal and political dimensions', *Global Environmental Change*, vol 10, no 4, pp313–317

COMMITTEE ON AGRICULTURE

Indonesia (2001) Fifth special session of the Committee on Agriculture, Statement by Indonesia, 13 February 2001, G/AG/NG/W/115

Republic of Korea (2001) Proposal for WTO negotiations on agriculture, Submitted by the Republic of Korea, 9 January 2001, G/AG/NG/W/98

United States (2000) Proposal for comprehensive long-term agricultural trade reform, Submission from the United States, 23 June 2000, G/AG/NG/W/15

DISPUTE SETTLEMENT

Argentina (2003) European Communities – Measures Affecting the Approval and Marketing of Biotech Products – Request for the Establishment of a Panel by Argentina Preview, 8 August 2003, WT/DS293/17 (other documents related to case are searchable with the document symbols WT/DS291/*, WT/DS292/* and WT/DS293/*; for parties' submissions and *amicus curiae* briefs, see www.trade-environment.org/page/theme/tewto/biotechcase.htm)

Canada (2003) European Communities – Measures Affecting the Approval and Marketing of Biotech Products – Request for the Establishment of a Panel by Canada, 8 August 2003, WT/DS292/17 (other documents related to case are searchable with the document symbol WT/DS292/*)

United States (2003) European Communities – Measures Affecting the Approval and Marketing of Biotech Products – Request for the Establishment of a Panel by the United States, 8 August 2003, WT/DS291/23 (other documents related to case are searchable with the document symbol WT/DS291/*)

FOOD SECURITY AND POVERTY ALLEVIATION

Abdalla, A, Berry, P, Connell, P, Tran, Q T and Buetre, B (2003) *Agricultural Biotechnology: Potential for Use in Developing Countries*, Australian Bureau of Agricultural and Resource Economics, Canberra, Australia

Anderson, K and Jackson, L E (2004) *Implications of Genetically Modified Food Technology Policies for Sub-Saharan Africa*, World Bank Working Paper 3411

Atanassov, A, Bahieldin, A, Brink, J, Burachik, M, Cohen, J I, Dhawan, V, Ebora, R V, Falck-Zepeda, J, Herrera-Estrella, L, Komen, J, Low, F C, Omaliko, E, Odhiambo, B, Quemada, H, Peng, Y, Sampaio, M J, Sithole-Niang, I, Sittenfeld, A, Smale, M, Sutrisno, Valyasevi, R, Zafar, Y and Zambrano P (2004) *To Reach the Poor – Results from the ISNAR-IFPRI Next Harvest Study on Genetically Modified Crops, Public Research, and Policy Implications*, International Food Policy Research Institute, Washington, DC

Berg, T, Syed, M, Opsahl Ferstad, H-G, Tsegaye, B and Waktola, A (2003) *Biotechnology in Developing Countries: Needs and Modes of Competence Building.* Noragric Report No 14-A, Noragric – Agricultural University of Norway, Ås, Norway

Borlaug, N E (2000) 'Ending world hunger: The promise of biotechnology and the threat of antiscience zealotry', *Plant Physiology*, vol 124, pp487–490

Chrispeels, M (2000) 'Biotechnology and the poor', *Plant Physiology*, vol 124, pp3–6

Cohen, J I (2001) 'Harnessing biotechnology for the poor: Challenges ahead for capacity, safety and public investment', *Journal of Human Development*, vol 2, pp239–263

Cohen J, Komen, J and Falck Zepeda, J (2004) *National Agricultural Biotechnology Research Capacity in Developing Countries*, Agricultural and Development Economics Division (ESA), UN Food and Agriculture Organization, Rome

CSTD (2001) *Synthesis Report on the CSTD Panels on National Capacity-Building in Biotechnology*, E/CN16/2001/2, United Nations Commission on Science and Technology

DBT (2003) *Genetically Modified Crops in Developing Countries – Challenges for the Development Aid*, Danish Board of Technology, Copenhagen

Dutfield, G (2000) 'Biodiversity in industrial research and development: Implications for developing countries', *International Journal of Biotechnology*, vol 2, nos 1/2/3, pp103–114

FAO (2004) *The State of Food and Agriculture 2003–04: Agricultural Biotechnology, Meeting the Needs of the Poor?*, UN Food and Agriculture Organization, Rome

IDS (2003) *Democratising Biotechnology: Genetically Modified Crops in Developing Countries*, Policy Briefings Series, Institute of Development Studies, Brighton, UK

IFPRI (2003) *Food Safety in Food Security and Food Trade*, 2020 Focus 10, International Food Policy Research Institute, Washington, DC

IFATPC (2004) *GM Technology: Assessing the Issues Confronting Developing Countries*, International Food and Agricultural Trade Policy Council, Washington, DC

Mugabe, J (2000) 'Biotechnology in developing countries and countries with economies in transition – strategic capacity building considerations', Background paper prepared for the United Nations Conference on Trade and Development, Geneva

Nielsen, C P, Robinson, S and Thierfelder, K (2001) 'Genetic engineering and trade: Panacea or dilemma for developing countries', *World Development*, vol 29, no 8, pp1307–1324

Nuffield Council on Bioethics (2003) *The Use of Genetically Modified Crops in Developing Countries.* A follow-up Discussion Paper to the 1999 Report 'Genetically modified crops: The ethical and social issues', Nuffield Council, London

Panos Institute (2005) *The GM debate – Who decides? An Analysis of Decision-Making About Genetically Modified Crops in Developing Countries*, Panos Report No 49, London

Phillips, P W B (2001) 'Will biotechnology feed the world's hungry?, *International Journal*, vol 56, no 4, pp665–677

Pinstrup-Andersen, P and Cohen, M J (2000) 'Agricultural biotechnology: Risks and opportunities for developing country food security', *International Journal of Biotechnology*, vol 2, nos 1/2/3, pp145–163

Pinstrup-Andersen, P and Schioler, E (2000) *Seeds of Contention: World Hunger and the Global Controversy over GM Crops*, The Johns Hopkins University Press, Baltimore, Maryland

Pray, C E and Naseem, A (2003) *Biotechnology R&D: Policy Options to Ensure Access and Benefits for the Poor*, ESA Working Paper No 03-08. UN Food and Agriculture Organization, Rome

Rosegrant, M W and Cline, S A (2003) 'Global food security: Challenges and policies', *Science*, vol 302, pp1917–1919

Scoones, I (2002) 'Agricultural biotechnology and food security: Exploring the debate', *IDS Working Paper 145*, Institute of Development Studies, Brighton, UK

Serageldin, I (1999) 'Biotechnology and food security in the 21st Century', *Science*, vol 285, no 5426, pp387–389

Spillane, C (2000) 'Could agricultural biotechnology contribute to poverty alleviation?' *AgBiotechNet*, vol 2, March, pp1–39

Thomson J (2002) *Genes for Africa: Genetically Modified Crops in the Developing World*, UCT Press

TWN (2003) *Genetically Modified Crops and Sustainable Poverty Alleviation in Sub-Saharan Africa: An Assessment of Current Evidence*, Third World Network Africa, Accra, Ghana

Zarrilli, S (2005) *International Trade in GMOs and GM Products: National and Multilateral Legal Frameworks, Policy Issues in International Trade and Commodities*, Study Series No 29, United Nations Conference on Trade and Development, Geneva

GENERAL

Anderson, K, Damania, R, Jackson, L A (2004) *Trade, Standards and the Political Economy of Genetically Modified Food*, World Bank Policy Research Working Paper 3395, Washington, DC

Charles, D (2001) *Lords of the Harvest – Biotech, Big Money, and the Future of Food*, Perseus Publishing, Cambridge, US

Devlin, A (2003) 'An overview of biotechnology statistics in selected countries', *STI Working Paper 2003/13*, Directorate for Science, Technology and Industry, OECD

GM Science Review Panel (2003) *GM Science Review – First report: An Open Review of the Science Relevant to GM Crops and Food Based on Interests and Concerns of the Public*, GM Science Review Panel, London

ICC Joint Working Party on BioSociety (2001) *A Global Roadmap for Modern Biotechnology*, International Chamber of Commerce, Paris, France

James, C (2004) 'Global status of commercialized transgenic crops: 2004', *ISAAA Briefs No 32*, ISAAA, Ithaca, New York

Juma, C (2000) 'Biotechnology in the global economy', *International Journal of Biotechnology*, vol 2, nos 1/2/3, pp1–6

Moeller, D R (2001) *GMO Liability Threats for Farmers – Legal Issues Surrounding the Planting of Genetically Modified Crops*, Institute for Agriculture and Trade Policy, St Paul, Minnesota

Newell, P (2002) 'Biotechnology and the politics of regulation', *IDS Working Paper 146*, Institute of Development Studies, Brighton, UK

Pardey, P G (2001) *The Future of Food – Biotechnology Markets and Policies in an International Setting*, Johns Hopkins University Press, Baltimore, Maryland

Pew Initiative (2003) *University–Industry Relationships: Framing the Issues for Academic Research in Agricultural Biotechnology*, Pew Initiative on Food and Biotechnology and Portland State University, Research Triangle Park, North Carolina, US

Runge, C F and Ryan, B (2004) *The Global Diffusion of Plant Biotechnology: International Adoption and Research in 2004*, Council on Biotechnology Information, Washington, DC

Serageldin, I and Persley, G J (2003) *Biotechnology and Sustainable Development: Voices of the South and North*, CABI Publishing, Glasgow, UK

Strategy Unit (2003) *Field Work: Weighing up the Costs and Benefits of GM crops*, UK Cabinet Office, www.strategy.gov.uk/downloads/su/gm/pdf.htm

Taylor, N, Kent, L and Fauquet, C (2004) 'Special issue: Progress, achievements and constraints for plant biotechnology in developing countries', *AgBioForum – The Journal of Agrobiotechnology Management & Economics*

Traxler, G (2004) *The Economic Impacts of Biotechnology-Based Technological Innovations*, Agricultural and Development Economics Division (ESA), UN Food and Agriculture Organization, Rome

UNDP (2001) *Human Development Report 2001*, United National Development Programme, Oxford University Press, New York

Health

American Medical Association (2000) *Genetically Modified Foods and Crops*, American Medical Association, Chicago, IL

Atherton, K (2002) *Genetically Modified Crops – Assessing Safety*, Taylor and Francis, London

Buchanan, B B (2001) 'Genetic engineering and the allergy issue', *Plant Physiology*, vol 126, no 1, May, pp5–7

Donaldson, L and May, R (1999) *Health Implications of Genetically Modified Foods*, Department of Health, London

FAO/WHO (1996) *Biotechnology and Food Safety*, Report of a Joint FAO/WHO consultation, UN Food and Agriculture Organization and World Health Organization, Rome

FAO/WHO (2000) *Safety Aspects of Genetically Modified Foods of Plant Origin*, UN Food and Agriculture Organization and World Health Organization, Geneva

FAO/WHO (2001) *Evaluation of Allergenicity of Genetically Modified Foods*, UN Food and Agriculture Organization and World Health Organization, Rome

National Academies (2004) *Safety of Genetically Engineered Foods: Approaches to Assessing Unintended Health Effects*, National Research Council and Institute of Medicine, Washington, DC

Royal Society (1998) *Genetically Modified Plants for Food Use*, Royal Society, London

Royal Society (2002) *Genetically Modified Plants for Food Use and Human Health: An Update*, Policy Document 4/02, Royal Society, London

Thorsteinsdóttir, H, Quach, H U, Martin, D K, Singer, P A and Daar A (2004) 'Health biotechnology innovation in developing countries', *Nature Biotechnology Supplement*, vol 22, no 12

WHO (2005) *Modern Food Biotechnology, Human Health and Development: An Evidence-Based Study*, World Health Organization, Geneva

INTELLECTUAL PROPERTY RIGHTS

Biber-Klemm, S (2000) 'Biotechnology and traditional knowledge: In search of equity', *International Journal of Biotechnology*, vol 2, nos 1/2/3, pp85–102

Canadian Biotechnology Advisory Committee (2002) *Biotechnology and Intellectual Property: Patenting of Higher Life Forms and Related Issues*, Report to the Government of Canada Biotechnology Ministerial Coordinating Committee

Curci Staffler, J (2002) *Towards a Reconciliation Between the Convention on Biological Diversity and TRIPS Agreement: An Interface among Intellectual Property Rights on Biotechnology, Traditional Knowledge and Benefit Sharing*, Université de Genève, Institut Universitaire de Hautes Etudes Internationales, Geneva

Dutfield, G (2000) *Intellectual Property Rights, Trade and Biodiversity*, Earthscan, London

Dutfield, G (2004) *Intellectual Property, Biogenetic Resources and Traditional Knowledge*, Earthscan, London

European Commission (2002) *Development and Implications of Patent Law in the Field of Biotechnology and Genetic Engineering*, Report from the Commission to the European Parliament and the Council, COM(2002) 545 final, Brussels

Ewens, L E (2000) 'Seed wars: Biotechnology, intellectual property, and the quest for high yield seeds', *Boston College International and Comparative Law Review*, vol 23, no 2

FAO (2002) *Public Agricultural Research: The Impact of IPRS on Biotechnology in Developing Countries*, Report of an Expert Workshop, Rome, 24–27 June 2002, UN Food and Agriculture Organization, Rome

Kesan, J (2000) 'Intellectual property protection and agricultural biotechnology: A multidisciplinary perspective', *American Behavioral Scientist*, vol 44, no 3, pp464–503

Kowalski, S P, Ebora, R V, Kryder, R D and Potter, R H (2002) 'Transgenic crops, biotechnology and ownership rights: What scientists need to know', *The Plant Journal* vol 31, no 4, pp407–421

Llewelyn, M (2000) 'The patentability of biological material: Continuing contradiction and confusion', *European Intellectual Property Review*, vol 22, no 5, pp191–197

OECD (2002) *Genetic Inventions, Intellectual Property Rights and Licensing Practices: Evidence and Policies*, Organisation for Economic Co-operation and Development, Paris

Olembo, N K, Sese, L, Mwasi, M and Henson-Appollonio, V (2004) *Intellectual Property Protection and Biotechnology: Issues and Processes for African Consensus*, prepared for the African Policy Dialogues on Biotechnology – Southern Africa, Zimbabwe, 20–21 September

Pardey, P, Wright, B and Nottenburg, C (2001) 'Are intellectual property rights stifling agricultural biotechnology in developing countries?', *International Food Policy Research Institute (IFPRI) Annual Report 2000–2001*, Washington, DC

Tansey, G (2002) 'Food security, biotechnology and intellectual property: Unpacking some issues around TRIPS', *Discussion Paper No 4*, Quaker United Nations Office, Geneva

Taylor, M R and Cayford, J (2003) *American Patent Policy, Biotechnology, and African Agriculture: The Case for Policy Change*, Resources for the Future, Washington, DC

Wendt, J and Izquierdo, J (2001) 'Biotechnology and development: A balance between IPR-protection and Benefit-Sharing', *Electronic Journal of Biotechnology*, vol 4, no 3

Yamin, F (2003) 'Intellectual property rights, biotechnology and food security', *IDS Working Paper 203*, Institute of Development Studies, Brighton, UK

PRECAUTION

Bergkamp, L (2001) *Biotech Food and the Precautionary Principle under EU and WTO Law*, Hunton & Williams, Brussels

Groth, E III (2000) *Science, Precaution and Food Safety: How Can We Do Better?*, Consumers Union, Yonkers, NY

Goklany, I M (2000) 'Applying the precautionary principle to genetically modified crops', *Policy Study 157*, Center for the Study of American Business, Washington University, St Louis, Missouri

Giampietro, M (2002) 'The precautionary principle and ecological hazards of genetically modified organisms', *Ambio*, vol 31, no 6, pp466–470

Katz, D (2001) 'The mismatch between the Biosafety Protocol and the precautionary principle', *Georgetown International Environmental Law Review*, vol 13, pp949–982

Lehmann, V (2002) *From Rio to Johannesburg and Beyond: Globalizing Precaution for Genetically Modified Organisms*, Heinrich Böll Foundation, Washington, DC

Paarlberg, R L (2001) *The Politics of Precaution – Genetically Modified Crops in Developing Countries*, International Food Policy Research Institute, Washington, DC

PREPARATIONS FOR THE SEATTLE MINISTERIAL CONFERENCE

United States (1999) Negotiations on Agriculture – Measures Affecting Trade in Agricultural Biotechnology Products, 4 August 1999, WT/GC/W/288

Canada (1999) Proposal for Establishment of a Working Party on Biotechnology in WTO, 12 October 1999, WT/GC/W/359

Japan (1999) Proposal on Genetically Modified Organisms (GMOs), 12 October 1999, WT/GC/W/365

SOCIAL AND ETHICAL ISSUES

Action Aid (2001) *Robbing Coffee's Cradle – GM Coffee and its Threat to Poor Farmers*, Action Aid, London

Bruce, D M (2002) 'A social contract for biotechnology: Shared visions for risky technologies?', *Journal of Agricultural and Environmental Ethics*, vol 15, no 3, pp279–289

Comstock, G (2001) *Ethics and Genetically Modified Foods*, Iowa State University, Ames

FAO (2001) *Ethical Issues in Food and Agriculture*, UN Food and Agricultural Organization, Rome

Nuffield Council on Bioethics (1999) *Genetically Modified Crops: The Ethical and Social Issues*, Nuffield Council, London

Skerritt, J H (2000) 'Genetically modified plants: Developing countries and the public acceptance debate', *AgBiotechNet*, vol 2, ABN 040, pp1–4

SPS AND TBT COMMITTEES

(Members' notifications to the SPS and TBT Committees are searchable at http://docsonline.wto.org/ using the documents symbols G/SPS/N/* and G/TBT/Notif/* respectively)

Argentina (2002) Response from the European Commission to comments submitted by WTO Members under notifications G/SPS/N/EEC/149 and 150, Submission by Argentina, 4 November 2002, G/SPS/GEN/354

European Commission (2002) Response from the European Commission to comments submitted by WTO Members under notifications G/SPS/N/EEC/150, and/or G/TBT/N/EEC/7 on food and feed products produced from genetically modified organisms, Submission by the European Communities, 26 July 2002, G/SPS/GEN/338 and G/TBT/W/180

FAO (2001) 'Biosecurity in food and agriculture', 14 March 2001, G/SPS/GEN/239

New Zealand (2001) 'Biosecurity risk analysis policy statement', Information paper from the government of New Zealand, 2 March 2001, G/SPS/GEN/233

TRADE IN GMOS

Appleton, A E (2000) 'The labelling of GMO products pursuant to international trade rules', *New York University Environmental Law Journal*, vol 8, no 3, pp566–578

Baumüller, H (2003) *Domestic Import Regulations for Genetically Modified Organisms and their Compatibility with WTO Rules – Some Key Issues*, IISD-ICTSD Trade Knowledge Network, Winnipeg, Manitoba, Canada

Bernauer, T (2003) *Genes, Trade, and Regulation: The Seeds of Conflict in Food Biotechnology*, Princeton University Press

Bernauer, T (2005) 'Causes and consequences of international trade conflict over agricultural biotechnology', *International Journal of Biotechnology*, vol 7, nos 1/2/3, pp7–28

Bredahl, M E and Kalaitzandonakes, N (2001) 'Biotechnology: Can we trade it?', *The Estey Centre Journal of International Law and Trade Policy*, vol 2, vol 1, pp75–92

Foster, M, Berry, P and Hogan, J (2003) *Market Access Issues for GM Products – Implications for Australia*, ABARE eReport 03.13 to the Department of Agriculture, Fisheries and Forestry – Australia, Canberra

Gaisford, J D (2002) 'Agricultural biotechnology and the FTAA: Issues and opportunities', *The Estey Centre Journal of International Law and Trade Policy*, vol 3, no 2, pp228–345

Musselli, I and Zarrilli, S (2002) 'Non-trade concerns and the WTO jurisprudence in the Asbestos Case – Possible relevance for international trade in genetically modified organisms', *The Journal of World Intellectual Property*, vol 3, pp373–393

Nielsen, C and Anderson, K (2000) *GMOs, Trade Policy, and Welfare in Rich and Poor Countries*, Policy Discussion Paper No 0021, Centre for Economic Policy Research, University of Adelaide, Australia

Oehmke, J, Maredia, M and Weatherspoon, D (2001) 'The effects of biotechnology policy on trade and growth', *The Estey Centre Journal of International Law and Trade Policy*, vol 2, no 2, pp283–306

Paarlberg, R L (2002) *The US–EU Trade Conflict over GM foods: Implications for Poor Countries*, Weatherhead Center for International Affairs, Harvard University

Persley, G J and MacIntyre, L R (2001) *Agricultural Biotechnology: Country Case Studies – A Decade of Development*, CABI Publishing, Wallingford, UK

Sheldon, I and Josling, T (2002) *Bio-technology Regulations and the WTO*, Working Paper No 02-2, International Agricultural Trade Research Consortium (IATRC)

Sindico, F (2005) *The GMO Dispute Before the WTO: Legal Implications for the Trade and Environment Debate*, Fondazione Eni Enrico Mattei, Milan, Italy

TRIPs COUNCIL

(For a more comprehensive list, see www.iprsonline.org/submissions/)

Brazil, Cuba, Ecuador, India, Peru, Thailand and Venezuela (2004) The Relationship between the TRIPS Agreement and the Convention on Biological Diversity and the Protection of Traditional Knowledge – Checklist of Issues, 2 March 2004, IP/C/W/420

The African Group (2003) Taking Forward the Review of Article 27.3(b) of the TRIPS Agreement, 4 June 2003, IP/C/W/404

Brazil, Bolivia, Cuba, Dominican Republic, Ecuador, India, Thailand, Peru and Venezuela (2003) The Relationship between the TRIPS Agreement and the Convention on Biological Diversity and the Protection of Traditional Knowledge, 28 May 2003, IP/C/W/403

Switzerland (2003) Article 27.3(b), the Relationship between the TRIPS Agreement and the Convention on Biological Diversity, and the Protection of Traditional Knowledge, 28 May 2003, IP/C/W/400

European Communities (2002) 'Review of the Article 27.3(b) of the TRIPS Agreement and the relationship between the TRIPS Agreement and the Convention on Biological Diversity (CBD) and the protection of traditional knowledge and folklore', Communication from the European Communities and their Member States, 17 October 2002, IP/C/W/383

United States (2001) Views of the United States on the Relationship between the Convention on Biological Diversity and the TRIPS Agreement, 13 June 2001, IP/C/W/257

Japan (2000) Review of the Provisions of Article 27.3(b) – Japan's View, 11 December 2000, IP/C/W/236

WTO DOCUMENTS

(Available at http://docsonline.wto.org/)

WTO (2001) Ministerial Declaration adopted at the Fourth WTO Ministerial Conference 14 November 2001, WT/MIN(01)/DEC/W/1

Index